CODE NAME KINDRED SPIRIT

CODE NAME
KINDRED SPIRIT

INSIDE THE CHINESE NUCLEAR ESPIONAGE SCANDAL

NOTRA TRULOCK

ENCOUNTER BOOKS

SAN FRANCISCO

First edition published in 2002 by Encounter Books, an activity of Encounter for Culture and Education, Inc., a nonprofit tax exempt corporation.

Encounter Books website address: www.encounterbooks.com

Manufactured in the United States and printed on acid-free paper.

The paper used in this publication meets the minimum requirements of ANSI/NISO Z39.48-1992 (R 1997)*(Permanence of Paper)*.

FIRST EDITION

Library of Congress Cataloging-in-Publication Data

Code name Kindred Spirit : inside the Chinese nuclear espionage scandal / Notra Trulock.
    p.   cm.
    Includes bibliographical references and index.
    ISBN 1-893554-51-1 (alk. paper)
    1. Trulock, Notra.   2. Intelligence agents—United States—Biography.   3. Lee, Wen Ho.   4. Espionage, Chinese—New Mexico—Los Alamos—History—20th century.   5. Espionage, Chinese—New Mexico—Los Alamos—History—21st century.   6. Nuclear weapons—United States.   7. Intercontinental ballistic missiles—United States.   8. Los Alamos National Laboratory—Security measures.   I. Title.

UB271.C6 T78 2003
327.1251073'092—dc21
[B]

        2002067856

10 9 8 7 6 5 4 3 2 1

ESPIONAGE: *The practice of gathering, transmitting, or losing through gross negligence information relating to the defense of the U.S. with the intent that or with reason to believe that the information will be used to the injury of the U.S. or the advantage of a foreign nation.*

Contents

Author's Note

wrote this book for two reasons. First, I hope that someday my
children will read it and understand why our lives came apart
in the aftermath of the investigations into Wen Ho Lee and Chinese espionage. Second, I wanted to try to set the record straight
as to what actually happened from 1995 to 2001. Public accounts
of this story in the media and elsewhere are shot through with distortions, falsehoods and outright lies, especially with regard to my
role in this case and my motivations as head of intelligence at the
U.S. Department of Energy. In writing the book, I have relied not
just on my memory of events, but also on interviews with other
participants in the case, intelligence experts, congressional investigators, and even some media people. I used official government
reports, congressional testimony and reports, and eyewitness
accounts to reconstruct events and timelines.

I have come to understand the worldview of Franz Kafka much
better as a result of what happened to *Code Name Kindred Spirit*
after the manuscript was completed. As is required for someone
with the level of security clearance I once had, I submitted the work
to the government for a classification review. As a former intelligence officer, I knew this was going to happen; I also knew that the
purpose of such a review is to prevent unauthorized disclosure of
classified information. Any intelligence agency, such as the CIA or
the FBI, mentioned in the manuscript gets a bite at the apple if that

agency's "equities" are involved. Thus the review can be time-consuming and often becomes subject to litigation.

There are a number of precedent-setting cases in this area of the law. Frank Snepp, a former CIA officer who wrote a memoir of the last days of the Vietnam War, didn't follow the rules. The government didn't stop him from publishing, but did win a judgment that blocked him from receiving any royalties. Consequently, he has never received a dime from his book. The government rarely seeks an injunction against publication, although that is an option; but as the Snepp cases demonstrates, there are other remedies that can deter would-be authors from flouting their obligations.

Yet there are certain prohibitions that theoretically protect against government overreach. Most importantly, the intelligence agencies must complete their review in a timely fashion and are expressly forbidden from censoring information on the grounds that it would be embarrassing to agencies or individuals. The period for review is usually set at 30 to 45 days, although government lawyers regularly find ways around this. Whenever it is finally completed, authors are supposed to anticipate a fair review, which focuses only on the protection of classified information.

When I ran Department of Energy Intelligence, I occasionally had the unpleasant but necessary duty of referring published articles or books to the FBI out of concern that classified information had been revealed in these materials. In all these instances, a review determined that classified information had indeed been compromised; in one case, the compromise resulted in the loss of a capability that had cost taxpayers millions of dollars. Nevertheless, the government took no action against the offending individuals, all of whom retained their security clearances. I know of no case during the Clinton administration when the FBI or the Justice Department took action against authors for compromising classified information, even when the Intelligence Community had concluded that significant compromises had occurred. In one recent case, the compromise was egregious and extremely harmful to U.S. national security, and it could have put lives at risk. A criminal referral was made to the FBI. Yet no action has been taken against the persons involved. As I discovered when I submitted my own manuscript, the government seems to reserve its energies for ensuring that material that could embarrass it never sees the light of day.

I took care to ensure that there was no classified information in *Code Name Kindred Spirit*. In order to guard against any inadvertent disclosure, I submitted the manuscript to the Department of Energy's Office of Intelligence for review in February 2002. There it sat as days turned into weeks and weeks into months. Energy Department officials made no effort to initiate a review, claiming that it was not their responsibility. After repeated phone calls from me and my lawyer, Energy finally sent the manuscript to the National Security Agency to oversee the government's review. NSA tried to move the review expeditiously. It distributed copies to the CIA, FBI, Department of Justice and, ironically, back to the Energy Department. And there the process stalled again.

The months turned into more months, with no word back from these other agencies. So, acting on advice from R. James Woolsey, the former CIA director, Peter Collier, my publisher, retained the services of Mark S. Zaid, a Washington lawyer who specializes in this type of case. Mark made the difference for us. He had recently won a major victory in a similar case involving the government's refusal to clear a manuscript and he was able to leverage that victory on our behalf.

Before Mark came on the scene, it seemed obvious that some officials had decided to drag the process out indefinitely and kill this book by sitting on it. Once Mark became involved, the government picked up the pace of its review. He enjoyed a good working relationship with a number of government classification experts and that helped. Nevertheless, several times Mark had to threaten legal action in order to speed up the FBI, CIA and Energy Department censors. Typically, the government would respond at the last minute, just as Mark was headed to court. Sort of an elaborate— and expensive—game of chicken.

In late August, I finally saw the results of the government's review of the manuscript. On the one hand, there were not as many deletions ("redactions") in the manuscript as I had expected. I was, however, shocked at some of the deletions the government did make. In particular, there were nearly three dozen instances in which the government "reclassified" information that had already been properly declassified and released to the public. Most of these involved direct quotations from the Bellows Report or the Cox Report, and in each case I had properly sourced and footnoted them. When Energy and CIA tried to get this information out of my book, it was a flat-out violation of the federal regulations that govern classified information. I was not about to put up with it. In an exchange of correspondence, CIA backed off on its deletion of this material. But this all took time and resulted in significant publication delays.

In other cases, in the truly Kafkaesque landscape that I was forced to travel through, the government refused to permit my use of unclassified information from articles published in the *New York Times* or popular magazines with circulation in the millions. The government's bizarre rationale for requiring deletions of material already read by millions of average Americans was that if I quoted it, my "past position, knowledge and experience" would confirm the authenticity of the information.

Classification regulations clearly state that information already in the public domain is not supposed to be subject to classification. But on this point—one of principle rather than substance—the government wore me down; it has dozens of lawyers and untold resources, and it relies on the reluctance of individual citizens to resort to the courts to fight its rulings.

The worst offender in this review was the U.S. Department of Energy, where most of the events described in this book took place. The department has a long record of abuses of classification and security. Energy officials are notorious for using trumped-up security issues to retaliate against the department's critics. In my case, personal grievances and individual vendettas interfered with due process in vetting this book. Energy Department officials completely ignored requests from NSA for responses to outstanding issues. Then Energy officials insisted that they couldn't talk to me about their "concerns" because I don't currently have a security clearance! They insisted that I apply for a security clearance before they would discuss their "concerns" with me.

The last time I applied for an Energy clearance, more than a year passed before it was granted, despite the fact that I had held Top Secret clearances for twenty years. This time around, obtaining a security clearance from Energy would likely stretch over many, many months. This would postpone and further delay publication. Which of course was the point. One senior security official was overheard to say, "Screw Trulock, why should we let him make any money off his book?"

At the end of the day, thanks largely to Mark Zaid and Peter Collier, we were able to agree on an approved manuscript. Both sides made some compromises; the government backed off on some of its more outrageous demands and the integrity of the narrative was preserved. As noted above, NSA acted professionally and honorably, and the other agencies came around after Mark got involved. But authors should not have to "lawyer up" in order to get their manuscripts through review. The government should worry about the accidental (or purposeful) release of sensitive data, not about embarrassment to itself. But as the reader will discover in the pages ahead, when it came to Wen Ho Lee and the Chinese espionage scandal, the government had very much to be embarrassed about indeed.

Cast of Main Characters

Clinton White House

Leon Panetta, Chief of Staff, Clinton I

John Podesta, Chief of Staff, Clinton II

Sandy Berger, Assistant National Security Advisor, Clinton I; National Security Advisor, Clinton II

Rand Beers, Senior Director, Intelligence Policy, National Security Council, Clinton II

Gary Samore, Senior Director, Nonproliferation Policy, National Security Council, Clinton II

Warren Rudman, Chairman, President's Foreign Intelligence Advisory Board, Clinton II

Department of Energy

Hazel O'Leary, Secretary, Clinton I

Federico Pena, Secretary, Clinton II, 1997–1998

Bill Richardson, Secretary, Clinton II, 1998–2000

Charles Curtis, Deputy Secretary, Clinton I

Elizabeth Moler, Deputy Secretary, Clinton II, 1997–1999

Ernie Moniz, Under Secretary, Clinton II, 1998–2000

Elgie Holstein, Chief of Staff, Clinton II, 1997–1998

Paul Richenbach, Special Assistant to Moler, 1997–1999

Vic Reis, Assistant Secretary, Defense Programs, 1993–1999

Joan Rohfling, Director, Office of Nonproliferation and National Security, 1994; Special Advisor to Secretary Pena, then Secretary Richardson, 1997–1999

Ken Baker, Deputy Director, Office of Nonproliferation and National Security, 1993–

Ed Curran, FBI Agent; Director, Office of Counterintelligence, 1998–2000

Ric Bloodsworth, Deputy Director, Office of Counterintelligence, 1995–1999

Chuck Washington, Office of Counterintelligence, 1993–1999

Dan Bruno, Chief Investigator, Office of Counterintelligence, 1992–

Ed McCallum, Director, Office of Safeguards and Security, 1990–1999

Los Alamos National Laboratory

Sig Hecker, Director, 1984–1998

John Brøwne, Director, 1998–

Steve Younger, Associate Director, Nuclear Weapons Program, 1994–1999

John Richter, nuclear weapons designer, identified W88 as U.S. warhead targeted by Chinese, 1995; retired 1999

Mike Henderson, nuclear weapons designer, chief of Kindred Spirit Analysis Group, 1995

Tom Cook, experimental physicist, intelligence analyst, participant in Kindred Spirit, 1997–1999

Peter Lee, scientist, 1984–1990

Wen Ho Lee, X Division, 1982–1999, three-time subject of FBI counterintelligence investigations

Sylvia Lee, wife of Wen Ho Lee, data entry specialist, hostess for Chinese visitors

Danny Stillman, Chief, International Technology Division; resigned 1993

Terry Hawkins, Deputy, then Chief, International Technology Division, 1993–

Larry Booth, International Technology Division, co-author of first Kindred Spirit memo, 1995

Bobby Henson, International Technology Division, co-author of first Kindred Spirit memo, 1995

Bob Vrooman, Director, Los Alamos Counterintelligence

Terry Craig, Deputy Director, Los Alamos Counterintelligence

Federal Bureau of Investigation

Louis Freeh, Director, 1993–2001

John Lewis, Director for Counterintelligence, 1995–1997, then Assistant Director, National Security Division; retired 1998

Neil Gallagher, Assistant Director, National Security Division, 1998–2001

Jerry Doyle, Chief, Global Section, National Security Division, 1995–1996

Steve Dillard, Chief, Global Section, National Security Division, 1996–1998

"Jack Kerry," Unit Chief, National Security Division, 1995–

"F. Jeff Maines," Special Agent, assisted Dan Bruno during Kindred Spirit Administrative Inquiry, 1995–1996

"Dick Lowenthal," Lead Agent, FBI Santa Fe Residency, 1996–1997

"Greg Smith," Supervisory Special Agent, National Security Division

"Cathy Cortes," Lead Agent, Santa Fe Residency, 1998–1999

"Joe Lacy," Special Agent, Santa Fe Residency, replaced "Lowenthal" as Lead Agent on Kindred Spirit case

"Jay Steele," Supervisory Special Agent, Albuquerque Field Office, "Lowenthal's" supervisor

Dave Kitchen, Special Agent in Charge, Albuquerque Field Office, authored "not guilty" memo for Wen Ho Lee

Will Lueckenhoff, Assistant Special Agent in Charge, Albuquerque Field Office, co-authored Lee memo

Central Intelligence Agency

John Deutch, Director, 1994–1997

George Tenet, Deputy Director, 1995–1997, then Director, 1997–

Paul Redmond, Associate Director for Counterintelligence; retired 1997

Media

Jim Risen, *New York Times*

Bill Broad, *New York Times*

Carla Robbins, *Wall Street Journal*

Walter Pincus, *Washington Post*

Vernon Loeb, *Washington Post*

Sheryl Attkinson, *CBS News*

Leslie Stahl, *60 Minutes*

Richard Bonin, producer, *60 Minutes*

Tim Russert, *Meet the Press*

Nuclear Weapons Terminology*

Primary: the first stage of a nuclear weapon. The primary uses chemical high explosives and nuclear materials, such as plutonium, to start a nuclear reaction that produces sufficient energy to drive the secondary stage. The primary contains the "pit," which is a spherical hollow metal assembly that contains plutonium.

Secondary: the second stage of a nuclear weapon. The secondary uses the energy produced by the primary to trigger a thermonuclear burn (nuclear fusion reaction). It is this thermonuclear burn that drives the ultimate destructive force of the nuclear weapon.

Source Code: the human readable set of instructions that can be given to a computer to perform a calculation simulating a physical event. Los Alamos National Laboratory source codes are usually written in a "high level language" and are then translated into instructions to be acted on directly by the computer. The physics package within the source code addresses matters such as detonation, high explosive burn, and weapon aging and degradation. Thermonuclear weapon design source codes model and simulate events which closely resemble test data from past nuclear weapons tests.

---

*These definitions are taken from the government's indictment of Wen Ho Lee.

The codes are calibrated through reference to live testing experience.

Input Deck/Input File: a set of instructions read by a computer to set up a nuclear weapon to be simulated. An input deck/input file typically contains exact dimensions and other geometrical information about the materials and the initial conditions of those materials for a particular nuclear weapon.

Data Files: these contain information relating to the physical and radioactive properties of materials at different temperatures and densities.

Map and Figures

Prologue

Making a martyr of [Wen Ho] Lee required making a villain out of
Notra Trulock, the whistleblower who called attention to the abysmal
security at our secret labs.
  —William Safire
    New York Times
    September 25, 2000

I had spent the day with my lawyers trying to figure out why the FBI was launching a full-scale investigation of me. When I got home, my golden retriever, Casey, had a big gash on his head, and dried blood matted his coat. Looking around, I had the chilling realization that someone had definitely been in our townhouse. This was not a simple break-in by kids looking for stereo gear or television sets. Books and papers, all of my working files, were scattered about on the floor. At first glance, nothing seemed to be missing, but somebody had surely been searching through them. Had the same people hit Casey and left him cut and bloody?

My head was spinning. Just a few days earlier, around dinnertime on a stormy Friday evening in July 2000, two armed FBI agents had come into my home, interrogated me for about an hour and then confiscated my computer—unannounced, no explanation given, and no search warrant. They didn't read me my rights; they just keep firing questions at me. The FBI, assisted by Department of Energy security officials, had "visited" my roommate at her office downtown that afternoon and coerced her "consent" to enter the home and take the computer. They held her a virtual hostage in her office, monitored all her phone calls, including those from her children, and threatened her with "busting down the door" of our townhouse and bringing TV camera crews along to film all this for the *News at Eleven.* She was terrified.

After the agents had left with the computer hard drive, which contained all my banking, tax, business and personal records, my friend told me that the FBI was accusing me of stealing classified documents and distributing classified information via e-mail to ... god knows who. "Who did he talk to? Who did he send e-mails to? Who were his friends? Did he send e-mails overseas?" The FBI agents pounded away on her for hours that day. "They think you took classified documents and are using them at home, just like John Deutch and Wen Ho Lee," she told me. Deutch, a former director of central intelligence, and Lee, the Los Alamos scientist then under indictment for spying, were both accused of "mishandling" classified information. Now the FBI acted as though I were up to the same thing. It didn't make sense. I had recently published a magazine article that was very critical of FBI and Justice Department officials for their inept handling of a Chinese nuclear espionage investigation, but I was scrupulous about keeping classified information out of the article. But the FBI was serious. Its agents took the unprecedented step of searching the computers of U.S. senators and their staffs for any e-mails from me.

I wish I could say that this break-in was the only clip in the highlight film of my life in the Bill Clinton era. But there had been a preview, about two years before, when two uniformed federal police officers wearing side arms and body armor appeared at the door of my office in the basement of the Department of Energy in downtown Washington. I was then director of intelligence at the DOE and my office was deep inside a soundproof, highly secure vault complete with double sets of steel doors. Visitors without the appropriate security clearances had to be escorted whenever they went inside this vault. The purpose of the police officers' visit was to arrest me. A disgruntled employee had filed a complaint alleging that I had assaulted him, and the police were there to "take me out" on those charges. They backed off when witnesses who had been present at the meeting where it supposedly happened scoffed at these charges. At that time, the police apologized for the "inconvenience" and then left. Several weeks later I managed to get my hands on their final report, which said "the assault did not occur." So you would think that Energy Department officials would take action against the employee, right? They did; he was transferred, given a cash bonus, and later granted a huge settlement by Secretary Bill Richardson—even though repeated "investigations" failed to turn up even a shred of evidence against me.

But now the FBI was accusing me of something far more serious than assault: compromising classified information. One doesn't expect the FBI to appreciate irony. But during my thirty years in the intelligence and national security field, I had worked on some of the most sensitive programs inside the U.S. government and had been in charge of special security to safeguard intelligence information at huge Department of Energy facilities employing thousands. Now the FBI was accusing me of violating the security oaths that I had enforced all those years. It least I think they were. Days turned into weeks, weeks into months, but I never heard from the FBI again after the agents had come barging into the townhouse. So, I really don't know what, if anything, I was accused of. Many people thought a new Bush administration would clear this up quickly, but Attorney General John Ashcroft's Department of Justice has ignored personal appeals from his former colleagues on Capitol Hill and other close political associates to dismiss this case and help restore my reputation. With each passing day, it looks more and more as if the objective of the raid was to retaliate for my daring to criticize the Bureau's performance in the Wen Ho Lee case and to make sure that I never worked in Washington again. They still have the computer—and all my personal records.

But that was hardly the end of it. As part of the fallout from the government's prosecution of Wen Ho Lee, his lawyers and supporters branded me a racist and a bigot in a very public fashion. Mainstream media like the *Washington Post,* the *New York Times* and *CBS News* have repeated the most outrageous allegations against me, including my "bias" against minorities generally and ethnic Chinese in particular, and my alleged abuse of security to harm careers and destroy the reputations of minorities who worked for me. Lee's lawyers constructed a defense strategy intended to depict me as the "Mark Fuhrman" of the Wen Ho Lee prosecution. His defenders claimed that I "singled out" Lee as the only suspect in the loss of national security information solely on the basis of his ethnicity. After you are smeared like this, try getting a job anywhere, especially in "diversity-sensitive" Washington, D.C. These false allegations have left me with no job, bankrupt and deeply worried about my children's future.

And for what? What was the Wen Ho Lee case all about, and what had I done to justify all this abuse? Under my direction, in 1995, a team of Energy Department scientists had uncovered a campaign of Chinese nuclear espionage against our national laboratory complex stretching back nearly two decades. We found hard evidence that the Chinese had acquired highly classified information on our W88 thermonuclear warhead, the most modern in the world; the neutron bomb; and other U.S. nuclear warheads—seven in all. As the director of intelligence, I also led the fight to reform security and counterintelligence at the DOE, which had one of the worst security records in the government. The existence of serious problems at the national laboratories was hardly a secret in Washington, but I was the first one willing to force the government to take action to plug the gaping holes in security at the labs. This action, however, was like closing the barn door after the horse has already left. We will never really know how many secrets about our nuclear weapons were stolen over the past three decades.

I refused to look the other way when confronted with evidence of Chinese nuclear espionage, even though I was ordered by my superiors in the Energy Department to bury it. The evidence proved to be the tip of the iceberg of assaults by the People's Republic of China on the U.S. defense science and technology community—assaults that continue to this day. I tried to put a stop to decades of neglect, mismanagement and blatant disregard for the protection of our most precious secrets concerning the design and development of nuclear weapons. Our security for these secrets was so bad, in fact, that government reports would later conclude that espionage and security breaches had occurred repeatedly and for years had gone undetected by those supposedly responsible for guarding this information.

I don't mean to say that I made the government take notice of these issues single-handedly. I had help from some officials within the FBI, at CIA, and even inside the Energy Department. Some of our elected representatives, like Congressmen Duncan Hunter from

California and Curt Weldon from Pennsylvania and Senator Arlen Specter, also from Pennsylvania, pushed through critical legislation that helped plug the gaps. But because I was the boss, the director of intelligence at DOE and responsible for counterintelligence at Energy's national labs, I became the point man in the struggle to stop the theft of our nuclear secrets.

As part of the collateral damage of this assignment, I became one of the most visible casualties of the fierce debate inside the U.S. government over the nature of future challenges to our national security from the People's Republic of China. Should we view China as a "strategic partner" or a "strategic competitor?" The Clinton administration embraced the former view with a vengeance, ignoring any and all intelligence information to the contrary.

One of the great ironies of the Clinton era is that while the administration was deeply hostile to U.S. nuclear weapons, it mostly looked the other way while a host of "rogue states" sought and acquired many of the ingredients for at least a fledgling nuclear capability. The PRC was the most blatant in doing this, but South Asia also "went nuclear" on the Clinton watch and Iran made important strides in developing both a nuclear and a ballistic missile capability to threaten its neighbors.

And that is where I came in. The Chinese, the Iraqis and others found a ready—and in some cases willing—source of information, knowledge and expertise within the U.S. nuclear weapons complex to assist their efforts to create or modernize nuclear weapons. The careless and haphazard approach to security and counterintelligence within the Energy Department complex offered a feast for hostile foreign intelligence services. Tasked by their scientific communities with acquiring the means to close the technological gap with the United States, these services looked to the DOE nuclear weapons labs as a sort of one-stop shopping source.

Why did the Clinton administration and many of its friends on Capitol Hill, in the media and in academia constantly equate the "end of the Cold War" with the end of efforts by foreign intelligence services to acquire our scientific and technical secrets? A combination of naïveté and wishful thinking, I guess. The appetite of foreign scientific communities and their respective intelligence services did not diminish with the end of the Cold War; if anything, it grew. Certainly their job became easier as Clinton appointees opened up our nuclear weapons laboratories to scientists from our former Cold War opponents and emphasized "international scientific collaboration," whose major achievement was to expose our scientists to foreign intelligence collectors. As a result, our national nuclear labs were suddenly flooded with visitors from China, Russia, India, even Iran and Iraq—many of them staying on for two years or more. Our ability to track them and enforce security measures and safeguards was overwhelmed by their sheer numbers. But the issue was not so much the presence of these scientists as the labs' utter disregard of even the basic rules for protecting secrets.

Of course, this story takes place within the context of other, equally disturbing trends in U.S. national security. The performance of agencies responsible for counterespionage within the United States on the Clinton administration's watch was so poor, especially against "nontraditional threats," that it raised questions about whether we can protect our most precious secrets in this new era. More than one after-action report found blunders, mistakes, miscommunication, mismanagement, negligence and outright incompetence in the government's handling of the PRC nuclear espionage scandal. As one such report concluded, the Chinese espionage investigation "was never a high priority" for the FBI or the Clinton administration as a whole, although "what was at issue was one of the gravest and most consequential purported acts of espionage ever investigated by the FBI."[1]

Very serious questions remain about the government's actions against the only "suspect" in the Chinese nuclear espionage ever investigated by the FBI: Wen Ho Lee. Frankly, I don't know if Lee "did it," that is, gave the PRC our nuclear secrets. I do know that he was a walking security nightmare who violated nearly every security rule in existence at Los Alamos National Laboratory. He certainly had opportunity, access and perhaps even motivation—the Holy Trinity of espionage. I do know that he lied repeatedly when questioned by government officials about his contacts with PRC nuclear scientists, the classified information they were seeking from him, and the assistance he provided to them. He admitted helping the Chinese with computer codes and software that even he acknowledged could be used in nuclear weapons applications. He failed an FBI polygraph on questions involving the W88 nuclear warhead.

The circumstantial evidence on Wen Ho Lee merited an aggressive counterintelligence investigation, but the FBI's handling of this case was an unmitigated disaster from beginning to end. It was an investigation in name only. The Bureau never applied the tools or procedures common to a full-scale espionage case: never conducted a financial analysis; never established surveillance, even episodically, on its main suspect; never conducted "trash covers"; and never interviewed the suspect's co-workers or supervisors. Faced with evidence of illicit computer activity, the Bureau never searched Lee's computer, nor did it even monitor his usage. In spite of its potential significance, two years passed before FBI director Louis Freeh even became aware of this case. Months would pass with little or no action by the FBI case agents. The Justice Department rejected FBI attempts to establish technical surveillance of the suspect's telephone and computer usage, a very rare occurrence in the history of such efforts, and the FBI never was able to obtain such coverage, even when it feared that Lee might tip off foreign agents. But a well-known federal prosecutor, with a long track record of successful espionage convictions, later determined that there was sufficient "probable cause to believe that Wen Ho Lee was an agent of a foreign power ... currently engaged in clandestine intelligence gathering activities for or on behalf of the PRC."[2]

As it was about to close its investigation, the FBI discovered that Wen Ho Lee had compromised nearly all of our nuclear warhead design secrets in one of the greatest breaches in the history of U.S. national security. He placed all these secrets on an unprotected computer network, which was repeatedly attacked by computer hackers, several of them known to be working for foreign governments. Despite such disturbing facts, the government still doesn't know if Lee's files were accessed from outside the lab. But the government does know that these files contained *exactly* the information that the Chinese needed to modernize their nuclear arsenal. And the government knows that China's intelligence services targeted Los Alamos National Lab for the acquisition of these secrets.

Many of the FBI actions during its four-year investigation of Lee are simply inexplicable. Let me give one example: It is customary to maintain surveillance on a suspect after the FBI has polygraphed that suspect, in case he attempts to flee or takes some other action that further implicates him. Yet in Wen Ho Lee's case, after the FBI told him he was an espionage suspect in early 1999, local agents made no effort to keep him under surveillance. If they had done so, the FBI would have detected Lee erasing millions of bytes of classified information he had placed on the unclassified Los Alamos computer network or on computer tapes, and sneaking back into his now off-limits office to destroy incriminating evidence of his massive security violations.

One explanation for the Bureau's performance was its long history with Wen Ho Lee and his wife, Sylvia. The Lees would claim that they had collected information on Chinese nuclear scientists during the 1980s and provided this information to the FBI and other U.S. intelligence agencies. Wen Ho Lee admitted helping Chinese scientists fix their nuclear weapons codes during his trips to China, but failed to report these interactions to the lab or the Bureau upon his return. This has led many to suspect that Lee "doubled" the FBI. The Bureau and the Justice Department have gone to extraordinary lengths to suppress any information about this chapter of the Kindred Spirit story.

Equally distressing was the response of government officials when finally ordered by the President of the United States to close security vulnerabilities and reform counterintelligence at the nation's nuclear weapons labs. "Cynicism," "arrogant disregard for authority" and a "staggering pattern of denial" characterized the Energy Department's response to those presidential mandates.[3] Months after President Bill Clinton had finally ordered major security and counterintelligence reforms, Energy Department and lab officials remained "unconvinced of Presidential authority."[4] Months before, the number two official in the Energy Department had ignored the FBI director's recommendation to remove Wen Ho Lee from access to nuclear secrets. She later claimed that she thought Director Louis Freeh, who twice urged the Energy Department to take action against Lee, was not speaking on behalf of the FBI. Nearly every single Energy Department official referred to in this book still works at the department in a significant capacity today. Should we now accept government assurances that our nuclear secrets are safe?

Not only was the FBI's investigation of Lee inept and mismanaged, the Justice Department's prosecution of him on allegations of mishandling classified information was nothing short of bizarre. One day Wen Ho Lee was in solitary confinement, a serious danger to national security because he wouldn't tell what he did with computer tapes he had made containing reams of nuclear secrets. The next day he was a free man, the victim of racism and overzealousness. Yes, he is a convicted felon, but he has his full laboratory pension (despite being fired in 1999), he got a lucrative book deal, and he may even be the star of an upcoming movie. And is the United States any closer to learning what really happened to all those nuclear secrets on the missing tapes?

Those tapes contained electronic blueprints of our nuclear warheads, giving their exact shapes and dimensions as well as the materials used in their construction. They had computer codes and databases holding all of the precious information collected over forty years from more than a thousand live nuclear tests conducted by the United States. The tapes contained everything necessary to simulate the actual performance of these warheads. At the very last minute before his release, the prosecution and Lee's own lawyers learned for the first time that he had made twice as many tapes as previously believed and maybe even more. Do we know what happened to those tapes? Lee has stuck to his story that he destroyed them, but the FBI has only his word for it. This from a man whom the FBI's files, stretching back twenty years, labeled as someone who would answer such questions "truthfully only when confronted with irrefutable evidence or the threat of a polygraph."[5] The FBI searched a huge garbage dump outside of Los Alamos looking for the tapes, but opted not to polygraph Wen Ho Lee to test his claims. But what the Justice Department suspects may be inferred from its offer of immunity from prosecution to Lee's wife if only she would give up the tapes.

What made the government walk away from its case in early September 2000? Was it the impending presidential election? Norman Mineta, a Clinton administration cabinet official, visited a key Lee family member before the plea bargain was struck and just before the presidential race kicked off in earnest. Many suspect that PRC contributions to the 1996 Clinton campaign were a factor in the government's overall handling of this case. There is good reason to believe that political motivations shaped both the FBI's and the Justice Department's behavior in the Wen Ho Lee case. Twice during the Clinton administration, the Justice Department refused to prosecute U.S. nuclear lab scientists on charges of spying for China and opted instead for lesser charges of mishandling classified information—without implicating the Chinese government in any way. Much of the FBI's strange behavior can be explained by fear within the Bureau of offending the Chinese government, a fear that was allowed to "undermine a critical FBI investigation about Chinese espionage."[6]

The most serious implication of the Chinese espionage case is the effect it has had on the federal security and counterintelligence community, already suffering from a severe failure of leadership. Throughout the case, FBI agents expressed their fear of lawsuits by Lee against them for simply doing their jobs. What future security official or counterintelligence officer will act on evidence of espionage by the People's Republic of China or any other nation that can call on a large community of political activists in the United States and a powerful lobby in Washington? Counterterrorism programs were hamstrung by worries about offending similar activist groups, at least before September 11, 2001. What CI officer would put his career and his family's financial security on the line, knowing that his government will abandon him in a heartbeat once the specter of "racism" or ethnic profiling is raised? The simple fact that the tactic worked so well in the Lee defense ensures that it will be used again and again.

After the tragic attacks against the World Trade Center and the Pentagon, it was commonplace to hear that "everything has changed." But has it? One of the worst consequences of the Clinton era for our national security was the complacency that pervaded both the government and American society. This complacency encouraged the deterioration of security and "threat awareness" at government agencies and facilities responsible for protecting American citizens and American secrets. Our nation's nuclear laboratories were not the only government institutions to feel the deadening hand of the Clinton administration when it came to security and counterintelligence. Decisions made by Clinton officials, implemented by bureaucrats concerned only for their own promotions and raises, and then allowed to remain unchallenged by a Congress that seemed asleep at the switch will haunt this country for years to come. Our Intelligence Community, suffering from its own leadership crisis, failed to detect plans for an attack that killed more Americans than Pearl Harbor. The CIA was formed specifically to prevent another Pearl Harbor. It failed—in no small measure because of decisions taken by Bill Clinton and his administration. Many of the problems that plagued FBI efforts against Chinese nuclear espionage resurfaced in the weeks and months leading up to September 11. Solutions to the errors experienced during the Lee case were proposed, even legislatively mandated, but the Bureau failed to implement these quickly enough and so repeated some of its mistakes—this time at a cost of over three thousand American lives.

While the Clinton administration could not manage national security, it surely could manage the news. Of course, the Chinese nuclear espionage scandal was overshadowed by all the President's other scandals. Suspicions of PRC espionage could hardly compete with news accounts of presidential semen on a blue Gap dress, but the administration had lots of help from sympathetic journalists. The *Washington Post,* the "company" newspaper in D.C., and *CBS News* did some of the worst reporting. The *New York Times* has taken a lot of heat for its coverage, but whatever mistakes it made pale in comparison with the distortions and fabrications published by the *Post* on almost a daily basis. The *Post* repeatedly misquoted official reports and launched a scorched-earth campaign, relying on anonymous "officials," to promote its line that no espionage had occurred and that racism was responsible for Wen Ho Lee's predicament.

Last, but by no means least, there was the role of Congress in the whole affair. In response to its oversight obligations in potentially one of the most serious espionage cases since World War II, Congress proved to be nearly as inept as the Clinton administration. There was no central, coordinated investigation of the scandal or of the administration's failure to disclose information to the Hill. Instead, competing committees conducted their own inquiries, each turning up important elements of the scandal, but never combining their efforts to provide the American public with a coherent picture of what had happened on the Clinton watch. The role of the armed services and intelligence oversight committees in both houses was negligible despite the serious implications of this case for national security. The "legislative" solution to security and counterintelligence vulnerabilities that created the problem in the first place produced a Rube-Goldberg-like organization that left the Department of Energy and its labs less secure than before the scandal.

This book is about what I saw during the Chinese nuclear espionage scandal. It is a story of cover-ups and concealment, missed opportunities, bungled investigations, and malfeasance. Intelligence professionals with long and distinguished careers were forced into retirement; others had their professional reputations tarnished and smeared and, as a result, would retreat into other, less dangerous intelligence disciplines. At the same time, Clinton political appointees and even career federal officials lied repeatedly under oath before congressional committees and to supposedly independent government investigators. Most of these federal officials were promoted, awarded raises and bonuses, and moved ahead in their careers as a reward from grateful political appointees for participating in this cover-up. Throughout this period, a class of pampered and privileged scientists continued to feed at the public trough, but categorically refused to accept even the most modest security and counterintelligence measures to protect the nation's nuclear assets. Secrets that American taxpayers spent billions of dollars to develop were given away by an administration bent on achieving ephemeral arms-control objectives.

This is also a story of what can happen to one person who tries to do his job in Washington today. Presented with documentary evidence of PRC nuclear espionage, I couldn't look away or ignore either this theft or the vulnerabilities at the DOE national labs that made it possible. Everybody in Washington knows the risks of speaking truth to power. I would be reminded of those risks over and over again during what still remains the most alarming and least understood scandal of the Clinton era.

ONE

The Making of an Intelligence Officer

In personal terms, the handling of this case is very much the story of the Energy Department intelligence official who first raised questions about the Los Alamos case, Notra Trulock.
—*New York Times*
     March 6, 1999

I always get asked about two things: how I got into intelligence work and how I got my first name. Answering the second question first, I am the third Trulock to carry the name Notra, although none of us is certain of its origin. My dad thinks some great-great-aunt stuck it on my grandfather, but no one seems to know what it means or how she came up with it. My dad hated it, but still inflicted it on me. When it came time for me to name my son, he was disappointed that I broke the streak. I have gotten some laughs out of it, especially with regard to its presumed "ethnic" origin; people have guessed, wildly, that it's Romanian or Hungarian.

Actually, I had a pretty conventional midwestern upbringing, and I always seemed—at least to myself—an unlikely candidate to be attacked as a racist or xenophobe by the *Washington Post* or the *New York Times.* My dad was a city fireman in Indianapolis, as was my grandfather. I also have a cousin who was an Indianapolis city fireman. As I look back, I am struck by the manner in which they all approached their job. After the tragedy of September 11, 2001, people now understand that a fireman's job is one of the most dangerous in the land. Dad went about his work with little fanfare, however; he rarely mentioned it and never regaled us with tales of his own bravery or that of his father. Occasionally, as a small boy running errands with him, I would hear snatches of conversation about some fireman's deeds. I understand that my cousin is a bona fide hero and has saved a number of lives in the course of duty, but I sure didn't hear this from him. These men don't brag about their work or their exploits; it's all just part of doing their job.

Mom stayed at home with us until around the time I was in the sixth grade, when she went back to work as a secretary. She is very intelligent, the brains of the family and an avid reader. I was always impressed at how quickly she could become knowledgeable about the Civil War or the history of doll making. After my brother and I left home, she finally started her own doll-making business along with her sister. My dad later became a gunsmith, and both flourished as entrepreneurs.

I grew up on the far outskirts of Indianapolis across the street from a soybean field. My first love as a boy was baseball. In contrast to the organized leagues my kids compete in today, we played every day in a big field down the street. We had Little League, but the weekly games hardly satisfied my appetite for the sport. I spent hours knocking rocks into that soybean field pretending that I was hitting home runs off Whitey Ford of the Yankees or Billy Pierce of the White Sox. Since we were Hoosiers, we also played an awful lot of basketball. But baseball was my first love.

I also read constantly: adventure stories, sports stories, biographies of sports heroes. Television was hardly the major presence in our lives that it typically is today, so I filled my time with stories of the heroics of Babe Ruth, Stan Musial, Chip Hilton and the Hardy Boys. Gradually, however, my tastes shifted to history and historical biographies. William Shirer's *Rise and Fall of the Third Reich* made a lasting impression on me, as did Bruce Catton's series on the Civil War. Books about the Kennedy administration sparked my interest in politics and especially foreign policy.

What is today called a "slacker" was then just an "under-achiever." Whichever term you use, I was a mediocre student. My parents tried hard to motivate me, but my head was always somewhere else. Still, I was the first Trulock, and certainly the first one named Notra, to attend college. I ended up at Indiana University majoring in political science and history during the late 1960s, when the "cultural revolution" that had hit elsewhere years earlier finally rolled into Bloomington. I was a fraternity boy and in the fall of 1967 we were wearing blue blazers with fraternity patches to class; by the following spring, the blazers were gone, replaced by the standard-issue radical outfit—Levis and boots. IU experienced every type of campus radicalism: antiwar protests, black student uprisings, and so on. My favorite was the educational reform movement. Grades were "bad" by definition, and by my senior year, many professors allowed students to grade their own efforts. Not surprisingly, these courses, mostly in the sociology and English departments, were very popular.

The backdrop for all this energy on campus, of course, was the war in Vietnam. Although I had been a Goldwater Republican in high school, I too gradually came to oppose the war—for sound geopolitical reasons, or so I thought. I believed that the war, especially by 1968–69, was ruining our chances for better relations with Russia and hurting our standing in NATO and elsewhere. The truth was that my college buddies and I didn't want to get killed for nothing, but at least I had constructed a high-minded reason for opposing the war. I also learned to parrot the standard antiwar critique about this being a civil war waged by idealistic peasant nationalists. When I joined the National Security Agency in May 1975, just as Saigon was falling, I was shocked to learn how naïve and just plain wrong I had been.

Some of my professors at IU thought I might have a career as a college professor. How they expected I could ever get through graduate school with my mediocre grades and poor study habits is beyond me. I had some vague notions of becoming a lawyer, but for the most part I just drifted.

One episode did shape my outlook later in life. As I said, I was a member of a fraternity, the oldest and one of the most prestigious on campus. Of course, the fraternity was lily-white, but by the time I was a junior and an officer of the fraternity, a number of us decided we should integrate the house. More and more African-Americans were coming through during the "open rush" periods and we identified a number of excellent candidates for membership. We finally settled on one individual who had it all: good grades, good personality, and a jock to boot.

Every candidate for membership had to be unanimously approved. Word spread that we were trying to "integrate" the fraternity, and resistance became fierce. At the final meeting to approve "bids" for prospective members, one of the seniors blackballed our nominee. His reason: color, pure and simple. I was outraged; I had never encountered such blind, stupid prejudice, although I was to see it many more times in the future. I promptly resigned my post and moved out of the house.

I was subject to the first draft lottery and hit the jackpot with a low number—52, as I recall. When I finally got around to checking with my draft board to see when I might be called up, I learned that I could expect to be in basic training by the end of the summer of 1970, the year I graduated. I briefly considered the National Guard, but Mom told me that Dad, who had enlisted in the Navy in World War II, didn't think it would be honorable duty. It bothered me to think that I might somehow dishonor him. Then I remembered that when I had taken my draft physical earlier in the fall 1969, I had been notified that I had qualified for an outfit called the Army Security Agency. I had never heard of this agency, but my first visit to an ASA recruiter in early summer, 1970, was definitely a turning point in my life.

During that meeting, I took still more tests. One of them measured language aptitude. Frankly, I didn't think I had any, so I was surprised when the ASA recruiter told me I had "maxed" the test. He said that I could "write my own ticket" and asked what I wanted to do in the way of language training. I asked the recruiter without hesitation which language would keep me out of Vietnam. Russian, he said, and I replied that Russian sounded good to me. I had to submit to my first background investigation in order to gain the needed security clearances to be admitted to ASA. Over the next few months, I heard from several of my college buddies that FBI agents were asking questions about my activities and friends and so on. Most of them thought it was pretty cool and assumed I was going off to be a spy.

It was far more mundane than that. After basic training at scenic Fort Leonard Wood, Missouri, the Army shipped me out to Monterey, California, for a year's worth of Russian language training. I started off the school year with my usual half-ass study habits, but soon got the shock of my life. The flunkout rate at the Defense Language Institute (DLI) was high, and those who didn't make it went to Advanced Infantry Training and then straight to Vietnam. I started burning the midnight oil and, for the first time since grade school, studied as if my life depended on it. I managed to bring my grade average high enough to stay in school and get a duty tour in Germany.

I did about eighteen months at an isolated post in the Bavarian Alps. I traveled quite a bit and got to see some of Europe. I had planned to go to Munich for the 1972 Olympics, but I had to work, so was not there when the tragic massacre of the Israeli athletes took place. The local scenery was breathtaking. I will always remember coming home from a midnight shift one winter Sunday morning. The snow was blowing hard and there was no traffic whatsoever. I stopped the car and got out to take in the sight. Just then a fox stepped out from the woods into the road about 150 yards ahead. The wind blew my scent away from him, although he was very alert. Then a smaller fox, probably a female, and some "kits" stepped out onto the road. I will never forget that picture. Soon the wind shifted, the male sensed me and they were gone in a flash.

Vietnam was winding down and some of the units were rotated straight from the jungles to Germany. I saw the beginnings of the "hollow Army," as it came to be known later in the seventies. In addition to the racial problems, drug use was rampant among the troops. We were sure to see stoned troopers during any trip to the big PXs at Nuremberg or Frankfurt. The Army's efforts to stamp out drugs always seemed to produce more users than ever before. At least once in my seventeen months, the Army ran an exercise to "rescue" us in the event of a Warsaw Pact invasion. An armored unit, I don't remember what size, was supposed to coordinate such an operation early one morning when I was on duty. The helicopter troop carriers and helicopter gun ships arrived bright and early. The gun ships were buzzing around the site, which got our counterparts over in Czechoslovakia very stirred up. The armored elements were supposed to arrive about the same time, but didn't show up until about four that afternoon. I talked to the unit commander, a captain about my age, and he told me they got "lost" on the way up, which explained why they were about six hours late. Needless to say, that didn't give us a warm feeling about our prospects in the event of an invasion.

The Army was downsizing after Vietnam and offered us four-year enlistees a year off for good behavior. They didn't have to ask me twice. Back home, I briefly considered law school again, but there seemed to be a glut of lawyers, all of them at least four years ahead of me in both their education and establishing their careers. I really had only three objectives when I got out: quit smoking, never play cards again, and never go near the Army or anything that even smacked of the military.

I ended up in Chicago in a sales training program. I made a lot of friends, but the work was just not stimulating enough. The long-term money prospects were good, but I wasn't sure I could hold out. I began to recall fondly the Russian language course in Monterey and even some of the work in Germany. Pretty soon, I was hauling out my textbooks and trying to read Russian language newspapers and books. After a year or so, I applied to the CIA and also to the Defense Intelligence Agency. I never heard back from DIA, but I did get a tape in the mail from CIA. I was supposed to transcribe what I heard on the tape and send it back. Too weird, I thought, so I threw the tape in the trash. Then I remembered the National Security Agency, the Defense Department agency that controlled ASA. It had always been a mystery to us. From time to time, NSA civilians would show up at our site in Germany, nose around for a while and then disappear again. NSA was still a supersecret organization at this time, in the mid-1970s. (It was commonly referred to as "No Such Agency" around Washington.) I applied, and to my surprise not only got a response but was invited to fly out to Maryland for an interview. I redoubled my efforts to brush up on my Russian and visited Fort Meade, the home of NSA, in the early fall of 1974. I did well enough on the Russian test to be offered a job.

I reported for duty at the National Security Agency in May 1975, when the agency was starting to publish a series of retrospective articles about its involvement in Vietnam going back to the beginning of the war. Every one of them gave the lie to the antiwar teach-ins and even the formal course work I had digested at Indiana in the late 1960s. This had been no "civil war," but a war controlled from the north since the very beginning. But I also wondered at the terrible job the Johnson administration did at telling the real story behind our involvement. I guess the necessity of protecting intelligence "sources and methods" overrode the need of the American people to know what was really going on in Vietnam.

At NSA I began as a transcriber. Surely I must have been one of the worst transcribers in the entire recorded history of the agency. My knowledge of Russian was fairly good; I could read it and even speak it pretty well. I could converse with my Russian language instructors, but I could not hear it on those tapes at all. I was just plain awful. I was desperate to find another job at NSA. But just like the Army, NSA had some very strange bureaucratic rules. Someone in the NSA hierarchy had decided to hold the line and not allow anyone to transfer out of the transcription career field. This meant that no matter how inept I was at it, I was doomed to be a transcriber.

I was close to quitting when I got my first big break. A man named Joe Nogal, since deceased, gave me an opportunity to become a watch officer in the National SIGINT Operations Center (NSOC). My exact duties there are probably still classified, but I can say that I loved the work. I did analysis and assessments, wrote reports and did lots of collection "coordination" and tasking. I was eager and aggressive, and many of the other watch officers were mid-career types, there primarily to escape the routine of a day job. They were all hardworking professionals, but not averse to letting some young eager beaver carry the load for a while. My "production" was high, and was graded by Nogal and others as being of high quality as well. Especially on afternoon and midnight shifts, after the bosses had gone home, I had a lot of autonomy and I tried to make the most of it. I also spent as much time as possible reading into the history of NSA and combing through the historical files on NSA operations and reports. It was fascinating stuff that the American public will never really know about or understand. This "super-secret" agency's contribution to our national security is inestimable. After I became director of the Department of Energy's intelligence office, I always supported community awards and medals for NSA employees. I even convinced the DOE deputy secretary to offer to support NSA's budget requests on Capitol Hill.

When I was at NSA in the late 1970s, we were the masters of the universe within the Intelligence Community. After my stint in NSOC, I went back to day duty in an analysis shop. Once again, the work was simply fascinating—as were the people. It is common knowledge within the Beltway that some of the smartest people to be found in Washington work out at Fort Meade, the home of NSA. I think this must be true; my fellow analysts were a special group. Most have since retired or gone on to other jobs.

Though I made my promotion ahead of the curve, by 1979 I had decided it was time to move on. I really didn't want to slog through the ranks, worrying about time in grade and all that other bureaucratic crap. I focused on the private sector, or what is commonly known as the "Beltway bandits." These are private companies located mostly around the Washington, D.C., area that sell analytic and technical services to the government. These companies have "morphed" numerous times in the past two decades and now focus mostly on information technologies and systems integration. In the late 1970s, they did a lot of hard-core analytic work using computer simulations and various other analytic techniques and tools. Nuclear weapons and nuclear security issues were the driving force of many of these companies, although advanced conventional weaponry of the type later featured in the Gulf War started to emerge at about this time.

By the mid-1980s, I had drifted into the arcane world of military Sovietology. This basically involved close and careful scrutiny of the writings and publications of Soviet military writers, who were actually fairly forthcoming about their thoughts on strategy, operations, doctrine and tactics. It was possible to tease nuances and formulations out of their work that could help us better understand how the Soviet military thought about the nature of warfare, threat assessments, foreign weapons systems and operations, and general strategy. During this period, I worked for the Foreign Systems Research Center in Denver, Colorado. The FSRC had one of the most extensive libraries of Russian-language military materials in existence in the West. The staff was full of Russian-language specialists, many with backgrounds similar to mine.

The arrival of the Reagan administration opened up new vistas for this type of research. For years, under President Carter and his predecessors, little real attention had been devoted to this body of materials. But Reagan officials understood that for the most part, the U.S. Intelligence Community's idea of analysis was simply imposing Western assumptions onto Russian thinking. In review after review of intelligence reports from the time around the Soviet invasion of Afghanistan, for example, one could find statements like: "no rational decision makers would invade a third world country in the aftermath of the U.S. experience in Vietnam." Well, in retrospect, the Russians probably wished they had adopted that view, but they were driven by their own set of assumptions, tempered by their own history and culture, and did not necessarily share our view of the world.

The nuclear balance between the Soviet Union and the United States is one good example of how pre-Reagan-era thinking missed the mark. While it is true that both sides lived according to some rules of the road governing their actions with regard to nuclear weapons, it is also true that the Soviet nuclear buildup and a ballistic missile defense around Moscow showed that the Russians were operating on a different set of assumptions from the U.S. policy of mutual assured destruction. They were planning to fight and survive a nuclear exchange. The new Reagan officials understood this instinctively and were receptive to new work in this area. Consequently, we flourished out in Denver for a period during the 1980s.

We worked on a number of groundbreaking studies, including potential Soviet responses to new U.S. military concepts and weapons. The work was exciting but difficult, almost Talmudic in nature. Competition among the specialists was fierce and great care had to be taken to ensure the authenticity of research reports. Any publication was subject to intensive fact and especially footnote checking by one's competitors. God help you if one of them found a mistake or an incorrect citation. More than once, some analysts were caught distorting the essence of a particular paragraph in a Russian text or misquoting a source outright. They paid a high price.

By far the most interesting work I did during this period was on the topic of the revolution in military affairs. The subject was nearly unknown in the West until the Russians started writing about it in the early 1980s. In fact, the thrust of the Russian work cut across the grain of U.S. assessments of Soviet military might at that time. This was when the Russian military was portrayed as being "ten feet tall" and spending unlimited quantities of rubles on building power. The Soviet military had, in fact, made great strides in the late 1960s and throughout the 1970s. At a minimum, the Soviets had achieved strategic nuclear parity with the United States.

They had developed a powerful, strategically important navy; their conventional arms were being upgraded; and even their air forces were modernizing at a fast pace. Moreover, the Soviet political leadership seemed to understand the potential diplomatic and political virtues of military power. They became more intent on asserting their prerogatives in an ever-increasing arc around the periphery of the Soviet Union. Afghanistan was only the latest in a series of Soviet extensions of military power and influence. The Soviets had actively intervened in the Horn of Africa, had provided the transport for Cuban forces to Angola, and were reaching into Central America, right on the U.S. doorstep.

Surprisingly, however, traces of pessimism were beginning to creep into Soviet military literature in the mid-1980s. Soviet thinkers such as Marshal Nikolay Ogarkov were beginning to write about a military-technical revolution that they feared might bypass them. The Soviets pointed to developments in electronics, computers and telecommunications—all the ingredients of the information age—as having the potential to change the very nature of warfare. Time and speed of operations would be the critical determinants of success on the future battlefield. Weapons would be more accurate and lethal and, as a result of communications and computers, there would be a greatly shortened cycle between the detection and the destruction of a target. With the advent of satellites and over-the-horizon sensors, even vast distances would no longer provide safety from such precision strikes.

It became apparent to some of us following this literature that the Soviets were talking about developments in the West, and particularly in the United States, that had the potential to negate their expensive buildup of conventional forces and might prove too difficult for them to counter. In short, the Soviet military feared that their investment and the attendant benefits of power and prestige could be overtaken by U.S. technological developments.

Selling that story to the Reagan Pentagon was not easy. Had it not been for one man, Andrew Marshall, the story would likely have gone unnoticed. Mr. Marshall was and still is the primary intellectual force in the Pentagon. Defense secretaries and their staffs ignore him at their peril. Naturally his influence has ebbed and flowed over time depending on the intelligence and intellectual curiosity of whoever happens to be the current secretary of defense. Marshall has mentored many of the nation's brightest young defense intellectuals and is widely credited with being the father of a number of defense strategies employed by the United States over time. He has been one of the strongest proponents of shifting America's defense posture away from Europe to confront new threats from the East—especially the Peoples' Republic of China. He is a longtime critic of the ineffectiveness of the U.S. Intelligence Community. He was the driving force behind Competitive Strategies, an idea that sought to play upon the systemic weaknesses of the Soviet Union and encourage it to waste resources on unproductive ventures. The Reagan administration's Strategic Defense Initiative, whatever its original intent, certainly had the additional benefit of driving Soviet spending to the brink of bankruptcy.

I am proud that I did some of the original work on this aspect of defense strategy under the sponsorship of Andy Marshall. One of my reports for him became a standard reference text at the nation's war colleges and even in some universities. In the last years of the Reagan Pentagon, a report entitled "Discriminate Deterrence" used some of the original research I had done on Soviet perceptions of the revolution in military affairs. One entire annex was devoted to the theme of Soviet thinking on these developments. Unfortunately, the report was dead on arrival at the Pentagon, but later I learned that the Chinese had studied it intensively. Nice to know that someone is reading your stuff.

Besides working for Marshall, I also came to the attention of Albert Wohlstetter, one of the defense intellectual giants of our time. Wohlstetter had made a name for himself in the 1950s with a number of important defense studies about our nuclear posture. His wife, Alberta, wrote the seminal study on the role of surprise in warfare based on the Pearl Harbor attack. Wohlstetter, now deceased, became interested in some work I was doing on Soviet thinking about nuclear strategy and operations. He became a very influential patron and opened a number of opportunities to me. In one of his articles in the prestigious journal *Foreign Affairs,* he labeled me as one of several bright young specialists on Soviet military thinking doing cutting-edge research. This was heady stuff for someone from my background, especially given the fact that I really had no formal academic training in this discipline. But I worked hard, was careful about my research and sources, and tried to be meticulous about my writing style. I wasn't really interested in supporting a particular political agenda or point of view; I just wanted to write what I believed and what I could support through solid research. In fact, on a number of issues, especially those involving nuclear strategy and conventional warfare, I tangled repeatedly with the "conservatives" in the field.

As the 1980s came to a close, I left the contract research world and worked for a year at the National Defense University. In 1990 I was selected to be on the U.S. delegation to a conference on military doctrine in Vienna. This was the largest gathering of European heads of military, I think, since the Vienna Conference in 1815. Officially, I was there to support General Colin Powell, the head of the delegation, although in truth the general, an impressive man, was hardly interested in what I or any other delegation member had to say. I did have the opportunity to meet and interact with many officials from the Soviet Union and from the Warsaw Pact. I learned much from this experience, although the Warsaw Pact and even the Soviet Union were soon to disappear onto the dustbin of history.

IN 1990 MY CAREER took a fateful, perhaps even fatal, turn when I accepted an offer to work at Los Alamos National Laboratory in New Mexico. After making the cross-country trip, our family found itself in a southwestern paradise. The light was different from anywhere else I had been, and the sunsets and sunrises were so breathtaking it was almost possible to think you were imagining them. My daughter, then six, used to say that the mountain vistas must surely be paintings, because nothing natural could be so beautiful. I came to appreciate why so many artists made their way to New Mexico.

It was fascinating to walk around the lab and think about the great works done there during World War II. I enjoyed having visitors because it was an excuse to arrange for guided tours by some of the old-timers. I enjoyed these at least as much as the visitors. During one tour, our guide led us to the site where the first atomic bomb was assembled before it was moved down to Alamogordo for testing. Such a historic site, but now there is a Dumpster sitting almost exactly where the atomic age was born.

At the same time, Los Alamos, a small town set up in the mountains, is very isolated—deliberately so, of course. I'm told it has more Ph.D.s, more churches and more travel agencies per capita than any other place in the country. One joke we heard early on about Los Alamos was that if a husband died, the first call the grieving widow made was to the real estate agent, then the undertaker. Los Alamos in the early 1990s turned out to be a depressing place, actually. The lab's leadership was weak and its mission, designing and developing nuclear weapons, was clearly in doubt. Few people in the military or the Bush administration as a whole cared much about nuclear weapons; in fact, most were intent on getting rid of them as quickly as possible.

President Bush's energy secretary, James Watkins, a retired navy admiral, seemed more determined to enforce a zero-defects mentality on the labs than to deal with the labs' future. Watkins sent a "Tiger Team" to inspect the labs in 1992, focusing primarily on safety and environmental cleanup. We spent hours checking electrical plugs and learning where the fire extinguisher was and how to dial emergency numbers. I think the lab must have spent millions of dollars preparing for the Tiger Team's arrival and then millions more fixing the deficiencies it uncovered. It seemed like mostly a waste of time; in retrospect, we were fiddling while Rome burned. It's too bad that Watkins didn't spend some of that energy on security and counterintelligence.

I was part of a policy group, the Center for National Security Studies, that had been formed to support the lab director. As with any such organization, the Center's influence depended on access. It had been established in the mid-1980s under a director named Don Kerr, who seemed to value the support. Sig Hecker, the director during my tenure, seemed to have little appreciation for our advice. Consequently, the value of the Center diminished over time and it was eventually disbanded after I left the laboratory. I must say that I got along well with Hecker, and he always made time to listen to what I had to offer regarding developments in Russia or Washington. But I saw the handwriting on the wall for the Center not long after I arrived, and so I began to cast around for other work elsewhere in the lab.

Despite my experience and background, I had practically no contact with the Los Alamos intelligence organization, euphemistically titled the International Technology (IT) Division. This was a strange collection of aging scientists and lab misfits; secretive to a fault, these guys were mostly intelligence wannabes. They were fiercely competitive with their biggest rival, the intelligence section at Livermore National Laboratory, known as "Z-division." IT's harshest invective was reserved not for a foreign espionage operation, but for a Z-division report or Z-division personnel. IT tried to convince its Washington customers, mostly in the Pentagon or at the Defense Intelligence Agency, that it drew on the expertise of the entire national lab network and could therefore give the customer access to decades of experience and the brainpower of the whole laboratory. In truth, IT almost never brought in scientists from outside its own small shop to work on government projects, so the government was buying the same old rehashed thinking from the same old scientists time after time.

I thought that I could build some bridges and maybe open some new areas of work for these guys. Andy Marshall had suggested that perhaps I could bring the lab into Washington-area deliberations about new foreign technologies—work that the labs had done in the past, but in a fashion too arcane to be of any real value to the decision makers. After all, the lab had many world-class experts on new materials and computer technologies, but IT had failed to master the ability to put these developments in terms that laymen could understand. I found, however, no interest whatsoever in any type of collaborative work at IT. My interactions and dealings with the management and scientists were always cordial; they just seemed unable to find common ground between their areas of expertise and my background. So I decided to create my own business opportunities and tap into this expertise for myself. I had retained all my security clearances and my network of contacts in the Washington area.

One topic that had particularly intrigued me was the issue of nuclear security in the former Soviet Union. As the Soviet empire and even Russia seemed to be coming apart, I wondered about the safety of its vast nuclear arsenal. What, if any, were the implications of the breakup for the Soviet military and for the integrity of the Soviet nuclear command and control system? What about the nuclear guards, technicians and others who comprised the swollen bureaucracy supporting the nuclear infrastructure? What would be their fate and how might that affect nuclear security—both theirs and ours? On my first trip back to Washington, I found some kindred souls interested in this issue at the National Intelligence Council and at the Department of Energy's Office of Foreign Intelligence. The National Intelligence Council is a collection of senior experts from within the U.S. Intelligence Community organized along both regional and functional lines, and its experts produce highly authoritative assessments on topics of interest to the President and his senior national security advisors. Larry Gershwin, from the NIC, and Jay Steward, at DOE, both expressed an interest in delving further into this subject. I was pleased that someone in Washington was giving some thought to such "worst-case" scenarios.

Steward already had some research on the stability of the Russian security system for nuclear weapons under way at the labs. He asked me to join in and try to make the results understandable to a policy customer looking to comprehend the big picture. The lab team's results were "not ready for prime time" and lacked any real intelligence input. I provided that, redid the briefing and was selected by Steward to brief Secretary Watkins at the DOE. About halfway through the briefing, Watkins woke up to the potential implications of the message that nuclear security in Russia was at risk, and he ordered Steward to undertake a broader study. We also provided the message to Gershwin and recommended that a National Intelligence Estimate (NIE) be commissioned to study this issue.

NIEs used to be the ultimate product of the U.S. Intelligence Community and, once adopted, they became the official view of the director of central intelligence (DCI), the overlord of all the intelligence agencies that compromise the Intelligence Community. Every year, the NIC experts would produce dozens of such assessments on topics ranging from trends in Soviet strategic nuclear forces to the prospects for systemic political change in Mexico. The NIEs covered foreign political, economic and military developments and were supposed to forecast trends over a set period of time, which could extend from about six months to ten years into the future. President Reagan's first DCI, William Casey, had taken NIEs very seriously, although it is said that he was not above changing judgments that did not suit his personal views. In mid-1991, I was selected to be one of the main drafters of an NIE on the security of nuclear weapons in the former Soviet Union. I worked on this estimate nearly fulltime over the next two years and spent much of that time on airplanes traveling to and from Washington. During this period, I worked closely with CIA analysts serving on the NIC as well as analysts from other intelligence agencies. I also think I was the first person from the labs to be selected as a principal NIE drafter in many years.

That last point did create some interesting problems for me. Back at the lab, the IT analysts were disturbed that someone from outside their organization had been invited to work on what they saw as their area of expertise. I tried to defuse their hostility by involving as many IT experts as possible in the ongoing project. To their credit, IT managers did provide appropriate workspace and support whenever I needed to review intelligence materials too sensitive to be kept in my own office. Meanwhile, the analysts from the CIA Directorate of Intelligence also resented the intrusion from an outsider. The CIA became an extremely recalcitrant player in the development of this assessment, and its analysts resisted and sought to water down any sort of meaningful conclusion or key judgment nearly every step of the way.

CIA analysts seemed unwilling or unable to think "outside the box" and were overly tied to what was the conventional wisdom of the period, i.e., Russian nuclear security was not at risk. Later on, when the conventional wisdom shifted to the other extreme of almost overstating the risk, I was amused to see the CIA embrace this new position with all the ardor of a recent convert. At that earlier point, however, the CIA and the State Department were nearly indistinguishable in their views and recommendations. "See no evil, hear no evil" would best describe the CIA's attitude toward the breakdown of control over Russian nuclear weapons in those days.

The most emotionally charged issue in disputes about the safety and security of nuclear weapons revolved around the political and territorial integrity of Russia. During the period when I was working on this estimate, the Soviet Union dissolved and broke up into a multitude of new states. Some of these, such as Ukraine, Belarus and Kazakhstan, still had nuclear weapons deployed on their territory. Internally, Russia's regions were restive and anxious to be free of Moscow's domination—especially in the area of taxation and economic control. Consequently, the issue of the possible disintegration of Russia became an important consideration in the fate of Russia's nuclear arsenal, which was spread across the vast expanse of the former Soviet Union.

Members of the Bush administration, however, had no interest in discussing the subject. The administration was counting on first Mikhail Gorbachev and then Boris Yeltsin to hold the old empire together, and was unwilling even to think about disintegration scenarios. Following their lead, the CIA pooh-poohed any possibility of a threat to nuclear security stemming from such a breakup. At the very time when some of the best Soviet analysts in the business—outside the government—were thinking very hard about the centrifugal forces in Russia and the demise of Moscow's control over its regions, CIA analysts were refusing to address the issue. "Worst-case scenarios" and "overly alarmist" were the usual CIA putdowns; I would experience these again during the disputes over Chinese nuclear espionage.

We had to contend not only with CIA, but with Russia itself, whose unfolding devolution constantly forced us back to the drawing board. The August 1991 coup in Moscow held a number of important developments for nuclear security, which some are still debating to this day. We also witnessed a serious deterioration in security for the Russian nuclear arsenal during this period. The Russians were learning the public relations game and fed lots of misinformation into the system about how secure their weapons were, and policymakers wishing to emphasize Moscow's hold on things used these Russian statements as rebuttal to our "worst-case" fears.

The NIE finally was published in late 1993 or early 1994. We were very concerned about the security of Russia's nuclear weapons and also worried about an unauthorized launch of Russian missiles against the United States. We feared that the growing Russian mafia might steal a nuclear weapon and sell it to a group of terrorists or to Iran or Iraq. Under sponsorship of Steward at the Department of Energy, I had been briefing policymakers in the Pentagon and even some congressional staffers around Washington on some of the conclusions and key judgments of our work for about six months at that point. We always underscored that ours was a DOE position and should not be confused with an official Intelligence Community position on this topic. Our reception was somewhat mixed; some Bush officials, especially within DOE, simply refused to accept that anything was wrong with Russian nuclear security. After all, their Russian counterparts had assured them that all was well. For the most part, official Washington took note of our conclusions and moved on, hoping that everything would turn out well without our having to do anything about it.

By far the most positive response we received came from NATO's secretary general, Manfred Woerner. In mid-1993, after the new administration had been sworn in, we traveled to Brussels to brief him, members of his staff and the U.S. delegation to NATO. The secretary general took our message very seriously, as did the non-U.S. members of his staff. The U.S. delegation, however, went ballistic because we had been allowed to come over with this "alarmist" and overly pessimistic story. A cable war ensued, with lots of finger pointing and name calling. Of course, our trip had been blessed by Bill Clinton's new Energy Department secretary, Hazel O'Leary, and approved by the State Department. The Intelligence Community knew our message full well, but nobody had thought to give the U.S. delegation a heads-up. They were caught off-guard and flatfooted in front of their European counterparts and, like bureaucrats anywhere, they were pissed. Not surprisingly, that was the beginning of the end of DOE's work on the subject of deterioration in Russian nuclear weapons security.

But for all the trouble, I do believe that our efforts in this matter did have an impact and maybe even made a difference. We certainly were among the first to raise the awareness of the U.S. political system to the threat represented by loosened nuclear security in Russia. Prominent defense experts like James Schlesinger, a former defense secretary, director of central intelligence and energy secretary, picked up the theme and began to carry the message on Capitol Hill. Senators Sam Nunn and Richard Lugar sponsored legislation to assist the Russians in securing their nuclear arsenal and the issue continues to be of concern to U.S. policymakers today. It also helped position DOE to play an important role in one of the biggest security debates of the early to mid 1990s.

FOR MY WORK on this project, in 1993 I was awarded both a Los Alamos Distinguished Performance Award, one of only about seven given to individuals that year, and an Intelligence Community Seal Medallion by the CIA director, James Woolsey. Given my later experiences with the Los Alamos lab, I bet they wish they could take that award back. Ironically, the metal stripping on the award began to peel off the plaque almost immediately. Just a coincidence, I guess.

One last thing about my time at Los Alamos. In early 1993, the IT director, Danny Stillman, stepped down and Los Alamos began a "search" for a new intelligence director. I strongly suspected that the job was "wired" for Stillman's deputy, a retired Air Force colonel named Terry Hawkins. But what the heck, I thought, I'll throw my hat in that ring. I had some fresh ideas about where Los Alamos intelligence should be heading and I had the support of some key intelligence managers back in Washington. I had a good interview with the selecting official, an associate director named John Browne, who later became the lab director. Some time passed and one day a friend who worked in the lab director's office showed up at my door. He said that Browne had selected me to be the new IT director, but that lab director Sig Hecker had been furious over this choice. Moreover, word had leaked out and Hecker was getting calls from former lab scientists from all over who were outraged that this job would go to a "nonscientist." It didn't; Hawkins emerged as the new IT director.

By this time, the Clinton administration was settling into office and Clinton political appointees were beginning to show up at the Energy Department. I had spent three years in Los Alamos, much of it on an airplane, and while the mileage benefits were nice, I was tired and wanted to spend more time with my kids. Seeking a transfer to Washington, I found a sponsor, an official named Ken Baker, who ironically would later become one of my worst enemies in the DOE bureaucracy. Finally I arrived back in Washington in October 1993. I had hoped to work on intelligence issues for an assistant secretary appointee, but I was sent downstairs to work in the DOE Intelligence secure compartmented information facility (SCIF). The SCIF was a cramped, windowless vault with air quality about like that of a World War II submarine. What a dump! It was to be my home for the next six years.

During the Bush administration, DOE Intelligence had been an independent office reporting directly to the secretary. But Hazel O'Leary didn't like this arrangement, especially after she got a look at the office's leadership. They just weren't quick enough on their feet for her and couldn't answer some of her most basic questions. There was also considerable suspicion that she and her new staff were skeptical about the value of intelligence in general and uncertain as to whether an "intelligence office" was consistent with her emphasis on "openness." So she consolidated intelligence into a larger office concerned primarily with policy issues. This was known first as the DOE Office of Intelligence and National Security, but that was later changed to the Office of Nonproliferation and National Security. Along with DOE's intelligence activity, this larger office was responsible for security affairs, arms control and emergency management. O'Leary hired a former staff director from Capitol Hill, Jack Keliher, to run this conglomeration, but he only lasted about a year or so before he ran afoul of her. It was never quite clear what he had done to earn her displeasure, but there was some speculation that he was still too much of a "Cold Warrior" for O'Leary.

In the four years that the intelligence activity was part of this larger office, there were three different directors, all political appointees. The Office of Nonproliferation and National Security was considered by many to be the most dysfunctional office in DOE; there were just too many competing interests and the leadership was too weak to make it run efficiently. Worse yet, DOE had the intelligence activity subordinate to a larger organization responsible for making policy, always a prescription for disaster. Conflicts between the mandates of policy and the "facts" that intelligence often turns up are nearly inevitable. Too often, policymakers just want to bury these intelligence "facts" when they prove inconvenient. Therefore, in every other Washington agency, intelligence is a separate and independent activity that reports directly to the cabinet officer who heads that agency. Even the State Department. Inevitably, DOE became one of the worst offenders in the politicization of intelligence.

By 1993 the leadership of the Intelligence Office was in complete turmoil. During the Bush administration, a former congressman from Virginia named Bob Daniel had been appointed director.

The title also carried with it the role of senior intelligence officer of the Department of Energy. Theoretically this made the job second in importance only to the secretary's on all matters pertaining to intelligence and counterintelligence. But Daniel had left, of course, in the housecleaning that followed the change of administration after Bill Clinton defeated George Bush in 1992. I had given O'Leary her first intelligence briefing on Russian nuclear security, and I was the first Los Alamos representative to have any contact with her. I found her to be quite personable and engaging. She seemed very interested in our subject matter and approved our visit to Europe and NATO, but I was not to see her again for nearly a year.

Jack Keliher asked me to try to help the current director of intelligence, a former Army buddy of his named Jim Ford. He was a career federal employee who was selected to be Bob Daniel's deputy in 1992. He was not a political appointee, but as a friend of Keliher's he had moved up to the top job in intelligence in 1993 after Daniel left. I was to learn that DOE Intelligence had been a swamp of backstabbing and the other bureaucratic martial arts practiced in Washington. During this time, the Intelligence Office was responsible for foreign intelligence and counterintelligence as well as something called the Office of Threat Assessment. Just what the latter did, I never really knew. I looked at some of their products and learned that they issued reports on outlaw motorcycle gangs in the American South and the potential threat from these gangs to DOE facilities. Forget the absurdity of it; such reporting on U.S. citizens by an intelligence activity is a serious violation of the law. I pushed Ford to get rid of this activity as soon as possible.

But of course nothing happened, as I would discover was the norm when DOE management was confronted with any tough issues. The internecine warfare that was ongoing in the Office of Intelligence was fascinating to watch, however. After every meeting of the key managers of the office—about four or five individuals in all— each would scurry back to his or her office to document every little tick and gesture by Jim Ford. Little of substantive value got accomplished during this period. The working employees were afraid to run afoul of any of the managers and so were disinclined to take any initiative whatsoever. I was most upset to see that leadership on the issue of Russian nuclear security had been handed over to

CIA. This was clearly a DOE issue and had afforded the office a chance to become an important contributor to national policy, so it seemed a shame to abandon it. Worse still, CIA was doing little more than repackaging and republishing work we had already done, and taking credit for raising the issue in the first place. After all, we were now about a year and a half downstream and a host of new initiatives, including intelligence collection activities, should have been set in motion. But CIA had failed to follow up on several good starts and, as we were later to learn, had even killed some promising efforts.

Meanwhile, the new political leadership was rapidly losing what little faith it had in the department's intelligence capability. At one point, Secretary O'Leary asked the intelligence people what they could tell her that she couldn't see on CNN. They were dumbstruck and had no answer.

Early in 1994, Keliher asked me for my recommendations about how to fix DOE Intelligence. I wrote a short memorandum arguing for a refocusing of priorities, a restructuring of the organization, and changes in the leadership mix in the office. I argued that the incumbent director could stay on provided that he had a strong deputy—an effort to keep Keliher from being prejudiced against my other recommendations—but that the other managers had to go. Further, I thought that counterintelligence and the Office of Threat Assessment should be removed from the intelligence portfolio; the latter office had nothing to do with intelligence and should have been eliminated altogether. Likewise, counterintelligence was too much of a distraction for Ford and was diluting the focus on foreign intelligence challenges. My strongest recommendation was: get rid of both these functions and focus on foreign intelligence.

To my surprise, Keliher called me and said he liked my ideas and wanted me to implement them. In May 1994, I was appointed director of intelligence at the Department of Energy. In early 1995, I also became responsible for managing the department's counterintelligence activity. The combination of these two functions put me in charge of all intelligence activities throughout the department and its widespread national laboratory complex, including about 2,500 people and a $35 million budget. The complex includes the now-infamous Los Alamos National Laboratory, as well as twelve other major, multipurpose national laboratories, repositories of the nation's nuclear secrets, acquired through decades of research, development and testing—at an expenditure of billions of taxpayer dollars. The labs also have developed world-class computing capabilities and provided much of the funding for the development of our supercomputers. As the director of counterintelligence, I was responsible for protecting those secrets from foreign intelligence services, such as China's Ministry of State Security.

THE DOE OFFICE OF INTELLIGENCE had never been a major player within the U.S. Intelligence Community, having always taken a back seat to the Central Intelligence Agency, the Defense Intelligence Agency and others. But I thought most of the key intelligence challenges of the 1990s and the new century were actually "DOE issues." DOE and the labs had a major role to play in intelligence on the spread of nuclear weapons, the security of nuclear weapons and nuclear material in the former Soviet Union, and foreign developments in technology, especially computing, biotechnology and materials technologies. We had just won the Gulf War, which was fought over access to a continuing supply of energy. I expected that energy security would become a critical issue in the coming decade. The Intelligence Community had yet to use the world-class expertise of the labs effectively in a major, integrated fashion on the tough intelligence problems now confronting us. Most agencies preferred to work with the labs on a "piecework" basis and often selected scientists to work on projects more for their willingness to agree with agency positions than for their technical skills. The labs rarely spoke with one voice, hardly ever coordinated their work plans, and consistently failed to live up to expectations. And they were very expensive.

Still, I was very bullish on how we could contribute intelligence support to the new Clinton administration. Although in many respects this represented the pinnacle of my career, I took the director's job in order to achieve specific goals and objectives. Besides, I had some additional motivation: Keliher told me that I had about six months to get the Office of Intelligence "fixed" or Secretary O'Leary would probably shut it down. Since I was not a career bureaucrat who had come up through the ranks and I really didn't have a stake in some existing priorities or policies, I thought I could break new ground for DOE Intelligence. I figured this was as high in the Intelligence Community's management structure as I would get. I didn't have the political connections or the big national reputation necessary to become, for example, the CIA director. My game plan was to rebuild Energy Intelligence and make it an important contributor to the Intelligence Community, then leave for a quiet job in the private sector or an analytic position somewhere else in the Community.

First and foremost, I wanted to develop good, solid intelligence assessments that would help our policymakers understand the world around them, warn them of emerging problems and challenges, and motivate them to develop policies to secure national security objectives. My prime directive was to make sure that our customers, especially the secretary, were not surprised. We would provide intelligence that helped her to anticipate upcoming problems or situations and then it was up to her to formulate policies and plans to manage these situations.

My original plan for Keliher had split counterintelligence out of the Office of Intelligence and transferred it to the Office of Security Affairs. I wanted no part of the murky world inhabited by CI officers and considered it to be little more than a distraction from the real work of intelligence. Ironically, the Justice Department's Office of Intelligence Policy Review overruled my recommendation and, after about a year, CI came back under my direct management.

It would later be said that I was inexperienced in counterintelligence and that this caused all the "problems." True, I had no prior experience or formal training in CI. In fact, I didn't want the CI job. Once it came under my control, I realized I had a real mess on my hands. The office was rife with personnel problems and petty bickering; it was just plain dysfunctional. A single example will suffice. One of the most highly touted CI analysts was asked to produce an assessment of the CI threat in Georgia. The analyst demurred, saying that Atlanta is a safe city and asking why we should be worried about the CI threat there. It sounds like a joke that an intelligence professional wouldn't understand the reference to the former Soviet republic. I wish it had been.

So I relied on an experienced CIA counterintelligence expert already on site. When he left for retirement, we found another expert fresh from an assignment on the CIA spy Aldrich Ames damage assessment team. He was experienced, able and held in high esteem within the counterintelligence community, and he proved to be an excellent CI manager. Unfortunately, we were unable to interest the FBI in sending over someone to help us. The FBI had had a bitter experience with DOE dating back to the late 1980s. DOE federal employees were openly hostile to FBI agents in their midst and made life for these agents miserable. The FBI agents on detail to DOE got almost no cooperation from their DOE counterintelligence office mates and were cut off from nearly all contact with higher DOE managers. I tried to reestablish the DOE-FBI relationship, but the damage had been done by the time I came along.

With a few very notable exceptions, the existing DOE federal cadre in the Office of Intelligence was poorly motivated and just waiting out their time until retirement. I promoted the exceptions, turned over most of the management duties to them and then recruited from CIA and the labs to fill the gaps. Within about six months, most of the time servers and clock watchers had departed, and a team combining strong intelligence analytic skills and decades of experience in the design, development and testing of nuclear weapons was in place. People often scoff at the notion of hardworking federal employees, but I can say that no group I'd seen in either the government or the private sector ever worked harder than these people. It was common to find people working weekends and evenings just to stay ahead of the flow of intelligence information into our office or to prepare reports and briefings for the upcoming week.

Keliher had given me about six months to "save" the office; otherwise, the secretary's bean counters would probably reinvent DOE Intelligence out of existence. In fact, we did make major strides in putting it on the map. Our work provided the stimulus for major U.S. programs to secure nuclear warheads and materials in Russia. We led the community in a major reevaluation of North Korea's nuclear program. We broke new ground in the Intelligence Community's assessments about Russian nuclear weapons, Russian programs to maintain these weapons under the Comprehensive Test Ban Treaty, and new Russian nuclear testing at their facility in the Barents Sea. We tried for a year to warn the Intelligence Community of the coming "nuclearization" of South Asia, but the Indian and Pakistani nuclear tests of mid-1998 still took everyone by surprise.

All in all, by the mid-1990s DOE Intelligence had become a force within the Intelligence Community, and policymakers at the National Security Council, the Pentagon and the State Department were coming to rely increasingly on our assessments. I used to tell our intelligence officers that articles in the *Washington Times* and elsewhere based on leaks of our reports meant that we had finally arrived. On at least one occasion, our efforts spared the department a major embarrassment and may even have saved some lives. I wish I could say that all our efforts made a major impact on Clinton policymakers, but many of our findings and conclusions cut across administration policy preferences.

But the biggest story we uncovered was unquestionably evidence of Chinese nuclear espionage

TWO

Setting the Stage

The widening gap between the level of security and the severity of the threat resulted in cases where sensitive nuclear weapons information was certainly lost to espionage.... The extent to which these serious lapses may have damaged American security is incalculable.
—President's Foreign Intelligence Advisory Board
August 1999

The Department of Energy was formed in 1977 during the Carter administration to meet the perceived energy crisis and combined the Energy Research and Development Administration, the Federal Energy Administration and elements of several other cabinet-level agencies. But it was also the successor to the Atomic Energy Commission, formed after World War II to manage the growing nuclear weapons laboratory complex. It is through this complex that the Department of Energy designs, develops, tests and maintains our nuclear arsenal, which is still the backbone of our national deterrent. The department's annual budget is in excess of $20 billion, and it runs largely on the strength of its laboratory contractors, which number about 260 for every federal employee on the DOE payroll. The laboratories and power administrations that comprise this complex are spread out over much of the United States, but the nuclear weapons labs and production facilities form its backbone (see map on page 40). The power and influence within DOE Headquarters wielded by scientists from these labs, and especially Los Alamos, Livermore and Sandia National Labs, far exceed their share of the annual DOE budget.

While the Energy Department was not a major player in national security debates over Kosovo, for example, it did take an important role in U.S. relations with Russia and the other states of the former Soviet Union. It became an instrument of policy on such

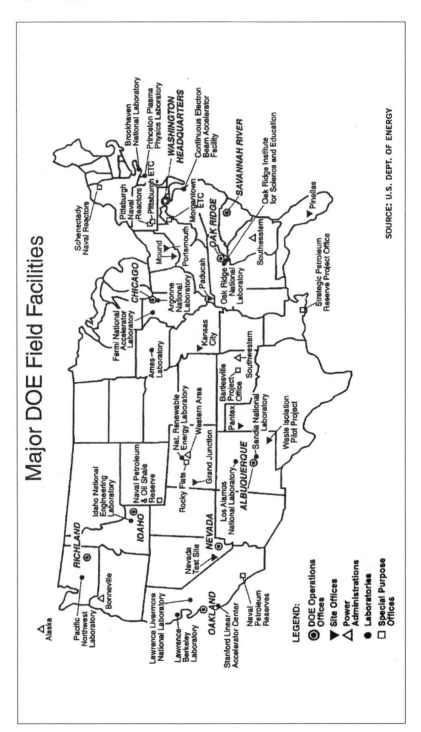

Major DOE Field Facilities

SOURCE: U.S. DEPT. OF ENERGY

issues as arms control, nuclear security and energy supply. The
Energy Department's national laboratories supplied cutting-edge
technologies to the Intelligence Community, the military and law
enforcement agencies in the battle against terrorism and foreign
and domestic computer attacks. One of my divisions had both technologies and staff deploying frequently to crises in Bosnia, Chile
and the Middle East.

But more importantly, the Energy Department and the national
labs like Los Alamos are the keepers of our most priceless nuclear
secrets. American taxpayers have spent billions of dollars developing these secrets. The United States conducted over one thousand nuclear tests at facilities in the Pacific Ocean and then at the
Nevada Test Site near Las Vegas. Each such test was also the occasion for countless non-nuclear experiments, computer simulations
and man-hours of research. As a result of all these experiments, the
labs are the keepers of the secrets on every facet of the development of nuclear weapons. These secrets are contained in thousands
of classified documents and recorded in enormous computer files
that are maintained on the labs' classified computer networks. These
files contain the records and results of every nuclear test conducted
by the United States since World War II, nuclear warhead design
specifics and other secrets about how U.S. nuclear warheads are
designed and how they work. The labs researched and developed
techniques for the production of the fissile material needed to fuel
nuclear weapons. Lab scientists explored virtually every fissile
material production technique imaginable over the past fifty-plus
years. The labs settled on breeding and production of plutonium
from so-called nuclear production reactors and various processes
to enrich uranium. But research units within the labs continue to
explore other methods for the production of fissile materials, including the use of powerful lasers. Lab scientists developed alternative
methods for reprocessing spent fuel from nuclear reactors for the
production of plutonium. When I was at Los Alamos in the early
1990s, the annual budget just for that lab alone was reputed to be
over $1 billion.

During my time at the Energy Department, there was frequent
turnover in the leadership of the Clinton administration's national
security apparatus. I served three secretaries of energy, three

secretaries of defense and two national security advisors. Despite their nuclear responsibilities, none of the three energy secretaries had any experience or background in national security, nuclear weapons policy or intelligence.[1] There were also three different CIA directors during this period. It is common knowledge that the administration was not really interested in national security and especially intelligence. I can personally attest to that, particularly with regard to intelligence, which was considered something to be manipulated and shaped to serve policy interests. Believe it or not, that is almost a direct quote from one of the CIA directors of this period.

The Clinton administration will not be remembered for its stewardship of national security. Bill Clinton came into power just after the death of the Soviet Union. Many thought the United States and the world were entering a "strategic pause," that is, a period in which international relations would be reordered to accommodate the new global realities. But as attention shifted away from Soviet pretensions, it seemed that a new threat emerged almost weekly. First, it was the proliferation of weapons of mass destruction. But although millions, maybe billions of dollars were appropriated for new technologies and policymakers constantly came up with new slogans like "counterproliferation," in the end the administration achieved precious little. Trying to "buy" countries like Pakistan, North Korea and even China out of their nuclear-missile ambitions just didn't work. So proliferation gradually faded in importance, to be replaced by terrorism and then cyberterrorism. True to form, lots of money got spent, a fair amount by the DOE national labs, but the failures were plain for all to see on September 11, 2001. For a while the Clinton administration flirted with making AIDS or global pollution or some other "nontraditional" issue the central focus of its threat assessments. Like a hyperactive child, it was unable to focus its attention. As a result, we suffered catastrophic losses in the war against terrorism and we may have lost forever the campaign to stop the spread of weapons of mass destruction and the missiles to deliver these weapons.

The U.S. Intelligence Community floundered during this time, lurching from one "threat" to another. Some of the Intelligence Community's leadership complained bitterly about the lack of any clear focus or direction from "downtown," that is, the White House. The National Security Council throughout this period was widely considered inept and rudderless. One Presidential Directive did seek to establish "intelligence priorities," but it mostly rubber-stamped the traditional emphasis on the former Soviet Union and other "traditional" threats. Its inattention to such things as intelligence collection was a disaster, if for no other reason than that Africa and the so-called Third World dropped off its map. I vividly remember one Pentagon intelligence representative saying that for the Pentagon, at least, Africa no longer existed. Never mind that U.S. forces would repeatedly deploy into Africa on what came to be known as "NEOs," or nationals extraction operations, to get Americans out of the cauldron that boiled over there again and again during the 1990s. But it also meant that U.S. forces would go into harm's way (as in Somalia in 1993) without intelligence products like maps, language skills and "on-the-ground" intelligence. This ineptitude didn't start in the Clinton administration, but it certainly got much worse in the 1990s.

Globalization and the "threat" to American business from foreign competitors were taken more seriously by the White House. As the Defense Department downsized, U.S. defense contractors had to find other markets for their products. Similarly, computer firms wanted to expand into new markets and sought to throw off export controls that restricted their entry into China and elsewhere. Little thought was given to preserving the edge that science and technology had provided U.S. national security over the years. Commercial diplomacy gradually became the centerpiece of the Clinton foreign policy and the execution of that policy shifted to the Commerce Department.

The Energy Department also became a player in commercial diplomacy, as Secretary O'Leary traveled the world in search of energy deals with South Africa, India and China. Many thought she was openly competing with Ron Brown, the secretary of commerce, to see who could open up the most markets for American business. As with Brown, her junkets to South Africa and elsewhere were packed with businessmen, often from the small, disadvantaged category, willing to pay for the opportunity to find new markets in those distant lands. It was commonly understood within the Energy bureaucracy, and at Commerce as well, that these seats were purchased with contributions to the Democratic National Committee or other "worthy" causes. Cabinet officials always travel with security officials and bodyguards, but it became customary for O'Leary's travel team to kick these officials off the plane in order to open up more seats for paying businessmen.

Traditional concerns about national security took a back seat to the new "commercial realities" in the consideration of what we would export. And the cabinet agencies that had previously managed export controls, State and Defense, gave way to the Department of Commerce, which led the fight to relax export controls on supercomputers, satellites, communications and a host of other high-tech products. American science and technology would be used in an attempt to entice countries like the People's Republic of China to open their markets and adopt behaviors appropriate for the "community of nations." In the search for new markets, very little attention was given to protecting the advantage that the science and technology sector had provided U.S. national security throughout the Cold War.

This change of emphasis created many of the "whistleblowers" in the Clinton administration—frustrated export control experts who had previously won the war to prevent high-tech exports to the Soviets and their allies in the Cold War were now pushed aside by political appointees interested only in the bottom line. One example: there was a battle-royal over the export of fiber-optic production capabilities to the PRC in the mid-1990s. The export controllers lost the battle and then watched with amazement as the PRC used its new capability to build a fiber-optic military command and control network for Iraq. Later, the Clinton administration had to conduct air strikes on Iraq to knock that network out of commission.

And so it went.

In addition to bizarre interpretations of export control, the end of the Cold War brought forth other examples of outright silliness on the part of the Clinton administration. "Openness" and "declassification" became the driving force in many national security organizations, even CIA and the Pentagon. The President instituted policies involving "bulk" declassification of records, that is, declassification by the linear foot rather than through a careful review of each document. Millions of pages of "declassified" material were pushed out the front door of various agencies, including the armed services, CIA, the Energy Department and the Pentagon. An ever-larger share of budget appropriations went toward the costs of "declassification." At DOE, for example, the funding requirements of declassification would consume an increasing share of the security budget. Millions were spent on sending documents out the door, and then millions more were spent on retrieving and reclassifying many of these same documents later.

Inevitably, hundreds of pages of materials containing classified details on nuclear warhead designs would be discovered in repositories around Washington, D.C., that were open to anyone with a U.S. driver's license, regardless of citizenship. These documents were found to contain details on U.S. nuclear warhead designs and nuclear tests. The Energy Department, which led the charge to declassify documents, would later find that the following types of nuclear warhead data, all of which should have remained classified Secret/Restricted Data, had been "inadvertently" released:

- Mass and dimensions of fissile materials
- Quantity of high explosives
- Number of detonators
- Detonation simultaneity requirements
- Tamper materials
- Contribution of boosting to performance
- How small a weapon can be designed
- Fissile material compression information
- Design for a levitated pit
- Yield of an individual device stage
- Yield-to-weight ratio
- Methods of yield selection
- Nuclear device weight
- Materials in a nuclear assembly system

Many of these documents were twenty-five years old or more and described older, less sophisticated U.S. nuclear warheads. But such details were exactly the types of data sought by would-be nuclear states or terrorists because these designs were less challenging to develop. At least some of this material found its way onto the Internet.

Finally, the notion that espionage continued to represent a very real threat to America's scientific and technological prowess was considered a joke by many in the Clinton administration. Combined with declassification, its definition of "openness" generally meant relaxed security procedures and a deemphasis of the traditional means of safeguarding our secrets. Security and counterintelligence budgets were cut to the bone, continuing a trend that had already started during the first Bush administration. In 1992, for instance, the FBI announced plans to transfer three hundred trained agents out of counterintelligence to violent crime cases. Clinton's new FBI director, Louis Freeh, continued that trend and "downsized" CI even more. Freeh emphasized street crime, drugs, gangs and white-collar crime. Many seasoned counterintelligence agents left the Bureau in disgust, and, as we learned later, the sections devoted to Chinese counterespionage were especially hard hit both at Headquarters and in the field.

The list of security mistakes and lapses—beyond declassification—that occurred during the Clinton years is staggering. The administration nearly destroyed the Defense Security Service, which is responsible for conducting security background checks on Defense and military personnel. By slashing its budget deeply, the administration created a huge backlog in security investigations and updates, thus increasing the vulnerability of the Defense Department and the military services to espionage. A bungled computer modernization program further hobbled DSS's mission and added to the turmoil surrounding this critical defense agency. The Pentagon's intelligence agency, known as the Defense Intelligence Agency (DIA), issued "no-escort" badges to Russian military intelligence agents, allowing them to roam the halls of the Pentagon unhindered by "burdensome" security.[2] DIA also abolished one of the government's strongest centers of intelligence on foreign science and technology.

The Central Intelligence Agency gutted its own Science and Technology Directorate, which had been responsible for many of the most successful technical intelligence collection programs during the Cold War. (The U2 spy plane, the use of satellites to gather all types of intelligence data, and many other supersecret technical developments had come out of this CIA organization.) The Clinton administration installed a Sandia National Lab scientist as the head of this directorate; her background was in computers and the development of computer-based analytic tools. Ill equipped to lead the diverse technical developments within the directorate, she hurt the CIA's ability to stay on the cutting edge of intelligence collection capabilities. Many of the organization's most creative people opted for retirement. Important technical collection initiatives were abandoned, which blinded us to critical clues about foreign nuclear developments.

The Commerce Department became particularly notorious for its lax security. Everyone remembers John Huang, the Clinton fundraiser who held a Top Secret clearance while he worked at Commerce. He was under investigation for years for allegedly funneling secrets to the Lippo Group and the PRC. Huang was known to be an avid consumer of intelligence reports, especially anything concerning energy developments in Asia. As it happened, I had some of the best Asian energy specialists in the Intelligence Community and we published regularly on developments in China and throughout the Asia-Pacific region. We later learned that more than a few of these reports made their way to Huang's clients in Asia. But other Clinton appointees at Commerce took dozens of classified documents on satellites, encryption and intelligence matters with them when they left the department.

The State Department "lost" laptop computers containing highly sensitive "special" intelligence, and Russian listening devices were discovered in a conference room frequented by the secretary of state. Russian diplomats and journalists were given "no-escort" badges that allowed them to roam freely through the building— the Cold War being over, after all. Likewise, State permitted contractors to move through the building unescorted. Given the sophistication of the listening devices and especially their clever concealment, one of these "contractors" must have been responsible for their installation.

And then there was the Department of Energy. No agency embraced "openness" more than Energy. Hazel O'Leary established this policy early on and DOE bureaucrats implemented it with a passion. In an Orwellian change, the DOE Office of Classification became the Office of Declassification[3] and the bureaucrat heading up this effort became a zealous advocate of pushing ever more classified information out into the public domain. Neither the Office of Intelligence nor the Counterintelligence Office was consulted before Secretary O'Leary's first big dump of classified information into the public domain in 1994. Subsequently, we learned that some scientists in the labs had bitterly resisted declassification of much of this material, but were rolled by lab managers and DOE bureaucrats eager to please their new masters. Why? Because promotions and cash awards were distributed to those who most readily embraced and implemented this new policy. Ironically, the same DOE official who led the charge on declassification and was awarded a $20,000 bonus for his efforts had been one of the most vigorous proponents of strengthened security and safeguards during the Bush administration. Contractors were hired to speed up the declassification and were paid on the basis of "pages declassified."

Inside the bureaucracy, many old-timers privately complained about this policy, but to criticize it openly was a sure ticket to early retirement or worse. It was not until much later that we in intelligence were able to persuade the "declassifiers" that much of the material going into the public domain could actually help a would-be proliferator develop nuclear weapons. Yes, much of the material was twenty years old or more, but many potential proliferators were at very early stages of their own programs and could benefit most from material considered obsolete or outdated by U.S. scientists.

The new team at DOE displayed a casual disdain for security in general. Shortly after her arrival, Secretary O'Leary cleaned out the holdover bureaucrats, whom she characterized as "old white guys with cuff links." Her new nuclear advisors were selected from the various antinuclear nongovernmental organizations (NGO) around town. In fact, her main advisor on these issues, and later chief of staff of the department, was a National Resources Defense Council lawyer who had spent most of his career suing the Department of Energy to force it to reveal more information on environmental cleanup or nuclear weapons plans. Not surprisingly, after the arrival of the O'Leary team, Freedom of Information requests for classified documents shot up. Security officials believed that O'Leary's advisors were pinpointing critical documents for requests by various antinuclear groups around Washington.

To demonstrate her own emphasis on openness, O'Leary removed the glass doors leading into the DOE secretarial suite on the seventh floor of the Headquarters building in downtown Washington, disarmed the guard force that maintained security at Headquarters, and reduced the security detail that accompanied her on trips. Later, when a stalker pursued her, she reinstated the enclosure on the secretarial suite and placed a guard outside that entrance. Her now-infamous decision to change badge colors was symptomatic of the O'Leary approach to security. Previously, DOE badges came in different colors to indicate the level of the security clearance held by the wearer and also to identify foreign nationals present on the lab campuses. Security officials told me that O'Leary considered the DOE badging system to be discriminatory and wagered that "persons of color" were more likely to hold lower-level badges than Caucasians. So DOE security went off and did a study. The result: "persons of color" at DOE Headquarters held proportionately more high-level security badges than did Caucasians. O'Leary lost her wager, but changed the badging system anyway. Hours were spent picking just the right color for the new badges and then finding just the right shade of green (her favorite color). The total cost of the new system is one piece of information that DOE will never declassify. It was implemented not only at DOE Headquarters in Washington, but also at all the lab locations throughout the country. Foreign visitors and postdoctoral assignees—even those from high-risk, sensitive countries—would now wear the same color of badge as longtime lab scientists.

At least once, O'Leary handed over a classified diagram of the U.S. W87 nuclear warhead, deployed on the Peacekeeper ICBM. The diagram was subsequently published in *U.S News & World Report,* which prompted a security investigation to find and punish the source of the leak. When the trail led back to Secretary O'Leary, the investigation was dropped. The diagram, subsequently published repeatedly, was probably classified Secret/Restricted Data, but O'Leary simply crossed out the classification markings before handing it to the reporter.[4]

As part of the openness campaign, O'Leary also loosened restrictions on those entering the building to visit the Freedom of Information Act library, where declassified documents were maintained. The building is a controlled-access facility—that is, escorts are required for visitors at all times. However, if a visitor showed up and told the guards that the FOIA library was his destination, the guards were instructed to permit him to pass through security without the usual restrictions. The guards were also instructed not to challenge visitors as to nationality or affiliation. Russians, Chinese and others could gain access to the building without the usual security precautions. Inevitably, an individual under surveillance by the FBI would come here to shake off his "tail." Security officials told me that diplomats would show up at the front door of DOE, announce their intention to visit the FOIA library, and be waved through security. When following FBI agents tried to enter, however, the guards would demand to see credentials and delay the agents' access to the building. Meanwhile, the diplomat under surveillance could slip out one of the building's many exits.

Secretary O'Leary's staff held regular meetings to inform her constituents—or stakeholders, in the jargon of the time—of progress in cleaning up the department and exposing past DOE and lab transgressions. An assortment of nongovernmental organizations, including Greenpeace, the Union of Concerned Scientists and other mostly left-leaning groups, would assemble at the department to take briefings from officials on such topics as environmental cleanup, nuclear testing and arms control initiatives. Some of these meetings were surreal and left many wondering just who was running the department. Bearded and Levi-clad Greenpeace activists, looking like leftovers from the 1960s, would demand ever more information about DOE's nuclear testing history, regardless of how this information was classified. Even some of O'Leary's closest advisors finally lost patience with these organizations. Nothing the department could do by way of declassification ever seemed to be enough for these people.

REPORTS ABOUT SECURITY vulnerabilities at the nuclear labs first began to surface in the late 1970s, shortly after the formation of the Department of Energy. These were primarily concerned with what is known as "guards, gates and guns," the physical security measures intended to protect nuclear materials and classified information stored at the labs. But there was also great concern about the labs' ability to protect classified information. A visiting graduate student, for example, once found classified documents containing the design details of our most advanced nuclear warheads on the publicly accessible shelves of the Los Alamos National Lab library. Congressman John Dingell, then chairman of the House Energy and Commerce Subcommittee on Oversight and Investigations, was a major thorn in the side of DOE and lab security officials, constantly prodding the department about security lapses and vulnerabilities. Not surprisingly, therefore, this aspect of lab security garnered most of the attention of senior DOE officials and most of the resources devoted to protecting the labs.

But beginning in the O'Leary years, security officials fought—and lost—a running battle over funding for security at the labs. Reductions in security funding were the order of the day and the annual reports to the White House on the status of safeguards and security at the labs, a holdover requirement from the Bush administration, were delayed year after year. The reports were completed on time, but since they portrayed an aging and increasingly deficient security system, political appointees simply refused to forward them to the White House.

Visitors to the labs can't help but be impressed by the physical security apparatus. They encounter lots of armed guards, barbedwire fences and badge readers, which give the labs the appearance of being secure. Yet these systems consistently failed to measure up to the requirements established by Energy Department and Pentagon security experts. The battle lines were generally drawn between security officials at DOE Headquarters in Washington and lab managers in the field. These managers and their program sponsors at Headquarters wanted to spend money on science and research and development, and proposed that money come out of security to fund these programs. DOE also poured money into new security programs for the protection of nuclear materials throughout the former Soviet Union. Various DOE programs were starved to free up funds for this project, but security in Russia was usually pitted against security at U.S. sites. This became especially galling in light of Russia's refusal to spend its own resources on protecting its stockpiles of nuclear materials—resources that went instead into the deployment of new strategic missiles and nuclear warhead programs. Most managers, however, regarded funds spent on security for U.S. lab sites as wasted money.

For their part, security officials worked up ever more complex threat scenarios to demonstrate the vulnerability of nuclear materials so they could illustrate the dangers of reduced funding and relaxed security. These scenarios involved terrorist attacks on lab facilities or thefts by insiders. Review after review, done by experts from inside DOE and the Pentagon, consistently found security at the labs to be inadequate. And these officials were repeatedly able to show that lab security could not survive attacks by trained terrorist forces. At one point in the mid-1990s, for example, Livermore National Lab eliminated its SWAT team, opting to rely on the local sheriff's department for protection against terrorists. So DOE security officials promptly turned U.S. Navy SEALs loose in an effort to penetrate Livermore security. In their war game, the SEALs wiped out the local sheriff's department in record time. But as with every other bit of bad news, the results of this game never saw the light of day.

By 1996, the trends in DOE security were established: severe budget reductions, diminished technical resources, increased responsibilities and reduced mission training all served to undermine the protection of the nuclear materials and classified information at the labs. The combination of these factors and the lack of management attention had put classified and sensitive unclassified information related to special nuclear materials and weapons production increasingly at risk.

When I was at Los Alamos from 1990 to 1993, there was a mood of quiet desperation, expressed in the common refrain, "Now that the Cold War is over, what do we do?" The Bush administration had stopped nuclear testing in 1992 and future testing seemed unlikely. The effect on lab morale was palpable and the lack of a clear mission or purpose dispirited nearly everyone in Los Alamos. The U.S. military seemed utterly uninterested in nuclear weapons, so the labs had also lost their primary client. The Bush administration's unilateral reductions of nuclear weapons beginning in

1992 seemed to represent the future—not only no new tests, but no new "starts" (lab shorthand for new nuclear weapons designs) either. The military's experience in the Gulf War, which saw devastating effects achieved by conventional firepower, seemed to underscore the declining value of nuclear weapons. How to sustain the lab's $1 billion budget and continue to attract new scientific talent? Moreover, the scientific cadre was approaching or had already reached retirement age. Without an overarching purpose, lab managers worried about sustaining their budgets, programs and staffs—and, consequently, their own careers as managers.

While the arrival of the Clintonites was viewed with considerable trepidation, in many respects the new administration actually did much to nurture and sustain the labs. The old guard at the labs had mostly retired or been pushed out, and the new management cadres willingly adapted themselves to the new regime. For some, the answer was to spin off lab technologies to private industry through Cooperative Research and Development Agreements. These CRADAs generated about $215 million in revenues by 1995, but gradually lost their appeal for both the labs and industry. Many in Congress considered CRADAs to be a diversion from the labs' true mission, nuclear weapons design and development, and some believed the labs were giving away sensitive technologies developed at taxpayer expense. But the Clinton administration set out to employ the labs to pursue its agenda of arms control and "denuclearization."

"Denuclearization" represented the clear, if unspoken, objective of many in the Clinton administration and especially the political appointees in the Energy Department. While this might seem paradoxical, what better way to get rid of nuclear weapons altogether than put the "denuclearizers" in charge of the nation's expertise and knowledge about such weapons? This objective was furthered by the dominance of the nuclear weapons design labs in the U.S. system. Energy Department officials allowed themselves to become dependent on advice and policy recommendations from managers at the weapons design labs: Los Alamos, Livermore and Sandia. The primary objective of this "advice" was to save jobs at the science labs. But as a result, the "production complex"—that is, the blue-collar sites that actually make the nuclear materials and assemble the weapons—was allowed to run down dramatically. We could do science, but we couldn't remanufacture our weapons. Our ability to make essential components for our weapons, such as "pits" and electrical components, practically disappeared in the 1990s.

As part of the denuclearization campaign, the administration's primary arms control objective was the signing and ratification of a Comprehensive Test Ban Treaty. The premise was to prevent any nation from testing a nuclear weapon and thereby stop the spread of these weapons. The treaty had very passionate advocates, but an equal number of opponents who understood full well that rudimentary nuclear weapons could be developed without resort to testing, especially if expertise and experience could be "borrowed" from a nuclear state. But the labs held the key to this central administration goal. If lab scientists could be persuaded to testify before Congress that they could assure the safety and reliability of U.S. nuclear weapons without testing, the administration calculated that Senate opposition to the treaty could be overcome. So the labs held enormous leverage over the administration and they struck a bargain along the lines of "support our continued existence at steady funding levels and we will support the treaty."

The labs hit upon an alternative to testing based on computer simulations that would replicate the performance of a warhead under live conditions. In the old days, the labs monitored the stockpile by pulling a warhead out of the arsenal, taking it to the Nevada test range and shooting it off. Now they would do this by computer and without live testing to provide a reality check. The labs dubbed this new program "Science Based Stockpile Stewardship." This took an enormous amount of computer power, and it required "reinventing" much of the science underlying nuclear detonations, because scientists would need to translate thousands of the details of such detonations into computer code. Part of this program involved a greater opening to universities and outside research labs, particularly in the area of computer science. The labs' computer networks were linked up with university networks and data flowed freely back and forth. The need for theoretical physicists, computer scientists and code development experts shot up. As it worked out— and this is a key part of the story—many of the lab hires in support of the new program were foreign nationals doing postdoctoral work at American universities. Many were very qualified technically and they would work for less than their American counterparts.

The administration also had to convince other countries to back the Comprehensive Test Ban Treaty. White House officials were eager to use access to the labs as "bait" to entice Russia, China, India and others into this and other arms control agreements. When I was at Los Alamos, I always thought it ironic that so many of our weapons scientists were also among the most fervent proponents of arms control, frequently "lending" their scientific credentials to policymakers in pursuit of the most specious arms control objectives. In return for being able to use the lab scientists to "educate" Russian or Chinese nuclear scientists on the benefits of arms control, the labs got increasing taxpayer dollars for arms control verification technologies. As a result, scientists from the weapons labs were eager to open "dialogues" with their Russian and Chinese counterparts, especially the Russians. Visits to previously closed Russian nuclear weapons facilities were eagerly anticipated and became the new status symbol among lab scientists. To facilitate such visits and "build confidence," we reciprocated by opening up our labs to foreign scientists in an unprecedented fashion. The parade of visiting scientists from China and Russia expanded dramatically in the early 1990s. Lab managers would later claim that this policy was merely a continuation of initiatives begun in the Bush administration, but in fact, opening the labs and relaxing security restrictions was almost wholly an achievement of Clinton administration political appointees.

The requirement for background security checks on these foreign visitors, particularly those from places on the DOE Sensitive Country List such as China or Russia, was relaxed or removed completely. Previously, any such visit would require a check at least to determine whether there were intelligence officers in a visiting delegation. Under the new policy, such a check was required only if the visit was to a classified part of the lab or was made for the purpose of discussing classified information. But the absurdity of that requirement is obvious: why would a lab visitor from China, say, be taken into a classified area or hold classified discussions with U.S. scientists during his visit in the first place?

And finally it must be said that the efforts of the Clinton administration were aided greatly by the labs' protection racket on Capitol Hill. Senators and congressmen with labs in their home states or districts fought like tigers to protect their constituencies. They readily agreed to the new mission—Science Based Stockpile Stewardship—as long as the President's annual budget requests did not decrease their labs' take. They sought and obtained funding for major new construction projects at the labs, such as expansive office buildings and high-tech testing facilities, despite the declining value of nuclear weapons in U.S. national security. The labs grew bolder and more resistant to any efforts to enforce compliance with security or counterintelligence guidance from Washington because they knew they could count on "their" senator or congressman to back them up. Los Alamos and Livermore, in particular, had a strong sense of entitlement to federal funding, which they pursued while using the "academic freedom" afforded by their affiliation with the University of California to avoid criticism. Most managers learned quickly that actually trying to manage the labs was not a career-enhancing move. This was especially true in the case of security.

To me, the emphasis on physical security, while important, was misplaced. I won't deny the importance of protecting nuclear materials stored at the labs or the value of guards and gates to deter insiders from carrying documents out of classified areas, although that policy turned out to be a stunning failure. But it always seemed to me that the threat from foreign intelligence services collecting information from lab scientists was much more real than the most elaborate security scenarios involving assaults or intrusions from outside. And much harder to defend against.

WHY SHOULD ANYONE be shocked at the notion of espionage efforts against the DOE labs? After all, the most damaging spy case in U.S. history took place at Los Alamos in the 1940s; it is only with the opening of Russian intelligence files and the publication of secret decrypts by the NSA that we have begun to comprehend the full magnitude of the theft accomplished by the Fuchs-Rosenberg-Greenglass espionage ring and Ted Hall. Spies from Russia, China and elsewhere have managed to penetrate lab security on a number of occasions since World War II, but most of these instances are unknown to the American public because the FBI and the Justice Department have declined to prosecute those few they do catch.

Nor should anyone be particularly shocked that foreign espionage could succeed at the nuclear weapons labs. The labs' track record on security—stretching back decades—has been shockingly bad. One of the cases revealed in the course of the Wen Ho Lee investigation involved the Russian theft of quieting technology for the naval reactors intended for our nuclear submarine forces in the late 1970s. An enterprising reporter pieced together the details of the case; his report indicated that the damage to the United States was calculated in billions of taxpayer dollars. The government declined to prosecute, as is often the case, for fear of further compromise of classified information. I found a copy of a letter in my safe from Admiral Hyman Rickover, the father of U.S. naval nuclear power, to the energy secretary, expressing his deep personal regrets that the United States had refused to prosecute the individuals involved. Rickover felt the loss of this technology, according to his letter, to be like "the loss of a child." Other cases are locked up in FBI or CIA files and will never be revealed to the American public, for some good and some not so good reasons.

Report after report warned successive DOE secretaries and lab directors about foreign intelligence threats and the likelihood that these threats could actually increase in the aftermath of the Cold War. Despite the long history of espionage efforts directed at the national labs, these managers seemed unable to shake off complacency. As early as 1985 or 1986, the Los Alamos director was warned about Chinese penetrations of his lab and the fact that the Chinese had already accumulated a surprising amount of classified information about nuclear weapons programs there. Lab scientists returning from visits to China were surprised at how knowledgeable their Chinese counterparts were about classified details of U.S. nuclear weapons programs. Apparently no one, either at the labs or in any responsible federal position in Washington, was concerned enough to begin an investigation or put limitations on U.S.-Chinese exchanges. The FBI may have regularly "debriefed" lab travelers, but the FBI never shared with us what, if anything, was done with the information held in its files. These files may have contained many important clues to Chinese espionage efforts and techniques against the labs. But the Bureau's refusal to share these files with us limited our ability to convince lab scientists that the Chinese (or Russian or any other country's) spy threats were real. Many of the senior scientists at the weapons labs were convinced that they were immune from such threats and they took great offense at any suggestion to the contrary.

In fact, an astonishing amount of information of value to countries with nascent nuclear programs is published by the labs or revealed in the course of international scientific conventions and symposia. Foreign scientists and intelligence officers are constantly "collecting" against unwitting U.S. lab scientists at such meetings. For example, numerous post–Gulf War studies determined that Iraqi nuclear scientists had profited in a number of different ways from interactions with DOE lab scientists at symposia and through the education programs of the International Atomic Energy Agency. A book entitled *Saddam's Bombmaker* is an interesting firsthand account of the role of foreign assistance in the development of Iraq's nuclear complex. In addition to French and German help, the book cites numerous examples of unwitting assistance to the Iraqis from the U.S. national labs. In a passage sure to resonate with those concerned about Hazel O'Leary's declassification projects, the author cites the value of reports from the Manhattan Project, given to the Iraqis in the 1950s under the Atoms for Peace program. The Iraqi author says, "I was sure that if U.S. officials knew how valuable its Manhattan Project reports would be to us years later, they would have kicked themselves." At another point, he discusses problems the Iraqis were having developing "lenses" or shaped explosives used to compress nuclear materials to a supercritical size, but then he says:

> Fortunately, a conference on high-tech explosives was scheduled for the United States in 1989, sponsored by none other than the major U.S. nuclear weapons labs, Los Alamos and Lawrence Livermore. It was open and unclassified (its program guide even included advertisements for nuclear triggers, which would put us on the path to getting them). We decided to send some people from the plant to America to learn about lenses.

Later, the Iraqi scientist boasts about replicating the explosives technologies "with the help of information" his people had acquired at this conference.[5] I wonder how many Americans know that the Iraqi nuclear weapons program was helped with expertise and information learned at conferences sponsored by the two premier U.S. nuclear weapons design labs.

The book discusses another topic near and dear to the lab scientists' hearts: the International Atomic Energy Agency. This is a United Nations organization that promotes the peaceful uses of nuclear energy. It is also supposed to enforce international safeguards on fissile material and prevent the production of nuclear weapons fuel. It does this through inspections, although many of the "inspectors" are from rogue states with covert nuclear weapons programs, such as Iraq and Iran. There is a long history between the U.S. national labs and the IAEA, based in Vienna, a favored destination for lab scientists. They can take a two-year sabbatical leave at IAEA, providing technical assistance to its programs. Other scientists travel to Vienna to shop their latest inventions and R&D developments to an international audience. These visits caused the U.S. Intelligence Community major heartburn for two reasons.

First, many scientists on sabbatical had access to sensitive U.S. intelligence information about foreign nuclear programs, often the very programs they went to Vienna to work on. How to prevent these scientists from "inadvertently" disclosing this information in the course of their daily activities or in "harmless" discussions with their international counterparts was a constant challenge. Although lab scientists were supposed to be "read out" of their security clearances during their stay in Vienna, we had at least one case of a scientist keeping his access to intelligence information and returning to his home lab periodically to read up on all the latest reports. We had a hard time convincing his supervisor of the importance of following very simple rules on this subject.

The second area of major concern regarded the potential compromise of sensitive nuclear detection capabilities. Over the years, the labs developed very powerful sensors for the detection of nuclear materials and affluents. Now, lab scientists convinced the IAEA to procure such capabilities from the United States, which in turn would generate funding for these scientists. Sound crazy? You bet, but it happened repeatedly. It's no wonder, then, that *Saddam's Bombmaker* speaks glowingly of the assistance the Iraqi program derived from the IAEA—and from the U.S. weapons labs.

Finally, it is under the cover of IAEA inspection training that scientists, engineers, and intelligence officers from countries that routinely sponsor terrorism against the United States are permitted to visit the DOE national labs. Iranians, Iraqis, Syrians, Yemenis, plus Russians, Chinese and others are trained at the DOE national labs in New Mexico on security procedures and safeguards that the United States uses to protect its own nuclear weapons and materials. Many of these security technologies and procedures are used in other sensitive U.S. facilities, both here and abroad. It is commonly understood that IAEA inspectors learn enough about these techniques to reverse-engineer these systems and then apply them in attacks on U.S. facilities.

The best post–Gulf War reports on the Iraqis' exploitation of U.S. nuclear weapons secrets were done within DOE, but were suppressed by the department's arms controllers and have never seen the light of day. I had a bootleg copy of one such report on the Iraqis' acquisition of nuclear information from the national labs, but I was never able to get it widely distributed to the Intelligence Community. I think the Energy Department arms controllers feared that dissemination of this information might increase the pressure to cut back on lab interactions with their foreign counterparts. An Energy Department intelligence officer told me that all existing copies of the report were destroyed after I left the department.

Foreign scientists can order unclassified lab reports and these requests can sometimes be valuable for determining the directions of a would-be nuclear proliferator. After the Gulf War, DOE started monitoring such requests for lab reports, papers and information, and managed to accumulate quite a database by the mid-1990s. DOE Intelligence, however, was never allowed to access this database; when the arms controllers ran out of money, we proposed to pick up funding for the project, but they opted to destroy the database rather than share it with us. Perverse!

The end of the Cold War did nothing to reduce or diminish these threats. If anything, access to the labs' achievements in science and technology became even more valuable to foreign intelligence services. These services relied not just on intelligence officers, although U.S. Intelligence Community records show that over 250 known or suspected agents visited DOE labs in the 1990s, in some cases for prolonged periods.[6] These services also used scientists, academicians, engineers and even businessmen to collect valuable information from the labs. Foreign intelligence services were able to exploit the labs' opening to American universities. Computer attacks by Russian, Chinese and other services on lab networks were often routed through universities tied into the lab networks. The benefits to a foreign nuclear program are obvious: the U.S. labs have explored every possible path to making fissile material for nuclear weapons and have developed and tested practically every known design of a nuclear warhead. Although Russia and China have become major sources of technology, knowledge and expertise for the rogue states interested in developing nuclear weapons, the United States stands out as the benchmark for many of these programs. Nothing is more valuable to the scientists in such programs than knowledge of how the United States did it. The savings in time, resources and manpower for the foreign nuclear programs that gain access to U.S. lab secrets are immeasurable—and lax security made that knowledge more readily accessible.

So the DOE labs, especially places like Los Alamos, Livermore, Oak Ridge and Sandia, will always be juicy targets for foreign intelligence collectors. It is important to understand, too, that the labs not only work on nuclear technologies, but do cutting-edge research in computational sciences, material sciences, non-nuclear military technologies and information technologies. The labs also do millions of dollars of work for the armed services, the Pentagon and the Intelligence Community, and all this represents high-value targets for potential adversaries.

Knowing this, one might expect DOE and the U.S. government to have invested heavily in counterintelligence in order to protect these critical secrets. Nothing could be further from the truth. In fact, counterintelligence at DOE and the labs is a relatively new mission, despite the long history of spy scandals within the complex. Growing concerns within the U.S. Intelligence Community finally led to the establishment of the Office of Counterintelligence at the

Energy Department in about 1992. These agencies were particularly concerned about the spread of new information technologies and the vulnerability of these technologies to outside penetration. Cyber security would prove to be a major weakness of the labs in the 1990s. Efforts to develop CI programs at the labs themselves began in the mid-1980s after a Livermore scientist was suspected of giving nuclear weapons secrets to China. The FBI agent who ran that case—who had formerly run an FBI San Francisco squad—established the first full-time CI program there, and Los Alamos initiated similar efforts around the same time. Prior to this, CI was an ad hoc mission at the labs.

The approaches taken by the two weapons labs' CI programs were very different. Livermore's program, headed by a former FBI agent named Bill Cleveland, emphasized protecting scientists from foreign intelligence operations and hired former FBI and CIA counterintelligence experts. Threat briefings and debriefings and close interaction with local FBI agents made this program effective and valuable. But budgetary pressures were starting to cut into its effectiveness by the early 1990s.

Los Alamos, however, went in a different direction. The head of that program was a former CIA officer named Robert Vrooman, who had come to Los Alamos in the early to mid 1980s from a position in the CIA's domestic contacts division. Vrooman was an odd choice. Unlike Cleveland, he had no prior counterintelligence experience when he took over the new Los Alamos program in the late 1980s.[7] Vrooman would later tell reporters that "he spent five years as the CIA liaison to Los Alamos," had played a "key role in sending Los Alamos scientists to China," and then "dashed off countless reports to agency headquarters outside Washington with secret details of Chinese nuclear weapons, gleaned by Los Alamos scientists."[8] During my dealings with him, he took a very relaxed view of the foreign intelligence risk to his lab. He professed to believe that neither Russia nor China represented a major espionage threat and that neither country was interested in U.S. nuclear warhead design information.[9] Vrooman would later explain his view of counterintelligence: "My biases were that lab scientists should talk to foreign scientists and vice versa. I have a bias toward collection; I think it's stupid to sit behind a wall and not know what the other guy is doing."[10] Unlike Livermore, Los Alamos appreciated the fact that Vrooman was not an "FBI guy," but "someone whose loyalty would lie with the lab."[11]

I thought that CI officers by definition are supposed to be ever watchful and vigilant, yet Vrooman seemed more concerned about accommodating lab managers unwilling to forego travel opportunities to China or Russia. As he says above, Vrooman was much more interested in the potential "take" from exchanges with foreign scientists—that is, the information that could be collected during such exchanges and handed over to authorities in Washington—than in protecting our scientists from such threats. And he was actively hostile to any "intrusion" from Washington bureaucrats into his domain. He led the charge at Los Alamos to loosen security restrictions on visitors to the lab—especially from China and Russia—and he personally signed new Los Alamos regulations eliminating Energy Department requirements for background checks on visiting scientists from sensitive countries.

The programs at Livermore and Los Alamos, and others established at Oak Ridge and elsewhere, were almost completely autonomous. No central control, no central coordination, no central policymaking apparatus. Each lab was on its own. While there was some information and data sharing, there was no central clearinghouse, nor would the labs accept guidance or policy direction from Washington. Consequently, it was not uncommon for an intelligence agent traveling with a foreign scientific delegation to be denied access to one lab, say, Livermore, but then gain entrance to the next lab, for instance, Los Alamos. Each lab had its own way of doing business, its own databases, and its own formats for conducting briefings and debriefings. Few of the labs ever forwarded CI information to DOE Headquarters, particularly if this information reflected poorly on senior lab managers.

It must be remembered that lab employees are contractors. At last count, there are nearly 120,000 of these employees, and about 65,000 have "Q" clearances, which authorize them to access Top Secret or Secret/Restricted Data or Secure Compartmented Information. The latter refers to special intelligence information, while Restricted Data refers to nuclear warhead design and manufacture, or the use of nuclear weapons as well as the production of special nuclear materials used in them. Nearly 40,000 other contractors have more limited-access clearances, known as "L" clearances, which provide them information at the Secret or Confidential/RD level.

The main nuclear warhead design labs, Los Alamos and Livermore, are "GOCOs," which means they are "government-owned, contractor-operated." The contractor in both cases is the University of California, which probably accounts for the academic atmosphere at these facilities. These labs are highly reluctant to take direction from Washington; but others, like Oak Ridge in Tennessee, are just as bad. To compound this problem, the lab CI officers are never scientists per se, although some pretend to be. For the most part, CI officials are retreads from other parts of the lab. Robert Vrooman's deputy and eventual replacement at Los Alamos, for instance, was a computer programmer who wanted a career change.

Given the hierarchy of lab professions in which the scientist is prince and the physicist is king, it isn't hard to see what a rough time counterintelligence officials would have dealing with these people. The contractor CI officials, particularly those at Los Alamos, were awed by these class distinctions and overly timid in the performance of their duties. Many scientists were openly offended by efforts to debrief them after their trips and refused outright to cooperate. Others were insulted by "threat briefings," considering themselves far too clever to be hoodwinked by some foreign intelligence thug. Still others regarded themselves as "citizens of the world," having more in common with their foreign counterparts than with ordinary Americans. In the words of one assessment:

> When it comes to a genuine understanding of and appreciation for the value of security and counterintelligence programs, especially in the context of America's nuclear arsenal and secrets, the DOE and its weapons labs have been Pollyannaish. The predominant attitude toward security and counterintelligence among many DOE and lab managers has ranged from half-hearted, grudging accommodation to smug disregard.[12]

The other thing that must be noted about CI is that it is a different intellectual discipline from security. Security types think in terms of locking things in physically—higher walls, more secure gates, more guards and dogs. Security officials can also measure their product. That is, they can test the readiness of alarm systems or the effectiveness of SWAT teams to repel intrusions. Over the years, the government has invested millions in developing alarm systems, detection devices and other extremely sophisticated means of preventing physical intrusions. Ironically, the labs have been at the forefront of this technology as part of their mission to enhance the security of nuclear weapons. The labs have also invested heavily in protecting information, although document control procedures and information handling requirements were loosened significantly in the early 1990s. Likewise, the labs were overly confident of their ability to protect against computer intrusions. I always thought it ironic to hear the labs brag about their expertise at computer security, given their own track record. The IT explosion in the early 1990s led to lab scientists exchanging e-mails with their counterparts all over the world. Thousands of such e-mails were sent daily from lab sites but none were monitored for content or even addressees. At one lab, it was estimated that 250,000 e-mails went out monthly and not a single one was monitored for security.

Counterintelligence, on the other hand, is oriented toward protecting the information and expertise contained in the brain of a scientist, intelligence officer or military planner. CIA traitor Aldrich Ames surely did pass along documents to his Russian handlers, but the most useful information he gave up was contained in his memory. He was able to reconstruct and compromise networks of agents working for the United States outside the guards, guns and gates protecting the CIA facilities in northern Virginia. Ames' reconstruction was then passed on to his Soviet case officer, with the predictable elimination of individuals working for us. The indictment of Robert Hanssen, the FBI counterintelligence expert, shows that he passed along classified documents and disks, but also letters that he had created outside the walls of FBI Headquarters. Both of these cases illustrate how ineffective even the best physical security can be against an insider threat.

Klaus Fuchs, the Manhattan Project spy, gave the Soviets a document of his own creation detailing information on the U.S. atomic bomb project. Ted Hall, also a member of the Los Alamos team in the 1940s, passed along similar documents to the Soviets.

These self-generated documents made a profound contribution to the Soviet atomic bomb project. In short, walls and fences are not sufficient protection against the compromise of ideas, concepts and details of technical experiments. Scientists know these particulars like they know their children's birthdays or their own social security numbers. They love to discuss such matters with other qualified scientists, whether face-to-face or long-distance by e-mail.

"Lab culture" also plays a role in the difficulties faced by CI officers. This term, heard a lot during the congressional hearings on Kindred Spirit in 1999, generally refers to the security climate at the weapons labs with their campus-like environment. Scientists freely met with their foreign colleagues on the lab campuses at Los Alamos and Livermore, and there was nothing to prevent a scientist from meeting his colleague at a location away from the lab, out of sight from lab security. This could and frequently did happen when scientists became impatient with security restrictions and regulations. Equipping a lab scientist to deal with efforts by scientists working for a foreign intelligence service to elicit information in such meetings was a constant challenge. Convincing that scientist that he was a target was even tougher.

Further compounding that problem was the reality that CI officers at the labs were also all contractors, but expected to report negative and sometimes derogatory information on their colleagues, supervisors or even neighbors. I witnessed many incidents in which CI officers were asked to report on the same people who wrote their performance appraisals, granted raises and approved budgets. The best programs took the view that they were attempting to protect the scientists by providing them with information and awareness to assist in warding off efforts at recruitment or elicitation. But such a relationship implied trust between the scientist, his management and the CI officer. Heavy-handed intrusions by DOE security or Headquarters' CI officials often killed such trust, which explains why lab CI officers were sometimes so reluctant to inform Washington of counterintelligence "anomalies."

These anomalies were supposed to be the subject of more intense CI scrutiny in the mid-1990s in the aftermath of the Ames case. Ames was a walking security red flag—a heavy drinker with profligate spending habits. He drove a red Jaguar convertible to work on a government GS-14 salary, and he paid cash for his home in a tonier section of northern Virginia. But none of his CIA colleagues thought to report this to security officials. Other examples of anomalies to be examined would include infidelity, bankruptcy, unexplained absences, failure to pass an FBI polygraph, and close and continuous contact with a foreign national, especially one from a "sensitive" country. From time to time, we would get wind of such an anomaly at DOE, but trying to run it to ground at the labs was always nearly impossible. Examples of lab scientists, even managers, who developed "zipper problems" during their trips to Russia were plentiful, but to my knowledge few of these were ever examined for CI implications.* Some lab scientists visited relatives in countries hostile to the United States or with known nuclear pretensions, but didn't bother to report these visits to security officials. If they did follow the rules and report these visits, then lab security officials rarely told DOE counterintelligence officials. (In one instance, I learned that a Los Alamos scientist with a Top Secret/RD clearance was being held in Iran from a congressional aide seeking my intervention with the State Department to gain the scientist's release.) Scientists supposedly under FBI investigation would travel to foreign countries without lab officials bothering to inform either the FBI or DOE counterintelligence officials.

The CI structure within DOE resembled a pyramid. The Washington Headquarters was supposed to be at the pinnacle; there was an intermediate level at DOE field operations offices in Albuquerque, Oak Ridge and Oakland; and then there were the contract CI officers at the labs. Theoretically, command and control was supposed to flow from Washington through the field sites to the labs. The reality is that the labs took direction from no one. One of the most frustrating aspects of trying to manage the labs was their refusal to provide vital CI information to Washington. If forced, lab managers and CI officers preferred to deal directly with local FBI representatives and cut DOE out altogether. More often, they just buried it.

---

*Once during a discussion with a senior FBI official, he said that half of official Washington would be under suspicion if the FBI investigated every report it received of "zipper problems in Russia."

When the Clinton administration took office in 1993, a beginning had been made on developing a complex-wide counterintelligence capability. For DOE, that capability was limited by the experience and orientation of the staff, however, and was viewed with a deep and abiding suspicion by the lab managers and scientists. Lab managers were cutting funding, trimming staff and piling additional duties on the remaining CI staff, including responsibility for record keeping on foreign visitors. Organizationally, CI staffs were pushed further down the management structure within the labs to the point that at Los Alamos, for example, CI reported to a manager whose primary responsibility was hallway maintenance. A CI officer would have to go through layers of management to report a problem to the lab director and he would need the approval of these managers before he could report a problem to DOE.

The CI programs at the labs in the early years of the Clinton administration were gradually being starved into submission. Funding cuts and staff reductions were the order of the day. What new staff there was came mostly from the security force that was being reduced. CI became a jobs program for lab staffers whose own programs had been abolished. After Bob Vrooman, the main CI person at Los Alamos came from a computer background, lacked any experience in the field, and, according to government reports, was later to commit perhaps the gravest single blunder in the entire Kindred Spirit case. At the same time, the labs' counterintelligence program was overwhelmed by the explosion of foreign scientists from sensitive countries like Russia and China. At some labs, CI officers gave up trying to interview scientists and simply sent them forms to fill out to satisfy the requirement for a CI "debriefing" after travel or a visit from a foreign scientist. By the time I got involved in 1995, counterintelligence at the labs was in freefall.

THREE

To Build a Better Bomb

By 2015, China is likely to have tens of missiles capable of targeting
the United States, including a few tens of more survivable, land- and
sea-based mobile missiles with smaller nuclear warheads—in part
influenced by U.S. technology gained through espionage.
   —"Foreign Missile Developments and the Ballistic Missile Threat
      to the United States through 2015,"
      U.S. National Intelligence Council, September 1999

Early in 1995, things seemed to be going well in the DOE
Intelligence shop. We had made a lot of progress since I
took over in May 1994 and the deathwatch for the Office
of Intelligence appeared to be over. Secretary O'Leary seemed
pleased with the support she was getting from us, and we had made
friends throughout the department and at the White House with
our work on Russian nuclear material security. One of the leaders
of U.S. efforts to help the Russians protect that material, Ken Luongo,
declared our reports to be the "bible" of his programs.

Russia and the proliferation problem had been the focus of
most of my efforts up to that point, along with managing the office,
implementing our equal opportunity programs, and trying to keep
the labs focused and productive. I never saw the Kindred Spirit
locomotive bearing down on me until it was in my face.

I knew, of course, that there were very different views on the
future of China and the security implications for the United States.
As Russia moved off center stage, some in the national security
community sought to project China as a rising superpower and a
major threat to U.S. interests around the world. At least before the
events of September 11, 2001, many agreed with the Senate Intelligence Committee assessment that "the Peoples' Republic of China
is perhaps the preeminent national security, foreign policy, and
intelligence challenge facing the United States in the post–Cold

War world."[1] During the 2000 presidential campaign, candidate George W. Bush labeled China a "strategic competitor." This is probably the most accurate description of the PRC. Its leaders do not share many of our assumptions about the world and they clearly want to establish their country's hegemony in what they consider its area of influence: East Asia and the Asia-Pacific region. How far beyond that area its objectives will extend is less clear. Policymakers who take the threat seriously are particularly concerned about the PRC military modernization, especially in technologies that would enable it to deter and, if necessary, defeat U.S. intervention in a Taiwan Strait crisis.

But there is another school of thought on China that takes a much more benign view of the PRC's future and seems to believe in the "convergence" theory, a staple of old political science views on the Cold War. That is, the more modern and the more a part of the world community China becomes, the more it will take on the characteristics of a "normal" nation-state—which is to say, the more it will look like us. Thriving international commerce, commercial market penetration by U.S. businesses, the triumphant spread of the Internet, and flourishing academic and business exchanges will all theoretically combine to bring about this transformation. According to such a view, the PRC should be seen as a "strategic partner," a position adopted by the Clinton administration. This notion had some very powerful proponents in academia, the business community, and surprisingly even in much of the Pentagon. The Clinton Defense Department seemed especially enamored with the idea that we should do absolutely nothing that might turn China into an enemy. Many of our military leaders viewed the Chinese as so hopelessly behind the United States in military capabilities that they would never catch us unless we acted in such a way as to provoke them. I don't think it's unfair to conclude that this benign interpretation of Beijing's intentions and behavior also dominated the CIA's view of the PRC.[2]

The DOE Intelligence Office subscribed to neither of these views, but it did have ongoing programs to follow China's nuclear weapons development. Much of the work was done on contract by Los Alamos. In part this was because Los Alamos scientists had made a number of trips to China and had been admitted to some of the PRC's nuclear facilities. This gave Los Alamos an edge in the competition with their counterparts at Livermore for intelligence research funding. At least once, Danny Stillman and Terry Hawkins took one of my predecessors, Bob Daniel, with them. I often wondered what the Chinese must have thought about the director of the Energy Department's intelligence office visiting them and about the implications of having such a high-ranking intelligence official traveling without a security escort in a country whose intelligence services were well known for eavesdropping and searching hotel rooms and baggage.

The key Los Alamos scientists doing the hard analytic work on China were Larry Booth and Bobby Henson. Both were long-time lab scientists, both had some nuclear warhead design experience, and both were well respected in the U.S. Intelligence Community. Booth had spent many years studying foreign nuclear weapons programs and his views on developments and trends in both the Russian and the Chinese nuclear programs were highly regarded in the Intelligence Community. I know less about Henson's lab experience, but I do know that he was more inclined to "think outside the box" than many scientists. Other labs helped out with assessments of PRC nuclear material production capabilities, command-and-control, and other nuclear weapons topics. Livermore handled most of the PRC nuclear proliferation issues, which were to become very important during the Clinton administration, although Oak Ridge did some groundbreaking work in this area.

At this point in time, frankly, I didn't pay that much attention to China. I was certainly aware of its strategic nuclear missile force, of course, and took quite seriously its ability to strike American cities with multimegaton warheads. But I thought the Chinese nuclear weapons program badly lagged behind those of Russia and the United States in sophistication and experience.

In any case, my overall impression was that we had the PRC nuclear intelligence target pretty well covered. Most of the work at Los Alamos was focused on understanding the purpose of China's latest round of nuclear testing, which continued into the mid-1990s, after we and the Russians had stopped. Up to that point, the PRC had done only about thirty live nuclear shots, in comparison with about a thousand for both Russia and the United States. I know there were some, especially academics, who claimed that the PRC made remarkable progress in their program, but neither Booth nor Henson shared that view. They characterized the Chinese nuclear program as "modest" at best and incapable of keeping up with the U.S. In their view, the Chinese program simply did not have the necessary experience, defined by the number of live nuclear tests, to produce modern nuclear warheads. This assessment was to become a central factor in the later deliberations on Kindred Spirit.

However, the PRC showed no sign of cutting back efforts to bring its nuclear program up to the level of the United States or Russia. Their continued testing provided an important window into Chinese intentions and accomplishments. By 1995, Booth and Henson were beginning to take a hard look at a testing series that the PRC had kicked off in 1992.[3] Their job was to try to figure out what were the main objectives of this round of testing. Both scientists spent considerable time puzzling through what the Chinese were up to, and their conclusions would begin a long nightmare for me.

ON APRIL 25, 1995, Booth and Henson sent me a Top Secret memo outlining their conclusions about the purpose of the Chinese tests. The memo is still classified,[4] but one report has noted, "These tests led to suspicions in the U.S. Intelligence Community that the PRC had stolen advanced U.S. thermonuclear warhead design information."[5] The two scientists believed that these tests were for the "purpose of developing smaller, lighter warheads for the PRC's new nuclear forces."[6]

I didn't think I could ignore such a stunning report, but I wasn't yet convinced that Booth and Henson were on the right track. Where could I turn for another, more authoritative assessment? The name that kept popping up was that of a Los Alamos scientist named John Richter. A nuclear warhead designer, Richter had decades of experience to his credit. I spoke with several other lab scientists at DOE and all agreed that Richter was the "go to" guy. And indeed, he had a truly impressive resumé. He had spent nearly forty years at Los Alamos, where he had led nuclear warhead development programs and nuclear explosive design groups. He had been the chief designer for forty nuclear test devices; in fact, he had more nuclear tests to his credit than the PRC had conducted up to that point. I also learned that John had spent a lot of time studying foreign nuclear developments and was familiar with intelligence materials. Moreover, his resumé noted that "he maintained a major nuclear explosive design code."[7] He seemed like the right guy to review Booth and Henson's work.[8]

John came back to Washington from Los Alamos in May and spent a few weeks holed up in our office in a special vaulted area, looking at all the relevant highly classified intelligence information. On May 25, 1999, I received yet another Top Secret/Eyes Only memo, this one signed by Richter as well. As was later reported, "the authors maintained their original assessment that espionage had occurred."[9] In testimony before Congress, I characterized the information in their memo as follows: "I was informed by three senior Los Alamos scientists of their concerns that the Chinese had acquired information, probably by espionage, from the U.S. that enabled them to develop and test a small modern nuclear device."[10]

Richter believed that the Chinese had acquired information on the U.S. W88 nuclear warhead and that this information had helped them achieve their breakthrough. The W88, designed and developed by Los Alamos for the U.S. Navy Trident D5 SLBM, is the most modern warhead in our arsenal, "a miniaturized, tapered thermonuclear warhead. It is the United States' most sophisticated strategic thermonuclear warhead."[11] Richter, in one of his many management jobs, had run the team that did the design work on the warhead.

Henson obviously provided some of the details of the memo to the *New York Times* for an article published in September 1999.[12] Based on conversations with Henson, a *Times* reporter wrote:

> The group looked more closely at a clue provided by [a] Chinese spy, who described the size of the bomb's atomic core with an analogy to a common household object, officials said in a new disclosure. Working from that, the scientists calculated a more precise size and Dr. Henson and Dr. Richter went through the American stockpile of nuclear arms, looking up measurements to see if any matched.

The atomic trigger of the W88, they discovered, was close enough in size to raise suspicions.

Given Richter's experience with the W88, I doubt that he had to pore through the American stockpile to match those measurements. Later *Times* articles covering the same ground for some reason omitted the key role played by Booth and cited only Henson.[13] I thought this extremely odd. I would have paid attention to Henson if he alone had brought me the warning, but Booth's involvement certainly lent much more credibility to his concerns. Booth would later remark that "Henson would not recognize a nuclear warhead's primary from his ass."[14] It was Booth's and ultimately Richter's assessment that forced my hand.[15]

At this point, I was required by Section 811 of the Intelligence Authorization Act of 1995 to report this matter to the FBI. ("The Federal Bureau of Investigation is advised immediately of any information, regardless of origin, which indicates that classified information is being, or may have been, disclosed in an unauthorized manner to a foreign power or an agent of a foreign power.")[16] A Congress disgusted by the CIA's handling of the Aldrich Ames spy case had levied this requirement. The agency had waited years before reporting its concerns about espionage in its ranks to the FBI, and Congress wanted to make sure that didn't happen again.

But first I had to break the news to my managers up the chain of command in DOE. My immediate supervisor at that time was a retired Air Force colonel named Ken Baker. He was a protégé of the former energy secretary James Schlesinger, and at that time the acting director of the Office of Nonproliferation and National Security, of which the Office of Intelligence was a part.[17] Baker seemed to understand and appreciate intelligence. I laid out the contents of the Los Alamos scientists' memo for him and he took their allegations of Chinese espionage and the theft of W88 information very seriously.

My next stop was the office of Charles Curtis, who was then the under secretary of energy, the number three spot in the department. He was a lawyer and had been head of the Federal Energy Regulation Commission in the late 1970s. He had come back into government with Bill Clinton, but didn't have the casual attitude about national security issues shared by so many other Clinton appointees. We had worked closely with him on the Russian nuclear material issue and he appreciated the intelligence support we provided him. Within DOE he had responsibility for national security programs: nuclear weapons, nonproliferation, arms control, security and intelligence.

Curtis looked increasingly grave as I laid out the scientists' conclusions. He asked a few questions, and I think he was well aware of John Richter's reputation. "What next?" was his main question. I told him about the Section 811 requirement to inform the FBI and he said I should do this as soon as possible.

In early June I first met with my counterintelligence managers. These included Don McIntyre, then the office director; our CIA detailee (whose name I cannot give); Dan Bruno, chief of the DOE counterintelligence investigations; and possibly others. I told them about the memo and probably had them read it. My main question to them was also, "Now what?" McIntyre recommended that we inform CIA, especially the Center for Counterintelligence, and create a special list to control access to this information (usually called a "Bigot list" in the intelligence business). He also proposed that we adopt a code name for this project. A short time later, he recommended the use of "Kindred Spirit" to denote all matters related to this issue. I don't know of any particular significance to this name; most likely it was next on an approved list of code names to cover special projects.

On June 23, 1995, McIntyre and I met with John Lewis, then the deputy assistant director for counterintelligence in the FBI's National Security Division. This division handled all the national security cases, especially those involving espionage. The NSD had won the war of the media over who had actually broken the Ames CIA spy case, so I was somewhat familiar with its activities. Also present was Jerry Doyle, an FBI section chief. I laid out our concerns and told Lewis of our plans for a peer review and the steps we had taken to protect the inquiry inside the department. He listened attentively and mentioned the longstanding concern within the FBI about the DOE labs and their loose approach to security. He seemed genuinely supportive, encouraged us to go ahead with a peer review of the three scientists' findings, and asked that we keep him posted over the summer. I invited the FBI to participate in the peer review, but Lewis declined.[18]

Back at DOE Headquarters, McIntyre had apparently commissioned Bruno to do some work developing an "investigative plan" for the conduct of Kindred Spirit. This was done without my knowledge. I don't mean this as the typical Washington bureaucratic dodge: had I known, I would certainly have told him to go ahead with that planning. But in all frankness, I hoped that a further peer review of the Richter-Booth-Henson findings would come back as inconclusive. I was aware of similar cases in recent years in which a foreign power was suspected of having acquired U.S. nuclear weapons data that aided its own program. In one such case a peer review was conducted, but concluded that there was no reason to believe that espionage had been involved. An espionage investigation was not in my plans for the office; I thought we had more important work to do on Russia and proliferation. And I simply didn't want to think the Chinese had conducted successful espionage against our nuclear weapons program.

PEER REVIEWS WERE a common practice within the labs; new scientific theories or new discoveries in nuclear weapons science were often vetted by a group of the theorist's peers. Usually a peer review brought together scientists from different labs so as to ensure a careful appraisal of the work. Given the history of competition between Livermore and Los Alamos, any peer review that included a mix of scientists would ensure a good scrub. So I intended to form a group comprising scientists from both labs, in addition to members of the Intelligence Community, if they would participate.[19]

My first task was to find someone to lead the peer review. I certainly wasn't going to do it and I didn't trust any of the Washington feds to handle the job. I wanted a true lab scientist, with experience in all facets of nuclear weapons design and testing. Mike Henderson's name came up. I had met him while I was at Los Alamos and he seemed like a decent guy, a somewhat crusty, typical old-line Los Alamos type. He had a big reputation and lots of nuclear design and testing experience. I would need Los Alamos director Sig Hecker's approval for Henderson's participation, so I flew down to New Mexico to meet with him. He was cordial as always, but grew somber when I described the contents of the scientists' memo, which I hadn't carried with me because of security restrictions. Hecker quickly approved Henderson for the job, especially after I promised to pay for his participation. I then met with Henderson and he accepted my invitation to head up the peer review. My guidance to him was simple: use the Richter memo as a working hypothesis and get the best judgment of the scientists as to whether the hypothesis had any merit. I should emphasize that we did not discuss the question of where any compromised information may have come from.

I told Henderson that he could assemble his team for the review. I don't know how he did this or what criteria he used. I did tell him I wanted "real nuclear weapons designers," not just the labs' intelligence analysts. Both nuclear warhead design labs had lots of intelligence specialists with expertise in areas related to nuclear weapons, but real design experience was scarcer. I wanted actual designers, experts in nuclear testing, and scientists with experience in code development and simulation. Scientists with hands-on experience in designing, testing and developing nuclear weapons would, I thought, be the best judges of China's accomplishments. I considered Henderson best suited to put this team together, so I let him come up with the key people. He snagged a Los Alamos designer named Reid Worlton and a Livermore designer named Bill Quirk.

I also invited participation from CIA and the Defense Intelligence Agency. CIA sent over a branch chief and a trained nuclear physicist who had spent some time at Livermore. DIA also sent one of its senior nuclear intelligence analysts, so I was satisfied with the Intelligence Community's participation. What I hoped for from this group was not so much technical expertise as an infusion of intelligence information that might not otherwise be available to us, plus experience in the handling of this information.

I think the first meeting of the Kindred Spirit Analysis Group, as it came to be known, was held in early July 1995.[20] The KSAG meeting took place in our secure vault inside the intelligence office in the basement of the DOE Headquarters Building in downtown Washington. I recall this as primarily an organizational meeting. My guidance was as clear as I could make it: Did the PRC achieve the results of its latest testing series with foreign assistance? Or did the Chinese have sufficient experience and capability to make the progress demonstrated in these tests on their own? And if the group believed that foreign assistance had been needed, did the Chinese have access to U.S. nuclear secrets? Pretty straightforward, I thought. I certainly did not expect the group to identify a specific lab or location within our weapons complex as a possible source. Just look at the intelligence and tell us if the PRC had made its great leap forward on its own or with illicit help—that was their mandate.

I didn't participate much in the deliberations of this meeting. It seemed as if every time I began to settle in and follow the proceedings, my secretary would pull me out of the meeting to put out some other fire. I don't know how long the meeting went on, but there were a number of tasks that came out of it.

First, the group wanted to draw up a timeline that would chart PRC nuclear tests, the key milestones in the development of U.S. nuclear warheads, and other similar categories of information. The idea was to try to see how much U.S. information the PRC had in its possession and how they had revealed that information to their U.S. counterparts.

When the timeline was compiled, it showed no smoking guns but some intriguing correlations. Scientific visits between the United States and China, suspected thefts or "compromises" of classified information, and key developments along the PRC warhead development timeline started to merge. The scientists also made a very detailed review of lab trip reports. Most of these reports were interesting for the types of questions the PRC scientists were asking our guys. Not surprisingly, no trip report ever revealed whether one of our scientists provided any direct assistance, but from the questions the Chinese were reported to be asking, it was evident that the PRC knew a lot about our program. An awful lot. Further, the level of sophistication of the PRC questions increased over time. Obviously, the PRC was getting smarter as the interactions with the U.S. labs continued.

Second, the group wanted to see if a former Livermore scientist could have been the source of W88 information. This is an official government description of that case:

> In the late 1970s, the PRC stole design information on the US
> W-70 warhead from Lawrence Livermore Laboratory. The U.S.
> Government first learned of this theft several months after it took

place. The PRC subsequently tested a neutron bomb in 1988. The FBI developed a suspect in the earlier theft. The suspect worked at Lawrence Livermore National Laboratory, and had access to classified information including designs for a number of U.S. thermonuclear weapons in the U.S. stockpile at that time.[21]

The counterintelligence chief at Livermore, Bill Cleveland, had been the FBI agent in charge of the investigation. We learned that the scientist's files had been maintained intact at Livermore, so some scientists from the Kindred Spirit group flew out to California to look for any indication that he had collected information on the W88 warhead. They returned with some good news and some bad. The good news: the scientist's files contained no documents related to the W88 warhead. The bad news: these files contained many other documents about U.S. nuclear warheads and warhead design concepts to which he should not have had access, such as information on U.S. nuclear command-and-control systems. Many of these documents were available only on a "need-to-know" basis and Livermore's records indicated that this scientist did not have the appropriate "need-to-know" to get these. He had obviously been collecting nuclear weapons reports and storing them inside his safe. How much of this he had passed along to the PRC will never be known.

He was allowed to resign from Livermore National Lab in 1981, and was never prosecuted. Cleveland told us that in order to prosecute, the FBI would have to either catch the suspect in the act—that is, apprehend him with classified documents on him or passing these to the Chinese—or obtain a confession. According to Cleveland, the FBI couldn't get him to confess and didn't catch him red-handed. After leaving the lab, he made a number of trips to the PRC in the 1980s.[22] The Kindred Spirit scientists were concerned that he could have passed along information to Chinese nuclear scientists on those trips. This would not be the last we would hear of the former Livermore scientist.

Finally, the Kindred Spirit group wanted to know more about the distribution of information on the W88 warhead throughout our nuclear weapons complex. This issue was later to become a major bone of contention, so I want to discuss it in some detail.

Richter knew that the W88 had entered its phase three development in the early 1980s—that is, after the competition between Los Alamos and Livermore had resulted in the Navy's selection of the Los Alamos design.[23] The scientists knew W88 information was at Los Alamos and probably at Livermore, but the group wanted to know what other locations might hold such information. So they tasked a scientist from the Sandia Laboratory named George Kominiak to determine, first, whether W88 information was in the public domain. At this point, the group had no idea what type of information might be out in public and readily available to the PRC. Richter's memo suggested that secret information had assisted the Chinese. Now the group wanted to make sure, especially as the PRC intelligence services were known to be assiduous collectors of our technical information published in journals and elsewhere. Second, Kominiak was supposed to review classified documents to determine the distribution of information about the W88 within the nuclear weapons complex. Classified information could be distributed both within the Energy Department and within the Defense Department. This was a U.S. Navy project, so the Navy could have provided classified information to its contractors. The Kindred Spirit group wanted to know just what kind of classified information had been spread around on the W88.

About this time, one of the scientists—I think it was Larry Booth—recalled a U.S. government report that addressed PRC efforts to obtain U.S. nuclear information.[24] He thought the report had been done sometime in the mid-1980s, possibly at the request of the director of Los Alamos. There was no way to know if Sig Hecker, who had become the director at about that time, had actually read the report. The CIA would later claim that the report documenting PRC efforts to obtain U.S. nuclear weapons information was only a "draft" and had never been "officially" published. Why not, I wondered?

In 1984, the Pentagon's Defense Intelligence Agency had done a similar report on this topic. This report was less detailed than the CIA product, but had about the same bottom line. It noted the disruptive impact of the Cultural Revolution on some of the PRC's nuclear weapon facilities and then forecast:

qualitative warhead improvements in terms of (1) increased warhead reliability and confidence, (2) development of more compact warheads, especially for tactical nuclear applications and possibly for MRV [multiple reentry vehicles] warheads, (3) increased hardening of warheads in a nuclear antiballistic missile environment, (4) tailored output devices, such as enhanced radiation, and (5) improved warhead safety, storage, and logistics procedures.[25]

And just how would the PRC attain these goals? According to the Defense Intelligence Agency report:

Qualitative improvements that the Chinese are developing for their nuclear warheads will **depend on the benefits that the Chinese are now deriving from both overt contact with U.S. scientists and technology, and the covert acquisition of U.S. technology.** [Emphasis added.][26]

Much later the report was declassified and posted on the National Security Archive's website.[27]

So here were two products of the U.S. Intelligence Community from the mid-1980s that established that the PRC's nuclear weapons program was benefiting directly from interactions with U.S. scientists at DOE nuclear weapons labs—both through aboveboard methods and by espionage. Yet it is clear in retrospect that the message of these reports had never gotten through either to policymakers or to DOE and lab managers. Too bad, because these reports should have alerted us to the risks of "openness" with the Chinese. In any case, these two reports from the Intelligence Community answered my main question to the Kindred Spirit Analysis Group: did the PRC's progress depend on foreign assistance? The answer was clearly yes, and that assistance was coming at least in part from within the DOE nuclear weapons labs.

I continued to wonder why such clear warnings about the risks of these interactions had been ignored by lab directors and high-ranking government officials for over a decade at this point. At least we now had some evidence of PRC acquisitions—although no one was prepared for what came next.

SOMETIME IN LATE JULY, Larry Booth and Carl Henry, another scientist from Los Alamos, attended a meeting of the CIA's China Working Group. This was an informal group that met from time to time to share the latest intelligence about PRC nuclear weapons developments. Booth came back from that meeting excited about some new information the CIA had acquired; he said there were "numbers" in a document that the Kindred Spirit group had to see.

The group had already met in late July and the discussion had been all over the map. It might best be characterized along the following lines: First, the intelligence convinced the group that the new series of PRC nuclear tests, begun in 1992, represented a departure from normal practice. How dramatic a departure was not so much the substance of the debate, as how the PRC had achieved it.

Some of our scientists argued that the Chinese could have accomplished all this without foreign assistance. They believed that some of the concepts associated with this achievement were known to them in the early 1980s, and we had determined that some of these could have come from the former Livermore scientist. Figuring about a decade's worth of effort leading up to the new testing, they thought that should have been enough time for the PRC to make such a breakthrough on its own. Livermore's Bill Quirk was the spokesman for this group.

Others, including John Richter and Bobby Henson, argued that the level of expertise in the PRC program before the 1992 testing series would not support such a breakthrough. The PRC lacked the live nuclear testing experience and diagnostics equipment to permit success in these tests. They should have had a lot of false starts and testing failures before they achieved success—the old trial-and-error method that characterized both U.S. and Russian developments. But there was no evidence that the PRC had been anything but successful in these endeavors. Therefore, according to this view, they must have had help. This debate was captured in a later official assessment of the activities of this group:

> While it is sometimes argued that eventually the PRC might have been able to produce and test an advanced and modern thermonuclear weapon on its own, the PRC had conducted only 45 nuclear tests in the more than 30 years from 1964 to 1996 (when

the PRC signed the Comprehensive Test Ban Treaty), which would have been insufficient for the PRC to have developed advanced thermonuclear warheads on its own. This compares to the approximately 1030 tests by the United States, 715 tests by the Soviet Union, and 210 by France.[28]

Furthermore, these scientists argued, the PRC just didn't have the kind of non-nuclear experimental tools to support such a development. On one of the recent trips to the PRC, one of our lab scientists had visited such facilities; when he came back he wrote a report concluding that the stuff the PRC showed him just wouldn't support modern experiments; either they didn't have such equipment, or they weren't showing it to us.[29] Fair enough.

On that note, the first session of the Kindred Spirit Analysis Group came to a close. No one, least of all me, thought there would be any consensus among this group. Most people who have dealt with the lab scientists know them to be a contentious lot, so this ongoing debate was commonplace. At this point, however, events took a dramatic turn.

Up to this time, our scientists' espionage concerns were based on "assessments" of intelligence data, just like those that analysts all over the Intelligence Community make every day. Given the expertise and experience of a John Richter, his assessment of course carried more weight than would that of a junior analyst at CIA. But then we were given a smoking gun: the now-infamous "walk-in document." This document, according to a later Senate report, "dated 1988, is said to lay out China's nuclear modernization plans" for the benefit of the PRC ministry responsible for designing and developing future Chinese missiles and missile nose cones.[30] The document's contents were stunning, to say the least.

Government declassifiers have tried to conceal the contents of the document by restricting public descriptions to "it provided some W88 information." The CIA, for example, considers classified any information about the accuracy of this report. As is often the case, however, official declassified descriptions of the contents have appeared that go well beyond this narrow and grudging summary. For example, one unclassified government report describes the document as follows:

In 1995, a U.S. intelligence agency obtained information that has come to be called the "walk-in" document. A copy of a classified PRC report, it contains a discussion of various U.S. nuclear warheads.

The document unquestionably contains some information that is still highly sensitive, including descriptions, in varying degrees of specificity, of technical characteristics of seven U.S. thermonuclear warheads.[31]

Yet another unclassified official report is even more direct:

In 1995, a "walk-in" approached the Central Intelligence Agency outside of the PRC and provided an official PRC document classified "Secret" that contained design information on the W88 Trident D5 warhead, the most modern in the U.S. arsenal, as well as technical information concerning other thermonuclear warheads.

. . . the CIA and other Intelligence Community analysts that reviewed the document concluded that it contained U.S. thermonuclear warhead design information.

The "walk-in" document recognized that the U.S. nuclear warheads represented the state-of-the-art against which PRC thermonuclear warheads should be measured.[32]

Former attorney general Janet Reno's declassified 1999 congressional testimony stated that the PRC had acquired "design information on the W88 Trident D5 warhead."[33] And yet a fourth government unclassified description of the document's contents stated: "In 1995, a U.S. Intelligence Agency received a document from a foreign source that suggested that design information related to a thermonuclear warhead currently stockpiled in the U.S. arsenal—the W-88—may have been compromised."[34]

David Wise, a journalist specializing in intelligence matters, has provided one account of its contents:

Alarmingly, the Chinese secret document, which bore a 1988 date, gave the exact width of the "short waist," or narrowest point of the W-88's primary. . . . Even more significantly, the document disclosed that the W-88s primary was "two-point aspherical."

. . .

It got worse. The document accurately gave the diameter of the secondary . . . and Chinese intelligence knew that unlike most other nukes, the primary of the W-88 was squeezed into the tapered tip of the warhead, forward of the secondary, a configuration that was supposed to be a closely held secret.[35]

The walk-in document came to the Kindred Spirit group sometime in early August 1995. Within the group it was immediately recognized for what it was—a smoking gun.[36] Booth and others wanted to ask follow-up questions about some of the revelations in the walk-in document, but were rebuffed by the CIA. In fact, the CIA refused to provide any details on how or where the document was acquired. There have been a number of "stories" over time about this, but most are bogus. The CIA has categorically refused to declassify the document and has been extremely vague about its origins. Much later, we learned that there was much more material provided by the "walk-in." For some reason, the CIA did almost nothing to process this material for nearly four years after it first showed up in Washington, sometime in early 1995.

Sources within CIA have claimed that the CIA director at the time, John Deutch, deliberately withheld the document from the Intelligence Community. Apparently, he had directed the chief of the unit that had first acquired the document to "sit on it" and not allow it to leave CIA. I was told that if Deutch had had his way, it never would have seen the light of day and it certainly would not have been provided to the Energy Department.[37] But now the scientists had it and its existence changed the views of many within the Kindred Spirit group.

When CIA analysts from the Directorate of Intelligence first acquired the document, they called a Los Alamos scientist named Alan Riley to verify the accuracy of the W88 information contained in it. Riley told them that the numbers checked out and that this information was (and still is) classified. What Riley probably didn't know was that senior CIA officials wanted to send FBI agents to Los Alamos to investigate him for gaining access to this information. These officials were suspicious of Los Alamos' ability to keep a secret and feared that Riley had shared information about the walk-in document with other scientists not authorized to know its contents. The officials urged the FBI to open an investigation on Riley, but I talked them out of it. It wasn't Riley's fault that analysts had called him and provided him with details about the document. If you want to investigate someone, I thought, investigate the CIA analysts who had called him in the first place.

Prior to the second meeting of the Kindred Spirit Analysis Group in late August, CIA officials shared the document with a small group of us at DOE Headquarters. The conclusion was inescapable: somehow the PRC had acquired classified information on our most modern nuclear warhead in the mid-1980s. Although I had already referred our espionage suspicions to the FBI, this document seemed to confirm our fears. In clear violation of their Section 811 obligations, CIA had refused to share the document with the FBI for reasons that have never been clear.* But even after this document showed up, the FBI still refused to open an investigation and wanted us to proceed with our peer review.

I also told Ken Baker and then Charles Curtis about the CIA's acquisition of the document. I know Curtis then had a discussion with DCI Deutch about the information in it. Curtis's phone call to Deutch had another, unintended consequence for Kindred Spirit, however. Afterward, Deutch was described as "livid" that CIA had provided the walk-in document to DOE. In a private meeting Deutch ripped the CIA analysts for sharing this information with us. They never returned to our meetings, nor did the DIA representative.

Had Deutch succeeded in bottling up this document, history would certainly have been different. The Kindred Spirit group would never have been able to agree on whether the Chinese had assistance, the FBI would have used such an inconclusive finding to deflect our requests for an investigation, and Chinese nuclear espionage would have gone on as before. Why Deutch sought to suppress such an obvious indication of PRC espionage against the U.S. nuclear weapons program is unknown. But the appearance of the document at DOE set off a chain reaction through the Clinton administration. Awareness of the "espionage" began to seep out.

---

*Section 811 was passed in response to the CIA's failure to notify the FBI of the Aldrich Ames case. Now, less than a year later, CIA was up to its old tricks again.

For example, after we informed Secretary O'Leary about the document, she called Leon Panetta, then chief of staff at the White House. Records uncovered later at CIA indicated that Panetta in turn called Deutch about the matter. So now the CIA and the FBI and the White House were aware of the existence of a smoking gun on PRC espionage. What happened? Actually, nothing much. Apparently Deutch promised to "get back" to Panetta, but never did.

At any rate, the August meeting of the Kindred Spirit group started off with the members examining the document. I sat in on one of these sessions because I wanted to hear the scientists' thoughts about all this. I distinctly remember Livermore's Bill Quirk exclaiming, "Well, obviously they got information on the W88. Why are we wasting our time arguing about whether they did all this by themselves? They've got all the information they need." Since he had been one of the most vocal proponents of the "they did it themselves" view, I thought his conclusion was significant.

At this point, the debate over whether the PRC had foreign assistance, specifically assistance from the United States, was over. I had not asked the group to determine where the PRC might have obtained such assistance, only whether the evidence would affirm the original suspicions that the Chinese had received foreign assistance. This, coupled with the Sandia scientist's report that this information was not available in the public domain and not widely disseminated within the nuclear weapons complex, closed off further discussion of this topic, at least in my presence. The next item on the agenda for the group was to try to determine the value of the information that the PRC had acquired.

As before, the debate covered a lot of ground. Some tried to measure it in terms of years saved, or number of nuclear tests or even resources saved. One group proposed "ten years," another group said "dozens of nuclear tests," but none of these measurements seemed to have any real substance. Later on, some analysts from one government agency would claim that nuclear espionage saved the PRC about two years and cited scientists at Livermore as its source, but Livermore refused to back that judgment. I had been through some of the wars over the Soviet economy and especially Soviet military spending earlier in my career, so I was skeptical about any measurement that purported to determine the savings in

U.S. currency or equivalents. Unfortunately, the KSAG could do no better than come up with the judgment that the acquisition had made a "material" contribution to the PRC's strategic nuclear modernization efforts.[38] My next question was, how? How did it impact the PRC program?

Along with the progress of the PRC's nuclear program, our group was also aware of China's efforts to upgrade and modernize its missile force.

> Road-mobile ballistic missiles and submarine-launched ballistic missiles require smaller, more advanced thermonuclear warheads. The Select Committee judges it is likely that the PRC will use a new, smaller thermonuclear warhead on its next generation road-mobile, solid-propellant ICBM, the DF-31.
>
> The DF-31 is likely to undergo its first test flight in 1999, and could be deployed as early as 2002. Introduction of the PRC's new, smaller thermonuclear warhead into PLA [People's Liberation Army] could coincide with the initial operational capability of the new road-mobile DF-31 ballistic missile system.
>
> The Select Committee judges that the PRC's thermonuclear warheads will exploit elements of the U.S. W-70 Lance or W-88 Trident D-5 warheads. While the PRC might not reproduce exact replicas of these U.S. thermonuclear warheads, elements of the PRC devices could be similar.[39]

Chinese interest in mobile missiles stemmed, in part, from the PLA's increasing worries about the credibility of its strategic nuclear deterrent. The PRC had not attempted, as far as we could tell, to build up its strategic nuclear missile force to the level of either the United States or the Soviet Union. Its strategic doctrine seemed to call for small numbers of ICBMs that would act as a second-strike deterrent to attacks by either the United States or the Soviets. The existing PRC force was assessed to be comparable to U.S. nuclear missile forces of the late 1950s or the early 1960s: large, liquid-fueled missiles with big, heavy warheads. For the deterrent to work, the PRC missile force had to be survivable, that is, capable of riding out a first strike by the United States or Russia. But in the mid-1980s, both countries were developing new missiles and improving their reconnaissance capabilities, and both seemed intent on deploying ballistic missile defense systems.* The Chinese were growing more concerned that their second-strike capability, the basis of their deterrent, would become vulnerable to a first strike by U.S. or Soviet missiles if these trends continued.[40] If true, this could disrupt long-range Chinese plans to reincorporate Taiwan, since without an effective, survivable nuclear deterrent, the PRC leadership probably believed that it could not hold off U.S. intervention in some future crisis over Taiwan. Its heavy investment in conventional military capability would be wasted if the PRC lacked a credible nuclear deterrent to back up these forces.

The Chinese began casting about for solutions to the growing vulnerability of their deterrent forces and settled on the same solution as the Soviets: develop and field long-range land- and sea-based mobile missiles. These missiles, constantly on the move, could "hide" from enemy reconnaissance systems and ride out a first strike in order to deliver a devastating retaliatory attack. But the nuclear warheads in the existing Chinese arsenal were much too large and heavy for deployment on mobile missiles. To successfully field such a capability, the Chinese needed to develop smaller warheads to fit into the nose cones of the reentry vehicles on the tips of these missiles.

The Kindred Spirit scientists argued that development of a small warhead suitable for deployment on such missiles could be a difficult challenge, but knowing what the U.S. achieved and how would be very beneficial, allowing the Chinese to avoid the false starts, blind alleys and cul-de-sacs that are a natural part of nuclear warhead program development. Having the kind of information indicated by the walk-in document would help the PRC program zero in on the correct path of development from the outset. At the time, no scientist in the KSAG expressed any dissent or reservations with this view, despite later assertions to the contrary. I cannot claim to have attended every session of the August meeting, but Henderson met with me and I also met with the group as a whole; no one dissented from that assessment. Richter also promoted

---

*The Soviets had already deployed such a defense around Moscow and were upgrading the system. President Reagan had announced his Strategic Defense Initiative by this time.

the view that the PRC now had a "roadmap" for its future development, although he later denied making such statements.

In early September, I asked the KSAG to wrap up its deliberations and document its thinking in a briefing that contained a summary of its observations, findings and conclusions. I heard later that the deliberations were rather intense, but there was a consensus on the bottom line. First, it was obvious that the People's Republic of China had acquired Secret/Restricted Data on the U.S. W88 thermonuclear warhead design. Second, "Compromise of [redacted] has been of material assistance to the PRC's strategic nuclear modernization efforts." And finally, the group concluded, "This technology enables earlier development of road mobile missiles to target the U.S."[41]

I can recall no conclusions or discussion as to who might have committed this compromise of our nuclear secrets. In particular, there was no discussion of where or how such information might have been obtained from within the U.S. nuclear weapons complex.

After the walk-in document showed up, discussions about Chinese acquisition of classified information ceased, as far as I knew. The debate shifted to just "how important" the information had been to the Chinese nuclear program. Bobby Henson was way out front, claiming that the Chinese had [redacted] the W88 design. Mike Henderson, the group leader, managed to bridge the gap between Henson and the other scientists with reference to a "material contribution." To my knowledge, the only dissent to that conclusion was Henson's. I was satisfied with the "material contribution" formulation as the best we could do given the state of our knowledge at the time.[42]

In late 1996, the FBI interviewed several of the participants in the development of these conclusions to record their recollections of these deliberations. These scientists told the FBI: "There had been no disagreement that 'Restricted Data' information had been acquired by the Chinese. The only disagreement was over how valuable the information was."[43] And even on this point, the scientists told the FBI: "Nor was there any dispute that this compromise had aided the Chinese nuclear weapons program by helping to establish what were attainable achievements and to avoid blind alleys in their own research and development program."[44]

I found those conclusions extremely powerful. Since the information in question was classified, it most likely was obtained by espionage. It is possible that a scientist could have lost a document that the PRC picked up somehow, but what was not debatable was that classified information had found its way into the hands of a foreign power. Nothing should obscure the hard facts that the PRC had acquired warhead design information on our most modern thermonuclear warhead and other nuclear warheads as well, and was using that information to develop and field missile systems that could be employed against the United States, its allies or U.S. forces in the Pacific region. My recollection is that the group met with Under Secretary Curtis later that fall to review its findings and conclusions. This meeting may have been held to prepare Curtis to discuss Chinese nuclear espionage with CIA director John Deutch, but it may also have been to prepare Curtis to discuss this case in an upcoming meeting with the weapons labs directors. He seemed satisfied that the scientists had done a thorough job and thanked the group for its work.[45]

Curtis reconvened this group of scientists in May 1996 to review, once again, the Kindred Spirit findings and conclusions. We were about to enter a new phase of our inquiry, including congressional notifications, and Curtis wanted to go over the scientists' judgments one last time. Mike Henderson delivered the presentation and Curtis put the scientists through their paces, with lots of good questions, but no scientist present expressed any dissent from the group's conclusions. I had repeatedly encouraged the scientists to speak up and share any reservations or disagreements they might have with Curtis at both the November and the May meetings. None did. The "walk-in document" had closed off that debate.

ONE OF THE QUESTIONS we were continually asked later in all the inquiries about the Clinton administration's handling of this case was "who knew about this and what did they know?" By this time—in addition to the CIA, the FBI and White House chief of staff Leon Panetta, DOE assistant secretary Vic Reis had informed the chairman of the Joint Chiefs of Staff, General John Shalikashvili, at the Pentagon in September 1995. Curtis and Reis both briefed the lab directors on the case in November 1995. Over the next two years, the circle of government officials knowledgeable about this security breach grew considerably.

But there was one obvious omission. By late spring 1996, or about a year after the first alert, we had yet to inform our elected representatives. In the case of intelligence matters, I was required by law to tell the intelligence oversight committees in both the Senate and the House what we had uncovered. At that time, Senator Arlen Specter (R-PA) and Congressman Larry Combest (R-TX) chaired these committees, respectively. Beginning around December 1995, or about eight months after our initial warnings, I became concerned that we had not yet fulfilled our reporting obligations to Congress. Our CIA friends agreed, as they had just suffered through a blistering from Congress over their failure to report the Aldrich Ames spy case in a timely fashion. I already had the materials prepared by Henderson and the Kindred Spirit group, and I thought these would be suitable for use on Capitol Hill.

But no one in the Energy Department or the administration was in a hurry to go to the Hill. Even though Curtis had already had a couple of discussions with CIA director Deutch, they were now talking about a "formal presentation" to him before we could notify Congress. Of course, every senior level official at the CIA had to review the material before Deutch could see it, so that took up a fair amount of time, too.

It was during this round of briefings that I met Paul Redmond, at that time an assistant to Deutch for counterintelligence. Redmond seemed like a throwback, grumpy and short-tempered, and I was surprised to find someone like him still working in a prominent position in the kinder, gentler Bill Clinton CIA. Redmond shared the credit for finally breaking the Aldrich Ames case in the early 1990s, and his contempt for the FBI's counterintelligence capability was intense. When he heard my summary of the Kindred Spirit findings, he said, "This is as bad as the Rosenberg case." On other occasions he would say that Kindred Spirit was as bad as the Ames case, since millions of Americans could someday die as a result of successful Chinese nuclear espionage. Redmond shoved aside the CIA bureaucracy more than once in order to keep the case moving forward.

When Deutch's schedule finally permitted the meeting to take place, sometime in March 1996 we gathered in his office in the Old

Executive Office Building, right next door to the White House. In addition to Curtis, Los Alamos director Sig Hecker, Vic Reis from DOE, Mike Henderson, the leader of the Kindred Spirit Analysis Group, Booth and another Los Alamos scientist, Carl Henry, attended the meeting. There was some banter between Reis and Deutch, mostly about nuclear testing. Deutch was a big fan of live testing and basically asked Reis that if he didn't test his weapons at the Nevada test site, how would the United States know whether the weapons really worked? Trying to do everything by computer was no substitute for live nuclear testing, according to Deutch.

The presentation went well and I wrapped up my briefing in about ten minutes. Deutch asked a couple of questions about what we meant by "material assistance," and that was it. None of the Los Alamos participants, including Hecker and Henderson, spoke. Curtis told Deutch of our concerns about informing Congress, but Deutch said he would take care of that and would inform the other players on the administration's national security team. We later learned that he didn't. I also recall George Tenet, then Deutch's deputy, sitting in his office across the hall, not having been invited to attend the meeting. Tenet later testified that the first time he heard of this matter was in August 1997 at the White House. By then, Tenet had already been the director of CIA for maybe a year or more. Did no one bother to tell him about what was happening at our nuclear labs when he moved up to the top job?

Shortly after the Deutch meeting, we met with Secretary O'Leary to update her on the case. At some point during the meeting, Curtis mentioned that we planned to tell Congress about Kindred Spirit. O'Leary brought every one up short when she asked, "And who has told the White House about all this?" Months had passed since Energy's last communication with the White House, but now Curtis was proposing telling a Republican-controlled Congress without first checking in with the White Hous.

This is how the first meeting with Sandy Berger came about. At that time Berger, a Washington lawyer and Democratic Party activist, was President Clinton's deputy national security advisor. His boss, Tony Lake, was out of town—I think in Moscow, making preparations for the President's first trip to Russia. I spiffed up our presentation materials by adding some PowerPoint charts, drawings and background information, and had our in-house graphics specialist make a title page that used the red PRC flag as a background. This came to be known as the "O'Leary briefing" because we had first presented it to her. It featured the Kindred Spirit group's conclusions about the probability of Chinese nuclear espionage right up front and then proceeded to explain the background and how the group had arrived at these conclusions. I included a diagram of the W88 warhead in order to depict the kinds of information the Chinese had acquired and also some pictures of the new PRC missiles that the Intelligence Community believed would be likely delivery candidates for new PRC nuclear warheads. I thought this would help clarify the message of the briefing.

The meeting was held on a beautiful springtime Saturday in the White House Situation Room. I met Curtis at DOE and then he drove us over in his old Saab. I'm sure he was a better lawyer than driver. We made it, but it was a pretty wild ride. After we arrived, we were escorted into the West Wing and waited there for Berger. Then we all trailed him into the Situation Room. Also in attendance: Vic Reis from the Energy Department, who was the "landlord" of the DOE weapons labs; the chief of CIA's Directorate of Operations; a reports officer from CIA's Operations Directorate; and Steve Andreesen, a man with a very high forehead in a perpetual frown who worked arms control and nuclear weapons issues for the National Security Council. He was a deputy to another NSC official named Bob Bell, a former congressional staffer for Senator Sam Nunn. Notable for its absence at our meeting was the FBI. The Bureau had been constantly updated on our progress and had been participating in our inquiries, so I expected at least one agent to be present. But no one was there from the FBI—and not for the last time.

Later on, Sandy Berger asserted that the discussion was very general and lacking in specifics. But Curtis refuted this and then Berger essentially abandoned that line. In truth, I gave him the same information about probable Chinese espionage, almost verbatim, that I had given CIA director Deutch. Afterwards there was some general discussion, and the CIA folks made a couple of broad observations. Berger told us to go ahead and notify Congress. He expressed his hope that the FBI would catch whoever was responsible, and that was it. Thanks very much for coming, goodbye. I don't know what type of reaction I expected, but Berger seemed distracted and didn't act especially concerned.

On the following Monday, Curtis and I were back in the Old Executive Office Building, meeting with Leon Fuerth, Vice President Al Gore's advisor. Curtis considered him to be one of the few people in the White House who truly cared about national security. And Fuerth was the only administration official, outside of CIA and the FBI, who did seem concerned and even somewhat thoughtful as I laid out the scientists' judgments about PRC espionage. He made a few suggestions for some additional areas of inquiry. I don't know if he ever told the Vice President.

By this time, April 1996, I had a new boss. A former congressional staffer from the House Armed Services Committee named Joan Rohfling had become the new director of the Office of Nonproliferation and National Security, relegating Ken Baker back to his deputy status. She had no previous management experience, but that is fairly typical in political appointments. She was a Curtis protégé and somewhat officious and overly concerned about her "prerogatives" as director, but we got on well—at least initially.

In early June 1996, Rohfling and I went back to the National Security Council to meet with Bob Bell, the senior director on the NSC who handled arms control and nuclear weapons issues. His main interest seemed to be the Comprehensive Test Ban Treaty. Rohfling explained that she wanted him to tell us who in the Pentagon should hear the Kindred Spirit briefing. Bell could hardly have cared less, but he finally suggested that we go talk to the defense under secretary for acquisition, Paul Kaminski. I thought it was odd that Bell did not recommend that we see officials with responsibilities for nuclear weapons policy or East Asian affairs in the Office of the Secretary of Defense, but he must have had his reasons. I recall the Kaminski meeting as being notable mostly for all the scale models of tanks, airplanes and warships that decorated his office. The Energy Department might have nuclear warheads, I remember thinking, but DOD had the really neat toys. As with nearly every Clinton political appointee, Kaminski suggested someone else to talk to, in this case the new director of the Ballistic Missile Defense Organization, and then thanked us for coming by.

Our first trip to Capitol Hill did not come until July 11, almost two months after we got the okay from Berger. I was beginning to believe that the Clinton administration just wasn't in a big hurry to do anything about this issue. Maybe they thought if they waited long enough, the Chinese problem would go away. At any rate, Rohfling made it clear that she wanted to do all the talking, and was taking me along for backup. We met with the Senate Intelligence Committee staffers in a special room in the Hart Senate Office Building. Rohfling conveyed a bare minimum of information. The staff director asked only one question: "Are there PRC nationals working at the labs?" Rohfling tried to dance around this by saying that we didn't think the foreign visitors program was the source of the problem, but rather it looked like an "insider" compromise. The guy just about ripped her head off—"That's not what I asked!" He then repeated his question. Rohfling meekly admitted, "Yes, there are PRC nationals at the labs." And that was about it.

We still had to do the House side of Congress, but that was not to occur until August. By that time, Rohfling had fallen out of favor with O'Leary and had been fired from her director's job. Ken Baker was the acting director once again. For some reason, I was asked to solo on the House briefing. This briefing was really strange. We didn't even see the Intelligence Committee staff director, as we had in the Senate. Instead we met with a staff assistant named Kathy Eberwein, who was responsible for oversight of Energy Department intelligence matters. She was accompanied by a lawyer serving with the staff. Their response was similar to all the others: terrible news, keep us informed. In retrospect, I'm not certain that Eberwein ever passed along news of PRC espionage to her boss or to the chairman of the committee, at that time Congressman Larry Combest (R-TX). Ironically, she later became deputy director of counterintelligence at the Energy Department under Bill Richardson

Not once were we asked to brief or meet with any individual senators or congressmen about this issue. No follow-up questions or meetings with the staff. It was difficult to understand why such an important issue seemed to generate so little interest on Capitol Hill. It was to be two years, in 1998, before any additional requests for more information came to us. I guess I could understand the Democrats being not too terribly concerned, but the Republicans controlled both the Senate and the House throughout this period. Yet there just didn't seem to be any interest, even when the leadership of both these committees changed in 1998. We thought surely a fire-breather like Senator Richard Shelby (R-AL), the new chairman of the Senate Intelligence Committee and a harsh critic of the administration's handling of intelligence, would want to look into all this. But no.

We did learn that the FBI had provided updates on their investigation to these committees. I think it's possible they told the Hill not to kick up too much dust that could interfere with an ongoing case. The Hill was overly deferential to the FBI on this, as on many other issues. And as we learned later, the FBI was doing almost nothing in its "investigation," so some healthy skepticism on the part of either the Senate or the House might have served to stir things up more. Our elected officials were not to learn until much later just how broad was the PRC assault on our nuclear weapons complex.

We made one more stop on our briefing tour in 1996. In November, Baker and I flew out to Omaha to meet with the commander in chief of the Strategic Command, successor to the Strategic Air Command. I guess the rationale for this meeting was that STRATCOM is the main customer for DOE's product—nuclear weapons—so maybe the customer ought to know that information about one of Energy's products was in a competitor's hands. We met with General Eugene Habiger, who ironically was later to become Bill Richardson's security czar at DOE. Another strange meeting, to say the least. Only General Habiger and one of his aides were present; his senior intelligence officer didn't even show up. I think Habiger understood most of what we told him, but he seemed much more interested in whether we could nominate any more targets in the PRC for his missiles than he was in the modernized weapons the Chinese were developing courtesy of the Energy Department labs.

So, by the end of the first Clinton administration in 1996, every single person and agency that needed to know this information had been told—or so I thought. I wouldn't find out until much later that FBI director Louis Freeh wouldn't learn about the case for another year, and the secretaries of state and commerce would have to wait three more years to find out. But most striking, it is very clear that neither Berger nor his boss, Tony Lake, told President Clinton; I have always wondered if Lake even knew. But my overriding impression at the end of 1996 was that senior officials within the administration really didn't want to know much about any of this. They could always fall back on the FBI's assurances that the matter was being probed aggressively and they didn't want to interfere with an ongoing investigation. News that the PRC had acquired classified design information on our most modern warhead should have set off alarm bells all over the Pentagon, in the White House and elsewhere. Damage assessments, vulnerability assessments, all sorts of things ought to have been starting up. For example, what if the PRC had sold our information to the Russians, information that would be useful in helping them tailor their ballistic missile defenses to exploit vulnerabilities in the W88 Trident D5? I had begun to suspect that the administration and even the military leadership in the Pentagon just didn't want to know.

FOUR

Who Done It?

[Wen Ho Lee] was doing things that were suspicious and lying while doing them. Either you become more suspicious when you encounter that, or you get out of the [counterintelligence] business.
  —Paul Moore, former FBI agent

While the Kindred Spirit group was wrapping up its work in September 1995, our counterintelligence guys were planning their next steps. With the PRC walk-in document in hand, I still wanted to refer the whole thing to the FBI. I had Dan Bruno sound out his counterparts on that topic once again, but he came back saying that the Bureau wanted DOE to do an "Administrative Inquiry" instead. We had exactly one "investigator," Bruno, and it was clear that he would have to cover a lot of territory. The FBI had dozens of trained counterintelligence investigators plus all of the legal resources that could be brought to bear in such an investigation. In truth, there is simply no reason for the FBI not to have taken over the case in 1995, as senior FBI officials later admitted.[1]

Sometime prior to my arrival at the Department of Energy, however, the counterintelligence office and the Bureau had signed a Memorandum of Understanding governing espionage investigations involving DOE or lab employees. The Energy Department had agreed to conduct Administrative Inquiries in the event that the FBI requested such assistance. I had reviewed the case files of past Administrative Inquiries when counterintelligence became my responsibility in 1995. These were all limited in scope and confined mostly to reviews of security files and travel records. In the Kindred Spirit case, we would do the grunt work of sorting through thousands of personnel files and records at the labs in an effort to identify potential investigative leads for the FBI to pursue. Frankly, we were stretched pretty thin by this time and I was worried that we wouldn't be able to give the FBI what it needed.

I wish I had simply drafted a letter for Secretary O'Leary to send to Janet Reno and Louis Freeh saying: "We think espionage against our nuclear weapons complex has occurred and we expect the FBI to take over and move out on this." But no one at DOE or the FBI was open to such a direct approach. The FBI's refusal to take on the case in 1995 left us with the option of either doing an inquiry or just letting the whole thing die. I didn't think then that it was my job to ignore the existence of a classified Chinese document with W88 warhead data in it. I still don't.

If we were going to have to do this inquiry, however, the last thing I wanted to do was screw up any subsequent FBI investigation. The FBI was notorious for blaming other agencies for mistakes that prevented it from "solving" a case or obtaining a conviction. I didn't want to face such recriminations later on. But how best to guard against some foul-up?

To me, the best protection would be to get the FBI to participate in the inquiry from the very beginning even if it refused to take control. I wanted Dan Bruno, who would be running the inquiry for us, to make sure the FBI was fully on board. I told him to give the key FBI Headquarters agents, Jerry Doyle, "Jack Kerry" and "Greg Smith," lots of briefings on his methodology and approach to the inquiry. I wanted the FBI to approve everything we would do. Better yet, I thought, let's try to get an FBI agent detailed to help us do the Administrative Inquiry. So, I met yet again with FBI associate director John Lewis along with section chief Doyle at their headquarters in September 1995. They already knew the Kindred Spirit working group's results and knew about the "walk-in document," and Lewis agreed that an Administrative Inquiry by the Energy Department would be the best place to start. I gave him a real sob story about all the personnel and funding cuts that Secretary O'Leary and her team had imposed on Energy counterintelligence. Then I hit him up for an FBI agent to help us on the inquiry. To my surprise, he agreed and offered one of their best China experts:

Special Agent "F. Jeff Maines." I had Ken Baker send a letter to the FBI assistant director, Robert Bryant, on September 25, 1995, documenting our agreement and putting our request in writing.[2]

"Maines" came very highly recommended to us as a real pro; at that time he was working out of the FBI office in Tampa. We would pay his travel and expenses and he would accompany Dan Bruno to the field sites to review records and files. I breathed a sigh of relief. How could the FBI possibly criticize Energy now, given that one of their best guys would be helping us out?

I think it's important to be clear on just what this Administrative Inquiry was and what it wasn't. First, Energy counterintelligence investigators, like Dan Bruno, have no police powers—that is, they can't force anyone to talk to them. They can't review bank records, conduct technical surveillance of telephones or computers, look at potential suspects' mail, or anything like that. By law, only the FBI has such investigative powers in espionage cases like this. The FBI was extremely sensitive about tipping off a potential "suspect," so it sharply restricted Dan's ability to interview anybody. For example, the FBI would not permit him to interview personnel in the Energy Department's Defense Programs office in Washington, which runs the weapons labs, for fear that these people would "blow" the investigation. So our role in the inquiry was limited to a file review. This inquiry would be little more than a records check, not unlike those done every day by the FBI and intelligence and defense agencies for the purpose of granting or updating security clearances for federal employees.

Bruno and "Maines," assisted by the lab counterintelligence officers, would compile lists of individuals at the labs or other Energy Department sites who worked with W88 information (access) and who traveled to the PRC or met with their counterparts from the PRC nuclear weapons establishment (opportunity). Access to relevant W88 information and opportunity to transmit, convey or inadvertently disclose that information to their PRC counterparts were the initial filters for winnowing down the list of potential investigative leads for the FBI. The "opportunity" aspect of this approach was based on the FBI's understanding of PRC intelligence collection methodologies. The FBI, supported by the Intelligence

Community, emphasized repeatedly the Chinese use of scientists to elicit classified information from their U.S. lab counterparts in face-to-face meetings, preferably on China's home court.

Later media accounts about the inquiry usually identified these two factors but omitted a third: security anomalies. As I mentioned earlier, there can't be many institutions with more "anomalies" of potential counterintelligence interest than the Energy Department and its labs. So a careful examination of personnel security files was a key element of the Administrative Inquiry into the loss of W88 information. The investigators were looking for such things as bankruptcy, infidelity, examples of excessive spending, close and continuous contact with foreign nationals, or indications of prior FBI interest—anything that could open a person to blackmail or financial enticements, or suggest a "propensity for espionage." A lab employee who had been the subject of an earlier FBI investigation and had been polygraphed by the FBI was a good example of an "anomaly" that would definitely draw our attention.

The FBI wanted Bruno and "Maines" to identify potential "investigative leads" for the Bureau to pursue in a full field investigation. That is, the inquiry we were undertaking would sort through the entire population of the labs with security clearances (about 100,000 with access to classified information) and try to narrow this down to a manageable set of leads, if any, for the FBI to follow. Later it was alleged that DOE should have identified documents that contained W88 information and the recipients for such documents throughout the entire nuclear weapons complex, including the Defense Department and defense contractors. In the case of the W88, this would have included the U.S. Navy program office in the Pentagon responsible for the development of the delivery system for the W88—the Trident D5 submarine-launched ballistic missile—and the Navy contractors responsible for development of the D5, the nose cone for the missile. But that is *not* what the FBI asked us to do. The FBI wanted the "who," not the "what." By law, DOE lacked the authority to expand its inquiry outside the Energy Department complex; it was up to the FBI to look at Defense and its contractors.

Bruno told the FBI that the DOE labs were not the only place where W88 information might be and the Bureau needed to look at the Pentagon and defense contractors. He constantly reminded them that DOE did not have the authority to look beyond the Energy Department and its labs, although the Bureau would later deny that Bruno urged them to look outside DOE.[3] "Yeah, we know that and we'll take care of it," was the Bureau's response. In retrospect, it would have been a good thing for Dan's team to compile a list of such documents; but there was no team, only Dan. We just didn't have the manpower, and the FBI wasn't interested in document lists or "locales." They wanted names and leads they could pursue. I think that using DOE in such a fashion would have been a waste of our already limited resources. The FBI could easily have gone to the U.S. Navy and gotten the list of W88 contractors and then examined contractor facilities for W88 documents. They had the resources and the authority to do that; we didn't.

One other point about this: We simply didn't know how much information the Chinese had actually acquired. The details in the CIA's walk-in document might represent the full extent of the information or simply the tip of the iceberg. The nature of the document was such that most scientists believed that the original Chinese authors had no reason to reveal everything they had collected, but only what their readership would need to know. We couldn't say whether the PRC had blueprints or what. I do know that Alan Riley, the scientist at Los Alamos who verified the accuracy of the W88 information described in the walk-document, told us that he was checking the W88 warhead blueprints. In 1984 there were about sixty copies of the W88 blueprints, all kept at Energy Department facilities. Over the course of the next couple of years, I must have asked Carl Henry and other Los Alamos scientists to verify the accuracy of the data contained in the walk-in document a dozen times.

Dan Bruno's plan had to identify which Energy Department sites the AI team would actually visit. With help from the FBI and from lab scientists on detail to our office, such as Carl Henry, he identified Los Alamos, Livermore and Sandia, the three nuclear weapons design facilities; warhead manufacturing sites like Pantex in Amarillo, Texas, where nuclear warheads are assembled; and Rocky Flats outside of Denver, where "pits" for the warheads were made. Dan and "Maines" also proposed to visit the Energy Department's Office of Defense Programs sites in Washington and the field operations sites in Albuquerque and Oakland. The time frame under consideration—1984 to 1988—covered the period when the warhead had been under development at Los Alamos, before it was delivered to the U.S. Navy in the early 1990s. The date of the walk-in document, 1988, was considered the latest that the compromise could have occurred.[4] John Richter and others pegged 1984 as the earliest date because at that point the Navy had selected the Los Alamos design and thus "fixed" the parameters of the warhead. Later we learned that the "earliest" date could have been pushed a bit further back into the early 1980s, but I don't know how much this would have affected the outcome of the Administrative Inquiry.

Dan asked the contract counterintelligence staffs at Pantex and Rocky Flats to check their records for travel by employees or managers to China or visits from Chinese nuclear scientists. But these were industrial production facilities, and Energy Department security officials considered the work performed at these sites too sensitive to permit visitors from countries such as Russia or China. Nor were the plant workers at these facilities allowed to travel to these countries. So there were no records to review at these two facilities. The FBI agreed that Bruno and "Maines" need not visit them, but promised to pick up these sites later, since the Bureau's investigative powers would allow it to do a more thorough job with interviews and so forth.

That left Los Alamos and Sandia in New Mexico, Livermore Lab in California, and the DOE field office sites at Albuquerque and Oakland, where personnel security files for the weapons lab contractors were maintained. The FBI told us to hold off reviewing the Defense Programs' federal employees at DOE Headquarters in Washington or at the field operations offices. They wanted the Administrative Inquiry to be as unobtrusive as possible so as not to alert any potential suspects. Defense Programs' personnel had a reputation for not being able to keep a secret, so the FBI was concerned that if word got out in these facilities, any later investigation might be blown. Bruno and "Maines" could go to Albuquerque or Oakland to review the security files of lab employees, but they were not to start pulling files on the federal employees working there.

So with the FBI's approval, there would be two site visits: one to New Mexico and one to California. Bruno and "Maines" would be looking for people who had access to the W88 information between 1984 and 1988 and who had traveled to the PRC nuclear weapons establishment or had interacted with PRC nuclear scientists visiting lab sites during that period.[5] They would then review security files to look for reports of prior security problems or "anomalies." Late in the fall, we held a meeting in our office at DOE Headquarters and Dan briefed his plan to the FBI. The purpose of this meeting was to ensure that the FBI approved his approach to the conduct of the Kindred Spirit Administrative Inquiry. If the FBI had any objections, I wanted to hear them.

Present at that meeting from the FBI Headquarters China Section were Jerry Doyle, "Jack Kerry," "Greg Smith" and "Maines." As usual, the FBI guys stood apart from the rest of us, if for no other reason than they dressed better. (I always wondered if the FBI got a clothing allowance.) Doyle and "Kerry" were tall, thin and Irish looking, and they spoke in a measured, careful manner. The FBI flew in the agent responsible for Los Alamos, "Dick Lowenthal," to attend this meeting. I had met "Lowenthal" while I was working there in the early 1990s; he was a short fellow and very secretive, like all the rest of the FBI types. Unusual for an FBI agent, "Smith" was very friendly and outgoing, with a good sense of humor. He was our main point of contact in the FBI's China Section, so we saw a good bit of him.

Energy was represented by Dan Bruno and Charles Washington, the latter about to become the acting director of the Counterintelligence Division. Los Alamos scientists Carl Henry and Larry Booth attended to assist Dan in explaining the findings of the Kindred Spirit working group. Bob Vrooman and Terry Craig from the Los Alamos counterintelligence shop were also there, but I don't remember if Livermore's Bill Cleveland attended. I recall very little discussion of what later came to be labeled the "predicate" of the Administrative Inquiry. We thought the FBI understood full well this predicate: the PRC had acquired classified data on the W88 nuclear warhead and we would be looking at Energy Department sites for the potential source of that compromise. Dan laid out his plan and the FBI's Doyle and "Kerry" approved our approach—without reservation. I do recall Dan once again reminding the FBI to look at the Defense Department.

Dan then sent messages out to the lab counterintelligence officers at Livermore, Los Alamos and Sandia requesting them to begin
pulling records that he and "Maines" would need for their search.
They made site visits in November and December 1995 to California and New Mexico to brief the labs on the Administrative Inquiry
and what they needed to conduct their review. I reported the results
of all these meetings up the line to my superiors, Ken Baker and
Charlie Curtis, who then approved the kickoff of the AI.

As far as I was concerned, we weren't looking for any super
spy; we were simply trying to narrow the field of potential suspects
for the FBI. A person or persons unknown had been passing classified nuclear warhead data to the Chinese and our job was to do
a preliminary inquiry to help the FBI sort out possible investigative leads within the DOE national lab complex that it could pursue in a full-blown investigation. What could be simpler or more
straightforward? The FBI argued that without an Administrative
Inquiry of this nature, the Bureau would have had to start its investigation from scratch. Of course, the FBI could easily have opened
what they term an Unknown Subject (UNSUB in FBI jargon) investigation at that point, but they chose not to—regrettably.

WHEN I ASSUMED responsibility for counterintelligence in 1995, I
asked for detailed information from CIA and the FBI regarding the
foreign intelligence threat to the DOE national laboratories. At that
time, there were no Intelligence Community reports documenting
the threat in a systematic way. Everything was pretty much ad hoc
and anecdotal. (It would be three more years before the community finally produced such a report.) After the initial suspicions
about Chinese espionage that spring, I requested further details on
Chinese intelligence operations. Our CIA officer, on loan to the
Energy Department, pulled this information together for me.

Both CIA and the FBI emphasized that the Chinese approached
spying differently from the Russians. We had long experience before
and during the Cold War with Soviet techniques: dead-drops, espionage cells, secret writing and all that. But the Chinese techniques
were "nontraditional" in that they concentrated more on eliciting
information from visiting scientists and other officials and less on
Soviet-style spycraft. According to CIA and the FBI, the Chinese

would employ scientists, academicians and students to collect information of interest. These people had more contact with American scientists and could ask better, more informed questions. Intelligence taskings would come from scientific or academic institutions engaged in research for the People's Liberation Army or from other governmental customers. But the scientists, professors and students from the Chinese Academy of Engineering Physics, which runs the Chinese nuclear weapons program, and related academic facilities like Fudan University would try to collect all types of information—classified or otherwise—from their U.S. counterparts.

The Chinese painstakingly collected lab and Energy Department unclassified technical reports, and visitors to Chinese facilities were struck by the thoroughness of their collections. In their own writings, the Chinese assessed these reports as "provid[ing] intelligence of great value."[6] The Chinese knew all about the labs' penchant for sloppy handling and "inadvertent" releases of classified documents, citing in particular the Los Alamos compromise of design details of several advanced nuclear warheads in the 1970s.

At that time, it was believed that the Chinese would not pay for information as the Russians had paid Aldrich Ames, Robert Hanssen and other U.S. spies. Instead, they would try to collect information from visiting scientists or high-ranking officials by engaging their visitors in wide-ranging and technical scientific dialogues. According to the FBI and CIA experts, these dialogues would often take the form of Chinese scientists seeking to elicit solutions to problems common to the field of nuclear weapons development. In the course of these dialogues, the Chinese would ask leading questions that the visiting scientist couldn't answer without disclosing classified information. The Chinese were perfectly willing to reveal some of their own secrets in order to "prime the pump" and get the visitor talking. "How did you solve the problem of x or y?" a senior Chinese nuclear scientist might inquire of his American colleague. Our scientists would constantly have to guard against engaging in "academic" discussions that gradually veered into classified matters. It was commonplace to invite the visiting scientist to make presentations and give seminars to select groups of his PRC counterparts and then be drawn into discussions of technical detail and information.[7] Such meetings usually occurred after a whirlwind tour of historical sites, like the Great Wall, and dinners held in honor of the visiting scientists.

The risks to both our scientists and our classified nuclear weapons information from this technique were summed up nicely in a 1999 government report:

> *The nature of the intelligence-gathering methods used by the People's Republic of China poses a special challenge to the U.S. in general and the weapons labs in particular.* More sophisticated than some of the blatant methods employed by the former Soviet bloc espionage services, PRC intelligence operatives know their strong suits and play them extremely well. Increasingly more nimble, discreet and transparent in their spying methods, the Chinese services have become very proficient in the art of seemingly innocuous elicitations of information. This modus operandi has proved very effective against unwitting and ill-prepared DOE personnel.[8]

We should not expect the Chinese to be clearing out dead drops like the Russians, but lab scientists visiting China should expect to have their baggage, computers and briefcases searched in their hotel rooms and would likely be subject to electronic surveillance during their trips. In fact, both the FBI and the CIA warned us that our lab scientists should expect a full-court press by Chinese scientists and/or intelligence officers during visits to Chinese nuclear facilities. Our records indicated that the Chinese could be quite persistent and sometimes harsh when they thought a visiting scientist was holding out on them. More than one U.S. scientist came back vowing never to return to China and urging the labs to halt the exchange program.[9]

When they explained these techniques, the FBI always referred to the George Keyworth case as an example. Keyworth was a very senior Los Alamos scientist who later became President Ronald Reagan's chief White House science advisor. He had been one of the earliest scientists traveling to China, and when he returned from his visit, he told how his hosts had badgered him for information about classified subjects, such as how the neutron bomb worked. Keyworth said he had resisted revealing classified information, but had provided the Chinese with an analogy. Whether this analogy, which concerned the techniques of "implosion," was classified was a matter of dispute between Keyworth and the government, but the Chinese made some rapid advancements in their neutron bomb program after Keyworth's visit. "Jack Kerry, " one of the FBI agents working with us, said that the Justice Department had prepared an indictment of Keyworth for disclosing classified information to the Chinese. According to "Kerry," it was only Keyworth's job in the Reagan White House that saved him. The FBI cited this as a classic example of how the Chinese would invite a prominent scientist to present lectures on harmless topics, and then lead the scientist into discussions in which classified details about nuclear weapons matters would be revealed. Lab scientists like Keyworth always thought they could easily fend off Chinese overtures for classified information and would continue to put themselves and U.S. secrets at risk by insisting on traveling to meet Chinese nuclear weapons scientists on their home turf.[10]

These visits and exchanges expanded during the Reagan administration, when the United States sought to develop China as a counterweight to the Soviets in the Far East. There were some memorable photographs of Chinese delegations at Los Alamos and Livermore and U.S. delegations in China. Initially, visits to China were limited to laboratory senior managers, but gradually the rank-and-file lab scientists began to travel at the invitation of their counterparts in China. Chinese scientists and intelligence officers trolled the labs and the international science symposia looking for scientists interested in visiting the People's Republic of China. One PRC institution in particular, the Chinese Academy of Engineering Physics' Institute of Applied Physics and Computational Mathematics in Beijing, became a popular stop for our scientists. The institute handled the computer simulations and mathematical modeling research in support of the nuclear warhead design work done at the Academy of Engineering Physics, which was the equivalent of Los Alamos but managed the overall nuclear weapons program. It also got into the arms control business in the early 1990s, probably to expand its opportunities to entice lab scientists to visit.

The FBI also emphasized the importance of Chinese-Americans to the PRC intelligence services. Paul Moore, a former FBI agent, has been circumspect in public, but behind closed doors he was more insistent on Chinese targeting of Asian-American scientists. His favorite message was that PRC collectors, in effect, "profile" U.S. targets, looking especially for organizations that have senior managers who are allowed to travel abroad and that employ large numbers of Chinese-Americans. He claimed that the Chinese have been successful against targets with such characteristics, like Silicon Valley and the U.S. national labs, and unsuccessful against U.S. institutions that don't, like the military. Special Agent "Maines," who would be accompanying Bruno, was also said to "know that the PRC had appealed to ethnic ties to Chinese-Americans in the past to obtain information."[11]

Our friends at CIA reinforced his message. They had had their own experience with a Chinese-American CIA employee, Larry Wu-tai Chin, who turned out to be a spy for the PRC. Chin had spied for decades from within the CIA, passing along political, economic and other types of classified government information to Beijing. After he was arrested, he committed suicide in his jail cell before the agency could fully interrogate him. The CIA's warning about Chinese ethnic targeting was even heavier-handed than the FBI's. But I never heard any counterintelligence officer—not even Paul Moore—say that the PRC "only" or "solely" targeted Asian-Americans or that Asian-Americans were any more susceptible to PRC spying than other lab scientists. Nobody I ever talked to inside the FBI or the Intelligence Community believed that.

Of course, we knew there were ongoing FBI investigations of suspicious actions by lab employees who were Asian-Americans. One was later revealed to be a former Los Alamos scientist named Peter Lee, who was prosecuted for providing classified nuclear weapons information to the Chinese when he was at Los Alamos National Lab in 1985. And of course, the early 1980s case at Livermore had also involved an Asian-American, suspected of passing secrets about the U.S. neutron bomb to the Chinese. But our review of the debriefings of traveling lab scientists plus our knowledge of the Keyworth case made me question any emphasis on Asian-Americans.

I didn't know, however, that Bruno had drafted an investigation plan in June 1995 to serve as a roadmap for the Kindred Spirit inquiry. His plan picked up where the scientists' working group would conclude and outlined an approach to the identification of lab sites and program staff with access to the suspected compromised information. But it also contained a passage that would come back to haunt him—and me:

> A critical element of this inquiry is the identification of personnel who worked on the various aspects of the design. An initial consideration will be to identify those US citizens, of Chinese heritage, who worked directly or peripherally with the design's development. (Note: this is a logical starting point based on the Intelligence Community's evaluation that the PRC targets and utilizes ethnic Chinese for espionage *rather* than personnel of non-Chinese origin.) [Emphasis added.]

I never saw this plan and certainly would not have approved the emphasis on "ethnic Chinese." I had never heard anyone make such a claim about PRC targeting practices and our experience indicated that such a focus would be too narrow. A later government review determined that Bruno's plan "was never implemented." There was no review that focused exclusively on Chinese-Americans.[12]

I DIRECTED THAT the Administrative Inquiry look at the records of the *entire population* of the labs, not just those of Asian-American scientists. With this direction, Dan Bruno and Special Agent "Jeff Maines" set off for New Mexico in February 1996. At Los Alamos, their first stop, they found two dozen boxes of lab travel records waiting for them. By now, the records were nearly a decade old and the Los Alamos staff, Bob Vrooman and Terry Craig, had not sorted them by country, only by year—1984 to 1988. Each trip by each scientist was catalogued in a single file, so there were hundreds of files for Bruno and "Maines" to work through in order to compile lists of lab scientists who had traveled to China and to identify Chinese visitors to Los Alamos, their lab hosts and other lab attendees. The latter task was complicated by the lab's record keeping, which was spotty at best in recording visitors from the PRC.

As they were preparing these lists, Los Alamos counterintelligence chief Bob Vrooman introduced them to a scientist named Bill Anderson, who ran the Los Alamos nuclear testing program and later worked for Vrooman in the lab counterintelligence office prior to his retirement in 1993. Anderson confirmed for Bruno and "Maines" that the W88 information of interest most likely resided at Los Alamos, Livermore, Sandia, Rocky Flats and Pantex—all the sites that Dan had identified earlier.[13] He also told Bruno that the information contained in the walk-in document had most likely come from the W88 blueprints and he didn't think that type of information was available in the mid-1980s at Sandia National Lab in Albuquerque.

At Los Alamos, W88 information was stored in the Applied Physics or X Division, where all of the lab's nuclear warhead design work was done. John Richter had been one of the stars of X Division and most of the Los Alamos members of the Kindred Spirit working group had worked in X Division at one time.

X Division facilities were scattered around the Los Alamos site, but division management and many X Division employees were housed on the second floor of TA43, the Main Administration Building. Access to X Division was strictly limited. Other than the intelligence office on the first floor, X Division was the other unit in TA43 that was locked off from the general lab population. X Division members worked behind a large, vaulted door; to gain access you had to call in for an employee or an administrative staff person to escort you to and from your destination. X Division also housed an inner documents vault, where nearly fifty thousand classified documents including warhead blueprints and other warhead design information were kept. This vault should not be confused with the "Blue Room," where Los Alamos had actual models of the nuclear warheads it had designed. That was on a lower floor in TA43, also behind a vault door.[14]

I recall Dan saying that they had to go through lab phone books from the mid-1980s to identify X Division employees from that period. Anderson helped them with this task, too; he gave them a list of all the nuclear tests performed in the development of the W88, along with names of the chief engineers, designers, radio chemists and others. Dan is a very meticulous guy who documents everything, so I was inclined to believe that he left no stone unturned.

So now Bruno and "Maines" had three lists: travelers to China, lab hosts and other lab scientists interacting with Chinese visitors to Los Alamos, and X Division scientists with W88 access—all from the years 1984 to 1988. When Los Alamos' counterintelligence chief Bob Vrooman saw these lists, he singled out an X Division nuclear code writer named Wen Ho Lee and his wife, Sylvia, also employed by the lab, for special attention. Vrooman told Bruno and "Maines" that the Lees had extensive contacts with PRC nuclear scientists, that they had traveled to China at least twice, and that their behavior upon returning from these trips was suspicious. The Lees were the only names that Vrooman recommended to Bruno and "Maines" for scrutiny. Nor did he provide any information about any other scientist on the list.[15]

When they completed their work in Los Alamos, their next stop was Sandia National Lab, despite Anderson's warning that it had nothing of interest. When they arrived, the lab counterintelligence officer, John Kirby, told Bruno and "Maines" that Sandia had not maintained travel or foreign visits records from the 1980s. They then drove over to the Albuquerque DOE field operations office, where they requested the files of about two dozen Los Alamos scientists, all of whom had met the criteria of travel or interaction with the Chinese and access to W88 information. Bruno and "Maines" uncovered numerous security anomalies and issues in these files that helped them further refine their lists. By mid-March, Bruno was back in Washington writing up the New Mexico portion of his report. Using both his and "Maines'" handwritten notes, he documented the results of their New Mexico trip and drew up lists of lab travelers to China and Chinese visitors to the lab, and a shorter list identifying Los Alamos scientists with security problems or issues. He asked the FBI to conduct background checks on the Chinese visitors to search for intelligence connections.

The records provided by Vrooman had yielded some seventy Los Alamos scientists who had visited China from 1984 to 1988; among these were the records of at least two individuals who didn't have security clearances. He had left it to Dan to do the grunt work of winnowing down this list to those with security clearances and access to W88 information. On March 14, 1996, Bruno sent his draft report to both "Greg Smith" at FBI Headquarters and Special Agent "Maines," who had returned to Tampa. Besides the New Mexico results, Dan also discussed their upcoming trip to California and plans to complete their site visits. "Maines" wrote back saying that Bruno's draft looked "great" and offered some additional comments, which Dan incorporated into his draft.[16]

"Maines" then made some additions to Dan's draft and sent the report to Bill Cleveland at Livermore on March 22, 1996. Cleveland had run an FBI squad at the San Francisco office, had managed the neutron bomb case, and was *the* expert on PRC espionage operations—especially against the weapons labs. "Maines" included the following statement in his draft: "At this early point in the inquiry, some LANL employees appear more suspect in this matter than others"; and it named "Wen Ho Lee, Sylvia Lee and [*redacted*] as suspects."[17] Bruno's draft had contained no such conclusion and, in retrospect, I think the FBI had decided that Wen Ho Lee was their man by mid-March 1996, if not earlier. It was about this time that Bruno brought Lee's name to my attention as a possible suspect. I had never heard of him before, even during the time I had spent at Los Alamos. I did check to see if he had ever held intelligence clearances; he hadn't.

The next stop for Bruno and "Maines" was supposed to have been Lawrence Livermore National Lab in Livermore, California, just outside San Francisco. I didn't learn until three years later, when all hell had broken loose, that "Maines" had been pulled off the assignment by the FBI and he didn't make the trip to California.[18] Neither Dan nor Chuck Washington, his supervisor, told me that the FBI had reneged on the deal to support us in the Administrative Inquiry. I think Dan finally made the trip sometime in late April or May. He went through the same process out there, identifying the key nuclear warhead design division, and compiling lists of Chinese visitors and lab visitors to China. The main difference from Los Alamos was that these Livermore counterintelligence guys were really professional, with lots of experience on PRC intelligence collection techniques. There was also a retired Livermore scientist helping him, Dale Neilson Sr., who had forgotten more about lab-related intelligence and counterintelligence matters than any of the rest of us will ever know.

One thing Bruno learned was that the blueprints for the W88 didn't show up at Livermore until 1990. How significant that was is hard to judge, because we couldn't say for sure that the PRC had acquired blueprints or other documents. Nor did it lead Bruno to exclude potential investigative leads from Livermore from his final list. He wrapped up this phase of the inquiry sometime around May

1, 1996, which meant that the whole Administrative Inquiry had taken about eight months, from October 1995 to May 1996.

Bruno returned to Washington after the Livermore visit and started writing up the final report. I had lots of other things on my plate then, but all the reports I was receiving from Chuck Washington, the new Counterintelligence Division director, indicated that the AI had gone well and that the FBI was satisfied with the job Bruno and "Maines" had done. In fact, they were chomping at the bit to get Dan's report.

I got my first look at it on May 16, 1996. Chuck Washington had edited Dan's draft and, according to Bruno, removed some key sections, which would later open the DOE Counterintelligence Office to much criticism from the FBI and the Justice Department.[19] As it was, the report was about an inch thick, with several attachments and different sections printed on different colors of paper, and it provided extensive detail on what Bruno and "Maines" had accomplished over the past several months. There were long lists of scientists and other personnel from both Livermore and Los Alamos in attached appendices. In a section printed on yellow paper entitled the "Internal Data Pages" (IDP) there were twelve names—the twelve investigative leads that Bruno and "Maines" had identified and thought the FBI should pursue.[20] The "leads" included scientists from both Livermore and Los Alamos, each with a narrative setting forth the information gleaned from their files that warranted their placement on this list. Dan noted that no records were available at the other facilities on his list, like Pantex, Rocky Flats and even Sandia. The report concluded by stating that DOE had finished everything it could do and now it was up to the FBI. Dan wrote:

> The writer believes that ECI [the DOE counterintelligence shop] has basically exhausted all logical "leads" regarding this inquiry which ECI is legally permitted to accomplish. Therefore, I strongly urge the FBI take the lead in this investigation.[21]

The key conclusions and list of potential "leads" of an AI were to be printed on yellow paper and these would be distributed only to the FBI. Within DOE, the yellow pages would be distributed outside the CI office only on a "by name" basis, and then only with my specific approval. Charlie Curtis and Ken Baker, my superiors, were the only people that I am sure saw the yellow pages. I didn't want the names of our twelve "investigative leads" floating around the Energy Department or the labs.

The yellow pages laid out Bruno's rationale for identifying the twelve individuals that DOE and "Maines" had concluded warranted further inquiry. All had access to W88 information, interactions with PRC nuclear scientists, and a track record of incredible travel or security problems. I recall that one was pro-Maoist, and had publicly advocated the forcible reunification of Taiwan with China.[22] Everyone who read the report, then and later, understood clearly why these twelve were recommended to the FBI for further review. Curtis and others asked me how some of these people ever got or kept their security clearances in the first place.

The lists that Bruno and "Maines" had prepared made no reference to the race or ethnicity of those named. There were scientists with English, Jewish, German and Asian surnames on the list. As I recall, about half the list had Asian-American surnames.[23]

CI division chief Washington forwarded the report to me with his own covering memorandum, noting the FBI's eagerness to get it: "I wanted to get the report to you ASAP, since the FBI said they would open [a full field investigation] after they received our report." Most of the one-page memo was about his recommendations for changes to the format of Bruno's draft report (see Appendix A). But one key paragraph stated the following:

> The report should be CLOSED, rather than PENDING, because no leads are set forth and in the IDP [internal date pages] it is stated that there is really nothing left to be done. We should consider publishing a CLOSED report and opening a Monitor Investigation to Monitor the FBI investigation, or open a Joint Investigation, based on a request for assistance from the FBI. Based on what we know now, I think we should not expend anymore OEI [Office of Energy Intelligence] on this without a tasking (verbal is ok; written is better) from the FBI, because we are mighty close to becoming involved in an espionage investigation, which we do not have the authority to do.[24]

I would later see this memo again in a place I would never have expected—it was classified, after all. I told Chuck Washington to make the changes he had recommended and then send it back to me. That completed, I signed the report out to the FBI on May 28, 1996.

At the time, a couple of things about the report did bother me a bit. First, it was poorly written and somewhat hard to follow, even though Washington claimed to have edited it. I was getting used to the fractured language used by the CI guys and the FBI, but I thought this report was difficult to read even by their lax standards. For example, there were several references in the report to the possibility that the PRC had acquired blueprints or other classified documents, but in other places it accurately restated the Kindred Spirit scientists' conclusions that W88 information had been compromised. I think the reference to blueprints was based on the information that Bill Anderson had provided Bruno and "Maines." I thought at the time this was a little strong, but Washington said that since it had come from an authoritative source interviewed during the course of the AI, the reference should remain in the report. I also believed, incorrectly as it turned out, that the FBI would follow all of these investigative leads and also investigate the DOD, the Navy and the Navy contractors. I guess we should have put that in writing, too. But Washington assured me that the FBI was interested only in the list of "names," which it wanted as soon as possible, and didn't care about the rest of the report.

The second thing that bothered me: Bruno included a section entitled something like "Investigator's Note" in which he discussed what he saw as Wen Ho Lee's opportunity, access and motivation— the Holy Trinity of espionage. Bruno didn't allege that the Lees were spies or anything like that; he was merely emphasizing that the FBI needed to take a close look at this couple, because:

> it is the opinion of the writer that Wen Ho Lee is the only individual identified during this inquiry who had opportunity, motivation, and legitimate access to both W-88 weapons systems information and the information reportedly received by the [PRC].[25]

Later, the FBI, including Director Louis Freeh, would claim that Bruno's investigative note was a "virtual indictment." That is attributing far too much weight to what Dan clearly labeled as the "opinion" of one Energy Department investigator. Freeh neglected to note that his own representative in the inquiry, Special Agent

"Maines," also believed that Lee was the most likely suspect by this time.[26] Freeh's allegations were just part of the campaign that the FBI was later to wage to cover up its own mistakes in this case. It is worth noting that Dan also wrote, "This by no means excludes any other DOE personnel as being possible suspects in this matter."[27]

Bruno sent copies of the report to Vrooman at Los Alamos and Bill Cleveland at Livermore. Vrooman would later deny reading the report, but his deputy, Terry Craig, contradicted him by recalling that they had both read and discussed it in May or June 1996.[28] Cleveland would say that he thought the report was a good, professional job.

There is one other event worthy of mention in the conduct of the Administrative Inquiry. I distinctly recall a meeting involving the FBI and our own counterintelligence people sometime near the end of the inquiry. The purpose of the meeting was for me to hear with my own ears whether the FBI or the lab CI types had any problems with the Administrative Inquiry report, methodology or approach—in short, to make sure one last time that we touched all the bases—and to find out if the Bureau or our CI experts had any reservations about the AI's findings. I recall the meeting taking place in our vault. I clearly remember Bruno, Chuck Washington, Vrooman and maybe Terry Craig from Los Alamos, and the FBI guys, Doyle, "Kerry" and "Smith," being there. I recall Dan going through the actions that he and "Maines" had accomplished over the past seven or eight months, and the FBI expressing its complete satisfaction with the outcome of the AI. Neither Washington nor Vrooman voiced any reservations or objections about the conduct of the inquiry or its findings.

After we had wrapped up our discussion, one of the FBI agents slapped the table with his hand and declared, "Wen Ho Lee is our guy and we're going to get him." Since I had barely heard of Lee at this point, I remember thinking the FBI must have a source that had independently fingered him. At this time I was unaware of the FBI's long history with Wen Ho and Sylvia Lee.[29] There was silence in the room after this comment and the meeting adjourned shortly thereafter. There was little doubt at that point that the FBI intended to prosecute Wen Ho Lee.

So that was about the extent of my role in the Administrative Inquiry, as Bruno has noted on a number of occasions. In retrospect, I relied too heavily on my "experienced" counterintelligence experts, to my eventual dismay. My mistake—if there was a mistake at all— was not in being too involved, but in not being involved enough.

AS DAN BRUNO WAS wrapping up the Kindred Spirit Administrative Inquiry, we learned that China had struck again; this time, the espionage target was technology associated with the neutron bomb.[30] Recall that the FBI believed the PRC had acquired the neutron bomb warhead design from a Livermore scientist around 1980. China successfully tested the warhead in 1988, but the report indicated that the Chinese were encountering some problems with the design and needed help.

John Richter and Carl Henry organized an "assessment" of this new information. Richter argued that if the Chinese were using the U.S. design, then they might have encountered the same performance problems that we experienced. Both Livermore and Los Alamos had come up with solutions to these problems, and Richter thought it "inconceivable" that the Chinese could have acquired this technology outside the lab complex. They wrapped up their assessment, which we promptly shared with the FBI.

But the FBI turned down our request for an investigation yet again and dumped it back in our laps. So on April 11, 1996, we opened a new Administrative Inquiry. Bruno was busy writing the Kindred Spirit report, so two other CI officers were dispatched to do the new inquiry. Steve Brown, a federal CI officer, and Bert Johnson, a contractor with long experience in counterintelligence investigations, visited Los Alamos and retraced Bruno's steps, reviewing documents and travel records. I don't recall who made site visits to Livermore and Sandia.

They learned that there had been a lab warhead designers' conference at Los Alamos in 1992, which included the presentation of a paper addressing solutions to the U.S. neutron warhead design. Richter speculated that it was this report and not a piece of hardware that the Chinese had actually acquired. The report was stored in the X Division classified documents vault, but the absence of controls on the door to the vault made it impossible to determine who had checked the report out, or when. Wen Ho Lee had attended that conference and Bruno's notes had recorded a 1992 visit to Hong Kong. Access and opportunity . . . again.

In late April, Dan sent me a memo that reported:

> Based upon the information representatives of the CI Division obtained at Los Alamos and Lawrence Livermore National Laboratories, concerning the "close hold" [redacted] information we received, I feel strongly that we should roll the info into subject Administrative Inquiry. Based upon the info we currently have, I do not believe these are separate issues perpetuated by different individuals.[31]

The "subject Administrative Inquiry" was Kindred Spirit. When we completed the AI in July, the FBI simply rolled the loss of the neutron bomb technology into their investigation of Wen Ho Lee.

WE FORMALLY HANDED over the report to FBI section chief Jerry Doyle on May 28, 1996. Unit chief "Jack Kerry" and Supervisory Special Agent "Greg Smith" read it "cover to cover."[32] No one from the FBI requested clarification, elaboration or additional information on any aspect of Dan's report. Doyle told me that the FBI would open a "full field investigation" and obtain technical surveillance of Wen Ho Lee's telephones and computers within thirty to sixty days. He promised us an aggressive, all-out investigation. It was obvious that they were focused exclusively on Lee. I reminded Doyle that there were other names on the list. He responded, "Yeah, we'll take a look at them too."

As part of their "full field investigation" they asked the Energy Department to take no actions that could alert Wen Ho Lee that the FBI was looking at him. "Non-alert status," the FBI later called this, although I never heard them use this term at the time. I wrote a "Next Steps Action" plan for my supervisor, Joan Rohfling, about the FBI request that we take no security measures or other actions that could alert the suspect without first obtaining FBI concurrence. The FBI's "investigative interests" took precedence over any concerns we had about protecting nuclear weapons secrets. I know it sounds odd, but that's the way the FBI wanted to play it; and with the approval of DOE senior management, including Curtis and Rohfling, that's how it went.

The FBI made the same request to Los Alamos director Sig Hecker in early July 1996. FBI section chief Doyle, accompanied by "Greg Smith" and FBI Albuquerque field office Special Agent in Charge (SAC) Tom Kneir and Assistant Special Agent in Charge Ronald Dick, met with Hecker, Terry Hawkins of Los Alamos' intelligence division, and Bob Vrooman and Terry Craig, the two lab counterintelligence officers. Doyle asked Hecker to leave Lee in place "for one year" and not to change his assignment for fear of tipping him off.[33] When Hecker asked how he could justify this, Doyle replied, "Lee has had access for ten years, so firing him would not do much now; and, if the lab did fire him it would have no legal justification to support this action."[34] I was aware of this meeting, but I didn't learn until 2001 that the FBI had asked Hecker to leave Lee in place for a year.

This was a fateful decision. Sometime during the Administrative Inquiry team's visit to Los Alamos in February, Bruno and "Maines" learned that X Division had no way to monitor access to its inner vault where blueprints and thousands of other classified documents on nuclear warheads were stored. They had wanted to examine the reports that X Division employees had looked at—various warhead blueprints and other W88 documents—but were told that in the early 1980s, X Division had stopped keeping track of which employees entered the vault or which documents they obtained. All access control devices on this vault had been removed, so the lab had no way of knowing whether employees were copying documents, taking them home, or what. (Faced with the same choice, Livermore opted to retain technical means to monitor such access.) All involved, including Los Alamos director Sig Hecker, decided what should have been obvious: X Division would immediately reinstall access control devices on this inner vault so there would be some record of who was going in and out. The FBI would then have means to monitor Wen Ho Lee's access to documents in this vault.

Los Alamos proposed to install a palm reader on the door. But before this could be done, we had to discuss it with the FBI. Jerry Doyle mulled it over and decided that Lee would have no reason to think that the device was aimed at him, since all X Division employees would have to register in order to get into the inner vault. They approved the installation and we assumed Los Alamos had fixed that problem. Four years later, we learned that Los Alamos never got around to actually installing the device on this door and had spent the money on something else, but left the lab director and us with the impression that the palm reader was in place.[35] So for another three years, Wen Ho Lee and everyone else enjoyed unfettered access to the nuclear secrets in the X Division vault.

But the FBI's request to maintain Wen Ho Lee in a non-alert status had a much worse consequence. In 1997, Lee downloaded classified W88 information onto a computer tape and then removed the tape from his X Division office.[36] The FBI didn't take any special measures to establish surveillance on Lee, and made a half-hearted effort to monitor his computer, but was rebuffed by Terry Craig, one of the lab CI officers. The computer tape containing all these W88 secrets has never been recovered.

LATER ON, THERE would be a lot of finger pointing about the consequences of "singling out" Wen Ho Lee. First, let's set the record straight: Lee was not singled out *to the exclusion* of other suspects. We sent a list of twelve "potential investigative leads" to the FBI and fully expected the Bureau to pursue each one.[37] For its own reasons, the bureau ignored ten of those leads. In fact, the FBI Albuquerque office would not open an investigation on these other leads until March 12, 1999, and then only at the insistence of FBI officials in Washington who ordered that the investigation be opened by the end of *that* business day.[38]

Given all that we know now, it would have been criminally negligent to exclude Wen Ho Lee from the list. Few dispute that. As a retired CIA counterintelligence expert put the matter in an e-mail in 1999:

> If WHL had been an Irishman he would have been a prima facie espionage suspect, given the circumstantial evidence surrounding him. Motive, opportunity, access—all were there. Pursuant [*sic*] to our treaty with the Bureau we were required to pass it on to them.[39]

Second, much has been made about Lee being "the" or "a" prime suspect. Based on what we knew about Lee at the time, why wouldn't this have been the case? After the FBI finally got serious about Kindred Spirit in 1998 and interviewed Lee, there was little room for doubt that he should have been "the" prime suspect. But in 1996 there was already quite enough to qualify him for this status.

Here is what Bruno and "Maines" turned up about Wen Ho Lee and Sylvia Lee in 1996: Born in Taiwan, Wen Ho Lee came to the United States and obtained a doctorate in mechanical engineering from Texas A&M University in 1969. He became a U.S. citizen in 1974 and joined Los Alamos in 1978. He had previously worked at Argonne National Lab facilities in Idaho and in Chicago. By 1982, Lee was a member of the Hydrodynamics Methods Group in Los Alamos' X Division. He developed computer codes and software used in the design of nuclear warheads. He was part of a team working on Langrangian mathematical codes used to develop the source codes employed in warhead development. (Source codes model and simulate every aspect of the complex physics process involved in creating a thermonuclear explosion. The source codes are written to design specific portions of a nuclear weapon—either the primary or the secondary components of a modern thermonuclear warhead.) Among the projects that Lee worked on in the early 1980s at Los Alamos was the W88 nuclear warhead.

Dan learned that Wen Ho Lee had already had two brushes with the FBI by 1996. There was a note in Lee's security file that the FBI had polygraphed him in the early 1980s after he had contacted an FBI espionage suspect in the Livermore investigation. The information in Lee's Energy Department file on this investigation was sparse, but Special Agent "Maines" knew all about it and urged Dan to include it in his write-up.

Lee had made two trips to China in the 1980s and had a history of extensive personal contacts with PRC nuclear scientists visiting Los Alamos during this period. Partially on the basis of this, Bob Vrooman had urged Bruno and "Maines" to take a closer look at both Wen Ho and Sylvia Lee. He told Dan that he considered both Lees' contacts with the Chinese to be "suspicious," but I don't know if he elaborated on those suspicions to Dan. Sylvia Lee had appointed herself unofficial hostess for Los Alamos interactions with the PRC during this period and had more extensive contacts with PRC nuclear scientists than anyone else at Los Alamos. Dan found indications of both personnel problems and security violations in her file. With regard to Wen Ho Lee's second brush with the FBI, we had some limited knowledge about an encounter between Lee and a high-ranking nuclear scientist during a visit by a PRC delegation to Los Alamos in 1994.[40] Lee had failed to include this official in the list of Chinese scientists he had met on his previous trips. The personal nature of his encounter with the official led the FBI to conclude that he had intentionally concealed his relationship with this individual.[41]

So Lee had suspicious contacts with PRC scientists; had failed to report at least one significant contact; had been the subject of FBI investigative interest at least twice; had been polygraphed by the FBI; and had access to the W88 information. No one else that Bruno or "Maines" ran across in their review came even close to that record. But there was more—much more—that the FBI and even our own lab CI officers, like Vrooman, knew about Wen Ho Lee but refused to share with us in 1996.

IT TURNED OUT that the 1982 brush with the FBI was much more involved than we were led to believe. We didn't know that the FBI had already run one full field counterintelligence investigation of Lee in December 1982, after he had been picked up in court-ordered electronic surveillance of a former Livermore scientist who was suspected of passing classified information to Beijing.[42] Lee told the Livermore scientist that he thought he could find out "who had squealed" on the scientist.[43] Another year passed before the FBI got around to interviewing Lee, who promptly denied attempting to contact the Livermore scientist. He told the Bureau that he didn't know the scientist in question and had never attempted to contact him. How could he, since the scientist had left Livermore Lab and Lee didn't know where he lived? The FBI suspected that Lee knew about the Livermore scientist through a mutual friend, possibly another scientist named Peter Lee, who was yet another PRC espionage suspect at that time out at Livermore. About a month later, the Bureau confronted Wen Ho Lee with evidence of his call to Livermore. Lee was forced to admit making the call, and claimed that he thought the

Livermore scientist was in trouble because of his dealings with Taiwan. Lee would later claim that he then offered to help the FBI with its investigation of the Livermore espionage suspect.

With the FBI listening, Lee placed three more phone calls to the Livermore suspect and then the FBI flew him out to California to meet the suspect. Lee said that the FBI gave him instructions before the meeting and then debriefed him afterward. The FBI's enlistment of Lee seems strange since the Livermore scientist was suspected of spying for the PRC, while Lee was claiming that his dealings were with Taiwan. Apparently there were concerns at the Bureau about exposing Lee to "very sensitive operational techniques," but the FBI used Lee against the scientist anyway.

The FBI has shrouded the outcome of this in secrecy, but they didn't get around to questioning Wen Ho Lee further about why he was contacting an espionage suspect until after his California meeting with the Livermore suspect. When the FBI finally polygraphed him, it became clear why Lee was anxious about Taiwan. He had been passing documents to the Taiwanese since the late 1970s and doing consulting work for them as well.[44] On several occasions, he had been in contact with a known intelligence officer at Taiwan's Coordination Council of North America, in Washington, D.C.[45] He fielded requests for specific documents and then mailed copies to the council's offices in Washington, D.C. A telephone records check turned up several calls to the council from his office in X Division; he initially denied making the calls, but recanted when confronted with these records. His supporters would later claim that these were harmless documents concerned primarily with reactor safety, and Lee himself would say that he only did it once.[46] But in 1983 the FBI determined that Lee had been providing documents to Taiwan since about 1978 and that although the documents were unclassified, they were also marked "sensitive" and carried NOFORN markings, that is, "Not for Foreign Dissemination." Moreover, Taiwan was on the DOE Sensitive Country List, as it was known to have an active nuclear weapons program. Lee had violated lab and Energy Department security regulations both by his contacts with the Coordination Council of North America and by the passing of the documents. Both acts were unauthorized and unreported—at least until the FBI caught him contacting the Livermore espionage suspect.

The FBI suspected that Lee was acting on behalf of Taiwan's intelligence service. Its full field investigation was sweeping: mail covers, surveillance and even a psychological profile that the FBI Behavior Science Unit at Quantico worked up on Lee.[47] Despite all this, the FBI claimed it couldn't make an espionage case and closed down its investigation in March 1984. The Bureau walked away from this episode with one crucial lesson learned, however: that Wen Ho Lee would "provide truthful answers only when confronted with irrefutable evidence (i.e., the FBI's awareness of his phone calls [to the Livermore espionage suspect and the Coordination Council]) or when faced with a polygraph."[48] Further, the FBI believed that Lee took satisfaction from sharing the results of his work with other scientists—regardless of their nationality. This conclusion should have alerted Los Alamos and the Energy Department to potential future problems with this employee, but it appears that the FBI never shared it with Energy.

When Los Alamos security officials learned of Wen Ho Lee's unauthorized contacts with the Taiwanese, however, they strongly recommended that Lee be removed from access to X Division's secrets. The director of Los Alamos' Safeguards and Security Division did a "threat assessment" that carried this conclusion:

> [Lee] works with the [two named] weapons design codes. These are both two dimensional hydrodynamics codes. Working on these codes allows him access to the input to any problem being run with these or similar codes.
>
> SUMMARY: The subjects [*sic*] current position allows him access to practically all current [nuclear warhead] design studies. I have worked in such a position for many years. The code developers have access to the designers, the input to the codes, and to classified documents related to the physics of the design. In particular, the code developers are especially interested in determining how well their codes will handle new design features.
>
> RECOMMENDATION: From OS [Office of Security] Division's standpoint, we should get him out of there.[49]

The hot "design" at Los Alamos in the early 1980s just happened to be the W88 warhead. This assessment should have been enough to change the history of this case.

For reasons never revealed, however, Los Alamos director Don Kerr rejected his security director's recommendation and allowed Lee to stay in X Division working on the W88 project. Why? One reason may be that Wen Ho Lee and his wife offered to assist the FBI the way he had helped them with the Livermore espionage suspect.[50] The Lees would later claim that the Bureau asked them to assist as "volunteer[s] without pay in the FBI's efforts to monitor Chinese scientists." They said that they served as "FBI Information Assets" from 1985 until 1991. Their main FBI contact was Special Agent "Dick Berk," to whom Sylvia provided background information on Chinese scientists they would meet at Los Alamos. Such information could tip off the Bureau to lab security breaches.

Instead of losing his clearances and then his job, Wen Ho Lee likely cut a deal with the FBI. In return for keeping his job at Los Alamos, he and his wife would pass the Bureau information they gathered on Chinese scientists. This deal had the approval of Director Don Kerr, who nonetheless demanded that information about the Lees' activities be kept strictly under wraps. In 1995–1996, during the Administrative Inquiry, we knew nothing about the Lees' relationship with the Bureau back in the 1980s.

Now Wen Ho and Sylvia Lee had the blessing of both the FBI and Los Alamos for travel, one of their favorite hobbies, and for developing scientific contacts with PRC nuclear experts. Wen Ho Lee met a number of Chinese nuclear scientists at a conference held at Hilton Head, South Carolina, in 1985, and he struck up a relationship with Li De Yuan, who had a background similar to Lee's and worked at the Institute of Applied Physics and Computational Mathematics in Beijing. Li was instrumental in Wen Ho Lee's future trips to Beijing, leading some to believe that Li had "recruited" Lee and may have been his case officer.[51] At any rate, the Lees were on their way to the PRC.

Wen Ho Lee was first invited there in 1986 to make a presentation at the Tenth International Conference on Fluid Dynamics in Beijing. After this, he was asked to give a seminar at Li's institute along with another Los Alamos scientist named Bob Clark. The FBI had met with the Lees beforehand to discuss their upcoming trip.

In 1988, Li De Yuan again invited Wen Ho Lee to Beijing, to give a paper at another conference. By now, Los Alamos had a formal counterintelligence program and had installed Bob Vrooman as its head. Vrooman approved Lee's trip, but was curious about the paper he would present. Wen Ho Lee told him that he had "borrowed" a colleague's unclassified paper, an answer that satisfied Vrooman. Vrooman did give him a defensive counterintelligence briefing, which included a reference to "some of the problems we have had with Chinese probing for help on nuclear weapons related issues."[52] Lee told Vrooman that the Chinese hadn't asked him anything on the 1986 trip and that he intended to take a ten-day vacation traveling in China after the conference, just as he had in 1986. As with the 1986 trip, the FBI paid Mrs. Lee's travel expenses and met with the Lees before they left. When they returned, the Bureau met with them again, and this time Mrs. Lee gave them a written report.[53]

When Wen Ho Lee returned from the 1988 trip to China, he told Vrooman that no one had asked him for classified information during this trip. He listed a number of PRC nuclear scientists, about fourteen in all, whom he had met, but Vrooman realized that Wen Ho Lee was now the only Los Alamos scientist who had traveled to China *twice* and then *not* reported back efforts to elicit classified information. On the 1986 trip, his friend Bob Clark had noted that Lee was busy making friends with Chinese scientists—"You might say he was friendlier than he should have been with these guys."[54] But Clark didn't report this to lab security or counterintelligence, which should have been very interested in Clark's observations.

Once again, Wen Ho Lee was being less than candid about his interactions with foreign nuclear scientists. On both the 1986 and the 1988 trip, Lee had indeed been asked by Chinese scientists for classified information about U.S. nuclear warhead designs. He would later claim that he refused to discuss classified information, but he admitted helping the PRC with some problems in computer coding. Both times, he had helped the Chinese fix problems with their hydrodynamic codes using information from the classified nuclear weapons codes he was working on at Los Alamos. Both times, he knew that the Chinese scientists asking for assistance on computer codes worked in the nuclear weapons program. Both times, Lee knew that the assistance he was providing would be useful to the PRC's nuclear weapons program.[55] Although he would proclaim that his assistance with these codes was harmless, he would later state that the hydrodynamic codes that he worked on helped to solve the most important problem in the U.S. nuclear warhead development program.[56]

In 1988, Hu Side, a rising PRC nuclear scientist, visited Lee in his Beijing hotel room. At that time, Hu was an explosives expert, but others would claim that he ran China's effort to miniaturize its nuclear warheads.[57] Hu asked Lee questions about nuclear warhead design concepts related to the W88 and other warheads in the U.S. arsenal. The questions themselves were significant and exactly the type of information the FBI was hoping Lee would pick up on his trips. But when he got home, he omitted Hu from his trip reports and debriefings and he denied that the Chinese had asked him for any classified information. Why? He would later claim that he was afraid he would "get into trouble," but of course the FBI had saved his Los Alamos job and sponsored his trip precisely for the purpose of collecting such information.

There was one other thing that Wen Ho Lee didn't bother to mention in his meetings with Vrooman or the FBI. In April 1988, he started moving files containing large amounts of classified nuclear weapons computer codes across a partition in the Los Alamos computer network onto the unclassified network. He would remove classification markings on the data and then simply transfer it out onto the unclassified computer network. Beginning in 1988, he moved nuclear weapons codes used to simulate the behavior of both primary and secondary devices over to the unclassified system, along with input files containing warhead dimensions and geometries, and utilities.[58] Was this illegal computer activity connected with his trips to China in 1986 and the impending 1988 visit? Wen Ho Lee said it was merely a coincidence.

Meanwhile, Bob Vrooman was also hearing complaints about Sylvia Lee's work performance. She was a data entry clerk working on an armor/anti-armor computer coding project, but she was behind on her part of the project. When her supervisor tried to speed her up, she told him she was too busy working for the FBI and the Los Alamos director on PRC lab-to-lab interactions. She was fielding correspondence from Chinese scientists seeking documents from Los Alamos and helping Los Alamos scientists with their own correspondence with their PRC counterparts. Her supervisor went to Vrooman to check this story out. Sure enough, Vrooman knew she was working for the FBI, although he has never admitted this.

But now Vrooman had a potential disaster on his hands. A Los Alamos scientist was traveling to the PRC and, upon returning, was claiming that the Chinese weren't asking for help. His wife was consumed with her "duties" with PRC nuclear scientists on behalf of the FBI, and her lab supervisors, who were paying her salary, were beginning to complain about this use of her time. So he flew back to Washington to share his concerns with the China specialists at FBI Headquarters. There he met with the FBI's top China experts, including Ray Wickman, "F. Jeff Maines" and "Greg "Smith." He also met with another FBI agent named "Jay Steele," who would later become the supervisory special agent in charge of the Kindred Spirit investigation. All of them knew about Wen Ho Lee and his track record. "Maines" and the rest advised him to deny any further travel requests from the Lees, but that seems to have been the extent of the FBI's advice. Despite Vrooman's suspicions, there is no record that the FBI took any further action at this time to look again at Wen Ho Lee and his behavior. Apparently none of the agents bothered to check the FBI's files on Lee or recalled the bottom line of the 1984 investigation: that Lee had been less than candid about these sorts of interactions in the past. In what was a foreshadowing of things to come, FBI Headquarters' instructions never made it out to Albuquerque, where local agents continued to employ the Lees until 1991, according to the press release issued by Lee's defense team in 2000.

When Vrooman returned to Los Alamos, he went to the director's office to check this part of Sylvia's story. The new director, Sig Hecker, "disowned" Sylvia and told Vrooman to get her out of the lab-to-lab interactions. But Sylvia ignored Vrooman's requests and continued to spend her time helping the PRC scientists in their dealings with Los Alamos. Vrooman learned that Wen Ho and Sylvia were hosting Chinese nuclear scientists at dinners in their home in White Rock during visits by PRC delegations to Los Alamos. The FBI had offered to pick up the tab for the hospitality that the Lees extended to their visitors.[59] Later, the FBI learned that Lee had discussed his work on hydrodynamic codes with a PRC scientist at one of these dinners.[60] Vrooman heard from other lab employees that the son of the director of the PRC's Institute of Applied Physics and Computational Mathematics was staying with the Lees during his visit to the United States, and another lab employee told him about a conversation she had overheard between Sylvia and the PRC Institute director. The Chinese dignitary was telling Sylvia what a good time they had had when they last met in Beijing. Had Wen Ho or Sylvia reported this contact when they returned?

In early 1989, Mrs. Lee received an invitation to speak at the International Conference on Experimental Fluid Mechanics in Chengdu, China. A strange invitation for a data entry clerk, but her husband was also invited to attend, again by Li De Yuan. Vrooman had seen enough and turned down the Lees' trip. But he had no luck stopping Sylvia's interactions with the PRC. She continued to translate letters for Los Alamos scientists and would show up unannounced during visits by PRC scientists to Los Alamos. She arranged for three prominent PRC nuclear scientists, including Hu Side, to receive a copy of an unclassified computer code written by another Los Alamos scientist. The Chinese wanted the code delivered to them while they were in San Diego and gave her instructions on which Los Alamos scientist was to bring it to them.

In late 1989, Vrooman tried once again to carry out the lab director's instructions. He met with Sylvia, her supervisor, and FBI agent "Dick Berk," and told her to cease all contacts with the PRC on behalf of Los Alamos. Vrooman wrote a memo dated December 13, 1989, in which he declared that another lab scientist would replace Mrs. Lee as the main point of contact with the PRC (see Appendix B). In the memo, he noted that he "was also concerned about the motives of the PRC in cultivating her as their point of contact." But then Vrooman agreed to allow her to continue dealing with the PRC: "Her personal relationship and correspondence with the PRC are her own business. By her own choice, she will keep ['Dick Berk'], FBI, apprised of these."[61]

Mrs. Lee was an employee of LANL at that time and had a Top Secret/RD security clearance. Any such contact with the PRC would hardly be "her own business" but very much the business of DOE, the lab and Vrooman. Yet Vrooman gave her the lab's blessing for continued interactions with PRC nuclear scientists. Once again, the FBI had intervened to save a Lee's job—this time Sylvia's.

Vrooman vowed to disapprove any future requests by the Lees for travel to China, and he got the associate director for nuclear weapons, Wen Ho Lee's ultimate supervisor, to do the same. But the travel restriction didn't apply to Hong Kong or Taiwan, and the Lees traveled to both in 1992. There is no record of Vrooman approving this trip; he may not even have been aware of it.

In February 1994, Hu Side, by now the chief of the PRC's nuclear program, led a delegation of Chinese nuclear scientists to Los Alamos as part of the renewed interactions between the labs and the PRC nuclear complex. One meeting was held in the Director's Conference Room on the fourth floor of the Main Administration Building. Participation was by invitation only, and Danny Stillman, one of Los Alamos' key scientists in the PRC–Los Alamos interactions, was taking attendance at the door. Wen Ho Lee showed up in coat and tie, uninvited, and managed to get past Stillman. By all accounts, Hu Side greeted him warmly, and their interaction led those lab scientists who were present to conclude that Lee was "well acquainted" with Hu. A quick check of Lee's trip reports showed that he had never reported meeting Hu on his trips to China, so Stillman referred the incident to the FBI. According to FBI records, Hu Side reportedly said of Lee, "We know him very well. He came to Beijing and helped us a lot . . . with various computational codes used in fluid dynamics which is a very important aspect of thermal nuclear [sic] weapons work."[62] In April 1994, the FBI opened another preliminary investigation on Wen Ho Lee.

Unreported contacts, denial that the Chinese had tried to elicit information from him, two FBI counterintelligence investigations in the space of about a decade, a history of unauthorized passage of sensitive documents to foreign scientists from sensitive countries, and statements made by the head of China's nuclear weapons program about the value of Lee's contributions to the Chinese program—no one else on the Administrative Inquiry list of potential investigative leads had such a track record. As Paul Moore, a former FBI counterintelligence expert, has said, "He [Lee] was doing things that were suspicious and lying while doing them. Either you become more suspicious when you encounter that, or you get out of the [counterintelligence] business."[63]

There was also a lot of controversy about Dan Bruno's investigative note in the Administrative Inquiry, which attributed access, opportunity and motive to Wen Ho Lee. Much of this focused on Lee's "motivation" to provide classified information and assistance to the Chinese nuclear weapons program. There were a number of hints that the FBI had first picked up in their early 1980s investigation and then expanded on in Kindred Spirit. There is reason to believe, for instance, that Lee was unhappy about his situation at Los Alamos. He thought his pay was low in comparison with Los Alamos scientists who had similar educational backgrounds and years of experience.[64] He was not considered a "high flyer" by his colleagues in X Division, but something of a plodder and "not the most brilliant scientist."[65] One senior Los Alamos nuclear weapons manager said he had never heard of Wen Ho Lee until the scandal broke in 1999 and had to go check the weapons program records to find out where he worked, even though Lee worked for the manager.

But his reception by the PRC scientists and by the Taiwanese before them was different. His explanation for providing sensitive documents to the Taiwanese was that he liked to participate in exchanges and dialogues with other scientists and that he routinely helped them.[66] During his first trip to Beijing in 1986, he "was excited and treated very well by his PRC counterparts."[67] He talked science with the cream of Beijing's nuclear weapons program. He entertained senior PRC nuclear dignitaries in his home, an honor not extended to him by their Los Alamos counterparts. Sylvia Lee clearly preferred dealing with PRC nuclear scientists to working on the mundane projects that paid her salary at Los Alamos. Dan Bruno thought that the assistance of both Lees to the PRC nuclear program was intended to "enhance [their] stature in the eyes of high-ranking PRC personnel."[68] In short, Wen Ho Lee's contributions to the Chinese nuclear program gained him recognition and status that he was unable to attain at Los Alamos.

The FBI agreed. Later the Albuquerque field office would point to Lee's provision of documents to the Taiwanese and his assistance to the PRC with computer codes, concluding that these acts showed "Wen Ho Lee's propensity to associate with foreign governments and provide information to foreign governments and therefore the propensity to aid in and commit acts of espionage."[69] If information is provided to a foreign country that could injure the United States or assist the other country, then espionage has been committed, regardless of whether the information was provided in the interest of "scientific exchanges" or for money, in the words of a later congressional report.

Obviously, none of this may have been sufficient to obtain an indictment, but that was never the purpose of the Administrative Inquiry. We expected it would be a point of departure for the FBI— but we were wrong.

AFTER MAY 1996, the Energy Department's inquiry was over and the espionage investigation was now in FBI hands. The FBI had retained the code name Kindred Spirit for its pursuit of the source of the W88 espionage. Given FBI section chief Doyle's eagerness to move out on the FBI's investigation, we sat back and waited to see what the FBI came up with. The case was assigned to the FBI's Albuquerque field office and was run out of the Santa Fe resident agency, down the hill from Los Alamos. This field office had some problems running counterintelligence operations in the past; most notably, it had allowed a former CIA officer suspected of spying for the Soviet Union to slip through its surveillance in 1985. He later turned up in Moscow and had compromised several U.S. intelligence operations against the Russians.[70] (John Lewis was still pained by any mention of this case when I met him a decade later.) Despite this embarrassment, Albuquerque's SAC, Tom Kneir, had vigorously implemented Louis Freeh's emphasis on crime busting at the expense of counterespionage. Gang activity, drug busting, Indian reservation and white collar crime all took precedence over counterespionage investigations, and the field office's counterintelligence agents were regularly assigned to work bank robberies and other crimes in addition to their CI duties. Given all the potential espionage targets in New Mexico—two national nuclear labs, U.S. Air Force bases and facilities, testing ranges, and the numerous defense contractors doing business with these facilities—downgrading the office's counterespionage squad seemed a poor management decision.

Albuquerque's handling of the Kindred Spirit case, potentially "one of the most serious breaches in national security in modern U.S. history," illustrated the risks of the FBI's new priorities.[71] Despite its gravity and FBI Headquarters' obvious desire to move aggressively, the Albuquerque SAC and "Jay Steele," the supervisory special agent in charge of the foreign counterintelligence squad, promptly put Kindred Spirit dead last on their list of Albuquerque's overall priorities. I met "Steele" during one of my trips to New Mexico. He looked as though he had stepped right out of a Western— tall and thin, with a thick mustache, just like a cowboy. He spent most of our meeting complaining about having to drive to southern New Mexico all the time to work on drug operations and gang activity. Counterintelligence didn't seem to be much of a priority for him. "Steele" considered the special agent assigned to the case, "Dick Lowenthal," a marginal performer, and neither "Lowenthal" nor his replacement ever worked the case on a full-time basis.[72] For nearly three years, the Albuquerque FBI field office would treat the Kindred Spirit investigation as a part-time duty.

Weeks turned into months, and by November 1996 we were getting word that nothing was happening on the case. "Dick Lowenthal" had yet to do anything, according to the information we were getting; we were told that he was experiencing personal difficulties, but I wondered why the FBI didn't just assign another agent. In truth, his managers piled other responsibilities on him that had nothing to do with counterespionage, so he never worked the case full-time. Meanwhile, the FBI's prime suspect was sitting down in Los Alamos' X Division untouched. My thinking about the FBI at the time was pretty much the following: "If you think it's Wen Ho Lee as you say, then go after him aggressively so that we can protect our nuclear secrets. Or clear him and start looking at some of the other leads we gave you." We also believed that the FBI was looking at the Defense Department, the Navy and the contractors. But the Bureau was just sitting on its hands. I couldn't understand the inaction.

It was also clear that the FBI discarded the other ten names on the list we sent in May 1996 and focused solely on Wen Ho and Sylvia Lee. "Greg Smith" later told me that when he started pulling together the FBI's records on Wen Ho Lee, he was surprised at how much the Bureau already knew about him and his activities. The FBI obviously knew a lot more about both Lees than we did, so maybe their decision was justified.[73] But how then to account for Albuquerque's treatment of the case? In her later criticism of the FBI's handling of this case, Attorney General Janet Reno stated that the FBI had "focused on 2, not the other [*number redacted*]. And they did not make any investigation with respect to the other [*number redacted*]." (The number was ten, as other sources indicated.) She thought the FBI had "perhaps other leads that could have been followed. There were other people that have a motivation, perhaps a greater motivation than Wen Ho Lee."[74] The FBI had decided that Wen Ho Lee was their man and focused what little investigative work it actually did on him.

Because 1996 was an election year, I suspected that the FBI was afraid of turning up anything that would embarrass an administration that had put so much stock in its "strategic partnership" with China. The Chinese campaign finance scandal had broken out that summer and the administration was under the gun for these revelations. I voiced these concerns only to my immediate staff, and they hooted me out of the room. "The FBI would never do anything like that," they said.

But by November 1996, Dan Bruno was telling me that the FBI Albuquerque office and the local agent, "Dick Lowenthal," still hadn't done anything on the case. The FBI wasn't just "dragging its feet"; its feet were encased in concrete. I told Bruno that he should communicate our "concerns" to "Greg Smith" over at FBI Headquarters. I would be willing to call Associate Director John Lewis, or better yet I could get Charlie Curtis, by then the deputy secretary at Energy, or even Secretary O'Leary to call Director Freeh. Naturally, that got FBI Headquarters stirred up and word came back that they got the message. Bruno relayed the following e-mail to me on November 21, 1966:

> I contacted ["Greg Smith"] and informed him of Notra's concerns and desire for a more aggressive approach on the case by Albuquerque. I also told him that Notra offered that if he (["Smith"]) believes it necessary, he would call John Lewis, etc. "Smith" told

me that he briefed his boss, "Jack Kerry," on the lack of action on this matter by [the local FBI agent, "Lowenthal"], the FBI FCI [foreign counterintelligence] agent that handles LANL. "Kerry" is reviewing the Kindred Spirit file and intended to take action to get this going again. After my call, "Smith" said he would pass on to "Kerry" Notra's concerns and would let me know what action FBI HQ is going to take to push Albuquerque field office on this case. He said that knowing Notra would, if asked, call Lewis, etc., was good to know and that he will keep that in his back pocket in case such a call is needed.

The FBI office in Albuquerque was not happy with our intervention, but we finally got some action—or so we thought.

We didn't know at the time that FBI Headquarters had suspended its Kindred Spirit investigation on July 31, 1996, just over two months after it had begun.[75] The suspension resulted from CIA's warning that the source of the "walk-in" document was "under control of the PRC intelligence services." The CIA had finally issued the document as an intelligence report in December 1995, after months of prodding and personal calls by Curtis to DCI Deutch. But in January, the CIA had put out its warning and pulled back all copies of the walk-in document, although there was some wording to the effect that DOE and the FBI could still use the information contained in the report. This basically came out of nowhere and to this day remains suspicious. Recall that Deutch didn't want this report to get into the hands of the Intelligence Community in the first place. Later, FBI agents said they didn't agree with the CIA's conclusion about the "source" being under control.

There was a lot of wild speculation about Chinese motivations for providing these documents to us. The PRC wanted to deter us; they wanted to mislead us and protect another, more important spy; and so on. Terry Hawkins, Los Alamos' China expert, argued that the Chinese were trying to harm the Energy Department nuclear labs by sowing suspicion and distrust. And on and on.

The only inkling we had of any of this was a request from the FBI for our assessment of the validity of the information contained in the document. Carl Henry, John Richter and some of our other lab detailees in Washington went back and once again checked all the data provided, both on Chinese systems and on U.S. systems, and came back reporting that it was all accurate. Once again, Alan Riley at Los Alamos verified the data through reference to blueprints, or so he told Henry. They drafted a letter for my signature to the FBI confirming our assessment that the information provided in the document was valid. Our letter went on to say that judgments about the credibility of the source of the document were not ours to make, but as for the nuclear weapons information, that was accurate to the best of our ability to determine. The FBI reopened their full field investigation on August 20, but "Even when it was restarted, it was not pursued with particular vigor in the latter part of 1996."[76] A Justice Department assessment of the FBI Albuquerque field office's performance on Kindred Spirit concluded that there was "a consistent failure to recognize or appreciate the gravity of the case."[77] But now a pattern had been established: months would go by with little or no action; we would complain and there would be a flurry of activity in Albuquerque or at FBI Headquarters; then silence again. This pattern would be consistent over the next three years of the case.[78]

But imagine my surprise at being totally out of the loop on all of this, despite being the Department of Energy's senior intelligence officer. This means that no one at DOE, including Secretary O'Leary and Charlie Curtis, knew that the FBI had stopped its investigation into the compromise of nuclear weapons secrets. Moreover, the FBI let Secretary O'Leary believe that it was acting vigorously in trying to resolve this case involving a lab and a lab scientist that was part of her cabinet responsibilities.

THE FBI DID MAKE one feeble attempt to gain access to Wen Ho Lee's computer in his office in X Division. As with so much else in this case, there is much confusion about this episode, mostly due to the very poor "memories" of the participants. But it is evident that "Dick Lowenthal," the local FBI agent running the case, wanted to take a look at Lee's computer—probably to examine Lee's e-mail history. "Lowenthal" could also have been looking for indications that Wen Ho Lee was downloading classified materials onto unclassified systems. (The information in the FBI's files from 1994 about Lee's assistance to the PRC with computer codes and software should have been sufficient justification for a search.) Whatever the case, "Lowenthal" was blocked from examining Lee's computer by Terry Craig, Bob Vrooman's deputy in the Los Alamos counterintelligence office. Craig believed that Lee had a "reasonable assumption" of privacy on his lab computer and that the FBI's access might violate Lee's Fourth Amendment rights. Craig promised to check whether Lee had signed a waiver or any other release form acknowledging the lab's or the government's authority to monitor his computer use. "Lowenthal" would consult FBI Headquarters about the legality of searching Lee's computer. Both promised to "get back" to each other, but they never did. The whole matter was forgotten—until three years later.[79]

This was a dreadful mistake, illustrative of how the FBI handled this espionage investigation from the beginning. This ranks as one of the most significant "missed opportunities" of the entire case. As noted earlier, Lee had already been transferring classified nuclear weapons design information to an unclassified Los Alamos network for nearly a decade at the time that "Lowenthal" tried to check his computer. And he would make yet another tape after this, in 1997. The bottom line: while Los Alamos and the FBI were screwing around trying to figure out whether Lee had signed some kind of waiver that would allow them to act, he was downloading onto an unclassified computer network and then onto computer tapes some of our most precious nuclear secrets. I suspect Craig was too intimidated by the X Division physicists to inquire as to whether Lee's computer was fair game for an FBI search. It was. Had he asked, X Division computer security officials could have shown him a waiver acknowledging that Lee knew his computer would be monitored, signed in 1995—more than a year before the Keystone Cops routine at the lab. There was nothing to stop the FBI from examining his computer activity, except incompetence and indolence.

Neither Craig nor the FBI breathed a word of this FBI request to us at DOE Headquarters. Nobody expects the FBI to share such information, but after all, Craig, Vrooman and the rest of the Los Alamos CI types were supposed to be working for us. We were paying their salaries, but apparently they didn't think they had any particular responsibility to report such interactions to us. Terry Craig would claim that the executive order that governs U.S. intelligence activities, EO 12333, prohibited him from looking at Wen

Ho Lee's computers once the FBI had opened an espionage investigation. That was ridiculous, however, since the order specifically required us to render any assistance requested by the FBI. But the Albuquerque FBI SAC, Special Supervisory Agent "Jay Steele," and Special Agent "Lowenthal" were happy to take no for an answer.

By April 1997, all of us at DOE Headquarters were more and more puzzled by just what was going on at Los Alamos. Two years had passed since Booth and Henson had raised the initial warnings, and nearly a year had gone by since we handed over the results of our Administrative Inquiry to the FBI and the Bureau opened its full investigation. But the Energy Department seemed to be the only party still concerned about Lee's continued access to nuclear secrets. Over at FBI Headquarters, Steve Dillard, Doyle's replacement as section chief, seemed satisfied with the pace of Albuquerque's investigation. He told the House and Senate Intelligence Committees on April 16, 1997, that the FBI was about "halfway through our anticipated two-year investigation and are about where we expected to be."[80] What two-year investigation? The FBI had told us nothing about a two-year investigation. So I sent Dan Bruno and Ric Bloodsworth out to Los Alamos in April 1997 to try to find out what the Bureau was doing.

There are several accounts of this meeting floating around. Ric forwarded an e-mail to me from Bruno documenting what had transpired, and this account is based on my recollections of what that e-mail contained. Vrooman and Terry Craig from Los Alamos and a new FBI case agent named "Joe Lacy" ("Lowenthal's" replacement) attended, and Ric and Dan met them up on the hill at Los Alamos. Also present was Ray Juzaitis, at that time the X Division chief and Lee's supervisor. This may have been the first time Juzaitis learned about the FBI's ongoing investigation of Lee, although FBI Albuquerque had received permission to brief him on the case back in September 1996.

In effect, a bargain was struck at this meeting. At the FBI's request, DOE would leave Lee in a "non-alert" status, still working in his office with the nuclear computer codes. Juzaitis told us that X Division was under the gun from DOE Headquarters to update all its computer codes for application in the new Stockpile Stewardship program and that Lee was the only guy in the division who had the experience to work on these so-called "legacy codes." This was the first time I learned that Lee had been involved with the W88 since 1982, when he first started working on nuclear weapons codes at Los Alamos, although the FBI and Los Alamos officials like Vrooman had known all along. Juzaitis said that Lee's work on this project had been instrumental to the success of the W88 and that he was an expert in this area. Not to assign him to the "legacy codes" project would raise questions and possibly tip off Lee that he was under investigation. But the FBI agreed to brief Lee's immediate supervisor on the Kindred Spirit investigation and have this supervisor keep a close watch on Lee's activities.[81]

In retrospect, this was pretty dumb, but we didn't know at the time that Lee had already downloaded onto unclassified systems a goldmine of information on nuclear weapons computer codes. Nor did DOE know about the FBI's information that Lee had been helping the Chinese with their nuclear weapons computer codes, or that the FBI had tried to look at Lee's computer but had been blocked by Terry Craig. Everyone was under the erroneous impression that X Division had installed a palm reader on its inner vault door so that the FBI could track Lee's access to blueprints and other W88 documents. Neither Vrooman nor Craig had followed up to ensure that X Division had installed the palm reader.

Worse yet, Lee's supervisors were not being completely honest about his access to classified information. They told the FBI that Lee was working on the legacy codes, when in fact he was probably part of a team modifying the design of the W88 warhead. The original design lacked some of the safety features standard in U.S. warheads. By 1997, Los Alamos had undertaken a new, safer design for the W88.[82]

When the FBI learned that Wen Ho Lee was part of that effort, it urged the lab to reconsider his assignment to that project. But Los Alamos refused to remove him from the project; Lee's supervisor told the FBI again that Lee had been "instrumental for the successful development of the W88." He was the expert in this area and Los Alamos had to have him on the W88 redesign team. The FBI's advice was rejected flat out: "any change at this time is pointless. Lee has known all about the most critical design information since 1988, and the new project does nothing to enhance the weapon."[83] Lee was probably running simulations to test the new designs, a task that was critical since the lab could no longer go to Nevada to conduct live testing of the warhead.

In return, "Lacy" promised that the FBI would step things up significantly. Its agents would go after Lee's bank accounts and travel activities; they would press for a court order to establish technical coverage of Lee's mail and telephone usage; and they would take an "aggressive" approach to interviewing his colleagues and neighbors. They promised that they would be wrapping everything up in short order.

Did any of this happen? The FBI looked at travel records abroad and found some "anomalies" like the trip to Hong Kong in 1992, and financial transactions at an American Express there that suggested to them that Lee might have traveled from Hong Kong into China. But the agents still didn't examine his lab computer and they didn't apply for the court order for telephone surveillance until July, about three months later.

At the meeting, another of the strange occurrences that characterized this case took place. Juzaitis mentioned that Lee had requested that a Chinese postdoctoral student be allowed to come to Los Alamos for the summer to help him with his project—the update of the legacy codes. Juzaitis wondered out loud at the meeting how the lab could authorize such assistance, since these codes were all classified. He promised to look into it and get back to Vrooman and Craig. I don't know if he ever did. Lee initially claimed that the legacy codes project would be unclassified, but when other members of X Division objected to his use of a PRC national to do this type of work, Lee simply wrote in on the request form another, more benign topic for the student to work on that summer. But it was Lee's request for a postdoctoral assistant that finally motivated the FBI to shake off its lethargy and pursue a surveillance warrant. Based on the FBI's representations to us about Chinese espionage tradecraft, the Bureau was correct to be concerned about Lee's request. The FBI suspected that Lee had invited the student to Los Alamos to give him access to classified information.[84] Despite all this, the student's visit was approved and he remained at Los Alamos working for Lee over the summer of 1997.[85] And the FBI never got a warrant to monitor Lee's interactions with the Chinese postdoc.

One other factor inhibiting progress on the Lee investigation at this time may have been concern about offending China. FBI officials tasked with opening an office in Beijing worried that an espionage prosecution of Wen Ho Lee might interfere with its overtures to Beijing. It was common knowledge that Director Freeh was intensely interested in opening FBI offices, known as LEGATs or legal attachés, in U.S. embassies abroad. This was one of Freeh's main objectives: to expand the reach and scope of the FBI's activities worldwide. Freeh's subordinates apparently allowed his desire for a LEGAT in Beijing to affect the Lee investigation.[86] The FBI covered up details of this interference in the investigation, but one later report concluded that "the National Security Division permitted [the FBI's] Criminal Investigations Division's admittedly legitimate concerns about China's sensitivities to undermine a critical FBI investigation about Chinese espionage."[87]

The same report says that Louis Freeh himself didn't know about the Kindred Spirit investigation until July 31, 1997—more than two years after we first gave the FBI a heads-up about Chinese espionage.[88] If this is true, it means that Freeh was almost the last person in government to know about this case, besides President Clinton. Attorney General Janet Reno and even members of Congress knew about it before Freeh, if that is believable.

So now it appears that the FBI had any number of incentives not to pursue the Lee investigation vigorously. First, it might interfere with Freeh's plans for an office in Beijing. Second, espionage investigations, especially those involving the PRC, were a low priority for the FBI, and the lowest in the Albuquerque field office. Third and more significant, there must have been a concern on the part of Albuquerque's senior FBI managers that their decade-long relationship with the Lees in the 1980s might be uncovered. Imagine the embarrassment if it was learned that the Lees had been using their relationship with the FBI as a cover for their assistance to the PRC nuclear establishment—while the FBI was paying for their travel and entertainment expenses!

AS IS TRUE of any manager with responsibility for two thousand people and a $35 million budget, I had a lot on my plate in 1996. Only some of it is relevant to the Kindred Spirit story. During that year, we made good progress on our programs to understand Russian nuclear weapons stewardship practices and procedures. Nonproliferation was becoming a major issue for the Clinton administration and Oak Ridge made a major contribution to identifying PRC proliferation assistance to Pakistan. We were also pressing ahead with our support to DOE's programs on Russian fissile material security and the report we had done the year before was being treated as the "bible" for these efforts.

Nevertheless, I was increasingly concerned about the state of the counterintelligence program within DOE and the labs. The more I learned about the labs' approach, the more I was convinced that we were on the verge of some major problems. In December 1995, I took my concerns to Under Secretary Curtis, telling him that we needed either more and better federal CI officers or more and better lab CI contractors, but preferably both. Given Vice President Gore's "reinventing government" initiative, we were under a hiring freeze. With the Republicans' tightfisted control of the Congress, Curtis thought we had no chance for more federal employees. But we could get money to support more lab contractors. Senator Pete Domenici of New Mexico and other congressional supporters of the labs were always for anything that ratcheted up the employment numbers in their home districts.

I had a very high regard for the professionalism of the Livermore CI program, so we took that as our model and designed a program that would provide funding for similar programs at all the labs with CI responsibilities. Curtis pushed our request through the Department of Energy's bean counters and the Office of Management and Budget. We made no reference to the Kindred Spirit issue in this package, but of course this was one of the driving factors behind our request. Instead, we talked generally about the increasing threat of foreign espionage and relied on FBI and CIA assessments to sell the package to Congress. I don't think we had to push too hard; the intelligence oversight committees in both houses were already aware of the Kindred Spirit issue and the House National Security Committee was also on top of the labs, urging them to be more security-conscious.

That spring I spent some time on the Hill defending our budgetary requests. The only resistance we encountered came from

Domenici's staff, which wanted to spend more money on science and research and thought our concerns about CI excessive. All the other signals were positive, however, that we would get most of our request in the new fiscal year budget. We started laying out our plans for how this money should be spent. In particular, we thought that we could pick up some retired FBI counterintelligence experts. The word was that Freeh was downsizing the CI mission and we hoped some of those he had let go would be interested in filling slots at the various labs.[89]

This was not to be—at least not until much later. The labs were just too cheap to pay retired FBI agents what they were worth and they wouldn't accept our "direction" to hire former agents. The labs set salary caps on CI positions at about $30,000 and refused to offer more, no matter what Energy Headquarters requested. Some of the labs or their local federal operations office turned the money down flat. At Oak Ridge, for example, the local feds had no desire for more counterintelligence funding, even though their lab program was in bad shape. They were probably afraid that money from Headquarters would open them up to more interference and control from Washington. Even though we now had the framework and financial support from Congress, we still were handicapped by the low quality of some of the lab and Headquarters CI staff. It would be three more years before the changes in staffing I envisioned in 1996 would finally take place.

But on the whole, I thought things were looking up. We had the support of Secretary O'Leary and Curtis to improve counterintelligence at the labs, and the department as a whole seemed to be coming around gradually on the risks associated with foreign intelligence threats. The FBI had promised action on the Kindred Spirit case. But there was one issue that continued to be nearly intractable for us: the expanding presence of foreign scientists at the national labs.

The issue just seemed to explode in the mid-1990s. Nobody would be surprised to see British scientists or even French, Germans or Japanese, but what the American public probably doesn't realize is that more than 25 percent of all the foreign scientists at the labs are from Russia, China, Iraq, India, Pakistan, Iran and other countries identified as "sensitive." The numbers of these scientists kept increasing each year of the two Clinton terms (see Figure 1).

By 1996, the department was coming under increasing scrutiny from Congress about Secretary O'Leary's openness policies, the declassification of massive amounts of documents, and the growing numbers of these foreign visitors from sensitive countries at the labs. Countries are deemed sensitive "because of national security, terrorism, regional instability, or nuclear proliferation concerns."[90] A look at DOE's sensitive country list illustrates these categories (see Figure 2). Notably absent from the list is France, although it is suspected of extensive efforts to collect classified or sensitive information from the labs. On my watch, the only objection ever raised by the State Department involved a visiting scientist from Israel. The department blocked the visit on the grounds that Israel had a weapons program and was known to be seeking access to classified

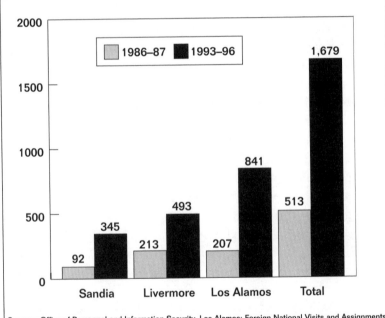

Sources: Office of Personnel and Information Security, Los Alamos; Foreign National Visits and Assignments Office, Livermore; Safeguards and Security Special Projects Team, Sandia; Office of International Technology Cooperation, DOE headquarters.

Figure 1.
Sensitive Foreign Countries: Average Annual Visits and Assignments to DOE Weapons Laboratories, Calendar Years 1986–87 and 1993–96.

DOE's List of Sensitive Countries

Algeria	Iran	Russia
Armenia	Iraq	Sudan
Azerbaijan	Israel	Syria
Belarus	Kazakhstan	Taiwan
China	Kyrgyzstan	Tajikistan
Cuba	Libya	Turkmenistan
Georgia	Moldova	Ukraine
(Republic of)	North Korea	Uzbekistan
India	Pakistan	

Figure 2.

information at the labs. The State Department never objected to visits by Russian or Chinese scientists, however, despite the fact that both countries fit the criteria it used to block the Israeli visit.

The sensitive country issue and particularly the controls and oversight to be exercised by Washington over the labs became a major headache for us. I had no dog in that fight until counterintelligence came under my management. Once that happened, however, I had to get involved. I had no particular view on the appropriateness of foreign visitors, but the lab managers wanted the visitors for a variety of reasons. As they explained to the Government Accounting Office (GAO), the labs were moving beyond nuclear weapons science into new areas of superconductivity, materials sciences, computational sciences and so forth. They wanted to be able to benefit from international developments in these fields and to ensure that lab scientists could fully participate in international conferences and other exchanges. From my point of view this was well and good, but we had already had some experience with the downside of such participation. The Iraqi success in acquiring lab information on high explosives at a 1989 conference, for example, should have made lab managers more wary of such "international" participation. But the management was absolutely adamant about keeping the labs open to foreign visitors, especially from sensitive countries. This included postgraduate students, or postdocs, about whom we were to learn more later.

We had inadvertently stepped into this controversy with our Kindred Spirit report to the Intelligence Committees on Capitol Hill in 1996. Our revelations may have triggered a new series of congressionally mandated studies by the FBI and the GAO. "Foreign visits to the labs" was suddenly a hot topic on Capitol Hill. The GAO was tasked with updating its 1988 study of DOE procedures for handling foreign visits and assignments by the House National Security Committee. On the other side of Capitol Hill, the Senate tasked the FBI to do a study of the Energy Department's counterintelligence programs, with a particular focus on counterintelligence safeguards on foreign visits and assignments.

The new GAO report came out in September 1996. About the same time, I learned that the foreign presence at the Energy Department labs was not a new concern to many on the Hill. Senator John Glenn of Ohio had been beating that drum since the late 1980s and had commissioned a GAO study back then. Nonproliferation was one of his hot-button issues and he thought the DOE labs were a major source of nuclear weapons information, mostly through their lax security procedures. He was also very concerned about how loosely the labs managed the foreign visits process. In at least one hearing, he told me about his concerns and made clear his view that he thought the labs would never clean up their act.

The September 1996 GAO report noted that in comparison with 1986–1987, the last reporting period, the number of foreign visitors at the labs had increased by 55 percent and the number of such visitors from sensitive countries had grown by 225 percent. I want to be clear on this: These numbers were just at the nuclear weapons labs—that is, Los Alamos, Sandia and Livermore—all of which had vitally important national security responsibilities for the maintenance of our nuclear stockpile and for the key secrets of our nuclear arsenal. At all three, the numbers of foreign visitors were growing and the numbers coming from sensitive countries were growing at a rate that seemed out of control.

The 1988 GAO report had found a number of problems with DOE's management of the foreign visitors program. These included: "inadequate prescreening of foreign visitors, poor identification and review of visits that could involve potentially sensitive subjects, and insufficient practices for approving, monitoring, and reporting foreign visits."[91] Late in the first Bush administration, some steps had been taken to mitigate these problems, including the formation of the CI office at DOE Headquarters. But now there was concern on Capitol Hill that our control procedures were getting loose and sloppy again, especially as the increasing numbers of foreign scientists threatened to overwhelm lab control resources and personnel.

In 1986–1987, sensitive-country visitors had been on the order of about 500 yearly, but by 1996, according to the GAO, there were nearly 1700 of these visitors yearly—and that number was continuing to climb. Nearly all of these were from China, India, Israel, Taiwan, and the states of the former Soviet Union, mostly Russia (see Figure 3). The biggest change in procedures had been the delegation of visit approval away from Headquarters to the labs. Background

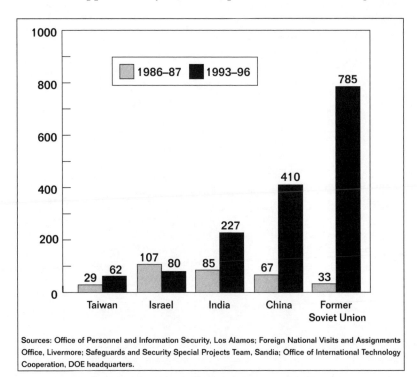

Sources: Office of Personnel and Information Security, Los Alamos; Foreign National Visits and Assignments Office, Livermore; Safeguards and Security Special Projects Team, Sandia; Office of International Technology Cooperation, DOE headquarters.

Figure 3.
Sensitive Foreign Countries with the Highest Average Annual Visits
and Assignments to DOE Weapons Laboratories,
Calendar Years 1986–87 and 1993–96.

checks were now to be only for assignees from a sensitive country staying for more than thirty days or visiting secure areas or discussing sensitive topics. Because of waivers granted to Los Alamos and Sandia, *nobody* was checked at these labs unless they intended to enter a secure area or discuss sensitive topics. A Chinese or Russian scientist could come to stay at either weapons lab for thirty days or more and never be checked. Livermore, to its credit, retained background checks on all visitors and assignees (see Figure 4).

The relaxation of security came about because the weapons labs complained that the background checks were too burdensome,

Type of visit	DOE headquarters	DOE field office	LLNL	LANL	SNL
1988 APPROVAL AUTHORITY					
High-level foreign officials	X				
Discussion of sensitive subjects	X				
Visits/assignments to secure areas					
From sensitive countries	X				
From nonsensitive countries		X			
Assignments to nonsecure areas					
From communist countries[a]	X				
From other sensitive countries		X			
From nonsensitive countries		X			
Visits to nonsecure areas					
From sensitive countries		X			
From nonsensitive countries			X	X	X
1996 APPROVAL AUTHORITY					
High-level foreign officials		X[b]			
Discussion of sensitive subjects		X[b]			
Visits/assignments to secure areas					
From sensitive countries	X				
From nonsensitive countries		X			
Assignments for nonsecure areas					
From sensitive countries			X	X	X
From nonsensitive countries			X	X	X
Visits to nonsecure areas					
From sensitive countries			X	X	X
From nonsensitive countries			X	X	X

[a] DOE's 1988 foreign visitor controls made a distinction between communist and other sensitive countries. DOE no longer makes such a distinction.
[b] DOE headquarters must concur with DOE field office approval of these visits.

Figure 4.
Comparison of Past and Current Authority to Approve Foreign Visitors.

required too much paperwork, and took too long to complete. When my office took over counterintelligence, we ran some spot checks on the process and found this complaint to be groundless. The FBI and CIA both were very responsive to our requests and we could turn around a background check in eight hours or less if necessary. The labs just didn't want to be bothered—and, at least at Los Alamos and Sandia, they weren't. Not surprisingly, the GAO investigation uncovered a number of instances in which foreign delegations showed up with known intelligence officers or scientists who had an intelligence background, and caught the labs unawares.

The lab management squealed when they thought Headquarters might tighten things up. Sig Hecker, the Los Alamos director, claimed that foreign visitors were essential to the "scientific culture" of the labs. He emphasized the contributions that a particular Chinese scientist had made to LANL's competitive position on superconductivity vis-à-vis the other labs. When I mentioned this to the CI specialists at the FBI, they just rolled their eyes. Other lab managers screamed bloody murder when they thought they might lose the ability to put Chinese or Indian postdocs to work on their programs. Let me be clear: these scientists were not working on classified lab projects, nor were they working in classified areas. Lab managers used them to do unclassified science mostly on computer-related projects; yet in many cases, the results of this work would then feed into a classified nuclear weapons program.

By mid-1996, it was evident that the Republican-controlled Congress was going to come down hard on the Energy Department's handling of the foreign visitors issue. I suspected that some of the members knew about the simmering Chinese espionage case and were using the visits issue as a stalking horse to get more stringent controls in place. Many, if not most, of the Republican members in both chambers disliked Secretary O'Leary and thought her policies symptomatic of the overall disregard and mismanagement of national security by the Clinton administration. The Republicans on the Hill thought they had an issue here that they could use to embarrass the President.

In early summer 1996, as the GAO was gearing up to do its study, Charlie Curtis asked me to come to his office to talk about all this. He was getting uneasy about the rumblings on the Hill and wondered what we might do to head off major trouble. My deputy at that time, MaryBeth Davis, had been promoting the idea of a study of the foreign visits and assignments program that would look at numbers, policies and procedures at each of the three weapons labs. I wasn't enthusiastic about it. CI was just part of the overall system of safeguards, but we shouldn't be making policy decisions about whom to let into the labs or when to deny access. The Office of Policy and International Affairs was responsible for managing this activity at the Energy Department; why not let them do the study? But the assistant secretary for that activity, one of the Clinton political appointees, had "starved" the foreign visits and assignments program office nearly into extinction.

Curtis thought our doing the study was a good idea. He promised to support us and issue guidance to the labs in his name. He wanted to look at numbers, policies, procedures, security and CI issues. Since the Chinese presence was going to be an issue, he asked us to focus on the numbers of PRC scientists at each weapons lab, including Oak Ridge, which was still in the bomb business, and Pacific Northwest Lab in Hanover, Washington, the site of the production reactors for the plutonium used in our bombs.

Curtis sent a letter to the lab directors and field office managers outlining his objectives and requesting their full cooperation. He noted the increasing congressional scrutiny and expressed his own surprise at the number of such visitors at the labs, especially from sensitive countries like China. He underscored the key point: the increasing numbers would not be of such concern if the labs could show that they were effectively managing the program and ensuring that safeguards and security measures were sound and in good working order.

We put together five teams of two persons each, most of them coming from the intelligence shop. A few counterintelligence people went, but MaryBeth Davis ran the show. Each team spent about a week at these sites. They compiled numbers, interviewed lab personnel involved in the management of foreign visitors, and talked to the "hosts" for some of these visitors. At the time, I thought this was a waste of manpower and a distraction from more important office priorities. But I was wrong.

We also had some of our scientists working in Washington take a close look at some of the topics the postdoctoral students from the PRC had proposed for study and compare these to known gaps in the PRC weapons program. They found a number of overlaps that seemed to show that even basic research done at the home of our weapons program could benefit the PRC's nuclear program. The scientists who did this work were John Richter and Carl Henry; I think a Livermore scientist assisted them as well.

Curtis had to fire off several "reminders" to some of the labs to get them to cough up the data we needed. Finally, he had to make some personal phone calls. I recall Oak Ridge being especially reluctant to help us in any way, although the rest of the labs cooperated at least at some level. It took a while to analyze all the data, but once we had, it was clear that the postdoc or assignments portion of the program seemed to present the most significant risks. Visitors tended to be at the labs for only three or four days and the security procedures for handling them seemed pretty solid. Same for high-level VIPs. We did turn up examples of scientists holding meetings with PRC counterparts away from the lab campus. (In one instance, a lab scientist hosted a meeting in his garage.) But on the whole, this part of the program seemed relatively secure.

It was a completely different story, however, when it came to assignments or postdoctoral students. By definition, these were visits lasting from thirty days up to as much as two years. But at Los Alamos, MaryBeth uncovered examples of assignees who still held Los Alamos badges more than two years after their assignment had been completed. Assignees basically had the run of the complex, save for the secure areas. As noted above, before 1993 all assignees had background checks, but now only Livermore continued that practice. Los Alamos and Sandia accepted postdocs and assignees from the People's Republic of China without any background checks. Many of these scientists were affiliated with the PRC weapons program, directly or indirectly. Some came from Chinese universities or institutes affiliated with the program; some came to the labs from an American university, especially from within the University of California system, after starting out at a PRC institute or university.

The lab "hosts" for these visitors were supposed to develop and implement a security plan specifying where the assignee could and couldn't go on the lab campus. In practice, many of the hosts were unaware of this responsibility while others admitted that they just turned the assignees loose and never checked on them again. As reflected in the later GAO reports, we also learned that lab security for areas in which assignees could roam was rather sloppy. For example, one inspection turned up boxes of "sensitive materials" in a hallway of a building frequented by PRC (and other) assignees. In another case, a newsletter containing classified information was distributed to the wrong recipient list, which included a number of PRC assignees obviously not cleared to receive this information.

A number of scientists volunteered some anecdotal information about security incidents as well. For example, we were told that Chinese scientists visiting Los Alamos had let it be known that they were paying for information about the supercomputers used in the lab's weapons program computing center. According to this account, they were casting their net broadly and a number of young American scientists had learned of these offers. Naturally, when we sought to investigate these reports, the lab clammed up and we got nowhere.

The FBI and CIA were greatly distressed by the growing numbers of PRC and other assignees at the labs. They told us many times that the PRC used these opportunities to "talent spot"—that is, identify American scientists who might have information valuable to the PRC's program and be interested in traveling to China. According to the FBI and CIA, the opportunity offered by the labs to share lunchrooms, exercise facilities, symposia and open forums would all increase such "talent spotting" opportunities. Terry Hawkins, the lab intelligence chief and resident China expert at Los Alamos, once told me that when a Stanford professor named John Lewis was writing his book on the Chinese nuclear bomb, he frequently visited Los Alamos and met with the lab's intelligence experts. When he came, the lab prepared an agenda for him, but the intelligence shop always prepared a special agenda for its meetings with Lewis. According to Hawkins' story, whenever Lewis traveled to Beijing, the Chinese accused him of being a U.S. spy. Once, to prove this contention, they waved a copy of the special intelligence agenda from Los Alamos at him. How did that piece of paper make it from the intelligence vault in Los Alamos all the way to China?

Our bottom line: regardless of how one assessed the potential value or risks of assignees, especially from sensitive countries, it was clear that the labs were doing a very poor job of safeguarding against potential disclosures of classified or sensitive information—inadvertently or otherwise. And by the way, most of these visitors had accounts on the labs' unclassified computer network and could access these accounts from off-site once they left the lab campus. This was the same network on which Wen Ho Lee had housed his nuclear weapons library since 1988.

Curtis wanted to call a meeting of all the relevant managers from these sites to discuss the findings of our study and come up with some initiatives or measures to mitigate problems and, hopefully, head off the reaction he expected from the Hill. By the time all our schedules could be synched up, it was November 1996. The election was over and we knew Hazel O'Leary was out as secretary for sure. But everyone was hoping that Curtis, by now the deputy secretary (no. 2 in the department) would get the top job.

The day of the meeting finally arrived and everyone paraded into my conference room. The lab directors were all there. The chiefs of the various DOE field offices also attended, along with Curtis's staff; Vic Reis, the assistant secretary for defense programs, who oversaw the weapons labs and managed the overall weapons program; and Ken Baker, my supervisor. Ric Bloodsworth and Chuck Washington were there from the counterintelligence shop. There were lots of big egos in the room, all thinking they might be performing for the next secretary—Charlie Curtis. The place was crowded, and it was fascinating to watch events unfold.

MaryBeth led off with a briefing of her findings. The only part that generated any real heat was the portion dealing with the potential contributions of postdoc research to the PRC's program. Hecker from Los Alamos, in particular, was irate and claimed that no *scientist* could ever make such "assertions." The irony, of course, is that Hecker's own people, including John Richter, had done the analysis on which this part of MaryBeth's briefing rested.

After the general discussion, Curtis asked for a show of hands as to how many considered the growing presence of PRC visitors and assignees at the labs a potential threat. (My recollection is that he used the word "threat," not "risk.") Exactly one lab director raised his hand: Bill Madia from Pacific Northwest Lab. Everyone else just shook his or her head, no. Curtis then said the magic words—that he himself considered it to be a threat. The reaction of everyone in the room was like one of those cartoon dogs trying to put the brakes on and getting turned around to go the other direction. Suddenly, everybody thought it was a threat and everyone starting talking about what to do next. They began to volunteer proposals and actions that could be taken to tighten up management and oversight of the program.

At this point, Curtis asked people to start focusing on "next steps." We had already worked up a list that included threat assessments, new automated data processing systems to track and manage foreign visitors, a new DOE order, and so forth. Hecker volunteered that it was a scandal that labs that were getting millions of dollars to do cutting-edge computer science couldn't even come up with a database of foreign visitors that was accessible from different sites around the complex. He made a very strong pitch to allow the labs to do their own assessments of the threat, which gave us some good laughs later when we saw some of the product—especially the Los Alamos assessment. (Ric Bloodsworth would later characterize it as "very shallow, very brief. No problem here, and if we ever do have one, we'll get in touch.")[92] We finally came up with four or five "initiatives" and Curtis put down some guidelines for future meetings. The meeting lasted a couple of hours, at least.

Afterward, Curtis had me up to his office and asked how I thought it had gone and whether we had accomplished everything we needed to, particularly to fend off the Hill. At the time, I thought the meeting was a success. Since then, I've thought it's too bad that Curtis didn't become the next secretary so he could have implemented those initiatives.

By the time we started work on the initiatives, it was evident that Curtis wasn't going to be nominated for the secretary position. The labs' interest in dealing with the foreign visitors evaporated almost immediately. The program was eventually transferred to Baker's organization, where it was to languish for three more years. The rest of the "Curtis Initiatives," as this drill came to be known, died a quiet death as the labs lost their incentive to follow through.

During 1997 and 1998, the numbers of foreign visitors continued to increase at the labs. In 1999 testimony, John Browne, the new

Los Alamos director, noted that in 1998 alone his lab had nearly a thousand sensitive-country visitors or assignees, and had employed nearly two hundred scientists from these countries. It had also seen a 20 percent increase in the number of visiting PRC scientists from 1995 to 1999.

In the new fiscal year 1997, the GAO decided to take a closer look at how the funding was being used by the labs. To my surprise, they determined two things: first, the labs had used this year's new funding as an excuse to reduce their own contributions to counterintelligence; and second, since this represented direct funding from Washington, it was subject to the same "taxes" as all other funding the labs received from Washington. Now at this point, we were figuring that for every $3 we gave the labs, we got back $1 in actual labor. The rake-off was significant. The GAO calculated that as a result of these two actions, some labs were actually spending less on CI than before. I just shook my head in wonderment. Of course, I had to defend the "cost of doing business" with labs to congressional investigators, some of whom had a field day with this. And why not? Here we are crying about CI and the espionage threat, asking for more money to help fix it and guard our nuclear secrets, and the labs end up taxing that money and spending less on CI than before.

Sometime in late 1997 or early 1998, I was meeting with Robin Staffins, a Livermore scientist on assignment in the Defense Programs office, who was telling me about a study done recently at Livermore that looked at the projects PRC scientists were working on, or at least were funded by nuclear weapons program monies. The number was quite high: as I recall, over one hundred Chinese scientists working mostly on computing projects associated with the DOE Strategic Computing initiative—unclassified research in support of what was ultimately a classified project. Lab director Bruce Tartar, however, had gotten nervous about the appearance of so many PRC scientists being on the weapons program payroll. So he pulled them off that funding source and paid for them out of overhead accounts.

I thought about this for a while and then it hit me that these Chinese scientists were being paid with funds that we were contributing through lab taxes on the counterintelligence program. The

CI programs were paying for the very people they were assigned to monitor. It was perverse. I wrote Staffins a memo outlining this "perception" problem and copied it to Baker. They were both pissed that I hadn't classified it to keep it out of the hands of the *Washington Post*. Baker admonished me not to send such a memo again, at least not an unclassified one.

Finally, in 1999, Congress imposed a moratorium on all foreign visits and assignments at the labs. Many people inside DOE Headquarters were very unhappy with this moratorium. They fought like tigers to open up the labs to foreign scientists again, and eventually succeeded.

FIVE

The Horse Has
Left the Barn

This makes campaign finance look like child's play.
—George Tenet
Director of Central Intelligence, 1997

By the end of 1997, the government would finally begin making an effort to confront the reality of Chinese nuclear espionage. That reality was underscored by the confession of a former lab scientist that he had provided classified nuclear weapons information to the PRC in the 1980s. But at the same time, advocates of accommodation with the PRC in the administration were ready to strike back hard at anyone who got in their way. The year 1997 saw the destruction of the careers of a number of distinguished intelligence professionals and it also marked the beginning of the end for me. I would become the subject of a smear campaign inside the government that resembled those the Clinton administration unleashed against Billy Dale of the White House travel office and others.

Secretary O'Leary left the department shortly after the New Year. For all the criticism of her, I hated to see her go. At least she was a known quantity. Curtis became the acting secretary, but it was already clear that he had no hopes of getting the top job. Not only was his main advocate on the Hill, Senator Pete Domenici, a Republican, but later Curtis told me that he was a registered Independent. And of course he was a middle-aged white male, something of a disadvantage in an administration committed to using minor departments, like DOE, to construct a cabinet that "looked like America." Curtis's loss was huge for the department. He was sometimes too deferential to the labs, but he was honest and had the best interests of the country at heart. And he was willing to deal with tough issues head on.

Early in the New Year, everyone thought that a woman named Elizabeth ("Betsy") Moler would come over from the Federal Energy Regulatory Commission to be the new secretary. Curtis introduced me to her once up on the seventh floor and told her to pay attention to me, that he had learned a lot about intelligence from my office. Although Moler came close, she never quite made it into the plush office on the seventh floor reserved for the secretary.

By Moler's account, she got the nod and was preparing for the announcement ceremony at the White House the next morning. She had her hair done and her mother flew into town. Betsy said that sometime in the middle of the night before the swearing-in ceremony—around 2:00 A.M.—her phone rang. It was a message from the White House: "Never mind." She said, and it was reported in the papers, that Henry Cisneros had intervened with the White House over the absence of Hispanics in the Clinton cabinet. Frantically, they called Federico Pena, the departing secretary of transportation, and implored him to take the job. He immediately took the "For Sale" sign off his front lawn. It was obvious that he was never too happy to be at DOE. Rumor had it that his wife hated Washington, and after Pena resigned once and for all in 1998 the family quickly moved back to Colorado.

When we heard he was the one, we started checking around to see what, if anything, Pena knew about intelligence or about national security, for that matter. Some of our people talked to a retired admiral who had provided intelligence support to him at Transportation and the word wasn't encouraging. But, we rationalized, how much intelligence did he need at Transportation? Of course, he had been tagged with the Air Florida debacle, and before that he was best known for the problems with the baggage handling system at the new Denver airport. (In fact, Pena had been mayor of Denver when I lived there in the mid-1980s.) After he came to DOE, people used to joke that the way to make our fissile material problems go away was to check the material into the Denver airport baggage system.

Anyway, the department's transition team was scrambling around trying to get his "briefing books" ready for his confirmation hearings, and my boss, Ken Baker, was desperate to get his "face time" with the new guy. We expected that surely Kindred Spirit would be one of the first things he would need to know. Days turned into weeks, then weeks into months. After some delays on Capitol Hill, Pena was finally confirmed as secretary on March 12, 1997. Surely now the call will come, we thought. But it never did.

I kept after Baker: "When are we going to tell him?" I would nag. Baker was obviously stalling and sought to blame Pena's chief of staff, a former staff member of the White House's National Economic Council named Elgie Holstein, for not putting us on Pena's calendar. Meanwhile, Baker was becoming paranoid about access to the secretary; nobody but he was allowed to venture into the secretarial suite on the seventh floor of the department. Several of Baker's office directors, including me, got reamed for venturing into that forbidden territory. In staff meetings, Baker repeatedly harped on following the "chain of command," saying he would approve anything that went to the new secretary.

Baker did bring Pena into the intelligence office at one point for a "meet and greet." Nice man, but somewhat impatient and totally clueless about intelligence. Whereas Curtis and O'Leary had some familiarity with intelligence at least, and were certainly willing to learn, Pena couldn't be bothered. O'Leary wanted a daily briefing and a briefing book, with lots of reports and cables. She would stay late to make sure she had read the book and used it to task her own people. Baker told us that Pena wanted one page with just the highlights of the day and that Baker would approve these before Pena saw them. We doubted that he even read them very often. Pena rarely made the time to meet with his intelligence briefers, who after waiting hours outside his office were repeatedly told to come back the next day or maybe the day after.

But mainly, we just couldn't understand the reluctance of Baker, Reis and ultimately Joan Rohfling to let Pena in on the secret: the FBI was conducting an investigation of a Los Alamos scientist on suspicion of espionage, and we had hard data that the PRC had acquired classified information on the most modern nuclear warhead in our arsenal. I used to think that when Pena went to a cabinet meeting, nearly every other agency head in the room knew about this (except perhaps for the President). How would he react if he heard about it first from one of those people, and not his own security officials?

It was during this time, remember, that the White House and the National Security Council were dead set on pushing the Comprehensive Test Ban Treaty to ratification in the U.S. Senate. At various times, CTBT was proclaimed to be the President's number one foreign policy goal. The administration needed the labs on board to placate Senate opposition to the treaty, and the key to the labs' acquiescence was the big bucks associated with the Science Based Stockpile Stewardship program (SBSS). We are talking about billions of dollars, not the usual bureaucratic chump change of several million here and there. A big part of the funding was to come from the Hill, but the Defense Department, the "customer" for the labs' nuclear weapons, was kicking in around $500 million or so a year. The campaign to sell this program to Congress and to the Defense Department went into full gear as we entered 1997.

It was at this time that I started getting instructions from my Energy Department superiors to "drop" Kindred Spirit. At several meetings over the winter and into the spring of 1997, Reis and Baker made it clear they wished we could just forget about Chinese nuclear espionage and make it all go away. This was history, after all, and as Baker said, "The horse has left the barn, so lets just forget about it."[1] Meanwhile, down in the intelligence shop we were getting all sorts of new information about PRC penetrations of our nuclear weapons program and PRC intelligence collection priorities and targets. We were sharing these with Baker and Reis, but their priority was keeping the lid on. They especially feared "leakage" of information about Chinese nuclear espionage to Capitol Hill.

I think Reis and Rohfling were also fearful of what the new secretary would do. They had already seen one example of what they considered Pena's "rash" behavior. He had abruptly canceled the contract for the operation of Brookhaven National Lab in New York after it was determined that the contractors running that lab had covered up information about environmental contamination of the area around it.[2] I think they worried that if he found out about Wen Ho Lee he would go off on the warhead design labs, Los Alamos and Livermore, and blow their efforts to obtain big bucks from Congress to fund Stockpile Stewardship. On at least one occasion in my presence, Reis claimed that Rohfling had told him to "bury" the Kindred Spirit scandal. Above all, Reis told me that he didn't want this information getting to Congress. He feared that knowledge of the labs' failure to protect our secrets would undercut any chance he had of selling Capitol Hill on SBSS. He was wrong, as events in 1999 were to show. He didn't count on people like Senator Pete Domenici's ability to deliver the pork, regardless of how bad things got at the labs.

I WANT TO EMPHASIZE that reports about PRC efforts to gain access to U.S. nuclear weapons information did not end in 1995. Over the next two years, we would receive more reports of Chinese nuclear espionage. Some of these reports told of past Chinese successes and others helped us forecast future collection targets at the two major weapons labs, Los Alamos and Livermore. For example, "In 1996, the U.S. Intelligence Community reported that the PRC had successfully stolen classified U.S technology from a U.S. Nuclear Weapons Laboratory about the neutron bomb."[3] We learned that the PRC acquired classified nuclear weapons information on the following additional U.S. warheads: the W87, used on the U.S. Peacekeeper missile; the W78, used on the U.S. Minuteman III missile; the W76, used on the U.S. Trident C-4 submarine-launched ballistic missile; the W62, used on the Minuteman III ICBM; and the W56, used on the Minuteman II ICBM.[4] (Note that all the U.S. warheads were intended for missiles, although the U.S. also makes warheads for its air-delivered bombs.) Finally, as was later reported, there were "other PRC thefts of U.S. thermonuclear weapons-related secrets," but the Clinton administration refused to permit publication of this information.[5]

Equally important, the PRC also sought tools such as supercomputers and computer codes to enable it to conduct nuclear simulations on high-performance computers.

The PRC has been using high performance computers for nuclear weapons applications. [These] HPCs may be powerful enough to help the PRC make use of design information that it stole from the United States, including design information for the W70

neutron bomb and the W88 Trident D-5 thermonuclear warhead—
without further physical testing.[6]

The Chinese had obtained these computers from the United States
after the Clinton administration relaxed export controls on them. In
1997 we also learned that a former lab scientist had provided the
PRC with classified information in the mid-1980s, when he worked
at Los Alamos. One of our Los Alamos experts determined that this
espionage "involved ... precisely the critical technologies important to a developing nuclear weapons state with an active testing
program."[7] Improved diagnostics capabilities were critical to continued progress on the newer PRC warheads; so we were particularly concerned when we learned that the PRC was seeking "access
to the Los Alamos National Laboratory based Dual Axis Radiographic
Hydrodynamic Test Facility, for the reason that it uses powerful X
rays to analyze the effects of implosions during non-nuclear tests."[8]

Of greatest concern to us were reports that we received during this period about the PRC's intent to acquire sophisticated U.S.
nuclear weapons codes that simulate the explosion of nuclear
devices. Our scientists believed that the Chinese had yet to conduct enough live nuclear tests to fill in all the suspected gaps in
their understanding of nuclear weapons science. But if they could
gain access to our nuclear computer codes and simulations and all
of the data collected from our decades of nuclear testing, then they
might not have to conduct additional nuclear tests. Our codes had
been calibrated over the years through reference to the results of
live testing in order to bring the codes and simulations as close to
live events as possible. The development of these codes cost the
American taxpayers hundreds of millions of dollars, so it was no
wonder that the PRC wanted to save itself time and money by acquiring this information. Los Alamos seemed to be squarely in the
crosshairs of the PRC computer code acquisition plans.

DESPITE THE FACT that we couldn't brief our new secretary, we
were still carrying the message around town. On March 20, 1997,
Baker and I briefed the vice chairman of the Joint Chiefs, Air Force
General Joseph Ralston, and the next day we briefed Harold Smith,
the assistant to the secretary of defense for nuclear, chemical and

biological warfare. Smith was the only official I came across who seemed to understand what a big deal this was, but by that time he was on his way out of office.

In April the FBI finished its report to Congress on DOE counterintelligence and sent a copy over to us. Federico Pena and FBI director Louis Freeh had a meeting about that time, and Freeh told Pena that he hoped there would be action on the Bureau's recommendations, which included a restructuring of the counterintelligence program, more funding for lab CI programs, and better security procedures for handling foreign visitors. Pena must have looked like a deer in the headlights; there is no way he could have known what Freeh was talking about. Baker had failed to tell Pena about the report in advance and he refused to permit us to provide an overview of its recommendations to Pena before his meeting with Freeh.

I had sent one of Pena's assistants a memo summarizing the key findings of the report. The Bureau had given us good marks for our efforts to upgrade counterintelligence at the labs, especially with regard to security awareness, training and analysis. But the report also emphasized the "endemic shortfalls" in the DOE program. These included:

- Too much authority over foreign visits and assignments delegated to the field.
- A conflict of interest inherent in requesting the labs to police themselves.
- The existing staff, even after the expanded program, is too small to meet the growing CI threat.
- Chain of command problems inherent in organizational structure of DOE and its CI program.
- The use of a contractor and a detailee to manage intelligence and CI demonstrates a lack of commitment by DOE to either activity.

The latter was a reference to Ric Bloodsworth and me. Baker refused to make permanent billets available to convert these positions to Energy Department federal positions. He thought that as long as he could hold out the threat of sending me back to Los Alamos, he could control the intelligence office. Likewise with Bloodsworth;

if he started pressing too hard on counterintelligence, Baker could just ship him back.

I implemented everything I could in the FBI recommendations and then started pushing Baker and Reis plus the labs to finish the job. Since "finishing the job" meant imposing some tighter restrictions on foreign visits and assignments, the labs were having none of that.

On the other side of the security house, the teams responsible for physical security were getting clobbered by budget cuts and a general rundown of security at the weapons labs. The guard forces at the labs had been particularly hard hit. The budget cuts had forced a 50 percent cut in guard force strength, and training was suffering. At Los Alamos, for example, security guards were failing even such basic tasks as weapons firing, baton use and handcuffing suspects.[9] We would get glimpses of this from time to time, but we had our own problems.

I was casting around for ideas as to how to get Reis, Baker and ultimately Pena's attention when I hit on the old Washington trick of forming a "Senior Advisory Group." A bunch of senior guys from outside the organization, well known and highly respected by that organization's leadership, would come in and spend about a month looking at the problem. They would then communicate the "solution" to your supervisors or the agency seniors. Unless you are a complete idiot, you only do this when you are certain they will tell your bosses what you want them to hear. By this time, I was pretty sure of that, so we put together just such a group.

We stacked the deck with intelligence "graybeards" like Dick Kerr, a former CIA deputy director, and Jim Williams, a former Defense Intelligence Agency director and counterintelligence expert. We were fortunate to get Jack Downing, who would later return to government to become the chief of CIA's Directorate of Operations. And we had another intelligence expert named Rich Haver, who had made his name in naval intelligence, but later was to be the director of the IC's Community Management Staff. We had a retired admiral who had been director of naval intelligence. In short, we had a well-respected group of experts. People like Reis and Baker might listen to them and maybe even follow their advice.

We talked to them about our problems and midway through the discussion, Haver blurted out, "The Chinese have been conducting a twenty-year assault on the DOE labs!" This senior advisory group had been around long enough to know a problem when they saw it, especially a political problem of immense proportions. The Republicans would have a field day if they found out about this, to say nothing of the continuing damage to our national security.

Several members of the group made field trips down to Los Alamos, where they were treated rather shabbily, as I remember. They also met with the Albuquerque FBI agents newly assigned to the case.[10] They came back very pessimistic. Los Alamos was clueless about its problems and arrogant to boot. This was probably the first time I heard anyone say that the labs didn't have a counterintelligence program up to even minimal standards. And the field office in Albuquerque had not assigned any experienced agents to the case.

This group wrote up their report, made some recommendations, and had some meetings with Baker and Reis. Kerr drafted an action plan, but it remained a draft until two years later, when he was able to implement some of his recommendations through the CIA. Most of the group was appalled by what they discovered at the labs; as one member wrote, "the consequences of a failure to establish an effective counterintelligence program relating to DOE are of such a strategic nature as to warrant briefings of the DCI, Attorney General, and the President's National Security Advisor." He thought this would put pressure on DOE and the labs to implement the FBI's recommendations, but he had never worked with the labs before and couldn't appreciate what we were up against. "Thanks for coming by" was essentially the response. They never got near the secretary.

During their trip to New Mexico, the advisory group had met with two new FBI agents recently assigned to the Kindred Spirit case. The "graybeards" told us that these agents were probably too inexperienced to handle such an investigation. But FBI officials in Albuquerque had misled their visitors by allowing them to think these agents were working on Kindred Spirit. They weren't.

In mid-1996, Supervisory Special Agent "Jay Steele" had asked FBI Headquarters for additional agents to put on the case. Jerry Doyle approved the request after meeting with Albuquerque SAC

Tom Kneir and ASAC Ron Dick in July. It was November before two new special agents, fresh out of the FBI training school at Quantico, arrived for duty at Albuquerque, where they were promptly assigned to a gang task force and an Indian reservation crimes squad, respectively, by ASAC Dick.[11] He believed the new agents would be more useful in these assignments, but would later claim that he didn't know they were supposed to be working on Kindred Spirit.[12]

More regrettably, when FBI Headquarters learned of the diversion of agents, it did "absolutely nothing about it." Unit chief "Jack Kerry" was afraid to inform his supervisors of the diversion, telling an investigative panel later on that doing so would have been "impolitic."

> He said the "culture" of the FBI is "very intolerant" of that kind of reporting and a field office has a great deal of "autonomy" as to how it assigns personnel. The "diversion of two bodies," he said, was not a "felony act" and happens all the time. In order for him to "drop [a] dime" on FBI-ALBQ, the conduct would have had to have been "illegal, immoral, fattening or contrary to public policy."[13]

And so the FBI's Kindred Spirit investigation would continue to languish.

BY MIDSUMMER we were at a dead end inside DOE. With Curtis gone, there was no adult supervision in the building and we couldn't get to Pena. The labs would scream bloody murder if anybody threatened to touch their foreign visits and assignments program. Meanwhile, the FBI had disappeared again on Kindred Spirit (we had heard nothing more from them since April) and Wen Ho Lee was still sitting in X Division accessing our nuclear secrets every day.

My options were to give up and go someplace else; go around the administration to Capitol Hill; or go outside the administration altogether and try to get some media interest in the story. None of these options seemed viable; and at that time, neither the director of the FBI nor the director of the CIA appeared willing or interested in intervening at the Department of Energy, as they were to do later that year.

My last hope was to find a sympathetic ear somewhere on the National Security Council and try to influence events inside DOE from over there. I chose this alternative because it allowed me to stay inside "the system." I hoped that intervention from the NSC would shake up DOE and make Pena become interested in implementing the FBI's recommendations.

Trying to protect our nuclear secrets against foreign intelligence threats, upgrading and reforming the labs' CI program and CI posture and, hopefully, in the process helping the security guys as well—that was my job. Wen Ho Lee was the FBI's problem at this point. My only interest in him was that the FBI either remove him from access to classified information or clear him.

Ric Bloodsworth, my deputy for counterintelligence, and I hit on the idea of going to see a National Security Council official named Randy Beers. Beers had the intelligence policy account on the NSC; I didn't know him but had heard good things about him. He had gotten a black eye in the news reports as the NSC official who failed to tell President Clinton about PRC efforts to buy influence in Washington.[14] But we had a chance to talk to the FBI agent involved and he vouched for Beers. We had virtually nothing to lose at this point, so we got on his calendar.

The meeting was set for July 3, 1997, a typically hot, muggy Washington summer day as I recall. Beers came into the meeting just back from a noon run, but looked pretty fresh. He knew what we wanted to talk about, having probably heard about it from the FBI. But he knew nothing about the intelligence information that supported the FBI Kindred Spirit investigation or how we had assembled a case that portrayed what Rich Haver had described as a twenty-year assault on the national labs. Coming on top of the Chinese campaign finance business, this must have been quite a shocker for Beers. After we gave him the broad outline of our story, he asked how he could help. I told him about our counterintelligence gaps, the ignored FBI recommendations, how we had been stonewalled on CI upgrades, and how this information had been kept from Pena.

To his great credit, Beers took it all in and started to sketch out a plan of action. Unlike nearly everyone else's response ("thanks for coming by"), he tried to draw a roadmap to fix this problem. The first step was to go back to DOE and tell Betsy Moler, the new deputy secretary, about the situation. (Moler had been given the number two slot as a consolation prize and probably a promise that she would move up if and when Pena departed.) Later, it turned out that Beers also was a buddy of Elgie Holstein, Pena's chief of staff, and gave him a call to make sure Holstein understood the seriousness of the problem. Needless to say, that broke the logjam.

Back at the department, I relayed Beers' message to Moler and, not surprisingly, next thing we knew, she, Baker, Reis and Holstein were down in my conference room hearing the bad news. I had updated the basic briefing to integrate all the new information that had turned up over the past year. As I laid out our story, Moler got very quiet and started looking at Baker and Reis. There was a brief discussion of who had kept Pena from hearing all this and Baker pointed his finger squarely at Holstein, who just shrugged. Holstein had no idea what Baker was talking about; he had made no such request to Holstein.[15]

Moler had to see the briefing twice, once on July 7 and again on July 11—perhaps because she didn't believe her own eyes the first time. Finally, Pena came down into the office to get the message himself. The briefing took place on July 14, nearly four months to the day since he had been sworn in, but more like six months since he had come over to DOE from Transportation. Pena later said, "That was the first occasion that this matter had been brought to my attention. I was absolutely stunned by it, I was shocked by it."[16] That is a fair characterization of his reaction. I thought he would go through the ceiling. "Why didn't I know about this before?" he thundered at us. His next question was, "What are we going to do about this?" I jumped on that one. "We have a full set of counterintelligence recommendations from the FBI ready to go," I replied. "I'm inclined to sign them right now," he said. "Whoa," Moler, Baker and Reis all chimed in together; this was moving way too fast. Moler told Pena that these recommendations weren't ready for prime time and had to be reviewed, etc., etc. Another missed opportunity to do the right thing.

I remember thinking that Pena could move decisively to cancel a lab contract if the issue was pollution, saying that "there need not be a trade-off between award-winning scientific research and environment, safety and health." But there would be no such action on a counterintelligence issue, even in the face of potentially far greater adverse consequences for the national security of the United States.

There was some discussion about the FBI's investigation; Pena didn't know about that either. He asked about the status and we told him what we knew. I told him about the April meeting with the FBI, Los Alamos' promise to limit Wen Ho Lee's access, and the 1996 "installation" of the monitoring device on the X Division documents vault. But I also shared with him our concerns about both the pace of the FBI's actions and Los Alamos' assurances that they had taken all agreed-to steps to safeguard our nuclear secrets. I told him about our difficulty in getting straight information out of Los Alamos and suggested that perhaps a query from him might get some action.

But Pena and Moler were both much more interested in "who knew" than in what we should do, and so we recounted for them all the senior officials we had briefed over the past two years. Moler was clearly displeased and said that was way too many. Too many? These were all Clinton appointed officials with real national security duties, I thought. But Pena decreed that henceforth, the message would go only to those officials he personally approved by name. Any briefing request had to be forwarded to Pena through Moler and they would approve or disapprove. "Shut this thing down" was the basic message. Pena left the conference room and I was not to see him again for another three months.

Moler was now in charge. I'd had a commanding officer in the military during my German tour that I thought was bad; he reminded everyone of Colonel Henry Blake in *M*A*S*H*. Moler made him look like General Patton. She was not just indecisive; she would *never* make a decision, and wanted to "study" everything to death. She also wanted any tough decision to be made by someone else— preferably someone at the White House.

Beers, at the NSC, wanted the word to get around to the cabinet officials with national security responsibilities, starting with the White House. By now, Sandy Berger had moved up to become the President's national security advisor and we were set up to go over the Kindred Spirit briefing with him again on July 29, 1997, in his West Wing office. Present were Berger; his deputy, Jim Steinberg; George Tenet, the new director of Central Intelligence; Paul Redmond, Tenet's deputy for counterintelligence; Beers and maybe one or two other NSC officials. Moler and Holstein came from DOE. I was the briefer. We had been told that FBI director Freeh would be there. But when we got to the waiting room outside Berger's office, there was nobody from the FBI. Tenet was clearly annoyed and mumbled something about "Louie" pulling this on him again.[17] I had no idea what that was about, but Tenet was on the verge of leaving; I think Redmond talked him into staying. He was later to say that this was the first time he had heard about Chinese nuclear espionage. It was true that he was not present when we briefed his predecessor, John Deutch, in March 1996. I couldn't believe that this was his introduction to Kindred Spirit, but maybe it was, given his surprised reaction.

Moler waltzed in about ten minutes after the briefing began, claiming that she had been meeting with some other NSC staffer about climate control. I was sitting to Berger's left and everyone else was sitting around a coffee table in Berger's West Wing office. I went through my briefing, handing Berger hard copies of the PowerPoint slides that I had prepared. With every new slide Berger sank a bit deeper in his chair. Tenet and Redmond were exchanging sidelong glances and rolling their eyes; Tenet finally whispered, loud enough for everyone in the room to hear, "This makes campaign finance look like child's play." The whole meeting lasted about an hour. I don't recall Berger asking any questions, but his deputy, Steinberg, did. Nothing memorable, but the tone was somewhat hostile. There was some reference, maybe from Berger, to the upcoming presidential summit between Clinton and the Chinese president, Jiang Zemin, in October.

But things did start popping after this. We hit the briefing circuit around town to carry the message over to Defense and Justice. Back at DOE, Bloodsworth and I were spending our time coming up with "options" on the 1997 FBI counterintelligence recommendations for Betsy Moler to review. By options, Moler meant more "study" and more after that. Finally, in exasperation, I proposed to her two options: one, declassify everything and let Russians, Chinese, everyone into the labs and give them access to all our nuclear secrets; or two, shut the labs down and then polygraph every scientist with a Top Secret clearance before we let them back in. I thought I had really stepped over the line this time and expected her to reprimand me. But she didn't bat an eye, and just asked us for more "study." It was obvious that Moler was stalling for time, and it was becoming increasingly clear that if counterintelligence at the Department of Energy was ever to be fixed, it would have to be done from the outside.

On August 1, I met with Associate Director John Lewis across town at the FBI. I had not seen Lewis for about a year, but after we went through all the new information we had put together, he said that something needed to be done about DOE. He remarked that for as long as he could remember, everyone knew that DOE security and CI was a problem, that DOE could never get a handle on the labs, and it was finally time to fix the mess over there. I can recall no discussion of the FBI's Kindred Spirit case at all.

By this time, DOE had become a member of the National Counterintelligence Policy Board, the most senior counterintelligence policy body in the government. Like much else, the CI Policy Board had been set up after the Aldrich Ames debacle. DOE had been admitted only on occasion, but I had persuaded the board's chairman to let us play a larger role. The board met monthly in a conference room in the Old Executive Office Building, right next door to the White House. I made yet another presentation at a board meeting asking for help and got many expressions of support, especially from the National Security Agency representative, Barbara McNamara. Fortunately, Lewis now chaired the board and he intended to use it to form a working group to review DOE's CI problems and come up with some recommendations.

During August 1997, we traveled to the offices of the secretary of defense, the attorney general, and the director of the FBI. I wondered why we were not telling the secretary of state and, in fact, this later became the source of some embarrassment to the administration, although these decisions were being made at the White House as far as I knew.

On August 7, 1997, we assembled in Secretary of Defense William Cohen's office, on the E Ring of the Pentagon, with a beautiful view out across the Potomac River.[18] The secretary was there, along with the under secretary of defense for policy, Walt Slocum, and Hal Smith plus maybe one other official were there from the Office of the Secretary of Defense. General James Jones, later to be commandant of the Marine Corps, was also present. I was struck by his size; he certainly had a commanding presence and his questions were sharp. Moler and maybe Holstein were there from DOE. We gathered around Cohen's conference table and walked through the presentation. At the outset, Cohen was phlegmatic, to say the least. But in contrast to Berger, with each passing slide he sat more upright in his chair, his body language screaming, "Oh, no!" Moler had fumbled through some introductory remarks and some words about all the "great things" Pena was doing to fix this problem. Hal Smith said some very nice things about his experience with DOE Intelligence and me. Far and away the most memorable remark, however, came from Cohen. He finally exclaimed, "No wonder Stockpile Stewardship costs so much! We're paying for two countries." (Recall that DOD had just ponied up about $500 million to DOE to support the program.) Everybody around the table, including me, thought that was pretty funny. A sideward glance at Moler, however, told me I had better not laugh out loud; she was not pleased with Cohen's observation. Bottom line of this meeting: thanks for coming by—although sometime later, DOD would start waking up to the problems all this represented for the Pentagon.

We traveled back to FBI Headquarters on August 12 to talk directly to Louis Freeh. I think this was the first time I met him. Dark and very intense, he gave off the impression of a no-nonsense guy. I must say his office and its anteroom were even more impressive than Cohen's. We met around a very large conference table in his office. FBI records indicate that Ken Baker attended this meeting. True to form, Moler was late. Freeh got tired of waiting for her to show up and we were about ten minutes into the presentation when she arrived. She offered some excuse, but Freeh basically blew her off. This meeting was memorable in many respects.

Freeh already knew what I was going to tell him because "Greg Smith" had prebriefed him. In front of Freeh on the conference table there was a large folder, probably the case file on Kindred Spirit. Toward the end of my presentation, Freeh pushed himself back from the table and started in on us. He told us that the FBI hadn't been able to get a court warrant for technical coverage on Wen Ho Lee's telephone and computer, but he didn't give up any details. (I knew nothing at the time about FBI's problems with the Justice Department that July, nor did I know that a year had passed before the FBI had even sought a warrant.) He also said something about how in his role as the "chief law enforcement officer of the U.S." he was of the opinion that obtaining a conviction of the Kindred Spirit suspect at that point would be too tough without the kind of evidence that surveillance could produce. So his advice to DOE was to take whatever measures were necessary to protect our nuclear secrets, especially our nuclear computer codes.

Wen Ho Lee's request for a PRC postdoctoral student to help him with the legacy codes had finally galvanized the FBI into action. The Bureau apparently feared that Lee would use the PRC student to pass classified nuclear weapons codes to China. Moler would later go to great lengths to deny that Freeh had made this recommendation to her. But when Freeh did so, Betsy responded that DOE had been deferring action at the FBI's request. Freeh shot back, "Take that right off the table." His meaning was clear: our April 1997 deal—that is, leave Lee in a "non-alert status" while the FBI got a warrant to do technical coverage—was now off. I didn't take Freeh's word to mean "fire him," as Moler later stated in one of her several accounts of this meeting.[19]

The other message Freeh gave us was that the time had come to fix the CI and security problems at the labs. Freeh was very insistent on this. "If DOE doesn't do it, then [Senators] Shelby and Kerry will do it for you. They will come up with a reform plan for Energy that you aren't going to like," he told Moler. Freeh's prediction that the Congress would impose "solutions" on DOE is exactly what happened.

I rode in Moler's chauffeured limo back to the department and explained to her the significance of Freeh's communication. The ball was now clearly in DOE's court. If I had had the authority, I would have stripped Wen Ho Lee of his clearance as soon as we got back to DOE Headquarters. But I only had authority over intelligence clearances and Lee had never had intelligence clearances. So this meant that the next steps would be in the realm of DOE's Office of Security Affairs. I told Moler, "Find a pretext to bring [Lee], find [a] pretext to do a polygraph, and if he refuses, take him out."[20] At the time, the boss of that office was Joe Mahaley, who reported to Ken Baker, as I did. So I told Moler that it was up to Baker and Mahaley to do the deed. When we got back to the department, Baker and I discussed Freeh's statements and what should happen next. He said that he would get with Moler and they would take care of this. They didn't, and Wen Ho Lee stayed in place for another *seventeen months* after this meeting.

Moler's response to Freeh's August 12 advice was the subject of much controversy later on. She would admit that she "heard" Freeh, but offered up a number of reasons why she didn't follow his advice.[21] Freeh's recommendation had not been a direct order, she would claim. Or, Freeh's recommendation didn't "make sense." The best one: she thought Freeh was "freelancing" and not really speaking on behalf of the FBI.[22] There is no record to show that she ever told Pena about Freeh's recommendation, and the Energy Department's chief of security claims that the first he learned of Freeh's recommendation was when he read it in a newspaper in 1999. So both Moler and Baker had dropped the ball.

But when I returned to my office, I told Bloodsworth that Freeh had said, "Nothing you do can interfere with [the] FBI case. Do what you've got to do. Take whatever administrative action that you want. It won't jeopardize the case."[23]

About a month later, in September 1997, Bloodsworth and I met with a CIA officer on detail at the FBI and told her that nothing had happened after the meeting with Freeh. She wrote her supervisors that Moler "still 'didn't get [the] picture' " and that she " 'will prob[ably] want the Bureau to be [the] thugs.' "[24]

On August 20, 1997, we met with Attorney General Janet Reno in her office at the Department of Justice. It was pouring rain that day and Baker and I had to wait outside the Justice building for Pena's chief of staff, Elgie Holstein, to show up. (Moler was on vacation.) John Lewis was present from the FBI. Eric Holder, Reno's deputy, also attended. Reno's office outdid all the others I had recently visited. It was beautiful, with a huge chandelier and all. Reno was extremely gracious to me; before I started she thanked me several times for coming over and repeated this afterwards. She was attentive during the briefing; I can clearly recall seeing her hands shaking from Parkinson's tremors. I don't recall any questions from her, although Holder did ask about a couple of things. Here again, I discussed only the intelligence information on PRC nuclear weapons development. At no time in my presence did Wen

Ho Lee's name or the FBI's investigation come up. Later I would be asked if I knew anything about an FBI official registering a protest with Reno about Justice blocking FBI efforts to obtain a warrant to monitor Lee. At that time, my answer had to be no. But I do recall Lewis staying on after we left, and the 1999 investigations show that he did so to ask for Reno's assistance on the warrant—to no avail, as it turned out.

This would be another of those strange events that characterized the entire Kindred Spirit investigation. Recall that the FBI had promised to obtain a warrant for technical coverage of Wen Ho Lee's telephones and computers in 1996—within 30 to 60 days after the initiation of the investigation. But more than a year had passed before the FBI even applied for the necessary warrant and then the application was denied by the Justice Department. The FBI would submit the application to Justice's Office of Intelligence Policy Review, which would approve the application or help the FBI improve it before forwarding it to the Foreign Intelligence Surveillance Court. This court met secretly to approve such warrants. Between 1979 and 1998, the FBI had submitted 11,201 applications for warrants—749 in 1997 alone.[25] Between 1995 and 1999, the Justice Department rejected only one application.[26]

Justice never formally turned down the FBI's application; it just wouldn't permit it to go forward to the court. Justice disputed the application on the basis of "currency" and "sufficiency," arguing that the particulars presented by the FBI were either too old or insufficient to meet a probable-cause standard. The FBI's application presented more than nineteen separate items, including:

- DOE counterintelligence and weapons experts had concluded that there was a great probability that the W-88 information had been compromised between 1984 and 1988 at the nuclear weapons division of the Los Alamos lab.*

---

*Janet Reno would later criticize the FBI for withholding information from OIPR. She testified that our AI had cited both Los Alamos and Livermore as sites where the compromise may have taken place. As evidence, she pointed to the list of potential suspects, which included both Los Alamos and Livermore scientists. But the FBI refused to show the AI to OIPR.

- It was standard PRC intelligence tradecraft to focus particularly upon targeting and recruitment of ethnic Chinese living in foreign countries (e.g., Chinese-Americans).
- It is common in PRC intelligence tradecraft to use academic delegations—rather than traditional intelligence officers—to collect information on science-related topics. It was, in fact, standard PRC intelligence tradecraft to use scientific delegations to identify and target scientists working at restricted U.S. facilities such as LANL, since they "have better access than PRC intelligence personnel to scientists and other counterparts at the United States National Laboratories."
- Sylvia Lee had extremely close contacts with visiting Chinese scientific delegations. Sylvia Lee, in fact, had volunteered to act as hostess for visiting Chinese scientific delegations at LANL when such visits first began in 1980, and had apparently had more extensive contacts and closer relationships with these delegations than anyone else at the laboratory. On one occasion, moreover, Wen Ho Lee had himself aggressively sought involvement with a visiting Chinese scientific delegation, insisting upon acting as an interpreter for the group despite his inability to perform this function very effectively.
- Sylvia Lee was involuntarily terminated at LANL during a reduction in force in 1995. Her personnel file indicated incidents of security violations and threats she allegedly made against coworkers.
- In 1986, Wen Ho Lee and his wife traveled to China on LANL business to deliver a paper on nuclear weapons-related science to a symposium in Beijing. He visited the Chinese laboratory—the Institute for Applied Physics and Computational Mathematics—that designs the PRC's nuclear weapons.
- The Lees visited the PRC—and IAPCM—on LANL business again 1988.
- It was standard PRC intelligence tradecraft, when targeting ethnic Chinese living overseas, to encourage travel to the "homeland"—particularly where visits to ancestral villages

and/or old family members could be arranged—as a way of trying to dilute loyalty to other countries and encouraging solidarity with the authorities in Beijing.

- The Lees took vacation time to travel elsewhere in China during their two trips there in 1986 and 1988.
- The FBI also learned of the Lees' purchase of unknown goods or services from a travel agent in Hong Kong while on a trip to that colony and to Taiwan in 1992. FBI agents speculated that this payment might have been for tickets for an unreported side trip across the border into the PRC.
- Though Wen Ho Lee had visited IAPCM in both 1986 and 1988 and had filled "contact reports" claiming to recount all of the Chinese scientists he met there, he had failed to disclose certain information that the FBI deemed significant. [This was a reference to his failure to report his contact with Hu Side in 1988.]
- Wen Ho Lee worked on specialized computer codes at Los Alamos—so-called "legacy codes" related to nuclear testing data—that were a particular target for Chinese intelligence.
- The FBI learned that during a visit to Los Alamos by scientists from IAPCM, Lee had discussed certain unclassified (but weapons-related) computer codes with the Chinese delegation. It was reported that Lee had helped the Chinese scientists with their codes by providing software and calculations relating to hydrodynamics.
- In 1997, Lee had requested permission to hire a graduate student, a Chinese national, to help him with work on "Lagrangian codes" at LANL. When the FBI evaluated this request, investigators were told by laboratory officials that there was no such thing as *unclassified* Lagrangian codes, which describe certain hydrodynamic processes and are used to model some aspects of nuclear weapons testing.
- In 1984, the FBI questioned Wen Ho Lee about his 1982 contact with a U.S. scientist at another DOE nuclear weapons laboratory who was under investigation.
- When questioned about this contact, Lee gave deceptive answers. After offering further explanations, Lee took a polygraph, claiming that he had been concerned only with

this other scientist's alleged passing of unclassified information to a foreign government against DOE and Nuclear Regulatory Commission regulations—something that Lee
admitted doing. (The FBI closed this investigation of Lee in
1984.)

- The FBI, as noted above, had begun another investigation
into Lee in the early 1990s, before the W88 compromise
came to light. This investigation was based upon an FBI
investigative lead that could reasonably be interpreted to
indicate that Lee had provided significant assistance to the
PRC.

- The FBI obtained a copy of a note on IAPCM letterhead
dated 1987 listing three LANL reports by their laboratory
publication number. On this note, in English, was a handwritten comment to "Linda" saying "[t]he Deputy Director
of this Institute asked [for] these paper[s]. His name is Dr.
Zheng Shaotang. Please check if they are unclassified and
send to them. Thanks a lot. Sylvia Lee."[27]

Reno and her deputies seem to have been the only officials in
Washington who believed this list was not enough. The FBI had
omitted some items to protect "sources and methods" and had also
failed to note that the Lees had assisted them in the 1980s as "informational assets." The FBI also refused to provide a copy of the DOE
Administrative Inquiry to the Justice Department. Nevertheless,
Reno's own internal review of the case later concluded:

> The final draft FISA application [redacted] on its face, established
> probable cause to believe that Wen Ho Lee was an agent of a for-
> eign power, that is to say, a United States Person currently engaged
> in clandestine intelligence gathering activities for or on behalf of
> the PRC which activities might involve violations of the crimi-
> nal laws of the United States and that his wife, Sylvia Lee, aided,
> abetted or conspired in such activities. Given what the FBI and
> OIPR (Office of Intelligence Policy Review) knew at the time, it
> should have resulted in the submission of a FISA application
> and the issuance of a FISA order.[28]

So why was the warrant stalled in Justice? Why didn't Freeh intervene with Reno to persuade her to permit it to go forward? And why did Justice quickly destroy all its files concerning the warrant? One other thing: the warrant did not mention Wen Ho Lee's computers, only his telephones. Later the FBI claimed that a warrant would have covered the computer as well, but others disagreed.

ONE OTHER ACTION came out of the July 29 meeting with Sandy Berger at the White House. He asked for a "quickie" assessment from CIA of the DOE presentation. This request marked the beginning of one of the most blatant efforts to politicize intelligence that I encountered in my career. By way of background, recall that I mentioned above that a presidential summit was scheduled for that October in Washington between Clinton and China's Jiang Zemin. In the runup to the summit, many intelligence careers were "terminated." Here's why:

The administration was looking for some accomplishments to promote at the summit, but these were rather tough to come by. DOE Intelligence, along with other agencies in town, had done some work on the PRC's energy futures and things looked rather bleak, both from a supply and from an environmental standpoint. China was a coal burner, and as a result Beijing was one of the world's most polluted cities. The State Department and the NSC must have gotten the idea that this would be a good place to focus; given the impressive GNP growth that China was experiencing at the time, the PRC market for energy should be booming over the next decade or so. China was also intent on using nuclear power, so there seemed to be a potential market for U.S. nuclear power firms. There had been no new nuclear power starts in the United States for years, so China seemed to represent an opportunity to keep this business alive. Both Westinghouse and Bechtel, two giant U.S. corporations, were hot to penetrate this market. The hitch was that legislation passed in the 1980s by a Democrat-controlled Congress prohibited any sales of nuclear-related technology to China unless the President could certify that China was not proliferating weapons of mass destruction.

China's proliferation record was, in fact, abysmal. One senior Intelligence Community official used to say that the Chinese would

sell anything to anyone. Pakistan and Iran were their primary customers, but they also provided technology and training to a host of
other "rogue states." It was widely believed that Pakistan had
acquired its first nuclear warhead design from China, but now the
Chinese were focusing more on training Pakistan and others in how
to produce their own fissile materials to make nuclear bomb fuel
and their own warheads and missiles.[29] Missile proliferation was
another area of contention, particularly China's sale of missiles to
Pakistan and Iran and others. In order for Clinton to authorize American corporations to sell nuclear power technologies to the Chinese, this behavior would have to stop—or appear to.

To that end, NSC senior director for nonproliferation Gary Samore
and State Department assistant secretary Bob Einhorn had been traveling to China to "educate" the Chinese on export control regulations,
the virtues of joining the missile technology control regime, and so
on. A number of DOE people from the arms control shop and the labs
had also been making these trips. The purpose of including DOE
seemed to be twofold: demonstrate to the PRC how lab experts could
make "valuable" contributions to arms control schemes; and convince the PRC nuclear establishment that it had a role to play in future
Comprehensive Test Ban Treaty deliberations. Of course, it gave the
PRC a great opportunity to do some more "talent spotting," but Samore
and Einhorn seemed willing to accept that risk.

The Chinese made a number of "concessions" and agreed to
sign up for the various international committees that police missile and nuclear sales. So Samore and Einhorn could come back to
Washington and spread the good word from China. They were
clearly more convinced by the pledges they were getting from their
PRC counterparts than by the information turned up by the U.S.
Intelligence Community. And of course, that information without
fail implied just the opposite: that there had been little or no mod-
ification in PRC proliferation behavior; they were just getting smarter
in the measures they took to conceal it from prying eyes. At that
time, Gordon Oehler, chief of the Nonproliferation Center at CIA,
wouldn't back down from his responsibilities to report accurately
the intelligence he was receiving on the PRC's continuing bad behavior. He wouldn't back down either in his message to the administration or in his presentations on Capitol Hill. He told Congress in

public testimony that the Clinton administration "regularly dismissed" information on Chinese missile sales to rogue states.[30] Obviously he would have to go, and go he did. Out of the blue, CIA announced that Gordon was retiring. He later told me that he took retirement after his supervisor promised the National Security Council that Oehler would not appear on the Hill again.

Intelligence Community analysts trying to publish National Intelligence Estimates on Chinese military science and technology ran afoul of Clinton administration policies emphasizing China as a "strategic partner." These estimates revealed the military benefits to China from U.S. technologies acquired through commercial projects with U.S. defense satellite firms, like Hughes Space and Communications, and other high-technology defense companies. Analysts were demoted and transferred to less politically sensitive intelligence projects. George Tenet, the director of Central Intelligence, personally intervened and stopped the publication of a number of reports that would have documented the benefits to China's military industries and its strategic missile force from U.S. technologies.[31]

With this background, you can understand the trepidation I felt with regard to the CIA's "quick look" at DOE's work on PRC nuclear weapons development. It was appropriate for Berger to ask the question, but as with so many such activities in the Clinton administration, it was the execution that was the problem. I met with Gary Samore at the White House on August 26 to go over the materials I had shown Berger. Several things were notable about this briefing. Samore made some observations about Chinese nuclear weapons developments that CIA analysts were later to relate to a congressional committee investigating PRC nuclear espionage— almost word for word. Put simply, Samore believed that the PRC was more than capable of making all the dramatic advances it had made over the last few years without outside help. Oh brother, I thought, we had already worked through this issue in copious detail two years earlier. I carefully described for him those deliberations and how the conclusions and judgments of the Kindred Spirit Analysis Group in my briefing were derived. Second, Samore made it abundantly clear that no matter what the Chinese did, the United States was not going to stop the DOE national lab scientists from interacting with their PRC counterparts. Samore said something to the effect that it was U.S. policy to use the DOE nuclear scientists to "engage" their counterparts in China and Russia and elsewhere, for that matter. Evidence of espionage or acquisition of nuclear weapons secrets was not going to stop that policy.

I thought this a remarkable statement, but Samore clearly meant it. "Go ahead, make all the security and CI fixes you want," he said, "but the lab-to-lab exchanges are going to continue." Spying was not going to get in the way of the Clinton administration's engagement policy with China. Period. When he was asked about this later by the reporters, Samore claimed that "If he had made such a comment in a briefing on the spy case, he was joking."[32]

Sometime in mid-August, Ric Bloodsworth and I went out to the agency and put all our cards on the table. I wondered why we were bothering, since we had already been through this crowd before in 1996 during the runup to briefing DCI Deutch. We saw mostly the same faces, including people serving on the China working group that our guys met with regularly.

CIA analysts from the Directorate of Intelligence drafted a paper and sometime in early September we were asked to come over to look at it. It was quite long and very disappointing. It said almost nothing about the walk-in document or any other intelligence that had turned up. Instead, it seemed to blame everything on the Russians. The Russians? We knew and had been following the interactions between the Russians and the Chinese, and had even written the first U.S. Intelligence Community paper on this topic in 1994 or 1995.

In hindsight, I suspect that Samore's tasking to this group was to come up with some alternative explanations for Chinese technological advances—that is, alternatives to assistance from the U.S. weapons labs. The agency strained mightily and came up with the Russians as the alternate bad guys. To meet Samore's requirements, the CIA had to cook some of the intelligence to make it come out this way. So the CIA assessment was shaded to portray Chinese achievements as either indigenous or resulting from Russian assistance. This allowed Samore to tell Sandy Berger that the intelligence was too murky and that Energy's conclusions were all based on worst-case scenarios.

When we came back to the DOE office, I was steamed. For one thing, the CIA had covered only the W88 compromise and made no mention whatsoever of any other PRC espionage successes. I ripped off a letter to George Tenet laying out my concerns and asking for another look at this important subject. I wrote: "We would be remiss in not expressing our concerns regarding both the overall analysis and several of the key conclusions. In our judgment, the DI paper contains a number of important flaws."[33] I never heard from Tenet, but the next time I saw the CIA paper it was much shorter, with much but not all of the offending distortion of intelligence gone, and a new set of "key judgments" attached, which ironically didn't match the evidence or the arguments set out in the paper itself. There were several different faces across the table representing CIA, many of which I didn't recognize. Now there was almost no disagreement between CIA and DOE on this set of key judgments; the disagreement that did exist was the product of analytic differences. I had no problems with "analytic differences"; I just objected to people fudging intelligence facts. To their credit, the CIA analysts supported our position regarding the need for security and CI reforms at the labs. But their political masters needed to minimize the PRC espionage, so they played along.[34]

Yet Samore was not content with a CIA analysis that played down Chinese targeting and acquisition of U.S. information. Any admission of Chinese nuclear espionage would prevent the President from giving the PRC a clean bill of health so that the sale of nuclear power plants to China could be authorized. Chinese nuclear espionage could also imperil the administration's ability to persuade the Senate to ratify the Comprehensive Test Ban Treaty. So Samore ran to Berger with word that the CIA "quick look" didn't support DOE's assessment, that the "picture was too inconclusive."

I always had a hard time understanding how anyone could argue that we were depicting a worst-case scenario. My discussions were always carefully qualified to spell out what we knew and what we didn't, as well as what the lab scientists thought about all this. But later I learned that Samore had represented my message along the following lines: the PRC had already produced the W88 and was currently deploying it on their new long-range ballistic missiles. I was shocked when I heard this from a high-ranking

Intelligence Community official in 1999. If this is what Samore was telling people around town, no wonder they thought I was a nut. And that didn't match the key judgments of the CIA paper, so I wondered if Samore had ever shown the actual paper to Berger.

At one point, Louis Freeh got wind of this supposed dispute between the CIA and the Energy Department. He asked his China specialists if they agreed with my findings and conclusions about Chinese nuclear espionage. Their response was that, generally, they did. These specialists, unit chief "Jack Kerry" and "Greg Smith," had witnessed some of the exchanges between CIA and Energy and were aware that the agency had been caught cooking some of the intelligence.[35]

We finally had an opportunity to argue all this out in front of Samore and Randy Beers in mid-October. In retrospect, this was a waste of time. Samore already had what he wanted and nothing we said at the meeting could change that. Frankly, I acted like a real jerk on this occasion. I tore into the CIA analysts there, accused them of dishonesty in the use of intelligence information, and so on. Not my finest hour. I should have just said thanks for all the "help" they were giving us to fix the security problems at the labs and left. Some battles are just not worth fighting. But there was one amusing incident at the meeting. One of the CIA guys, a trained physicist but with no hands-on experience in the design or development of nuclear weapons, started lecturing John Richter about how to build such weapons. The scene of this young CIA pup, who barely knew what a nuclear warhead looked like in real life, lecturing Richter, who had designed and tested forty such devices, was priceless. Even Samore was snickering.

In the space of a few short months, beginning in about July and extending through November, the Energy Department just got repeatedly hammered on the counterintelligence and security front. Besides the report of the National Counterintelligence Policy Board, on September 25 the General Accounting Office released the results of its study on controls on the DOE foreign visits and assignments program. The conclusions of the GAO study were old news to us: DOE's procedures for controlling visits and assignments were not implemented by the labs, and those controls the department did have in place had failed to prevent sensitive-country nationals from accessing sensitive and even classified information. The report criticized Los Alamos and Sandia for exercising their waivers with regard to background checks on such visitors, which meant that no foreign visitors were ever checked. The report cited examples of foreign intelligence agents entering the labs without the knowledge of either the labs or DOE, examples of the "compromise" of classified or sensitive information to foreign nationals through neglect or sloppy security procedures, and exchanges of sensitive information that were never identified by the labs to DOE.[36]

Nor were things going well on the other side of the security house. Throughout the fall, Moler and her DOE assistants were doing their best to bury a security assessment that would show significant lapses in physical security at the weapons labs. This is an excerpt from the cover letter to the report that finally went to the White House on or about November 6, 1997:

> . . . in all candor, we have been hampered in meeting [safeguards and security] obligations by organizational obstacles and competing internal interests. . . . by far, the most pressing issue is the Department's current unsatisfactory method for managing its safeguards and security program. Simply put, the current method does not work as intended.[37]

SOMETIME IN FALL 1997, Randy Beers and the people doing the outside CI study began to discuss how to make DOE do the right thing . . . finally. Pena clearly didn't have the guts to do this without the top cover of some sort of directive from the White House. An executive order and some other options were discussed, and then someone hit on the idea of issuing a Presidential Decision Directive.

Every administration uses such directives; they just call them different things so as to put their own mark on some action. An Internet site run by the Federation of American Scientists lists seventy-five such directives issued during the Clinton years, dealing with such topics as national space policy and international organized crime. Somebody, maybe Bloodsworth, observed that while the labs had ignored Pena and Moler, the secretary and deputy secretary of the Energy Department, perhaps they would pay attention to the President.

The recommendation for the PDD was set forth in the CI Policy Board's September report. The early drafts of the directive, with Bloodsworth participating for DOE, covered intelligence, counterintelligence and security. Each was to become an independent entity reporting directly to the energy secretary. In the future, a professional, preferably from the FBI, would run counterintelligence and the labs would have to hire professional CI people. Budgets would go up, controls on the foreign visits problem would be tightened and, finally, there were references to the use of polygraphs for the scientists.

Let me point out that few issues have been more screwed up than consideration of the polygraph for the labs. The "poly" is used extensively at most of the agencies with national security responsibilities. A "passed poly" is the price of admission for CIA and the National Security Agency. DOD uses the polygraph on its "special access" or black programs, and in selected cases at the Defense Intelligence Agency. Secretaries of state refuse to take a poly. That leaves DOE. In the past, it was mainly used as an instrument of the security goons; they were always hot to poly somebody, anybody, on whatever grounds—usually some security infraction or some issue that turned up on a background security check.

But many people, especially from CIA, wondered why they were regularly subjected to a polygraph, while the lab scientists who handled information every bit as sensitive never were. Nor did these scientists appear to have any restrictions on their travel; they could go just about anyplace, anytime, with only minimal restrictions. Often, if a CIA type looked suspicious after a foreign trip, the agency would just slap him or her on the polygraph box and clear up any problems. I am not a great fan of the poly. I have taken a couple and it's not a fun experience, nor is it necessarily foolproof. On the other hand, taken as one instrument in the security toolkit, the polygraph can be useful.

The early drafts of PDD 61 did have some words about the polygraph. All in all, these drafts looked pretty good. If actually implemented—always the tough part—the directive might help. But DOE fought a hard rearguard action against it.

Later on, Pena and Moler took credit for charging out on behalf of the PDD. In truth, Moler and her underlings fought it tooth and nail. First off, they absolutely refused to let security slip out of the control of their political appointees, so they demanded that security be taken out of the PDD. The White House rolled on that one. Next, Moler didn't want intelligence to become an independent office; she wanted it to stay under political control. To keep intelligence under the thumb of the political types, they needed to convince George Tenet, the CIA director. We had spent a lot of time with Tenet's people and they knew instinctively that subordinating intelligence to political considerations had a bad odor. Politicization of intelligence was sure to follow. So Tenet was insisting that intelligence must become an independent office. Moler and company fought hard, and, at one point, even claimed to have Tenet's agreement that the office would stay submerged in a policy shop. Tenet or one of his deputies actually called Beers from Rome to say that Moler was misrepresenting his position.

Pena and Moler later denied all of this, but it was essentially confirmed by a government report in 1999. To me, the real shocker was that the lab management—Sig Hecker at Los Alamos, Paul Robinson at Sandia and Bruce Tartar at Livermore—refused to concur with the findings of the PDD or the draft language, and urged DOE to do likewise.[38]

President Clinton finally signed Presidential Decision Directive 61 in February 11, 1998, about six months after the whole drill had begun. Some of the PDD's mandates have been made public. These include:

- Hiring counterintelligence professionals to be based at the weapons labs.
- Doubling the budget for counterintelligence.
- Changing the screening and the approval process for foreign scientists seeking access to DOE labs.
- Making the lab directors directly accountable for foreign visits and CI at their labs.
- Instituting more extensive security reviews—including the use of polygraphs—for DOE scientists working in sensitive programs.[39]

The PDD tried to clear away the layers of management between CI and the lab directors and the secretary in order to facilitate the timely reporting of CI concerns. It established accountability and clear lines of authority throughout the complex. It directed the secretary of defense, the attorney general and the FBI director all to stay engaged in CI reforms at Energy. Finally, it directed the National CI Policy Board to oversee the implementation of the new PDD. It all looked very good—on paper.

In October 1997, Louis Freeh and George Tenet came to visit Pena and Moler, to explain to them why all this was necessary. I was called in to do a "prebrief" for Pena, reminding him what this was all about. I hadn't seen him since July, but assumed Moler had been keeping him up to speed. But he didn't seem to know much about what had gone on since I had seen him last. Just as I was getting into the update, Tenet showed up with his entourage. I was supposed to leave, but Tenet motioned for me to stay on and Pena had no way of overruling him. Freeh showed up a little later and did most of the talking.

Pena took copious notes, to show he was really paying attention. Freeh told him about the CI Policy Board study, about how the DOE's CI program didn't meet even the minimal standards of a good program, and how they were there to help him. But first, Freeh told him once again that the "deal" between the FBI and DOE keeping Wen Ho Lee in a non-alert status at Los Alamos was off. A "script" prepared for Freeh's meeting with Pena and Moler contained the following:

> Before we get to our specific proposals, we want to stress with you the importance of taking immediate action, if not already done, to prevent any further damage by the "Kindred Spirit" subject with his current access to sensitive computer codes. As noted in previous conversations, the FBI investigation should not prevent you from taking whatever actions you think appropriate to remove him from his current position and access to sensitive programs.[40]

In other words, DOE should do whatever it considered necessary to protect its nuclear weapons secrets, especially its sensitive computer codes.

Neither Pena nor Moler even batted an eye; I think it went right over their heads. Later, neither Pena nor his chief of staff, Elgie Holstein, also present, could recall such a warning. Twice now in the space of just over two months, the director of the FBI had urged the Energy Department to take action to limit Wen Ho Lee's access to nuclear secrets, but the secretary and the deputy secretary of the department ignored his recommendations.

Freeh then went on with his presentation by saying that DOE needed a short-range and a long-range program. The short-range program was the work plan and steps set forth in the PDD. Freeh detailed these for Pena, who was still writing furiously. When he finished, Pena said something like, "Well ... what about the second phase?" Freeh just shook his head and told Pena to worry about implementing the first part of the program. Freeh offered to help Pena on Capitol Hill to get the funding that it would take to staff such a program.

Pena asked very few questions, and immediately tried to shift the discussion to Russian arms control with Tenet. I couldn't believe it. Here were Freeh and Tenet making a trip over to tell Pena that he and his predecessors had failed in their responsibilities to safeguard our nuclear secrets, and all he wanted to talk about was arms control with the Russians. Tenet just blew him off and left, shaking his head. One of his people told me that on the way back to the agency, Tenet said words to the effect that those people [Pena and Moler] "just don't get it."

Later we learned that the FBI Albuquerque office delivered the same message about removing Wen Ho Lee's clearances to Los Alamos counterintelligence chief Bob Vrooman the same day. Word of Freeh's August recommendation had reached Albuquerque by late September and Special Agent "Joe Lacy" had been told not to "allow DOE to use the Kindred Spirit case as an excuse for not taking action regarding the movement of Lee Wen-ho [sic] or the removal of his clearance." This guidance had come directly from FBI Headquarters: don't let the lab (Los Alamos) or DOE use our investigation as an excuse to do nothing.[41]

Their concern was well founded. Bob Vrooman refused to accept the FBI's recommendation and never even mentioned it to his supervisors or the lab director. FBI records of this meeting indicate that Vrooman claimed that Wen Ho Lee wasn't working on "anything new," and that Vrooman didn't think Lee's security clearance or his access to classified information should be removed.[42] Vrooman unilaterally decided to ignore the recommendation of the FBI director to remove Lee from his current position in order to protect sensitive nuclear secrets. He would later claim that he didn't want to interfere with the FBI's investigation(!). "Lacy," contrary to FBI Headquarters' instruction, docilely reported to his superiors that Vrooman "does not want to move subject or take his clearance away."[43] Vrooman misled "Lacy" with his claim that Lee wasn't working on anything new; the FBI knew he was working on the modified W88 warhead design.

On three separate occasions from August to October 1997, the FBI told Department of Energy officials that their earlier request for non-alert status for Wen Ho Lee was "off the table" and that Energy should remove Lee's access to nuclear secrets. The FBI had finally decided that the risks of his continued access outweighed the FBI's investigative objectives. Pena, Moler, Baker and Vrooman at Los Alamos did not share the FBI's anxiety; they ignored the Bureau and left Lee in place for another fifteen months.

My time was running out. Moler, Baker, and probably Pena were incensed that I had gone around them to the White House and, through the White House, had finally forced them to take action on DOE's counterintelligence and security vulnerabilities. Moler's contempt for me was palpable. Baker wanted to fire me, but some of his associates told me that he was terrified that if he did, I would "spill my guts" about all that was going on at DOE.

Now all sorts of allegations about my conduct and management of intelligence started to fly my way. Baker made some references to financial improprieties in Intelligence, but my budget guy shot all that down with ease. A co-worker in another office alleged that I had sexually harassed her, but when I demanded a formal inquiry, she withdrew her statements. The most repulsive stuff had to do with rumors about the personal lives of people in my office, which I refuse even to mention here. Then I was falsely accused of assaulting one of my employees, but Baker and Moler declined to take any action to discipline that employee for making false accusations to the police. All of this crap started after I had gone to the White House in July 1997 to bring NSC officials into the struggle to fix CI and security at the Energy Department.

I was cut out of more and more meetings with Moler and the people working on the security and counterintelligence reforms.

Whatever went on upstairs on the new PDD was always a mystery to me. But friends all over government, including at the NSC, would call to regale me with the latest in DOE's efforts to thwart the President's will.

Of course, it was only a matter of time until Pena tried to replace me or put someone over me to keep me "under control." That day came when an arms controller named Rose Gottemoeller showed up as the new director of the Office of Nonproliferation and National Security. She would be my boss now, at least until the PDD took effect. I had known Rose for some time, well back into the 1980s, I think. She had been a research assistant for years at the Rand Corporation until Ted Warner, who also had a high position in the Clinton Defense Department, pushed her out.

She had landed a job on the first Clinton administration National Security Council with responsibilities for Russia and the new republics. She served for about eighteen months there and then headed off to a nice job in London as the director of a prestigious research institute. We had got on well in the past, but during some of our early meetings at DOE she was clearly on guard. I can imagine the tales she had been told about me. Very early, probably in September or October, Baker had me brief her on Kindred Spirit. For this, Moler reprimanded Baker. She hadn't authorized Rose to get that briefing and she reminded Baker that she controlled access to it, not him.

A Pena press release, issued by the department on November 14, 1997, identified Gottemoeller's new responsibilities as including intelligence and security: "She directs, manages and coordinates all intelligence and safeguards and security activities for the Department. She serves as the Secretary's principal advisor on nonproliferation and intelligence matters."[44] Her duties regarding intelligence came directly from my own job description. With a stroke of the pen, Pena had transferred most of my important responsibilities to Rose. I was now out of the business of managing the department's intelligence activities. Gottemoeller herself removed me from interactions with other Intelligence Community agencies, like the National Security Agency, and I never saw the FBI again.

So I really don't know what deliberations were going on, if any, about Freeh's recommendations, repeated twice, to remove

Wen Ho Lee from his access to classified information. I do know that after November 14, 1997, it was now Rose Gottemoeller's job. Did she do it? Obviously not.

TO TOP IT ALL OFF, it was around this time that the FBI finally nailed a former lab scientist for passing classified nuclear weapons information to the PRC. This case had a number of striking parallels with the Wen Ho Lee case, including inexplicable behavior by Justice Department officials. The scientist in this instance, a naturalized U.S. citizen from Taiwan named Peter Lee (no relation to Wen Ho Lee), had been under observation by the FBI for many years, at least back into the early 1980s. He had worked at both Livermore and Los Alamos National Labs during the 1980s, and then had gone to TRW Inc., a defense contractor in California. In 1994 or 1995 he had reapplied to Los Alamos and had been graded at the top of all applicants; the FBI warned us off him, however, and eventually Peter Lee's application was rejected. Apparently the standards for obtaining such a warrant were lower at that time than later, when the FBI applied for one on Wen Ho Lee.

Peter Lee was a laser expert, and a good one according to the accounts we received from some of his lab contemporaries. He had come to the United States from Taiwan, gone to school for his advanced degrees here, and then begun work at Livermore Lab in California in 1976. In the early 1980s he worked on Livermore's efforts to simulate nuclear explosions through laser experiments, which was to become the lab's special area of expertise in the Stockpile Stewardship program in the 1990s. In 1984 Lee switched labs and went to Los Alamos, where he continued to work on these laser programs. FBI accounts indicate that he and Wen Ho Lee were acquainted. They both lived in White Rock, outside Los Alamos, but the extent of their relationship was unknown, at least to us in the Energy Department.

In January 1985, Peter Lee made a trip to Beijing. Here again some of the similarities with the Wen Ho Lee case are striking. PRC nuclear weapons scientists, including Chen Nengkuan, a longtime nuclear designer, appealed to him for assistance in his hotel room during that visit and asked him questions about his work and his approach to the solution of different technical problems. Court documents indicate that Lee knowingly shared classified information with his Chinese counterparts as he drew diagrams and discussed mathematical and experimental results related to U.S. laser fusion programs. It was this information about laser fusion that led to his eventual sentencing.

Bill Cleveland, the counterintelligence officer at Livermore, had helped the FBI catch Peter Lee and he shared some of the information from the FBI's interrogation of Lee with me. According to Bill, PRC nuclear scientists had visited Peter Lee in his hotel room. During this visit, they told him that the United States was very strong and China was weak, and that since Peter Lee was Chinese, he had an obligation to help protect China against the United States. They flattered him, told him he was a great scientist, and then asked him for help. He agreed and gave a number of lectures to PRC nuclear specialists. These lectures focused on the use of lasers to simulate nuclear explosions. I don't know how many times Lee traveled to China, but his most recent trip had been in the mid-1990s. By this time, he was employed by TRW Inc., working on a classified antisubmarine project for the U.S. Navy. He admitted passing classified information on this project to the Chinese as well.

For all this, he faced at least fifteen years and stiff fines in excess of $200,000. But instead, he got a year in a halfway house and a $20,000 fine. What happened?

First, the FBI needed to step up its efforts to nail Lee. They called him in for an interview that revealed that he had been less than forthcoming on his security forms about a recent trip he had made to Beijing. Although his forms showed that he was taking the trip for vacation and personal reasons, in fact he had lectured at the Institute of Applied Physics and Computational Mathematics. While there, he had discussed his current project on radar imaging in support of antisubmarine operations. He had brought an image with him to share with the Chinese, showing how this technology worked. After his lecture, he tore up the image and threw it away. This set off all kinds of warning bells, so the FBI obtained his permission to polygraph him. He pretty much bombed the polygraph and the FBI was off to the races.

All of this was taking place out in California and the FBI had called upon Livermore to help them with classified assessments and other technical assistance. We in the counterintelligence shop were following the case, but it was mostly run out of DOE Security and the nuclear weapons program. I don't recall the first time I had heard about it, but it was probably sometime in late summer, 1997. Our guys at Livermore, the retired FBI CI experts, told us that it was classic PRC collection. Go to a visiting scientist's hotel room and ask lots of questions, try to elicit classified answers and maybe get the guy to give some lectures to a selected group of PRC scientists. But for some reason, despite Lee's admissions of espionage, an indictment was very slow in coming down. Jonathan Shapiro, the assistant U.S. attorney in Los Angeles, where this case was "prosecuted," told congressional investigators and reporters that the Justice Department had him hold off on an indictment until after the Clinton-Jiang meeting in Washington in late October 1997. Shapiro had wanted to prosecute Peter Lee on espionage charges, but the Justice Department blocked that request as well. It's clear that the administration didn't want to embarrass Jiang or offend the Chinese government.

But there also seem to have been some problems with just what the FBI told the Defense Department and the Navy about this indictment. Defense and the Navy refused to join in on the indictment for fear of compromising some of their secrets in court. But in later discussions with the DOD's general counsel, after the dust had settled, she made it clear that the FBI hadn't told Defense everything about Peter Lee's indictment. In particular, she said that the FBI hadn't told her about the allegations of compromising classified nuclear information. The FBI had limited its information to just the allegations regarding Navy programs. The first she had heard about Lee's compromise of nuclear secrets was from DOE. Had she gotten the full story from the FBI, she said, her recommendation not to pursue an indictment on the Navy matter might have been different. I don't know why the FBI didn't tell her about Lee's nuclear espionage.

Finally, there is the role in Peter Lee's sentencing played by Livermore and DOE. Former Secretary O'Leary had declassified much of the laser fusion program in 1993, over the strenuous objections of many of the lab scientists; now Lee's defense was able to use this to argue that the severity of his crime was not major. Never mind that the information was still classified in 1985, when Lee provided it to the PRC. Further, some of Lee's former supervisors asserted that he didn't even have access to classified information; but we knew that wasn't true. The first damage assessment provided by Livermore and DOE Headquarters, mostly from Robin Staffins, a Livermore laser expert, was so thin that Shapiro was wondering what the big deal was and why he was even prosecuting Lee. The judge also got some ringing endorsements of Lee from PRC officials at the Chinese Academy of Sciences.

DOE Security came down to see us for another assessment of what Lee had given the PRC nuclear program that might have contributed to their progress. A LANL scientist named Tom Cook wrote a cogent, well-argued damage assessment that demonstrated how the information Lee had provided the PRC in the mid-1980s would benefit the PRC program. Tom wrote that the "data provided by Dr. Lee was of significant material assistance to the PRC in their nuclear weapons development program." He concluded that Lee's assistance had "directly enhanced the PRC nuclear weapons program to the detriment of U.S. national security."[45] That is espionage by any definition. Unfortunately, the Justice Department reached a plea bargain with Peter Lee before our assistance was sought and our assessment could be prepared.

In March 1998, we traveled out to Los Angeles for the sentencing. The Justice Department had already blocked Shapiro from filing an espionage case against Peter Lee, so he had to settle for a plea bargain. The FBI guys were hoping that he would spend some time in the midtown Los Angeles detention center, an ugly gray building not far from where we were at the federal courthouse. One night over there with all the rapists and murderers, the FBI claimed, and Peter Lee would sing like a bird. The FBI still wanted to know more about his involvement with the Chinese and anything else he could tell them about other American scientists assisting the PRC. But the judge had different ideas; Lee was sentenced to a halfway house someplace in Anaheim, a $20,000 fine and three thousand hours of community service. Shapiro and the FBI were very disappointed with this outcome.

In retrospect, it's clear that the Justice Department sabotaged the case against Peter Lee. Justice officials rejected efforts to prosecute him under the harshest of the espionage statutes for his disclosure of nuclear weapons secrets to the Chinese. Lee had also attempted to obstruct justice by obtaining falsified travel receipts from the Chinese to cover the fact that they had paid for his 1997 trip—after Lee had told the FBI that the trip was vacation-related and paid for by himself. The Justice Department never pursued this clear obstruction of justice. Peter Lee had failed an FBI polygraph on questions related to espionage and the provision of classified information to unauthorized persons. He had failed another polygraph seeking to learn whether he had lied to the FBI after his first polygraph. He had denied any knowledge of classified programs or publications, even though he was the author and editor of some of these publications.

Despite all this, Justice accepted a plea to lesser charges involving the 1985 provision of classified nuclear weapons information to the Chinese, and dropped any charge related to the 1997 anti-submarine compromise. Attorney General Janet Reno and Deputy Attorney General Eric Holder reportedly were not involved in the decision-making on this case. Justice officials would later plead "miscommunications" for the outcome of the Peter Lee case. But the message seemed obvious: if you get caught spying for the Chinese by the Clinton administration, you get off easy. The Justice Department and the White House were very allergic to any admission that China might be spying on the U.S. nuclear weapons labs.

From our standpoint, however, even the weak plea bargain had some positive aspects. Now we could go back to Moler and the lab directors with some evidence that the PRC was indeed preying on the labs. But when we got back to Washington, it was as if the Peter Lee case had dropped off the face of the earth. DOE management ignored the case and all its implications.

Further proof of the labs' disregard for security came in late August 1997, when a security official uncovered indications that arms controllers at Livermore were putting Top Secret intelligence information on computer servers cleared only up to the Secret level and then sending this information around the country. We in the intelligence shop had suspected that the labs were doing this, but had been blocked many times from inspecting these systems. What was so infuriating about this was that instead of just admitting what they had done, taking a security slap on the wrist and moving on, all of the senior officials involved acted like little kids caught with their hands in the cookie jar. Livermore's response was "who, me? not me"; and the senior DOE officials in charge of this program claimed no knowledge, even though we had uncovered memos detailing conversations among them about this compromise some six months earlier. Livermore even tried to go around DOE Headquarters and appeal to the National Security Agency for retroactive authority to do what they had done. Once this came to the attention of senior officials at Fort Meade, Livermore was left out to dry. I think this all finally got fixed, but the question remains: who could trust the labs?

The last significant event of the year involved the Department of Defense. In August we had discussed Kindred Spirit with Secretary Cohen, but it took a while for Defense to grasp the implications of what we had told him. Defense is a major customer for many of the labs' products in addition to nuclear weapons. Sensor technologies, computers, and non-nuclear high explosives are just some of the labs' products that feed into the Pentagon's military requirements. It was only a matter of time until Cohen's deputy John Hamre and others would want to know if their investments were safe.

Through late fall 1997 and into 1998, I met with a series of defense officials. On several occasions, I was paired up with other DOE Security officials, especially Ed McCallum, then head of Security's Office of Safeguards and Security. He was a former Army Green Beret and had quite a reputation for his temper. He was responsible for the "guards, gates and guns" part of DOE's security program as well as computer security. Needless to say, he was having no more success than I was trying to make DOE do the right thing. Taken together, the message we were conveying should have been shocking. Not only was DOE vulnerable to foreign intelligence services, but DOE physical security and especially computer security were equally bad.

McCallum was just then uncovering evidence that a lab scientist had placed sections of the "Green Book," a classified report on the DOE Stockpile Stewardship and Management Plan, on an unclassified network server and sent these sections out by unclassified e-mail. Its editor at Los Alamos (where else?) sent sections of the classified version around the country via the Internet. Federal security officials later told reporters that "every warhead in the current inventory is described in the Green Book" and "By definition, every warhead is compromised when it is put on an unclassified system, made accessible whenever it switches through different servers over the Internet and is then backed up."[46]

When I first heard McCallum's brief about security, I was amazed, and I believe he had the same feeling when he heard my Kindred Spirit brief. Baker had kept us away from McCallum and at one point Moler "ordered" Bloodsworth to have no dealings with McCallum. Now I knew why. The DOD officials looked stunned when McCallum finished.

We were called back several times, meeting mostly inside a part of the inner reaches of the Pentagon that belong to the Joint Chiefs of Staff. Finally, Deputy Defense Secretary Hamre came down and listened to the whole story. He and the other DOD officials were hopping mad that DOE had told them nothing about any of this. During one discussion about Chinese nationals working at the labs, Hamre exploded: "Someone please tell my why there are goddamned Chinese commies coming into our national labs!"

SIX

The Truth Comes Out

[DOE is] a large organization saturated with cynicism, an arrogant disregard for authority, and a staggering pattern of denial. For instance, even after President Clinton issued a Presidential Decision Directive *ordering* that the Department make fundamental changes in security procedures, compliance by Department bureaucrats was grudging and belated.
—PFIAB Report, 1999

The year 1998 will always be remembered as one in which a sitting President was impeached. As the impeachment proceedings were unfolding in the House, however, the Cox Committee was taking testimony on yet another scandal in another part of the Capitol. I suspect many Washington politicians in both parties are glad that Monica Lewinsky was the focus of attention and not the PRC's efforts to penetrate America's centers of defense science and technology and the American political process.

For the most part, however, I will always remember 1998 as yet another year of lost opportunities. On February 11, President Clinton ordered the secretary of energy to reform and restructure counterintelligence within the Department of Energy and the national labs. Presidential Decision Directive 61 stressed the importance of the department's "stewardship of vital national security capabilities, from nuclear weapons to leading edge research and development projects" and directed Federico Pena to implement an "effective and coordinated counterintelligence program" to protect these capabilities.[1] That such an order would have to be issued to a cabinet officer is a clear indication that DOE could not manage its own affairs. Finally, the administration had come to grips with the threat to the national labs and established clear lines of authority, accountability, reporting and oversight from the national counterintelligence community. But it would be another year before any of this would be implemented.

Betsy Moler and Rose Gottemoeller had managed to get all references to security pulled out of the final draft of PDD 61. A 1999 government report summed up their actions as follows:

> That there were disagreements over various issues is not surprising; that the DOE bureaucracy dug in its heels so deeply in resisting clearly needed reform is very disturbing. In fact, we believe that the NACIPB (National CI Policy Board), created by PDD in 1994, was a critical factor in ram-rodding the PDD through to signature. Before 1994, there was no real structure or effective process for handling these kinds of issues in a methodical way. Had the new structure not been in place and working, we doubt if the PDD would have made it.[2]

Ed Curran, a senior FBI counterintelligence expert, finally showed up at the Energy Department to head up the new counterintelligence office on April 1, 1998. I breathed a huge sigh of relief on that April Fool's Day. All the CI headaches, the petty personnel bickering and the dealings with recalcitrant lab managers were now Curran's responsibilities. He had just finished a tour at CIA, where he had led the efforts to catch yet another CIA officer spying for the Russians in 1996. Curran's first task was to do a study of counterintelligence at the labs, so he promptly set off on a ninety-day project, mostly by updating the previous work done by the FBI and making some lab visits. His finding: "DOE CI didn't meet even minimal standards." That was a sort of dog-bites-man story to us, but Curran thought it was a big deal. He submitted his report on July 1, at which point Moler decided she needed to study it some more. The report languished, buried in Under Secretary Ernie Moniz's office until December. A final implementation plan for counterintelligence reform wouldn't go to the labs until nearly a year after Curran reported to DOE for duty. Obviously, nobody in a leadership position at Energy was too concerned about all this. I guess Sandy Berger and the NSC basically forgot about it. They did have a lot on their minds then, what with the White House scandals.

Back in August 1997, after our second meeting with Berger, I had recommended several times that we return to Congress to provide an update on Kindred Spirit. Moler turned that idea down flat; in her opinion, we had fulfilled our reporting obligations in 1996. We didn't know at the time that the FBI was providing regular updates to the congressional intelligence oversight committees. Later these updates were said to number nineteen in total. Based on what I had seen of the FBI's oversight reporting, I'm sure the information they provided Congress was the bare minimum. Secretary Pena was said to have wanted to go to Congress with this new information, but Moler talked him out of it. Moler and the White House were calling the shots on Kindred Spirit.

One important aspect of the mandated reforms, however, was the necessity of asking Congress for more money. New people were to be added to the CI staff and more money was needed to support expanded CI programs at the labs. Congress wasn't about to just give us the money without some explanation, and since Curran wasn't up to speed on the background or rationale for additional funding, I was volunteered to lead the charge.

We met with congressional staffers soon after the PDD was signed by President Clinton and explained the background of the new requirements. Of course, Moler forbade me even to breathe the words "Kindred Spirit," so I talked about the foreign visitors and the emerging foreign intelligence threats to the labs. There were some skeptics, to be sure, but most of the staff went along with our requests.

By midsummer of 1998, however, Betsy Moler was having more trouble holding the line against returning to Congress to discuss Kindred Spirit. By this time, Pena had resigned and was on his way back to Denver. Moler was now acting secretary of energy.

In early July, a House Intelligence Committee staffer, Kathy Eberwein, called me and said the new committee chairman wanted to get an update on "Kindred Spirit." The committee was deliberating on the Intelligence Community budget authorization, and Porter Goss (R-FL), the new chairman, wanted to talk to us about our new CI program. Moler had designated Paul Richenbach as her action officer on this stuff, so I called him to give him a heads-up on Goss's request. He replied that he would get back to me, but he never did. Eberwein called again, and yet again. Both times I had to put her off by saying that the request was under consideration on the seventh floor, where Moler's office was located.

At almost exactly the same time, Assistant Secretary Vic Reis had tipped off one of Senator Pete Domenici's aides that we were hiding a secret that Domenici needed to know. DCI George Tenet was also openly wondering why DOE hadn't told Domenici, who had always been its patron saint. The aide, a young man named Alex Flynt, summoned me to his office the next day to tell him all about Kindred Spirit. "Whoa, this whole business has to be approved by Moler," I told him. So he promptly called her; I ran upstairs to give her a warning, but Flynt was already on the phone pressing her to approve his request. Moler was adamant: "No briefing, no way." She hung up saying, "I can't believe that I just told Pete Domenici no." Neither could I.

On top of all this, Defense Department officials were becoming restive about developments at Energy. Three senior Defense officials —Deputy Secretary John Hamre, Under Secretary for Acquisition Jacques Gansler, and Assistant Secretary Art Money—had "invited" Moler to the Pentagon to discuss Kindred Spirit.

Now, I wasn't a very good bureaucrat, as I didn't fastidiously document everything I did in "memos for the record." I had never before written a memo about briefing requests from Congress, but then DOE had never before turned down such a request. I had a bad feeling about this one. So I wrote up a memo documenting the requests we had received from Porter Goss in the House and from Senator Domenici. In it, I memorialized for Moler the requests from the House Committee on Intelligence and also from Alex Flynt for the Kindred Spirit briefing. Under the heading "Policy Impact," I wrote:

> **Potentially significant.** Any resulting Committees' concerns, how-ever, could be addressed by a status report on DOE's implemen-tation of PDD/NSC 61. Similarly, DOD is interested in DOE's plans and programs for safeguarding DOD equities in the National Lab-oratory complex.

In short, I thought that complying with the Hill's requests would enable us to manage any fallout. We could say, "Yes, we have a problem, but we're on top of it and here's what we're doing about it." Plus, we had been to Congress already in 1996, so no one could allege that we were holding out on the Hill.

I addressed the memo to Moler, and sent a copy to Ernie Moniz, the new under secretary. I had my executive assistant walk it upstairs and hand it directly to Richenbach. She later recalled that she had delivered a copy to Moniz's office and one to Moler's secretary, and had personally handed a copy to Richenbach. Still nothing happened. Betsy was ignoring Congress and me. (When Moler left the department in late 1998, the memo was found in her office safe.)

So I thought I would give it one more shot. By that time, we were in the middle of budget deliberations for fiscal year 1999. One of the final meetings to decide on future priorities was held in one of the big DOE conference rooms on the eighth floor of another wing of the Energy building. With Moler presiding, all the department's program managers were there, including the Navy admiral who ran Naval Reactors. (DOE shared responsibility with DOD for the construction and maintenance of the nuclear reactors that power our submarines and surface fighting ships.) In the course of the discussion, the admiral, resplendent in his summer white uniform, made his case for his budget requirements. He said something about having eighty or so operational ships and submarines deployed worldwide that depended upon DOE/Naval Reactors for support. Moler pulled herself up in her chair and said in an imperial tone that the admiral's requirements were neither more nor less important than anyone else's in the room. The other programs funded windmills and research on more efficient refrigerators, and Moler thought these were as important as the reactors powering our naval ships at sea? I cringed, and the admiral's face reddened with anger.

So maybe this wasn't the best time to remind her of Congress's briefing requests. But I did anyway. During a break, I asked for a private moment with Moler and Richenbach. I restated the Hill's request. She paused, looked at Richenbach, and said, "They only want to hurt the President on his China policy." No briefings. Betsy was no foreign policy expert, so she must have been under orders from Sandy Berger and the National Security Council to prevent Congress from learning any more than it already knew about Kindred Spirit. Berger and the White House were still trying to sell Congress on the Comprehensive Test Ban Treaty, and Congress was also taking up the annual Most Favored Nation trading debate about China. Republicans on Capitol Hill were becoming more critical of the administration's overall policies on China, and news about Chinese nuclear espionage would surely add more fuel to that fire.

There was to be one more instance in which Moler stopped Congress from learning about Kindred Spirit and the CI problems at the labs. This occurred in October 1998, just before she left the department for good. Congressman Duncan Hunter, the chair of the Military Procurement Subcommittee of the House Armed Services Committee, obviously smelled a rat in our reorganization plans and budget requests. Not surprisingly, he wanted to know what was going on. Hunter is a real defense hawk and has no patience with those who favor moderation, as the Clinton administration did, in dealing with Russia or China.

One day I got a call from one of our Congressional Affairs representatives, who told me that Hunter wanted to hold a session on DOE's counterintelligence budget request. He later sent me an e-mail confirming this and expanding on the request. In brief, Hunter wanted to know about the events that had led up to PDD 61. Nothing could have been clearer, but my quandary was twofold. First, Moler's gag order on Kindred Spirit was still in place. Second, I would be telling Hunter before I had reported to my own oversight committee, the House Permanent Select Committee on Intelligence, and its chairman, Porter Goss. I silently cursed Moler for putting me in this position and proceeded to write up my testimony.

I had been giving testimony before Congress for about four years now. All of my testimony was given in closed session; in each case, I wrote out a prepared statement, usually classified, and then made an oral presentation that was condensed from the longer statement. I always submitted my draft to our Congressional Affairs Office for review and approval. They usually sent it over to the Office of Management and Budget, where Energy's budget expert then reviewed the testimony. In four years, I had never had a word in my testimony changed by anyone. I think that people on the Hill trusted me and knew that I never lied to them. If I couldn't answer a question, I would tell them I didn't know and promised to answer for the record.

This time around, my written testimony summarized the types of threats to the labs from foreign intelligence services, and I was able to provide several examples of successful penetrations of our defenses. These were well known around the counterintelligence community and wouldn't have surprised anyone. I included some of the earlier examples of PRC targeting, like the 1980s Livermore case and the Peter Lee case, but I avoided any mention of Kindred Spirit.

To my surprise, Moler sent my testimony over to the National Security Council for "review." It was none other than Gary Samore who did the review and then started spreading word around that now I was claiming that Russia and others were targeting the national labs. Who didn't know that? But I guess we weren't supposed to remind Congress about it.

Moler called down to the office and told me to remove all the material about foreign intelligence penetrations of the labs from my testimony. We argued over just what I was to cover. Moler thought that Congressman Hunter wanted to talk about the foreign visits and assignments program. Sure, that was the subject of an open session of the hearing, but I was to testify in a closed hearing afterwards. Behind closed doors, he wanted to know why exactly we were asking for more money. He wanted to know specifically about the foreign intelligence threat to the labs. But Moler insisted that I bowdlerize my testimony. Moler or Gottemoeller also sent the testimony over to the Central Intelligence Agency for a review. That too was a first. But when I talked to the CIA's congressional people, they said that CIA was glad somebody was finally telling Congress the truth about the mess at the Energy Department.

Meanwhile the clock was ticking. Congressman Hunter's staff assistant, Pete Berry, started calling my office wanting to know about the status of my written submission. The more we stalled, the more suspicious he became. These guys were not stupid. Anytime an agency is dragging its feet like this, their first assumption is that higher-ups are tinkering with testimony—and they are usually right. Moler was doing more than tinkering; she was censoring. I followed her instructions, but I also left in some of the information about the foreign intelligence threat. I forwarded a copy to Congressional Affairs and wondered how I would get through this session.

The day of the scheduled hearing arrived, October 6, 1998, and we all traipsed up to the Hill: Gottemoeller and Moler in her limo and the rest of us crowded into a van. Moler was an uninvited and unwanted guest at this hearing. Hunter opened by remarking on the fact that her presence had not been requested, and that only after her second or third request did he agree that she could appear. She wanted to testify in both the open and the closed sessions. In the open session, the committee heard from the GAO about its recent reporting on the DOE foreign visits program. Nothing really new came out—the GAO making the case that DOE was too lax in its security and the DOE types extolling the virtues of having foreign scientists at the labs.

The real fireworks were saved for the closed session. Hunter opened by saying that his staff had learned that Moler had edited my remarks and had removed the very material the committee had requested. I thought, uh-oh, I'm in big trouble now. I hadn't tipped them off, but Moler would never believe that. She offered some lame excuses about her "understanding" of what the committee had requested and then told Hunter that she was ready to tell him anything he wanted to hear.

So Hunter proceeded to march me through explicit accounts of known espionage activities at the labs. He would ask "what else?" and I would offer up another example. He wasn't going to get Kindred Spirit out of me, but unless he stopped asking "what else" I would either have to lie to him or tell him I couldn't discuss Kindred Spirit. At that point, I expected him to go off on us. But he stopped short of that. Leaving the hearing room, Richenbach expressed relief that at least Hunter hadn't gotten Kindred Spirit out of us. But I knew I had been too clever by half and this would come back to bite me at some point down the road. I hadn't exactly lied, but I certainly had not been forthcoming. I hated the position Moler had put me in and I hated the fact that I hadn't done the right thing.

IN ADDITION TO impeaching a President, the Republican-controlled Congress mandated the establishment of two important commissions to take testimony and make judgments about key issues of contention within the Intelligence Community in 1998. The first focused on the future ballistic missile threat to the United States and the second on the threat from the PRC.

The Clinton administration had used a National Intelligence Estimate, written earlier in the 1990s, to downplay the ballistic missile threat and justify a reduction in its support for defense against such threats. The National Intelligence Estimate had triggered an uproar on Capitol Hill and several hearings had already roasted the CIA and the administration for wishing away the ballistic missile threat. That estimate had ignored the likelihood that Russia or China would assist the rogue states in their development of long-range ballistic missiles, despite the clear evidence of Russian assistance to countries such as Iran. Former CIA directors, like Robert Gates from the first Bush administration, had publicly testified to the mistakes and errors of that estimate.

But now Congress wanted an authoritative panel to look at the whole question from scratch. Chaired by Donald Rumsfeld, a past and future secretary of defense, the commission was staffed by well-known defense experts of both liberal and conservative persuasions. Members included Richard Garwin, a famous nuclear physicist, the usual retired Air Force generals, and prominent "defense intellectuals" like Paul Wolfowitz, who would later become the number two man in the Bush Defense Department. The commission also looked at U.S. intelligence collection and analysis capabilities and issued its report in July 1998, shredding former Intelligence Community assessments of the ballistic missile threat and concluding that the threat was real, that the IC had underestimated the scope and pace of ballistic missile developments, and that the Community was losing its capability to keep up with these developments. The Rumsfeld report was hard-hitting and the panel was unanimous in its findings, itself a remarkable feat and probably testimony to the panel's astonishment at just how badly the Intelligence Community had botched its earlier estimates.

At some point, one of the lab guys was called upon to give a presentation to the commission on some new PRC command-and-control developments. The presentation was only semicoherent, so I had to jump in to help out. In so doing, I had to make some observations about PRC nuclear weapons developments. It just so happened that Rich Haver, from our 1997 Senior Advisory Group, was also on this commission. I don't know if he told Rumsfeld anything about this, but they had obtained authority from the CIA director to see "everything," including DOE's big secret about the PRC's penetration of the labs. There are no references to Kindred Spirit in the commission's final report, but I later heard that Rumsfeld himself had gone to Newt Gringrich, then Speaker of the House, and told him about the issue. I always wondered if that was the origin of our summons to the Cox Committee, headed by Congressman Chris Cox (R-CA).[3]

I first heard about the Cox Committee in midsummer 1998. Officially titled "Select Committee on U.S. National Security and Military/Commercial Concerns with the People's Republic of China," it was mandated to review the performance of the U.S. government in protecting defense technologies and information or permitting their transfer to the PRC. Among the ten items the committee was to look at was the subject of PRC campaign financing and influence peddling: "Any effort by the Government of the People's Republic of China or any other person or entity to influence any of the foregoing matters through political contributions, commercial arrangements, or bribery, influence-peddling, or other illegal activities."[4]

I assumed when I read this that the Cox Committee was the outgrowth of reporting by the *New York Times* on the transfer of missile technologies and expertise to the PRC by Hughes, Loral and other U.S. corporations. This reporting had noted the coincidence of major campaign contributions by the chairman of Loral and the Clinton administration's subsequent relaxation of export control policies on satellites, which just happened to be manufactured by Loral and Hughes. But the way I read the charter, the committee would have license to look at Kindred Spirit as well. I wondered how Moler was going to block the Cox Committee from hearing about the FBI's Kindred Spirit investigation.

But she wouldn't get to make the call. Despite all she had done to help the White House by keeping Kindred Spirit under close wraps, away from the Republican-controlled Congress, and placating the labs by completely thwarting any security reforms and slow-rolling CI improvements, we heard in midsummer that Betsy would not be replacing Pena. Instead, United Nations ambassador and former New Mexico congressman Bill Richardson would be the new DOE secretary. One of Richardson's closest associates told people that Richardson thought he had a good shot at the Vice President slot on the Gore ticket. He had made a deal with John Podesta, then Clinton's White House chief of staff, to deliver the Hispanic vote in return for a place on the ticket. In order to make the Hispanic vote come over to Gore, he needed a cabinet position with plenty of domestic travel and an opportunity to disburse lots of money to constituents around the country. What better place to travel widely and spread cash around than DOE?

Richardson brought his own people with him, including a CIA officer named Larry Sanchez as the new director of intelligence. Richardson offered me the position of deputy director and asked me to run the office until Sanchez showed up. One thing was very clear from our early conversations: neither Richardson nor Sanchez knew anything about Kindred Spirit. Both walked in completely blind to what had been going on at DOE for the past four years and to the security problems that stretched back two decades or more. I think Sanchez was shocked when I first told him about Kindred Spirit, but to his credit he didn't try to sweep it under the rug. Likewise, my early dealings with Richardson were generally positive. Being a former congressman, he knew better than to try to withhold information from the Hill. So, generally, I figured that now we were free of Moler's gag order and could be more forthcoming in our presentations to Congress.

We had already made one appearance before the Cox Committee. In early September, we had been called to give new testimony on the PRC and supercomputers. Supercomputers were one of the thorniest issues in the whole Clinton administration overhaul of export control policies. Many on the Hill suspected that the White House had promised Silicon Valley producers of high performance computers greater access to international markets in return for campaign contributions. Whatever the case, restrictions on the export of such computers were considerably relaxed during the Clinton years. But this decision was not without its opponents even within this administration.

The issue first came to my attention in 1995, when IBM and perhaps one other computer maker had proposed the sale of high-performance computers to Russia, supposedly for weather and banking applications. The weather applications were suspect, given the similarities between the computer models used for atmospheric and climate change and those used to model nuclear detonations. So the DOE export control shop recommended against the sale. But I was contacted by officials from the National Security Agency to set up a meeting with Charlie Curtis on this topic. At the meeting, they made a pitch for DOE's support of the sale. Their rationale was that the supercomputer business in the United States was dying and international sales would help sustain this industry, so crucial to the future of the National Security Agency and the U.S. nuclear weapons program. And there were also proponents of the sale within DOE. Some believed that if the United States was serious about a "strategic partnership" with Russia, why not sell them these computers? Others recommended that the sale be made to help secure Russia's support for a Comprehensive Test Ban Treaty. And these arguments made some sense, I thought. We had learned quite a lot about the Russian nuclear weapons program in recent years. The program was sophisticated and well advanced. The Russians had taken a different path of development than the United States, but Russian warheads worked.[5]

We doubted that the Russians would bother to use the computers to produce more advanced nuclear warheads. Still, there were other military applications for these computers, like designing stealth applications for aircraft or advanced supersonic missiles, that most people agreed should make the sales to Russia off limits.

The Russians were unhappy, to say the least. It's clear that they had been promised by somebody in the Clinton administration that these sales would go through, and now we were stiffing them. Inevitably, of course, the Russians managed to purchase at least two high-performance computers from Silicon Graphics for use at one of their nuclear weapons labs. The Russians then bragged about their end run around U.S. export controls, which created a mini firestorm within the government and on Capitol Hill. (Silicon Graphics claimed that it didn't know the Russian nuclear weapons labs worked on nuclear weapons!) DOE Intelligence got dragged into this by the House Armed Services Committee (HASC), which tasked DOE and the Defense Intelligence Agency to do assessments of "the risks to U.S. national security resulting from previous exports of U.S. supercomputers."[6] After the usual internal DOE tussles over turf, the committee directed that it had intended DOE Intelligence to do this assessment. This meant that we needed access to records of such sales so we could do some concrete analysis instead of just waving our arms.

Trying to get this type of information out of the Commerce Department or DOE's export control shop was harder than stealing gold from Fort Knox. The Commerce Department and DOE made a big deal of protecting industry proprietary data, that is, information about sales and technical specifications of the exported computers. What did they think we were going to do with this data, make a killing on the stock market? We went back to the Armed Services Committee with the message that we couldn't do the study if Commerce didn't pony up the data. That initiated an exchange of threats between Congress, Commerce and DOE. Finally, we got some but not all of the data we needed. I gave the assignment to Tom Cook from Los Alamos, who put together a classified study for the Hill that we coordinated through all the key players within the Intelligence Community. The conclusions of this study were later declassified and published by the HASC; they also show up in the Cox Report. Tom's bottom line was that the impact of high-performance computer acquisition was driven by the complexity of the nuclear designs under development and the availability of high-quality, relevant nuclear test data. Of all the so-called Tier III countries, China stood to benefit most from such acquisitions. (Tier III countries included Russia, Israel, India and Pakistan in addition to China.) We were allowed to publish our bottom line in an unclassified paper that we issued in May 1998. We judged that "the PRC's acquisition and application of HPCs to nuclear weapons development have the greatest potential impact on the PRC's nuclear program."[7]

Tom made his case in an unclassified paper he wrote in December 1998: China had a modest number of nuclear weapons tests for its earlier warhead designs. Later, more advanced Chinese nuclear warhead designs had the benefit of only a limited number of tests and none of these had been conducted under material-aging conditions. This meant that the PRC had leapfrogged through warhead design classes and that computer-aided modeling could help them fill gaps in their understanding of the science underlying these new designs. High-performance computing power mattered since it could reduce the time required to run calculations and produce results that would more closely resemble actual practice. Of course, the Chinese would also need access to vast amounts of nuclear test data in order to refine their computer models and bring these closer to actual performance experience. The brilliance of Tom Cook came in his ability to present a very complex subject in terms even a layman could understand.

In congressional testimony in early 1997, Commerce officials revealed that in a little over a year, from January 1996 to March 1997, the PRC had acquired forty-six U.S. supercomputers. I remember clearly the expression of shock on the faces of the members and even other witnesses in the hearing room. Forty-six in a year! By May of 1999, that number had jumped to 603 high-performance computers.[8]

So it came as no surprise when the Cox Committee summoned us to testify on China's acquisitions of HPCs. The session was closed and attendance from the members was good. I recall Congressmen Chris Cox, Porter Goss and Curt Weldon from the Republican side and maybe John Spratt from the Democrats. I had prior experience with Goss, Weldon and Spratt, but I didn't know Cox or the others present. Cox was from California, had served in the Reagan White House, was the vice chairman of the House Commerce Committee, and was known to be very ambitious. The Commerce Committee gave him his entrée into this subject, since export controls are within that committee's jurisdiction. Tom did a great job explaining the complexities of the issue and why we thought the PRC would stand to benefit the most. The Cox Committee followed faithfully the outlines of Tom's presentation in its unclassified version of its report, published in May 1999.

I wondered how long it would be before the other shoe dropped and the committee came back to DOE for more information on the PRC's "new" nuclear warhead designs and how they'd made these technical breakthroughs. Sure enough, we were summoned once again to come up to Capitol Hill to discuss PRC nuclear weapons development. Our first time at bat was on November 12 in a conference room in the Cannon House Office Building on Capitol Hill. This meeting was to be for staff members of the Cox Committee, both Republican and Democrat. The administration was clearly growing uneasy, however, and we held meetings at CIA on November 9 and also with Secretary Richardson's people to go over our presentations.

The CIA was trying to orchestrate the presentations and clearly would have preferred that Larry Sanchez do all the talking. To his credit, Sanchez would have no part of that, being barely up to speed on even the basics of his new responsibilities. So a CIA analyst would give an overview of the history of the PRC nuclear weapons program and existing capabilities, and I would discuss the work we had done over the past four years on where we thought the PRC program was going, based on data it had acquired from U.S. sources. I would not, under any circumstances, discuss the FBI's Kindred Spirit case or any other aspects of espionage. The FBI would cover that subject in its own testimony to the committee.

At the first meeting, the room was filled with relatively young people, as most congressional staffers are. There were a few older guys in attendance, including Rep. Cox's chief of staff, Dean McGrath. I would see quite a lot of him later on. The CIA had several "back benchers," and I brought a number of lab scientists with me, including Los Alamos scientists Tom Cook and Carl Henry. The FBI was also present and gave an overview of all their ongoing investigations into PRC targeting of the DOE national labs, plus some other cases. I think the combined effect of my remarks and the FBI's presentation rocked the staffers and even the CIA types. They were in a big hurry to get out of the room, probably to get back to report the bad news to their management.

A few weeks passed and then we were called up to make a presentation to the full committee. The meeting was held on December 7. It was to be a Pearl Harbor for both Wen Ho Lee and me.

THE HEARING WAS HELD in a conference room off a main corridor leading into the Capitol Dome. As usual, the members were sitting up on an elevated dais looking down at us. The room itself was very ornate, with lots of wood and old pictures of former congressmen hanging on the walls. The attendance was fairly good: Cox, Goss, Weldon, Doug Bereuter from the Republican side, and Bobby Scott, Lucille Roybal-Allard and Norm Dicks from the Democrats. Dicks was a former chairman of the House Permanent Select Committee on Intelligence and was known both for being a straight shooter and for his volatility.

CIA led off, basically following the script that Gary Samore had laid out for them the preceding summer: what an impressive program the PRC had developed, how quickly they had made major advances, and so forth. For all that, however, the agency analyst then had to explain why the PRC nuclear program had slowed down so dramatically in the 1970s during Mao's Cultural Revolution and why the PRC lagged behind the rest of the nuclear states so badly. She fumbled through all that, and then it was my turn.

I won't say that the members were inattentive at first, just that I don't think Dicks or some of the others were prepared for what they were about to hear. My presentation was classified, but most of it was later declassified and published as Chapter 2 of Volume I of the unclassified Cox Report issued in May 1999, so I am allowed to speak about it here. I told them about the W88 and the type of classified information on the other six U.S. warheads that we had found in the PRC walk-in document; how the Chinese were using this data to develop smaller, modern thermonuclear warheads for their new mobile ballistic missiles; the Chinese acquisition of U.S. neutron bomb data; and the payoff to the Chinese strategic nuclear deterrent from all this.

As the final report shows, at no time did I tell the committee that the Chinese had "copied" the W88 warhead. The unclassified report is laced with my reservations about the PRC's application of stolen design information to its new generation of warheads. For example, I told the committee that "the PRC will exploit elements of the stolen U.S. design information for the development of the PRC's new generation strategic thermonuclear warheads."[9] And, "While the PRC might not reproduce exact replicas of these U.S. thermonuclear warheads, elements of the PRC's devices could be similar."[10] But I think the most important message was the warning I conveyed to the committee about the importance of protecting our "legacy codes."

> Given the limited number of nuclear tests that the PRC has conducted, the PRC likely needs additional empirical information about advanced thermonuclear weapon performance that it could obtain by stealing the U.S. "legacy" computer codes, such as those that were used by the Los Alamos National Laboratory to design the W-88 Trident D-5 warhead. The PRC may also need information about dynamic three-dimensional data on warhead packaging, primary and secondary coupling, and the chemical interactions of materials inside the warhead over time.

The Select Committee is concerned [reflecting my own fears] that no procedures are in place that would either prevent or detect the movement of classified information, including classified nuclear weapons design information or computer codes, to unclassified sections of the computer systems at U.S. national weapons laboratories.[11]

I think it's fair to say that the more I talked, the more agitated the members became, especially Norm Dicks. His face got redder and redder and it was clear that he was hearing all this for the first time. He took notes furiously and finally he stopped me.

"Did I just hear you say this?" he asked, and then read back portions of my testimony.

"Yes, you did," I replied.

Dicks then turned to his colleagues and said, "Everybody in town knows how screwed up DOE is, but nobody thought it was this bad."

Dicks may have been putting on a show for his colleagues, because it turned out that he was already aware of the Wen Ho Lee case. In his capacity as ranking minority member of the House Permanent Select Committee on Intelligence, he had been briefed by the FBI on the case in July of that year.[12]

Ed Curran, our new counterintelligence director, was along for the ride but was not scheduled to speak before the committee. Dicks called him up to the front table and proceeded to rip into both of us. How could we let things get so bad, why hadn't we fixed all this, and on and on. Both Ed and I said words to the effect that "Hey, we just got here, this stuff's been going on for years." Dicks was apoplectic and yelling at us that he was going to call his buddy Bill (Secretary Richardson) as soon as the hearing was over and get some answers. He would set Richardson straight on just what his priorities at DOE should be. As I recall, the FBI then testified about their investigations of DOE espionage cases, specifically, Livermore and Peter Lee. When they turned to Kindred Spirit, they had to acknowledge how little progress had been made on that case and that the suspect was still in place accessing classified information. Of course, they told the committee that Director Freeh had warned DOE in 1997 to remove the suspect's access to classified information and, of course, DOE hadn't complied. That set Dicks off again, and in the ensuing discussion, the FBI mentioned that the suspect was currently traveling in Taiwan.

I could tell from the look on Ed Curran's face that he didn't know about this. I certainly didn't, but now I was out of that loop. Ed was furious, to say the least. The lab had double-crossed DOE Headquarters again by not telling us about Lee's foreign travel.

Now Dicks was really on the warpath and he had company. He may have been miffed at being misled by the FBI; section chief Steve Dillard had told Dicks that the FBI had no indication that Wen Ho Lee had made any unauthorized disclosures of classified information and that Lee was involved in "maintenance activities" in support of the lab's Stockpile Stewardship program. How the FBI knew that Lee had made no unauthorized disclosures is unclear, given that the Bureau had no surveillance—technical or otherwise—on him. The FBI had yet to polygraph him or even conduct an interview of his colleagues. Perhaps Dicks realized at this point that the FBI had been too glib in its reassurances to him.

The Republicans mostly just sat back and watched the fireworks. Rep. Goss said he knew about this and mentioned that his efforts to learn more during the previous summer had been thwarted by DOE. The hearing finally wrapped up and Sanchez pronounced himself satisfied with my presentation.

Back at the department, Curran and Sanchez beat a path up to Richardson's office to give him the bad news. They both understood that they had a first-class problem on their hands. An FBI espionage suspect had been allowed to remain in place and not lose access to classified nuclear weapons information for nearly two and a half years. The FBI had next to nothing to show for its efforts, but the heat was going to be on DOE and Secretary Richardson for not protecting its secrets. Further, Ed Curran's ninety-day study was still languishing in the Office of the Secretary. Almost a year had passed since the PDD had been signed and little of what it mandated had actually been accomplished. On top of that, I had just laid out everything we had learned over the past four years about PRC targeting and acquisition of U.S. nuclear weapons information. This was the first time that such a presentation had been given to Congress, even though it should have been done three years earlier. The members of the Cox Committee now knew about Moler's successful efforts to block Congress from learning these facts. In short, Richardson had a real mess on his hands—none of it of his own making.

The first thing he had to do was get Curran's report out of deep freeze and ship it over to the national security advisor, Sandy Berger, as the PDD mandated. We were regaled with firsthand observations of how Richardson's assistants had to scurry all over the Office of the Secretary, which includes a number of suites and smaller offices, looking for the report. They finally found it buried in Ernie Moniz's in-box, pulled it out and ran it into Richardson's office. He signed and had it delivered over to the White House. When Rep. Dicks did call, Richardson told him that Ed's report had gone over to the White House a long time ago and they were getting ready to implement all the recommendations. I guess Dicks believed him.

Then discussion in the secretary's office turned to what to do about Wen Ho Lee. He was indeed in Taiwan and not slated to come back until late in the third week of December. What he was doing there and who authorized the trip was the subject of many phone calls to Los Alamos and considerable blue language from Curran.

Worse yet, this was Lee's second trip to Taiwan that year. He had traveled there in March 1998, and had obtained lab approval for that trip, but the lab didn't bother to inform our counterintelligence office in Washington or the FBI, at least until Lee was long gone. At this point, Lee had been under investigation for over two years; his supervisors in X Division knew he was under investigation and yet approved his travel abroad in March. We then learned that the lab had turned down his request to travel to Taiwan in December, allegedly to visit an ailing relative, with his airfare paid by a company named Asiatek in return for a presentation he was to make there.[13] Despite the lab's denial of authorization, Lee went anyway. It turned out that he was working on a consulting agreement with the Chung Shan Institute of Science and Technology in Taiwan and was paid about $5,000, which he deposited in a bank account in Taiwan.[14] None of this was reported to the lab. Chung Shan does defense research.[15] That Los Alamos would allow this to happen without telling Ed Curran, let alone getting his authorization, should have persuaded any skeptics once and for all that the lab just didn't take security seriously.

After the committee hearing, Curran and Sanchez questioned me closely about DOE's meetings with Freeh and the "advice" Freeh had given us about Lee. They both knew the FBI would be the first to tell the world that it had recommended that DOE take away his access but we had failed to follow Director Freeh's advice. Of course, they were right.

I think it was during this period that Curran came up with the idea to polygraph Wen Ho Lee on his return from Taiwan before the end of the year. I suspect the strategy was based on the assumption that he would fail or at least show deception, and then this result could be used to jerk his clearances and get him out of X Division. But they had to wait until he got back from Taiwan.

To make this even worse, Curran told me in mid-December that the FBI had run a sting operation against Wen Ho Lee.[16] I was surprised, because Freeh had led us to believe that the FBI had no further investigative interest in Dr. Lee, but FBI section chief Dillard hadn't bothered to tell us about it.

In fact, however, late in 1997, after Freeh's recommendation to remove Lee's clearances, FBI Headquarters sent a fifteen-step plan to Albuquerque to reinvigorate the Lee investigation. The plan directed local FBI officials to take the following investigative steps:

- Conduct Additional Interviews
  - Open inquiries on other individuals named in the DOE AI who met critical criteria.
  - Develop information on associate's background and interview the associate.
  - Interview co-workers, supervisors and neighbors.
- Conduct Physical Surveillance
- Conduct Other Investigative Techniques
  - Review information resulting from other investigative methods.
  - Review other investigations for lead purposes.
  - Implement alternative investigative methods.[17]

But the Albuquerque FBI office "almost completely ignored" the plan.[18] In fact, the local agents tried only two of Headquarters' recommendations, and it took nearly eight months for the FBI to put together the sting operation.[19]

In August 1998, an FBI agent called Lee from a location in Santa Fe, about twenty-five miles down the hill from Los Alamos.[20] The agent posed as an officer from the Ministry of Foreign Affairs and the Ministry of State Security, China's main intelligence organization. He asked Lee if there had been any repercussions for him as a result of the Peter Lee case. Wen Ho Lee agreed to meet the agent, but then called back to cancel. The agent called Lee twice— on August 18 and 19—and Lee took a pager number where he could contact the agent in the future and the name of his Santa Fe hotel, should Lee change his mind.

> The [undercover agent] then told Dr. Lee that one of the reasons he wanted to meet was to see if there was any material to take back to the PRC. After Dr. Lee said there was not any such material, the [undercover agent] said that since the material he brought back to China and the speech he gave were so helpful, did Lee have any plans in going to the PRC in the near future. Dr. Lee said that he would probably not be going to the PRC until after his retirement from LANL in one or two years. He did not, as one would expect, deny that he had previously sent material.[21]

Lee did not report this to security, but his wife, Sylvia, made a number of phone calls to the wives of lab scientists asking whether their husbands had been contacted. Lab CI officers had been alerted and gave Lee every opportunity to report the contact. When they finally questioned him about it, Lee failed to disclose the substance of the conversation or that the agent had given him a beeper number and named a hotel in Santa Fe for a proposed meeting. Lee said he had "intended" to report this contact, but hadn't gotten around to it yet.

The objectives of the operation were to "show that they [the Lees] are agents of a foreign power" and that they are "currently engaged in clandestine intelligence activity."[22] The operation was poorly planned and poorly executed, to say nothing of the fact that the FBI agent who contacted Wen Ho Lee spoke Cantonese rather than Mandarin.[23] Lee spoke Mandarin, which is the official language of the Chinese ministries, so he may have been suspicious from the outset. Although the main objectives were not fulfilled, the FBI nevertheless claimed to have developed about seven additional items of incriminating material against Lee. Further, Lee's failure to report the incident to Los Alamos counterintelligence officials and then his lack of candor when he finally did make a report enabled FBI officials to conclude that the operation had not been a total bust.[24]

As was now commonplace, however, the transcript of the sting operation was not fully analyzed for another three months, or about the time we were appearing before the Cox Committee in December. In fact, Curran thought the whole idea was dumb, doomed to fail, and especially poorly planned.[25] But the Bureau was still not ready to move on Wen Ho Lee.

The FBI also began to take seriously reports that Lee might be communicating surreptitiously with his Chinese handlers. One of Lee's neighbors had reported strange noises coming out of his telephone nearly four years earlier. Apparently, the neighbor suspected that signals coming from the Lees' TV satellite antenna were causing the interference. The FBI had dismissed the neighbor's reports, but now desperate, they had him keep a log of the interference. They could find no meaningful pattern.

The Headquarters' directive had also recommended trash covers and physical surveillance of Lee, steps that had proven very productive in the Aldrich Ames case; but FBI Albuquerque dismissed these recommendations as "impractical." Albuquerque also ignored about a dozen other suggestions from FBI Headquarters for additional action on the case, including setting up preliminary investigations on the other ten leads that we had provided the Bureau two years before.

AFTER THE GREAT UPHEAVAL at the first Cox Committee hearing on Pearl Harbor day, we got to do it all over again. This time we had the attention of the full committee, including Democrat John Spratt. The hearing, which was held on December 16, lasted all afternoon and into the evening. This date is infamous for another reason: that day President Clinton authorized the launch of cruise missiles against targets in Iraq, supposedly in retaliation for Iraq's barring of weapons inspections, but right in the middle of the House's impeachment deliberations. The House Judiciary Committee had already voted out the articles of impeachment and there was widespread speculation that Clinton was using the missile strikes to "wag the dog" and deflect attention from the House proceedings.

The other development of interest at about this time was the publication of a book titled *Year of the Rat*.[26] It provided details of PRC efforts to buy access to and influence in the Clinton White House. I had seen one of the authors on a popular C-SPAN show called *Washington Journal* and he had made some startling allegations about the role of PRC money in the Clinton administration.[27] I mentioned the book to one of Secretary Richardson's political appointees during a trip over to Capitol Hill; he just shook his head grimly and said something like "Just what we need." Scandals were beginning to pile up on top of scandals: Whitewater, Monica, Chinese campaign financing, and now Kindred Spirit.

Between our first appearance before the Cox Committee and the December 16 hearing, Chairman Cox had learned more about Wen Ho Lee and the Kindred Spirit case. The FBI China Section had a new chief named Chuck Middleton, and on December 11, he and unit chief "Jack Kerry" gave Cox a detailed briefing on the FBI's investigation. Cox asked questions about the difficulties the FBI was having in getting a warrant for technical surveillance on Lee. After the briefing was over, Middleton told his superiors back at the Bureau that Cox was "upset" with what he heard.[28] So now the FBI was beginning to feel the political heat coming off Capitol Hill as well.

At any rate, this hearing was memorable for going on and on as the CIA just kept digging a deeper and deeper hole for itself. The lead CIA analyst made assertion after assertion about PRC nuclear capabilities, mostly along the lines of "they can't do this, they can't do that." When challenged, she was unable to offer any intelligence evidence for these optimistic assertions. More than one congressman suggested the obvious: if we don't know, that should be our answer, not that they can't do something.

The truth was that there was much we didn't know. For more than a year, CIA had been holding what came to be known as "Hard Targets" working groups on China. Not once during that period had we been able to get any serious consideration of PRC nuclear production or warhead manufacturing facilities on the table. The agency was mesmerized by internal Chinese Communist Party politics and economic decision-making. At one meeting, I argued for an expansion of the group's focus and said that the Intelligence Community was letting its analytic and collection capabilities against PRC nuclear developments run down and nothing was being done to stop the bleeding. I was only echoing the Rumsfeld Commission's findings, but I was firmly told that this was not the place to air such complaints. I was never invited back again. Now the whole committee could see how deficient CIA's capabilities had become.

So was I the Cox Committee's star witness, as the *New York Times* would later claim? Certainly I was telling them things they had never heard before. None of the members were overly solicitous of me; after all, I was there representing a Democratic administration, even though intelligence is supposed to be apolitical. On the Democratic side, Rep. Scott and Rep. Roybal-Allard asked pretty good questions, despite their obvious lack of national security experience. The Republicans were rather subdued and mostly deferred to Rep. Dicks, who blasted away again, really letting us have it about DOE's sloppy security practices and inability to keep a secret.

But at this hearing, once again all testimony related to Wen Ho Lee and the FBI's investigation came from the FBI. Middleton and "Kerry" fielded all of the committee's questions. "Kerry" also testified about Lee's continued access to Los Alamos computer codes and nuclear secrets, and about DOE's failure to remove his access. This presentation undoubtedly spurred Curran to write Secretary Richardson about the need for immediate action on the Lee case.

Finally, there was a great deal of interest from the committee, particularly from Cox, on the question "who knew and when?" In particular, "when did Berger first tell President Clinton?" and who else in the administration knew and when? I didn't know, and no one else at the hearings could answer. At this hearing, Cox said that Berger had provided a written response to the committee saying that the President had not learned about PRC nuclear espionage until early 1998.[29] But later, as the media firestorm broke out, that was amended back to mid-1997 to make the administration look less naive. What's the truth? I would bet on February 1998.

That is when Clinton signed the PDD and Berger probably had to tell him why he was suddenly being asked to direct DOE to fix its counterintelligence program. This means, of course, that nearly three years had passed since suspicions of PRC nuclear espionage had been brought to the attention of the White House chief of staff, Leon Panetta, two years since we had told Berger the first time, and six months since DOE had told him the second time. Why did it take so long to inform the President about all this? Maybe he just didn't want to know. But I never understood how Panetta got off scot free from all the criticism Berger later endured. Except, of course, that Panetta was a former congressman from California, an ex-member of the club, and Berger was merely a Washington lawyer. Cox also asked us about briefings to the secretary of state and the secretary of commerce. And we had to tell him that DOE, at least, had briefed neither Warren Christopher nor Madeleine Albright nor the Commerce Department about any of this. The CIA officials present didn't know of any briefings either. (When we finally made the trip over to tell Secretary Albright about all this in 1999, after the *New York Times* articles about the Cox Report, she was not pleased to be hearing it for the first time. She looked around the room and asked some of the people who had been with Christopher, her predecessor, if they knew anything about it. They all shook their heads.)

NOW THAT ALL the testimony was in, Bill Richardson and DOE had a major disaster on their hands. My testimony to the Cox Committee revealed the scope and magnitude of PRC acquisition of our nuclear weapons secrets, and the FBI had told all about Director Freeh's warning to remove Wen Ho Lee from access to classified materials months earlier and about DOE's failure to follow his recommendation. The FBI, backed up by Ed Curran, had also revealed the low state of DOE counterintelligence and security, their recommendations for improvements made in 1997, and the fact that more than a year had passed and very little had been done to implement their plan. Curran told the commission that CI at DOE didn't even meet minimal standards: "There is not a counterintelligence program, nor has there been one at DOE for many, many years."[30]

The FBI also told the committee about the history of "problems" between itself and DOE:

> The FBI reportedly has sent several agents to the Department of Energy in the last 10 years to try to improve the counterintelligence program, but has repeatedly been unsuccessful. A significant

problem has been the lack of counterintelligence professionals, and a bureaucracy that "buried" them and left them without access to senior management or the Secretary of Energy.[31]

All in all, it was a devastating critique of DOE and its management of security and counterintelligence—stretching back over at least two decades.

Moreover, the committee immediately began to demand "documents" that verified my testimony. A document request ordering that DOE produce everything related to Kindred Spirit arrived at the department even before we got back there on the evening of December 16.

Richardson went over to the White House to tell John Podesta, Clinton's chief of staff, the bad news. Richardson had been busy calling Republican congressman trying to convince them not to vote for impeachment, but now he had his own problems. Podesta told him to slow roll all the document requests; the Cox Committee charter was due to run out by the end of December or in early January 1999, and DOE would just wait them out. These tactics had worked well for the administration before; why not now?

Over the previous four years, we had produced or compiled about 150 to 200 documents regarding Kindred Spirit. These were being held mostly by the lab scientists on detail to the intelligence shop in Washington. I pulled all these together and started making lists to respond to the Cox Committee's requests. Usually, requested documents, some highly classified, would go from my office to DOE's Office of Congressional Affairs. The OCA would take a quick look at the documents, then package them and deliver them to the appropriate location over on Capitol Hill. This time, the documents went out the front door of GA301, the Intelligence Office, but stopped and stayed in the OCA, on the DOE seventh floor. Many of these were later returned to the Intelligence Office after Richardson and company cleared the building in 2001, having never been forwarded to their destination.

We kept pushing the documents out the front door, but the Cox Committee kept complaining that it wasn't getting what it was asking for. Finally, Dean McGrath, the committee's staff director, called me and asked me to come up to meet with Rep. Cox. I was not to let anyone know about this meeting. We met in Cox's office off one of the corridors leading into the Capitol Dome. I think he thought I was withholding the documents, but I sketched out the process and told him I thought the documents were being held up on the seventh floor. And further, that the department had been told to "slow roll" the committee because the White House expected its charter to expire soon, and along with it the political threat that Cox represented. On the spot, Cox told McGrath to subpoena Richardson to show cause why he should not be held in contempt of Congress. The threat of a subpoena broke loose some, but by no means all of the requested documents.

But what to do about Wen Ho Lee? The FBI had told the Cox Committee all about DOE's handling of Lee and especially its failure to carry out Freeh's recommendations. Richardson was really in a bind now. He knew that if he didn't act, he would face unrelenting criticism, at least from Republicans in Congress and probably from the media. His game plan to get in the running as a possible vice presidential candidate depended on good press and favorable publicity. So he adopted the approach O'Leary had taken nearly three years earlier. Her theme had been, "It happened on their [the Republicans'] watch; we [the Democrats] are trying to fix it." Trying to sell that after the two years of bumbling and fumbling under Pena and Moler might be tough, but Richardson thought he could pull it off.

Besides, Ed Curran had a plan: as soon as Wen Ho Lee returned from Taiwan, polygraph him and then bust him out of X Division. That way, at least, he would no longer have access to nuclear secrets. It appears that Ed initially expected the FBI to do a confrontational interview with Lee upon his return on December 21, 1999. But the Albuquerque FBI agents begged off, claiming that they still weren't prepared to interview Lee after investigating him for nearly five years. It's likely that had Ed not forced the issue, Lee might still be working in X Division today while the FBI was still "planning its next steps."

The polygraph was scheduled for December 23 and administered by Wackenhut Security Systems, a private security firm on contract to the Energy Department.* I will never forget the look on

---

*In many espionage cases, the polygraph is the seminal event in the entire investigation. That the FBI allowed a private security firm to polygraph their only suspect in this critical espionage investigation is telling.

Ed's face when he walked into our office that afternoon and said that the word had come back from Los Alamos, where the polygraph had been administered, that Lee had passed with flying colors. My thoughts were only that the FBI had "wasted three years on this guy and now we were no closer to knowing the source of the W88 information in the walk-in document than we had been at the beginning.

DOE Security and Los Alamos started making plans to give Wen Ho Lee his security clearance back and let him return to his old X Division job. We heard that a letter of apology to Lee from Richardson was in preparation, although I don't think Richardson ever seriously considered it. But then things began to get weird. Suddenly Ed wasn't sure that Lee had actually passed the polygraph. The FBI wanted to see the raw results, but for some reason DOE's chief of security, Joe Mahaley, wouldn't let them have the transcripts.

So did Wen Ho Lee really pass the first DOE polygraph, given on December 23, 1998? His lawyers claim he did, DOE security says he did, and all his supporters in the media repeat these claims as gospel. What really happened on that wintry day?

First, documents revealed in the course of congressional hearings make it clear that Secretary Richardson wanted to remove Lee from his X Division post before the Cox Committee Report was published. For example, in October 2000, Senator Arlen Specter read into the Congressional Record the following information:

> . . . I refer first to an FBI document from Neil Gallagher which says "William Richardson, Secretary, Department of Energy, may call Director Freeh about this investigation on Monday, December 21, 1998. On December 17 and 18, DOE counterintelligence advised they wanted to try and neutralize their employee's access to classified information prior to the conclusion of the Cox Committee hearing this month"—and that's rubbed out and said, "prior to the" and written in "issuance of the final report by the Cox Committee."
>
> Then there's a deposition of ["Greg Smith"], FBI agent, which was taken in July 1999, which reads, in part, as follows from page 91, quote, "The Department of Energy was becoming more and more concerned about how they would appear and how they

were appearing during the committee meetings, and it was becoming very urgent for them to look like they were doing something.
Ergo, they decided 'on our own, we have to interrogate and interview Lee Wen Ho'—that's their articulation—'and we have to
jerk his clearance or his access and we expect the FBI—we're
begging the FBI, please resolve this investigation in the next 30
days or 60 days so we can fire this guy.' "

And on the next page, 92, quote, "There was a new Secretary
of Energy there who all of a sudden had a big need to show that
they were correcting all the problems, and if that meant immediately firing Lee Wen Ho, regardless of whatever the FBI was
doing, they were going to do it as soon as possible, so they were
taking their own action on this."[32]

From this, it is evident that Richardson already understood
the potential fallout from the Cox Committee and was moving hard
to get rid of his problem—Wen Ho Lee. And he wanted him out
before the Cox Report was issued. That way he could claim that he
had been on top of the espionage scandal as soon as he found out
about it; after all, he had only been on the job a few months.

The day after our last session with the Cox Committee on
December 16, R. P. Eddy, one of Bill Richardson's special assistants,
sent him a memo recommending that Wen Ho Lee be fired. Eddy
wrote: "The Cox Committee is seized with this, the case and the
slow response will be a big part of their report. If you took bold
action on this case soon it would be great evidence to them that
you are fixing this problem." He urged Richardson, "Call Louie
Freeh and tell them you are firing Lee."

> He [Lee] returns on 12/21 and will walk into the confrontational
> interview with the FBI. He will then know that he is made. He
> can legitimately be fired for not reporting foreign travel, [redacted],
> and lack of candor in previous counterintelligence interviews.
> This will show [that] you are getting rid of dirt, and your new
> counterintelligence plan has teeth.[33]

Not only would Louis Freeh's 1997 advice finally be implemented,
but Richardson was now being urged to go all the way and termi-
nate Lee's employment at Los Alamos.

Lee returned from Taiwan on December 21, 1998, but the FBI begged off the interview, saying they were not yet ready. Ed Curran had had enough, and he seized the initiative from the Bureau. On December 23, Lee was interviewed and polygraphed by Wackenhut in the Los Alamos Main Administration Building, TA43, inside the security perimeter on the Los Alamos campus. During the pre-exam interview, Lee began to remember details of his 1988 trip to Beijing that he had omitted from his trip report ten years earlier. For the first time, he revealed that PRC nuclear weapons chief Hu Side and a "Mr. Chin"* had asked him for classified information in 1988. He told the examiner that he had not reported this on his 1988 travel form because "there are no specific areas of the report, as he recalled, to reflect contact of this nature." He failed to mention that he had not told Bob Vrooman about these Chinese overtures when Vrooman had debriefed him in 1988. He said that he and the unidentified Mr. Chin corresponded for several years after that. He also mentioned the sting operation the preceding August. It's possible that incident tipped him off as to the FBI's interest in him and so he decided to make some "confessions" to head off a bigger investigation.

The polygraph consisted of four questions especially designed for Lee:

- Have you ever committed espionage against the United States?
- Have you ever provided any classified weapons data to any unauthorized person?
- Have you had any contact with anyone to commit espionage against the United States?
- Have you ever had personal contact with anyone you know who has committee espionage against the United States?

Lee's response to all four questions was "no." The examiner determined that he "was not deceptive when answering the questions"

---

*This is possibly Chen Nengkuan, a PRC scientist working for the China Academy of Engineering Physics. Chen had elicited classified information from Peter Lee in 1985 and had introduced him to other PRC nuclear scientists. Peter Lee discussed classified information with these scientists as well.

and told Lee, lab security and the FBI agents waiting outside the Los Alamos conference room that he had passed the test—with flying colors. The DOE examiner was very sure of his conclusions and apparently convinced the FBI agents present that the Bureau "was barking up the wrong tree."[34] These agents were aware of Lee's admission that in 1988 he had withheld information from Los Alamos and had been less than candid about his contacts with Chinese nuclear scientists, but they didn't interview him about any of that until three weeks later.

Ed Curran, however, had already decided to put Lee out of X Division. His access to his X Division office on the second floor of TA43 was suspended and he was assigned to T (Theoretical) Division, which is outside the security perimeter of Los Alamos.[35] Ed was able to use the admission Lee had made about an unreported contact in 1988 as the basis for his suspension. The Energy Department had finally implemented Louis Freeh's recommendation from over a year earlier. By 5:00 P.M. on December 23, 1998, Wen Ho Lee was locked out of his office on the X Division second floor, but he could still enter the secure area that housed TA43 and other secure areas of the lab. It would be two more months before he would be barred from entry to all the secure areas at Los Alamos. His office was now off limits and his X Division computer privileges had been revoked. Curran was halfway there.

But then Lee's behavior took a strange twist. That night, about 9:30 P.M., Lee passed through the TA43 security perimeter, took a side stairwell up to the X Division and tried three times to get through the vault door into his X Division office. Ten minutes later he tried a couple of times again. Each time, his badge didn't work and he was unable to get by the security system on the X Division door. He was back again early the next morning, at 3:31 A.M. on Christmas Eve. It is unlikely that he would have encountered anyone on the evening of the 23rd, and even more unlikely that anyone would have spotted him in the wee hours of Christmas Eve morning. But he had to pass through perimeter security to get into TA43. Clearly there was something in his office that Wen Ho Lee wanted, and badly.

Back in Washington, Curran and Mahaley were still arguing over the FBI's access to the raw transcripts of the polygraph. It would be late January before Curran's own polygraph expert, Dave Rentzelman, finally got a look at the Wackenhut transcripts and he didn't like what he saw—not the alleged exonerating results and not the way the test had been administered. The "control questions" were not appropriate, and Lee had some problems with several of the questions; in particular, his response to the question "have you ever provided any classified weapons data to any unauthorized person" was off the chart. But the examiner waved off Lee's erratic response as having been caused by a sneeze. At a minimum, Rentzelman recommended another exam with several more questions added.

Meanwhile, Mahaley was adamant that the FBI was not going to get the raw transcripts. His fallback position was to give the Bureau the summary sheets containing the scores that the Wackenhut polygrapher had assigned to Lee's answer. But the FBI and Curran wanted the raw transcripts. They were not to get them until January 22, 1999, and it was almost too late.

The lab reopened after the holiday on Monday, January 4, 1999, and Lee reported to his new office in a T Division trailer. Sometime that day, he managed to persuade Los Alamos' computer help desk to restore his computer privileges on the X Division server. No one from the lab security or counterintelligence office had thought to tell the help desk people that Lee's access had been suspended, and he wasn't about to tell them himself. So he was back in action on the X Division server. He began to cover his tracks all the way back to 1988 by erasing four files over the server. He also renewed his effort to get back into his X Division office, sometimes by "slip streaming" behind other employees through the vault door. Once he got in at 2:45 A.M. on January 14 (the government still hasn't explained how he managed to do this) and again at noon on the same day. Each time he got through the door unescorted, he was committing a security infraction by being in a space for which he had no proper access. On the 2:45 A.M. visit, he started up both his secure and unclassified computers in his old X Division office.

This must be one of the sorriest episodes in the history of Los Alamos. The man had had his X Division access suspended and his computer privileges terminated, but he was back on line almost immediately; he had gained access to his old office behind a vault door on several occasions and then fired up his classified X Division computer. If Wen Ho Lee, by this time a marked man, could pull this off, who else had enjoyed such easy access to the nation's nuclear secrets?

FBI special agent "Cathy Cortes," recently assigned to the Kindred Spirit investigation, finally got around to interviewing Lee at his White Rock home on January 17. In this interview, Lee revealed more contacts with nuclear weapons experts from the PRC's Institute of Applied Physics and Computational Mathematics in 1986 and again in 1988 than he had ever reported in debriefings or on trip reports. He also told "Cortes" about his encounter with Hu Side in 1988. Accompanying Hu to Lee's hotel room on the 1988 trip had been Zheng Shao Tang, at that time the deputy director of the IAPCM. Lee admitted that Hu asked questions about U.S. nuclear warhead design practices, including "two-point and multipoint detonation," but told "Cortes" that he refused to discuss these matters.[36] The FBI suspected that Lee had this contact as a result of its 1994 investigation. But now Lee admitted meeting Hu much earlier. "Cortes" didn't pursue any of Lee's new admissions. Her interview was *pro forma,* intended to close out the Lee investigation and get this case off the books.

Despite all these admissions, which showed that Lee had once again been deceptive about his contacts with PRC nuclear scientists and their requests for assistance, on January 22, 1999, FBI Albuquerque recommended that the Kindred Spirit investigation be shut down. Before the "Cortes" interview, the FBI Albuquerque office had begun preparing a report for transmission to Washington that cleared Wen Ho Lee of the W88 allegations.[37] Albuquerque Special Agent in Charge Dave Kitchen allowed Lee to write a statement clearing himself of any wrongdoing and then transmitted Lee's statements, some documentation related to the DOE polygraph, and his own assessment back to FBI Headquarters.

Kitchen's memo contains a number of memorable observations. For example, he dismissed allegations that Lee had supplied Hu Side or other PRC nuclear scientists with W88 information by declaring, "If they were co-conspirators in a plot to pass the W88 material, such activity would have come to light during the course of the [Wackenhut] polygraph examination." Kitchen declared that any help Lee had provided the Chinese was "unclassified and permissible." Since Lee was born in Taiwan, Kitchen concluded that he had "no particular reason to support China's nuclear weapons pogram from that point of view."[38]

Then Kitchen launched the FBI's campaign to shift the blame for their own failure to make progress in the Lee case back onto the Department of Energy. The Albuquerque FBI office was already pointing a finger at Ed Curran for denying them copies of the December 23 polygraph results. Now Kitchen would take aim at DOE's Administrative Inquiry from nearly three years earlier as the culprit in this case. Kitchen criticized the "selection criteria" by which Lee had been identified as being "too restrictive" and "misleading."[39] He said the lack of any evidence, any "smoking gun," meant that Wen Ho Lee was not guilty. Kitchen's assessment wound up with the following conclusion:

> In as much as Wen Ho Lee has been cooperative, passed the DOE polygraph and provided a sworn signed statement, FBI-AQ has no reason to believe Lee is being deceptive. Based on the FBI-AQ's investigation it does not appear that Lee is the individual responsible for passing the W88 information.[40]

As recently as November 1998, agents from the Albuquerque FBI office had written that his pattern of action "shows that Wen Ho Lee has the propensity to commit and engage in the crime of espionage including willingly providing documentation to foreign officials."[41] Now Kitchen was declaring Wen Ho Lee "not guilty."

But the DOE polygraph had not been subjected to a quality control review; in four years of "investigation" the FBI had conducted only one interview; Kitchen was willing to accept a signed statement from Lee as "proof" of his innocence; and his characterization of Lee as "cooperative" would prove to be a bad joke. The FBI had no intention of following up on Lee's admissions of his unreported contacts with Hu Side and others. They had not interviewed Lee's co-workers or supervisors. They had never looked at his computer, although their files contained information about his computer code and software assistance to the PRC. They had never been able to conduct technical surveillance of him. One report later characterized Kitchen's assessment as "nothing short of outrageous."[42]

The contrast between the FBI's handling of Peter Lee, who made essentially the same type of admissions to the Bureau, and Kindred Spirit is puzzling, to say the least.

In less than a month, both the FBI and the Energy Department's security officials made three grievous errors that would rebound on the government down the road. First, Energy had "misread" the results of the polygraph—deliberately or otherwise—and handed Wen Ho Lee's defenders a powerful card to use both in a trial and in their public relations campaign: "Wen Ho Lee had already passed a polygraph on these subjects." Second, SAC Kitchen's "not guilty" memo would also be used by Lee's supporters to show that even the FBI hadn't put much stock in the case against him. Bob Vrooman and others would repeatedly refer to Kitchen's memo as indicative of the fact that politicians in Washington were railroading Lee, despite the local FBI's assessment that Lee was innocent. And third, no one monitored Lee's movements or detected his efforts to get back into his X Division office, nor did anyone think to search the office.

So what accounts for SAC Kitchen's rush to get the Wen Ho Lee case off the books? The Energy Department was not the only agency in Washington concerned about acute embarrassment once the Cox Report came out. By late fall, during the Cox Committee deliberations, the Bureau had turned over the leadership of the FBI Albuquerque office. The office got a new special agent in charge (SAC), Dave Kitchen, and a new assistant SAC, Will Lueckenhoff. The Headquarters' China Section agents, "Kerry" and "Smith," had complained to Lueckenhoff about Albuquerque's bungled management of the case from its beginning in 1994: the diversion of agents; the insufficient manpower and resources devoted to the case; the lack of any follow-up to Headquarters' requests; and their frustration with the local agents assigned to the case. They both emphasized that this case was "big" and, more alarmingly, now the Cox Committee was starting to sniff around the Wen Ho Lee investigation. Lueckenhoff immediately called Kitchen and told him "we've got a problem."[43]

In mid-December, Headquarters agents had met with Rep. Cox again to discuss Wen Ho Lee and reported back Cox's displeasure over the FBI's handling of the case. It is also likely that Rep. Dicks heard the FBI's briefing and realized that the upbeat story he had gotten from section chief Steve Dillard earlier that summer about Wen Ho Lee's status might have been off the mark. And Dicks was a lot more emotional about these things than Chris Cox.

The new SAC took some steps to head off congressional criticism. He removed "Joe Lacy" from the case and assigned Special Agent "Cathy Cortes" to handle Kindred Spirit from this point on. He directed "Cortes" to try again to get technical coverage on Lee and put her to work on drafting a new request for transmission to the Justice Department. But he also allowed Energy to go ahead with its polygraph of Lee and claimed he wasn't ready to conduct an FBI interview of Lee when Curran requested the FBI to do so. He let Curran and Energy take the initiative—what little of it there was—away from him; Ed Curran was now calling the shots on the Kindred Spirit case.

No one expected that Wen Ho Lee would pass the Wackenhut polygraph in December, but once Wackenhut told Kitchen that he had, Kitchen could use that as a pretext to deflect any criticism coming their way from Congress. "What's the big deal? Wen Ho Lee was clearly the wrong guy; DOE had it all screwed up" would cover for any FBI mismanagement of the case by himself or his predecessors. Kitchen's rush to get the Lee case closed out and off the books, before the Cox Report would come out, makes sense in this context.

There is one other possibility, of course. Kitchen must have wondered if the Albuquerque FBI office's reportedly long relationship with the Lees colored his predecessors' handling of the case. Did they automatically assume, because of this relationship, that it simply couldn't be Wen Ho Lee? Bob Vrooman and other Los Alamos managers, who knew about the relationship, were now claiming that it couldn't have been Lee. Vrooman would have a lot to explain if it turned out that Lee had been passing secrets to the Chinese on his watch. Whatever the case, events were now unfolding that would make Kitchen and Vrooman look foolish and naive.

STILL OUTSIDE THE FENCE, Lee began deleting files from the X Division server on January 20, three days after his "final" interview with the FBI. On the 19th, the computer help desk told him how to get to the common file server, where all his old files were stored. He must have thought he was home free and now just needed to cover his tracks. On January 21, he contacted the Los Alamos computer help desk and wanted to know why the files he was deleting weren't "going away." He wanted the files to go away "immediately" and wasn't aware that the deleted files wouldn't "disappear" until the next time the server backed itself up. A help desk worker—had one been alerted to Lee's security situation—might have wondered why he was deleting so many files and triggered an alarm. But Los Alamos and the FBI continued to be asleep at the switch. In fact, the ever-helpful computer desk personnel told him how to delete the backup files created when he deleted the original copies, which he promptly did. It is obvious that no one was watching Lee—neither the FBI nor lab counterintelligence officers—and he was free to erase the evidence of his computer activity. He nearly got away with it.

The paperwork was almost complete for Lee to reenter X Division and resume his career as a nuclear weapons code developer, when Ed Curran got a phone call on February 2 from Chuck Middleton, an FBI section chief. Middleton told Curran, "There's a problem. We've got some really bad news. This is terrible. Quality control said he failed and needs further testing."[44]

The FBI polygraph quality control unit at Headquarters had finally got the raw transcripts of Lee's polygraph. By February 2, its quality control experts disagreed with Wackenhut's reading of the results and even the way the test had been conducted. "Inconclusive, if not deceptive" was their bottom line.[45] It seems that the control questions were structured in such a way as to minimize differences in reactions between these and the actual test questions. Thus Lee couldn't possibly have failed the Energy Department polygraph test—which helps explain why his scores were so good. The quality control people gave Curran a heads-up and he immediately reversed the restoration of Lee's clearances and accesses. He came down to the Intelligence Office to tell Sanchez about this new development and we all shook our heads in wonderment. "What in the hell was going on out in New Mexico?" I thought. Talk about the gang who couldn't shoot straight.

Now the FBI was back on the case, this time running it not from Albuquerque but from Headquarters in Washington. On

February 10, the FBI polygraphed Lee in a hotel room in Los Alamos. This time the questions were different. The FBI asked him whether he had passed specific nuclear weapons codes or W88 information to unauthorized persons.[46] He scored "deceptive," repeatedly, on these two questions. The weapons codes he was asked about were used to simulate and optimize the design of both the primaries and secondaries of thermonuclear weapons. They ran him through the exam one last time and then gave him the opportunity to explain why he might have failed the polygraph. Lee told the examiners that he had never worked on the W88, that he thought it had been designed at Livermore, and that all of his assistance to the Chinese had been unclassified and approved by Los Alamos. But he did reveal a little more about his interactions with PRC scientists. Dissatisfied with his answers, the FBI told Lee that he failed this polygraph and sent him home.

Shortly after that polygraph was over, Lee was back in his T Division office, deleting computer files like a madman. The FBI claims that he deleted over three hundred files by 9:30 that evening, including a file with the name of the Chinese postdoctoral student who had worked for him in 1997. He also tried to get back into X Division office again that evening.

The FBI finally decided that it had a viable espionage suspect who had just bombed a polygraph on questions specific to the purpose of the entire Kindred Spirit investigation—the W88 and nuclear codes and software. Moreover, Lee knew he was a suspect, because the FBI told him he flunked the polygraph. Also for the first time, Lee admitted helping PRC nuclear scientists fix some of their computer codes. He conceded that his assistance used equations and information from the classified nuclear codes he had been working on back at Los Alamos.[47] Lee admitted knowing that he had been providing assistance to PRC nuclear scientists, that he had helped the scientists "solve" their problems and that the information "could easily be used in developing nuclear weapons."[48] By definition, Wen Ho Lee was admitting that he had committed espionage by providing defense information that could be used to the advantage of a foreign nation. But then the FBI and DOE went away and left him alone for *another month.* No physical surveillance, no monitoring of his computer usage, no effort to obtain a warrant for technical coverage of his telephone, nothing. Nor is it clear that the FBI told lab security or counterintelligence officials about their renewed suspicions. Customarily the FBI keeps close tabs on suspects after such an occurrence, knowing the failed polygraph might provoke a suspect into incriminating actions—like flight, or massive file deletions from a computer network, or destroying incriminating evidence such as computer tapes. But the FBI still sat on its hands. Could this really just have been incompetence?

While the FBI and Los Alamos were napping, Wen Ho Lee was deleting files on February 10, 11 and 12. He also tried to get back into his old X Division office on February 2, 3, 8, 9 and 10. Later the FBI learned that he had gained unescorted access at least three and possibly four times during this period. What was he after? Probably computer tapes that he had made some time in the mid-1990s. Now that he had them, on February 16, he called the help desk again asking how to completely erase a file on a computer tape. The FBI reports that on the same day, he uploaded the contents of two tapes to the unclassified computer network from his office in T Division and then erased the files. Sometime before February 23, he again got access to his office by walking in with another X Division colleague. But when this lab scientist wouldn't allow Lee to remain in his office unmonitored, the FBI reports, Lee "angrily" left the floor.

On February 23, Ed Curran forced lab security to pull Lee's security badge. He would no longer be able to get into TA43, past the security guards. Finally, on March 5, the FBI was ready to interview Wen Ho Lee—nearly a month after he had failed the FBI polygraph. At this interview, Lee agreed to allow the FBI to search his former lab office in X Division. (Why did the FBI need Lee's permission to do a search of his office? It was on government property!)

Lee was interviewed again on March 7, 1999. This interview was pretty much a disaster—heavy-handed, threatening, shrill, with references to his children and family. It must have been ugly. Just a little over a month before, FBI SAC Kitchen had declared Wen Ho Lee not guilty; now Kitchen was threatening him with the electric chair if he didn't confess to espionage. Later, Lee's lawyers were able to exploit this interview to depict him as the victim of a vengeful and vindictive government.

But at least the FBI was finally moving—four years after the Energy Department's initial warnings and three years after the FBI opened a full investigation. The FBI Albuquerque office had done practically nothing on what could have been one of the most significant espionage cases in U.S. history. And things weren't much better at FBI Headquarters; Supervisory Special Agent "Greg Smith" and his unit chief, "Jack Kerry," complained about Albuquerque repeatedly to Steve Dillard, their section chief. Dillard refused to pass this along to his superiors: John Lewis, assistant director of the National Security Division; Robert Bryant, the FBI deputy director; and ultimately the FBI director, Louis Freeh. Director Freeh didn't even know about the Kindred Spirit case until July 31, 1997, and from October 1997 to September 1998 he heard about the case only one more time.[49] Dillard was the section chief during a critical twenty-one months of the Lee investigation and he is no less culpable for the FBI's failures in this case than the Albuquerque supervisors. The only excuse offered later was that "FBI culture" would penalize any Headquarters agent who reported such concerns about a field office's performance up the chain of command. In short, career ambitions took precedence over the requirements of "an investigation involving allegations of espionage as significant as any the United States Government is likely to face."[50]

ONCE ED CURRAN and the *New York Times* had forced their hand, FBI Albuquerque assigned capable CI agents to the case and in a few short weeks spanning February and March 1999, they put together what should have been a compelling case that Wen Ho Lee had been engaged in espionage on behalf of the People's Republic of China. They started from 1982 and learned that Lee had provided documents and assistance to Taiwan without authorization, concealed this from lab security, and lied to the FBI about it when initially questioned. They must have noted the FBI's conclusion from nearly two decades earlier that Lee "provided truthful answers only when confronted with irrefutable evidence . . . or when faced with a polygraph."

There should have been no doubt that Wen Ho Lee had access to critical W88 design information; one of his supervisors had said that Lee was the expert on the computational models used to

develop the W88 and could not be moved from his current project—supporting the design team modifying that warhead. The FBI
knew about Sylvia Lee's monopoly over lab contacts with the PRC
scientists and her role in providing technical reports from the Los
Alamos library to these scientists.[51] They knew she had provided
an unclassified computer code developed at Los Alamos to two
senior PRC nuclear officials, Hu Side and Zheng Shao Tang.

The records of the 1994 FBI preliminary inquiry into Lee's
encounter with Hu Side should have raised additional red flags.
Beyond his failure to report previous contacts with Hu, FBI sources,
including at least one by San Francisco's squad, reported that Lee
had helped China's nuclear weapons program with computer codes
and software. Hu's praise for Lee's assistance came when Hu was
the director of the Chinese Academy of Engineering Physics.

The nature of that assistance would become clear when Lee
began to dribble out details of his interactions with PRC nuclear
scientists after he was finally confronted by the FBI. At first, he
simply admitted to some additional contacts with officials from the
Institute of Applied Physics and Computational Mathematics, conducting a correspondence with these officials and developing a
close relationship with one, Li De Yuan, that went back to 1985.

He then admitted meeting Hu Side in 1988, when Hu and
IAPCM director Zheng Shao Tang visited his Beijing hotel room
and asked for classified information on U.S nuclear warhead designs.
A review of his 1988 travel reports showed that he had failed to
mention meeting Hu and omitted any reference to Zheng or Hu asking for classified information. His explanations that he forgot or
that there was no space on the trip report form for such information were unconvincing. Nor did he explain why he had not told
Vrooman during his post-trip debrief.

When the FBI finally learned that either Lee had failed the
Wackenhut polygraph or the polygraph was so badly flawed as to
be worthless, the Bureau decided to polygraph him again. This time
he certainly failed, particularly on questions about providing W88
information and classified nuclear weapons codes to unauthorized
persons. Now the nature of Lee's assistance, for which the Chinese
had been so grateful, began to come out. At least twice, IAPCM scientists had asked him for help in solving "mathematical problems."

Both times, Lee admitted helping these scientists using equations that were the same as those used in two Los Alamos computer codes to develop nuclear weapons like the W88. He admitted that in both instances his assistance could easily have been used for nuclear weapons developments, that he knew both scientists were from the PRC nuclear weapons program, and that his assistance had "solved or improved" their problems.[52] The FBI had also learned that Lee had helped IAPCM scientists with problems in their hydrodynamic codes during a visit to Los Alamos.

Wen Ho Lee's defenders would later try to pass off this assistance to the Chinese scientists as being harmless and applicable to many non-nuclear applications. But Lee was not a professor from a university physics faculty helping a graduate student solve a math problem. He worked in the heart of the design division of America's premier nuclear weapons laboratory, he held the lab's highest security clearances, and he had daily access to the nation's most precious nuclear secrets. He knew he wasn't helping a graduate student, but scientists from China's most important nuclear warhead modeling and simulation center, and he also knew that his help—contrary to his defenders' claims—had nuclear warhead applications.

The circumstantial evidence of Lee's espionage was piling up, at least as high as in the Peter Lee case. But just as in that case, however, the Justice Department and the FBI backed away from pursuing the espionage case against Wen Ho Lee.

FOR AT LEAST two years, we had been taking bets in my office on when this story would leak out into the media. I figured 1996 before the election for sure; but the Republicans ran such an inept campaign that even an espionage scandal wouldn't have helped them. Others bet on 1997, assuming that some of the Republicans on the Hill who bitterly opposed the administration's China policy would leak the news to try to upset the presidential summit. When the New York Times started publishing articles on the illegal transfers of missile design information and expertise to the PRC from U.S. satellite makers Loral and Hughes, we also figured that the W88 case was sure to follow. But still nothing had appeared.

We assumed that at least some of the fallout from the classified version of the Cox Report would be a series of leaks to the media to soften the eventual blow of publication of the report. I don't think I knew at the time of the hearings that the committee intended to publish an unclassified report. But the Cox Committee finally wrapped up its work and delivered a Top Secret version to the White House just after the New Year, 1999. Man, did the shit hit the fan when the National Security Council and various other Clinton administration types first saw the report! Gary Samore, who was still at the National Security Council, got the job of managing the administration's response, which consisted mostly of stonewalling the committee's request for declassification of the report until the NSC could figure out a way to make it all go away.

The Clinton administration had mastered the techniques of spinning the news: leak things out after the day's news cycle is over, on Friday evening before a long weekend, or just before a holiday. The Clintonites would dribble "news" out over a period of weeks or months and then, when a story finally broke, respond to reporters' inquiries with a "that's old news" answer. It had worked very well with many of the President's scandals, particularly those involving Whitewater and women, and it appeared that Samore was buying time to employ the strategy again.

I never saw the classified version of the whole report. Sanchez kept it in his safe and shared it with only a few other people in the office. Meanwhile, Cox and his staffers were wrestling with declassifiers from all over the government, especially from DOE. I did get to see some of the earlier portions of the declassified report—and there was nothing left but blank page after blank page. DOE classifiers had blacked out everything. Not just anything of substance, but *everything*.[53] Stalling for time, I thought. But all that was about to change.

The *New York Times* usually gets the "credit" for first breaking this story. But the *Wall Street Journal*'s Carla Robbins published a story entitled "China Received Secret Data on Advanced U.S. Warhead" in January 1999.[54] This article broke the news that the PRC had acquired W88 design information, that the FBI was investigating a suspect at one of the DOE's laboratories, that President Clinton had signed PDD 61 about a year earlier "calling for sweeping changes to the Energy Department's counterintelligence program," and that the DOE labs were reluctant to accept the mandates of the new PDD. Robbins' article noted the criticism of the administration for moving too slowly, but administration officials blamed the labs' fierce resistance to change. It was a good article, very balanced and not overly dramatic. All the basic facts were there, but the article was met with complete silence by the rest of the media and Capitol Hill.* No further coverage, no follow-up, no other news outlet picking up the story. Nothing.

Robbins later claimed that the article did not result from a White House leak and that she had a good source. Her misfortunate was to have the *Wall Street Journal* run the article on the exact day that President Clinton's impeachment trial began in the U.S. Senate. Later on, even her editors didn't realize that one of their own had broken what turned out to be a huge story. The Senate trial dominated the news coverage for another month, pretty well blotting out everything else of significance in Washington.

The President was finally, inevitably, acquitted on February 12, 1999. Five days later, the *Washington Post* added several details to the story in an article entitled "U.S. Cracking Down on Chinese Designs on Nuclear Data," by Walter Pincus.[55] A veteran reporter, Pincus was rumored to have extremely good contacts in the Intelligence Community, particularly among the senior leadership of the CIA and at the White House. He had broken a number of stories about the Intelligence Community during my time in Washington, but I had never met him or had any dealings with him. Pincus had learned the code name Kindred Spirit, and he was first to identify an "Asian-American" as the focus of the FBI's investigation. He noted that this was the third case involving Chinese espionage at the national labs, citing the Livermore and Peter Lee cases. The Cox Committee, the PDD, and even a veiled reference to the walk-in document—it was all there in his piece, but not on the front page. In fact, Pincus later related that he had a hard time getting the *Post* editors to publish the piece at all.

---

*The Robbins article was the first time Justice's Criminal Division learned about the case; the FBI had never told the Internal Security Section, which would make the final prosecution decision, about the investigation. It had repeatedly discussed the case with the White House and Congress, but not ISS.

As with Robbins' *Wall Street Journal* story, Pincus's revelations were again met with almost complete silence. Between the two articles, it had now been revealed that the PRC had acquired W88 nuclear warhead design information that could help the Chinese create smaller warheads for mobile missiles. The code name of the FBI's investigation was published and the fact that the FBI was focusing on an Asian-American at Los Alamos National Laboratory as a possible source for the espionage was now also in the public domain. Further, the articles noted that this was the third such case involving PRC espionage against the DOE national labs over the past two decades. The administration's efforts to mitigate the threats of PRC espionage, as embodied in PDD 61, and the labs' fierce resistance to the mandates of President Clinton's directives were revealed. The Cox Committee Report and at least some of its recommendations were outlined in the Pincus article. So what was missing? Save for the story of the internal struggles to get the administration to confront the problem and "personalities," practically nothing. Neither article named any names or identified any of the key players (with the exception of Chris Cox), and neither article dished the dirt. No sex, no real intrigue—none of the stuff that the media had learned to feed on during the Monica Lewinsky scandal.

THINGS WERE GOING from bad to worse for me. After my testimony to the Cox Committee, I was now a pariah inside the department and especially at the labs. My testimony had been vetted and approved by the department, and it was the FBI that revealed to the Cox Committee all the past cases of nuclear espionage and the lax security at the labs. But it was time to kill the messenger.

Damage control meetings went on daily up in Secretary Richardson's office and over at the National Security Council, with Gary Samore coordinating the administration's response. Larry Sanchez would report back highlights from some of the meetings he was attending. The Commerce Department representatives were deeply distressed by the Cox Report's "findings" and worried out loud about their ability to continue exporting high-performance computers to China.

The DOE plan for damage control was outlined in a memo written by Richardson's national security assistant, R. P. Eddy, dated

January 6, 1999, and entitled "Cox Commission Response" (see Appendix C). This memo makes me the scapegoat of the antici-pated embarrassment to the department, by claiming that all the assessments of the Chinese weapons program were strictly mine. There are repeated references to "Trulok's [sic] findings" and "Tru-lok's point of view." It appears that Eddy anticipated that the Cox Commission would leak its findings and the media campaign that Energy intended to conduct would claim that I alone was respon-sible for these assessments. Then Richardson would use Ed Cur-ran to spell out all the positive steps that the secretary was taking to fix the CI problems within the complex, emphasizing, "we are well under way to strengthening the program." The most common complaint from inside DOE was that "real" bomb designers hadn't worked on this project and that, somehow, my testimony was all the product of one person—me. Eddy's memo envisioned "using lab experts to make a new DOE review of the KS [Kindred Spirit materials] Trulok used to create his assessments." Then these "lab experts" would "create new more measured 'DOE position' on KS."

That really frosted me, so I ripped off a blistering memo to Secretary Richardson detailing the composition of the Kindred Spirit Analysis Group, the combined years of experience, the num-ber of nuclear tests and the number of warheads in our arsenal that members of this group had to their credit, and so on. How could anyone believe that all this was simply the product of one person? This effectively killed that notion, although some of Richardson's assistants then tried to argue that the "right" bomb designers hadn't reviewed the work. But I guess some of the cooler heads recognized how silly that argument would sound, so it was dropped. But the labs, especially Los Alamos, were not done yet trying to spin the intelligence information.

The next tack seemed to be to demonstrate that the information didn't necessarily come from the weapons labs, but could have come from any number of other places, especially DOD or the Navy con-tractors. Well, this wasn't exactly big news either. From the beginning we had told the FBI exactly that, and we had always operated on the assumption—wrong, as it turned out—that the FBI was investigating those other sources of information. Sandia National Lab, in particu-lar, went all out to find documents containing W88 information that had been distributed to the DOD contractor community in the mid-1980s. Not surprisingly, they found some, or so they claimed. Sanchez never showed these to me, so I don't know if these documents provided the type of detail contained in the walk-in document or were published between 1984 and 1988—the period that Dan Bruno and "F. Jeff Maines" had researched in 1996. But so what? To me, this was precisely what we had been telling the FBI all along. Nor did it mean that the PRC was not conducting espionage against the national labs.

DOE, the labs, the FBI and the administration as a whole were starting to circle the wagons. Coming off the other Clinton scandals, some probably saw all this as just another attempt to get the President. But I had no dog in that fight. I had voted for Clinton twice, although, like many in the Intelligence Community, I was disappointed by the way White House officials had politicized and manipulated us. But when I went to the White House to do the briefing in mid-1997, some officials there, like Randy Beers, responded promptly and addressed the problem in a head-on fashion. Even these officials had not anticipated how recalcitrant the labs could be, and Berger made a major mistake by transferring responsibility for this matter from Beers to Gary Samore. Instead of confronting the problem directly and claiming credit for fixing it, Samore tried to downplay all the evidence of PRC espionage. And he had to enlist the help of CIA in doing so. This manipulation is what ultimately led to the firestorm of criticism of how the administration handled the case, and it also left the administration with no choice but to destroy the message and the messenger. They were about to be handed a readymade target by the *New York Times*.

MARCH 6 WILL forever be a black day for me. I woke up very early that Saturday morning, probably 4:30 or 5:00 A.M., and read the *New York Times* story on the Internet.[56] The further into the story I got, the deeper my heart sank. By the end, I knew that my career was over and that I would never recover from what I had just read. For reasons that still mystify me, the *Times* had decided to make me the "hero of the story." No career intelligence type can ever survive such a blow.

I had been talking to one of the *Times* reporters, Jim Risen. I had read the articles of another *Times* reporter named Jeff Gerth on the illegal transfer of satellite and missile information to the PRC. Gerth and Risen were working on the PRC nuclear espionage story together and Risen seemed to be well plugged into the Intelligence Community. Unlike the *Washington Post*'s Walter Pincus, Risen was willing to write stories unfavorable to the White House that could only have come out of the Intelligence Community. One of Risen's stories, about some of the politicization that had been going on with CIA's reporting of corruption among Russian leaders like Viktor Chernomyrdin, caught my attention. Most of the Intelligence Community analysts working on Russia knew the White House just didn't want to hear about internal corruption in Russia or any other bad news. Risen had reported accurately on this and several other topics relating to the administration's manipulation of intelligence information.

He first called in December 1998, but I wasn't ready yet. He called again a couple of times in January. By February, I was getting increasingly frustrated with all the personal attacks inside DOE and also with the stonewalling. I seriously doubted that any of the Cox Report would ever see the light of day. When the *Wall Street Journal* and *Washington Post* articles were met with complete silence, I thought maybe it was time to talk to Risen. There has been an awful lot of BS spread around about my dealings with the *New York Times,* so I'll try to set the record straight.

First, I think it's accurate to say that I was "a" but hardly "the" source for the March 6 exposé. In my discussions with Jim Risen, it was evident that he already knew a lot about this case and that he also had very good sources somewhere in the Intelligence Community. What he didn't know was how the DOE, the labs and then finally the administration had compounded the problems by stonewalling and trying to make the whole issue just go away. I had firsthand experience with all this, and to me that was still the story. (I didn't yet know how badly the FBI had botched the whole Kindred Spirit investigation.) Risen already had all the stuff about the W88, he knew about the Asian-American suspect at Los Alamos, and he had also uncovered new details about both the FBI's and the White House's handling of the case. From what I could tell, he was talking to people at the FBI, CIA and even DOE. Later on, I was told that Secretary Richardson had spent a "fair amount of time" talking to the *Times* reporters about this case.

I was willing to characterize the manner in which former Secretary Pena and Betsy Moler had tried to bury the case and keep the news away from Congress. Risen had a number of sources on Samore, so I only had to confirm some of his pronouncements on the administration's China policy. The article caught fire primarily because it was so critical of the Clinton administration's handling of the whole episode. There was not a single word of criticism for officials in the first Clinton term. But those in the second term— Moler, Pena, Samore, Berger, et al.—caught hell. The overwhelming thrust of the article was that the administration had downplayed the "fact" of nuclear espionage so as not to interfere with higher-priority dealings with the PRC. This fit in neatly with the on-going controversy over PRC campaign contributions to the White House and the Democratic National Committee and the PRC's efforts to buy influence in the Clinton White House. Coupled with the earlier reports of White House intervention on behalf of big campaign contributors like Loral to ease restrictions on PRC launches of U.S. satellites, it all seemed to add up to the White House jeopardizing U.S. national security in return for cash from China and foreign donors with close connections to the PRC Peoples' Liberation Army.

Second, the *Times* article put a human face on this story: mine. The *Journal* and *Post* stories were dry, straightforward reporting with references to anonymous sources—fairly standard "inside the beltway" stuff. The *Times* story, on the other hand, named names, identified heroes and villains and, all in all, was pretty dramatic stuff. Coverups, denials, malfeasance, all the makings of a drama.

As I said above, my heart sank as I read through the story. It hit rock bottom when I saw the following: "In personal terms, the handling of this case is very much the story of the Energy Department intelligence official who first raised questions about the Los Alamos case, Notra Trulock."

When I read those words, I knew the administration would now turn its "politics of personal destruction" machine on me. I had talked to Risen "on background" and I had no interest in self-promotion or claiming any credit for anything I had done over the past four years. By making me out to be some sort of "hero," Risen and Gerth must have known they were setting me up to be brutalized by the Clinton administration and the rest of the media.

My daughter had a basketball game that day and I remember sitting on the bleachers watching her play, cheering for her but dying on the inside. I wanted to run and hide, just get away from the storm that I knew was coming my way. Why did I ever talk to these guys? Risen had told me that lots of people, both at the FBI and at the CIA, were crediting me with finally forcing the labs to do what everyone at those places thought should have been done years before. Risen said that George Tenet, the CIA director, had told him that he would give me a medal if he could. But I knew— and had said—that the credit belonged to Henson, Booth and Richter for first uncovering the espionage, to the Henderson Panel for validating their findings, and then to Charlie Curtis for taking the problem seriously and pushing for solutions to the labs' long-standing security problems. My only claim to fame was that I knew my job was not to cover up or bury this problem after Curtis left the department in early 1997, but to try to protect our nuclear secrets and to present honest and "unpoliticized" intelligence information to policymakers.

By mid-afternoon, my phone was ringing off the hook. Other reporters, TV news people, even some publishers wanting to sell "my story" began calling. Oh God, what if television cameras began camping out on my lawn, as they did to Ken Starr? His daughter went to the same school as mine, and several of my daughter's friends lived just up the street from Starr. The TV and other reporters had made life in Starr's neighborhood a nightmare; I sure didn't want that experience for my kids. Fortunately, my fears on that score at least were baseless.

But the telephone kept on ringing. I was taking no calls, and I didn't speak to any reporters over that weekend, although my wife did take a few calls. One in particular was intriguing, especially in light of later developments. Solly Granastein, Mike Wallace's producer from *60 Minutes,* called several times over that weekend, but I was afraid to call him back. I had already gotten in way over my head and now I just wanted it all to go away. I have often wondered how things would have turned out if I had done *60 Minutes* before Wen Ho Lee did.

MEANWHILE, THE ADMINISTRATION continued to stall the Cox Committee on final approval of a declassified version of the committee's report, while it produced its own version of the story of Chinese nuclear espionage. One of the Cox Report's recommendations was the production of an official government "damage assessment." Now the White House pushed George Tenet and the CIA to get off the dime and produce such an assessment. In fact, the White House issued a press release to announce the CIA assessment without even bothering to tell Tenet. Clearly the objective was to get something official out that would steal the thunder from the Cox Report, if and when the declassified version was ever released.

A national intelligence officer named Bob Walpole managed the damage assessment. Walpole was a CIA officer I knew from his days working on nonproliferation. He was a good choice, in my opinion. We'd had our differences in the past, but I thought he was honest. A team of analysts from various intelligence agencies, including Energy, was brought together and worked on the assessment for about a month. Larry Sanchez made me the official liaison between Energy and the assessment team, but I kept my distance. Everyone knew where I stood and I wanted to see what the assessment team came up with. We did have lab scientists working on the team: Tom Cook, Carl Henry, John Richter (I think), and a Livermore scientist named Cary Spencer, who kept pushing the most benign explanations for Chinese developments. In one case, his explanation for a measurement of a Chinese device that was exactly the same as its U.S. counterpart was "coincidence."

About halfway through, Walpole called me to say he was concerned that I wasn't going to like the outcome. When he described the assessment's preliminary findings, these tracked almost precisely what I had been saying for about two years now. So what was the problem? Walpole was surprised and went on to say that Gary Samore had told him that I was informing people that the Chinese had already manufactured a W88-like warhead and were deploying it on fielded missile systems. I was stunned; never had I made such an outlandish claim. No wonder Samore had told Sandy Berger that Energy was presenting a worst-case scenario. I polled every person I could think of who had seen my briefings, "Did I ever say anything that could have led you to believe . . . ?" and then repeated Samore's allegations. The response was unanimously "no."

AS THE WALPOLE GROUP was wrapping up its work, there was a stunning new development in the Wen Ho Lee case. After Lee had failed the February 17 FBI polygraph, the Bureau had taken another two weeks to get back to interviewing him and gaining his permission to search his office. When they did, agents found documents with the classification markings clipped off, others with the markings "obliterated" and still others printed out minus the required classification markings.[57] Worse yet, on March 23, one of the Los Alamos scientists assisting the FBI's search of Lee's office found a logbook with a list of files stored on the unclassified Los Alamos computer network. The scientists instantly recognized these as classified files, but when the scientists and the FBI went to the X Division server to look for them, the files were gone—deleted over the course of the last two months. They were able to pull Lee's directory off backup tapes and their worst fears were confirmed: Wen Ho Lee had been moving classified files across the firewall and storing them on an unclassified computer network since 1988.[58]

One Monday morning in early April, during the preparation of the Intelligence Community Damage Assessment, I met with Los Alamos scientist Steve White, who had spent the previous weekend "reconstructing" Wen Ho Lee's computer transfers. White had flown to Washington the night before to meet with the Walpole group, but he was still reeling from what he and others had discovered that weekend. White's testimony later during Lee's judicial proceedings reflected what he had told us in April:

> This is . . . its unimaginable. I could not believe it. I cannot—I still cannot. I have trouble believing it. Its just—all the codes, all the data, all the input files, all the libraries, the whole thing is there, the whole ball of wax, everything.[59]

When I saw him in April, he was still in a state of shock from what he and other Los Alamos scientists had uncovered. White said that Lee had moved all the computer codes used in developing Los Alamos nuclear warheads, all the input files containing the classified warhead dimensions, geometries and materials, and all the data and results of all the nuclear tests done to develop these warheads. One reason that White may have been so shocked is that he himself had given Wen Ho Lee the input decks to run with the computer codes when Lee had asked for them in the mid-1990s. He probably felt betrayed. Another scientist that Lee had asked for similar files about the same time turned him down; Lee didn't have a need to know that information. White's boss, Richard Krajcik, would later describe the "input deck" as an "electronic blueprint" of a nuclear warhead.[60]

Sometime later, the FBI and Los Alamos found some portable computer tapes in Lee's office and concluded that in 1993 Lee had started placing all of this data onto these tapes. He couldn't make tapes from his office inside the X Division, so he would visit a colleague outside the security fence and use his friend's tape drive. The friend gave Lee his access code and password so Lee could log on and download the files he had placed on the server onto tapes. Lee would visit his friend's office during lunch and after hours, telling him that he was downloading some files. He didn't tell the friend that the files were classified, as he would later say, because the friend didn't have a security clearance or the need to know.

In 1995, Energy Department security officials had become concerned about computer security in X Division and forced Los Alamos to physically separate the classified and unclassified systems. No longer could Lee move files across the partition as he had done before. But then the Los Alamos computer team installed a tape device on one of Lee's X Division computers. He would no longer have to go through the cumbersome process of moving files and then going outside the fence to download these onto tapes. Now he could do it right from his desk. A Los Alamos scientist went to look at Lee's office in X Division and told me that Wen Ho Lee had arranged his office so that his computer workstations could not be observed from the doorway, the view being blocked by bookcases. One workstation was for access to the unclassified X Division server and had the tape drive; the other was for access to the classified X Division server, code-named "Enchanted."

The FBI determined that Lee had wrapped up his downloading outside the fence by mid-1994, but would make at least one more tape in 1997. This time he had downloaded all the data on both the primary and the secondary components of one (unidentified) thermonuclear warhead and the very latest data on the W88 warhead. This tape apparently contained information on the newly modified W88 design and was characterized as "the most significant, according to Los Alamos experts, because it contains the most sensitive material of all those he created."[61] And for some reason, Lee hadn't bothered to erase the classified files that he had placed on the open computer network. These would remain out on an unprotected network until early 1999, in some cases for more than a decade.

Here was my worst nightmare. For three years, I had been warning anyone who would listen that the PRC was after our nuclear weapons codes, input files and so forth. Our information indicated that the PRC thought they could obtain these data from Los Alamos. Now the FBI had learned that all of this information, *exactly* the information the Chinese had been after, had been sitting on an unclassified, unprotected computer network for years, being regularly updated and expanded by Lee, and that there were also computer tapes with this information floating around somewhere. The unclassified computer networks at the labs were very vulnerable to hackers and attacks by foreign intelligence services. A 1998 government report listed 324 attacks on unclassified Energy Department computer networks from October 1997 to June 1998 alone. The report stated that outsiders acquired "complete access and total control to create, view modify or execute any and all information stored on the system."[62] Lee would later claim that he had applied three passwords to protect these files, as if somehow he had outsmarted computer hackers, at least some of whom were sponsored by foreign governments. Lee may have been less than candid about his passwords; reportedly he had applied only two, and one was "WHLee."[63] At least six times, the FBI learned, someone logged onto the Los Alamos computer using Wen Ho Lee's access code and password, always after Lee had been loading classified files on the unprotected network or making tapes. His daughter would later claim that she was logging on to play Dungeons and Dragons.[64] The FBI could never learn whether his files were accessed. Los Alamos monitoring systems could record "log-ons" from outside the lab, but not specific files accessed during these sessions. If the PRC or any other hacker did not get these files, it was just plain dumb luck.

At the time, this new information was extremely sensitive and the FBI refused to allow Walpole to use it in the unclassified version of the damage assessment. There was a short paragraph about Lee's computer transfers in the classified report, though hardly anyone in government was allowed to read this report. But the recriminations were sure to start flying when this came out.

WALPOLE AND TENET were scheduled to present their findings to the intelligence committees on both sides of Congress. Walpole invited me to attend, but Secretary Richardson turned that idea down flat. I don't know his reasons, but he wouldn't budge. Tenet and Walpole both appealed to him—to no avail. Finally, Sanchez met privately with him and persuaded Richardson to reverse his decision. I could attend the closed hearings, but was to make no public appearances whatsoever.

To make sure that the damage assessment scooped the Cox Report, the administration had produced an unclassified version of the assessment and Walpole announced its findings at a press conference in April (see Appendix D). The key finding of the unclassified assessment read:

> China obtained by espionage classified US nuclear weapons information that probably accelerated its program to develop future nuclear weapons. This collection program allowed China to focus successfully down critical paths and avoid less promising approaches to nuclear weapons designs.[65]

It went on to describe Chinese acquisitions of W88 information and data on a variety of U.S. nuclear warhead design concepts including the neutron bomb, and it noted that the national labs were targeted in the Chinese collection program. Walpole did give the administration an out by stating: "To date, the aggressive Chinese collection effort has not resulted in any apparent modernization of their deployed strategic force or any new nuclear weapons deployment." This was technically correct—to a point. The Chinese were working very hard to modernize their strategic force, but hadn't yet finished the testing required to make these new missiles operational. That was just around the corner. As for any new nuclear warhead deployment, the evidence is murkier. The Intelligence Community believed that the Chinese had never deployed the neutron bomb, but were later contradicted by a Chinese announcement reminding Taiwan and the United States that the PRC had indeed developed such a warhead. I think Walpole missed the point; the Chinese collection effort was about the future, about deployments of new weapons that would take place over the next decade or so. But the reference to no new deployments or no apparent modernization of their strategic forces was eagerly grabbed by administration spokesmen in their campaign to downplay the impact of Chinese nuclear espionage. Nevertheless, I was satisfied with the outcome of the classified damage assessment and even the unclassified version mostly tracked with our view of what had happened. Walpole gave his press conference and made appearances before Congress on April 21—more than a month before the declassified Cox Report was finally released.

The Top Secret Cox Report had first been submitted to the White House on January 4, 1999. The White House put out a statement in early February agreeing with the Cox recommendations on export control measures and the need to prevent the "unauthorized disclosure of sensitive military information." But then the administration sat on the report for another four months. At least once, it got help from the Republican-controlled House of Representatives, when the House voted to hold off release until after the visit of Prime Minister Zhu Rongji from China.[66] A week before the unclassified version was released, Cox and Norm Dicks presented the committee's findings in a closed meeting to a group of senators and congressmen. Naturally, the highlights of that briefing were immediately leaked to the *New York Times* and other journalists for publication the next day. So there wasn't much left for Cox and Dicks to announce; most of it had already been made public.

On May 26, 1999, Cox and the rest of the committee members held a press conference to release the declassified version of the report officially. Cox said that nearly 70 percent of the classified version had made it through the declassification process and all present hailed the bipartisanship and unanimity of the report's findings. Which lasted about five minutes. When it came his turn to speak, Representative John Spratt, a Democrat, said, "It's alarming. But is it accurate?" Even Dicks said the conclusions were "written in a worst-case fashion."

The White House released its response the same day, essentially adopting the committee's recommendations as its own.[67] The administration claimed that most of the recommendations had already been implemented, a standard ploy, and pointed to other measures, like the Presidential Decision Directive and Secretary Richardson's actions, as indicative of its aggressive approach to thwarting Chinese nuclear espionage and improving security and counterintelligence at the nuclear weapons labs.

The Cox Report got about two days' worth of news coverage and then it disappeared from the front pages of the *Washington Post* and other national media. Ironically, the Republican leadership in both the Senate and the House dropped the report like a hot potato. It was dead on arrival; the White House strategy had worked flawlessly.

SEVEN

Testimony

Certainly, they stole information relating to the W-88 and another
warhead, but beyond that, Tim, there is no evidence—and this is the
CIA damage assessment of April certified by Admiral Jeremiah, General Scowcroft—that there was any modernization, any modernization of the active strategic stockpile of China and any new weapons
development that have been deployed.
   —Energy Secretary Bill Richardson to Tim Russert
   Meet the Press
   May 30, 1999

After the *New York Times* article appeared, I was even
more an outcast than I had been after my Cox Report testimony. Former colleagues and even the few that I
counted as personal friends began to shy away from me. President
Clinton's political appointees at the DOE were telling people that
"I had single-handedly destroyed the Department of Energy." Everyone knew what was coming and nobody wanted to be "collateral
damage." The Clinton administration was about to go into its warroom mode and woe to anyone who got in its way. After one of my
early appearances before a closed congressional session to talk
about Kindred Spirit, Bill Richardson's assistant secretary for congressional affairs came back to the department telling the secretary
that I was a "very credible witness." I knew this wasn't meant as
praise; instead, the administration would have to destroy my credibility to make the Wen Ho Lee scandal go away—and that's exactly
what happened.

   I had already been looking around for another job in the Intelligence Community. CIA director George Tenet had assured me
repeatedly that I would have a job over at CIA or someplace in the
Community; now came the time to take him up on his promises. I
had applied for a couple of jobs at the agency and even had a couple of interviews. There were two or three opportunities that would
have been perfect, but Tenet wanted no part of me. So now what?

My main objective was to slip back into anonymity as quickly as possible. I did receive a nice offer from TRW Inc., but I didn't feel that I could take it until the drama played out.

Given the media attention generated by the *Times* story and particularly the references to DOE's refusal to provide information about Kindred Spirit to Congress, it was inevitable that the finale would come on Capitol Hill. Recall that three years had passed since our first notification of Congress. With the exception of the Cox Committee, there had been surprisingly little interest in this scandal on the Hill. After the Republicans captured both houses in 1994, some Republicans told me that no Clinton scandal would go uninvestigated. But they were too busy chasing Monica and the President's sex life to pay much attention to nuclear espionage.

The Wen Ho Lee story broke after the dust had begun to settle from the impeachment debacle. I suspect the Senate leadership was still smarting from criticism of its handling of the President's trial.[1] Regrettably, the leadership's performance this time around would prove equally poor. If any issue merited a select committee review and investigation, it was this. But Trent Lott, the Senate majority leader, bowed to pressure from within his ranks to allow several different committees to conduct their own hearings and write legislation. Instead of one consolidated investigation that could pull together all the different threads, committee hearings were going on all over Capitol Hill. I often wondered who if anyone was even maintaining an accurate record of all the revelations made during these hearings, particularly the closed ones. As in the Senate impeachment trial, politics once again would trump principle and even considerations of national security.

Senator Richard Shelby (R-AL), chairman of the Senate Select Committee on Intelligence, held some of the first hearings. But before this, I had several private meetings with various senators to explain what had happened. A DOE watchdog always accompanied me, but I still found ways to tell the story. The first meeting was with Fred Thompson, chairman of the Senate Governmental Affairs Committee (GAC), and Pete Domenici, of the Energy and Natural Resources Committee and also the Budget Committee. Domenici, of course, was the patron saint of the labs; but Thompson also had a major DOE lab in his home state of Tennessee.

Both senators had the same question: what had happened and why? Domenici in particular was crestfallen. Over the years, my staff and I had had a number of meetings with both him and Thompson to talk about Russia, proliferation and some other topics. Domenici and Thompson were both very appreciative of our help; Domenici even said that he learned more from us in one hour than in a whole series of briefings from the CIA. Several times, he said that many senators had come up to him and asked him what had happened, why hadn't he told them about spies at Los Alamos. It was clear that he didn't know anything about this. I had always thought that Vic Reis or a lab director would have clued him in, but evidently not, and Betsy Moler had denied his request for information in 1998.

The first set of hearings was behind closed doors in the Senate Intelligence Committee hearing room in the Hart Senate Office Building. The DOE delegation was supposed to go over together, but I guess Richardson didn't want to be seen with me. I was told to wait behind in my office until they called. I heard later that Richardson and Senator Bob Kerry (D-NE) got into a tiff about my absence, Kerry demanding to know where I was and Richardson retorting that he wasn't responsible for "managing my calendar." So I was summoned, but when I got there, Richardson literally turned his back on me, and the rest of the witnesses, including DCI George Tenet, also ignored me. One person came over to shake hands and ask how I was doing—Louis Freeh. I appreciated that gesture.

The secretary and the rest of the dignitaries took up most of the hearing time trying to explain away what had happened. Richardson did the Clinton "let's move on" routine and wanted everybody to focus on how much he had accomplished in fixing the security problems at the department. Cheered on by the Democrats on the panel, Richardson repeated his public assurances that everything was now okay and our nuclear secrets were secure. But the Republicans were having none of that. I finally came up to the witness table very late in the afternoon. All the administration dignitaries promptly departed, but most of the Republicans stayed and were joined by my home state senator, John Warner. As I laid out what had happened, Warner and others sat in stunned silence. At the end, Warner turned to Senator Shelby and said that never in his time on the Hill had he heard a story like mine.

The Senate Intelligence Committee held a few more hearings and did some investigations, but frankly not much came of it. The staff was rather timid and more than willing to take no for an answer from the administration in response to its document requests and other issues. Why the committee's leadership let this one slip away from them is a mystery.

At some point, Warner's people proposed holding open hearings on this scandal. I had never testified in public before; since it was intelligence-related, my testimony was always given behind closed doors. But Warner was intent on "informing the American public" of this scandal and how its government had tried to cover it up. I had a number of preliminary meetings with Les Brownlee, the staff director of the Senate Armed Services Committee, of which Warner was chairman. I told Brownlee that I thought this was a bad idea, but he assured me that Senator Warner knew that the White House would come after me and the Republican leadership was ready for that and they would "look out" for me.

The hearing was set for Monday, April 12, in one of the large hearing rooms in the Hart Senate Office Building. Warner and the committee were tied up with the deepening crisis in Kosovo and so the hearing was scheduled for late afternoon, around 4:00 P.M. I was nervous, to say the least.

The hearings were not too partisan—nothing like the Lewinsky affair. But a pattern was established from the beginning. The Republicans made the appropriate gestures to protect classified information and all that, but wanted nearly everything out on the public record. They would promise to go into closed sessions if need be, but then plowed right ahead asking the same questions. The Democrats, for their part, were "shocked" that we would ever discuss these things in open session; they professed great concern for national security and wanted to get into closed session as soon as possible. Get everything behind closed doors, so the media can't see what's going on—this seemed to be their strategy. They were partly successful due to the nature of this issue.

Some of the senators wanted to look at the FBI's handling of the case and the role of the Justice Department in turning down the

Bureau's requests for technical surveillance in open hearings. The FBI categorically refused to appear at a public hearing and even told one Senate committee chairman that a key FBI witness had been called out of town unexpectedly before one such hearing.

Before Senator Warner brought his Armed Services Committee hearing to order, there were photographers and reporters all over the place. Most of the reporters were decent and stayed away, but the photographers were circling around us taking picture after picture. It was unnerving, to say the least. Finally, the hearing was gaveled to order and Warner made an opening statement saying that its purpose was to "examine the Department of Energy's management and stewardship of highly sensitive information and materials over the past several years."[2] Warner had sought to add some provision to the defense authorization bill to establish better oversight of DOE security, but Betsy Moler had led the charge to water down that provision, and Warner's displeasure with her was evident:

> That legislation would have significantly improved DOE security. Unfortunately representatives, the high-ranking officials, one who will be present as a witness today, resisted that legislation to the point where it was in conference between the House and the Senate, and it evolved from that conference a severely weakened position. Today even that weakened requirement enacted by Congress and signed into law by the president has not been fully complied with by the Department of Energy.

This was nothing new to us, but was to become a constant theme. It didn't matter where the mandate to improve security and counterintelligence came from, the President or the Congress; DOE and the labs would ignore it.

Warner said that the public was entitled to know "whether senior members of this administration, in particular DOE officials, past, and I am not saying present, but certainly past, intentionally prevented full disclosure to the Congress of the extent of the alleged Chinese espionage at DOE facilities as it was alleged at that time." He went on:

> If there was in fact a conscious decision to withhold information from Congress or to downplay the consequences of potential espi-

onage efforts against our national labs, in order to protect possibly the administration's engagement policy with China, then the administration's motives and its ability to effectively manage its national security missions must be placed before the Congress and the nation's public.

Frankly, at that point I knew my goose was cooked. Although Warner's words sounded good, his constant references to "intentional," "conscious" and "alleged" all sounded like code words for giving the administration a free pass. Moler and her allies could claim it was all a misunderstanding, that I was just too zealous and had misinterpreted her statements and positions, that there had been miscommunication, and everybody could go home happy. I was kicking myself for ever getting involved in this charade.

That's not to say that some senators didn't really want to get to the bottom of this. Senator Jim Inhofe was a real tiger, as were his colleagues Jeff Sessions and Bob Smith. But for the most part, Warner pulled their teeth.

Senator Carl Levin (D-MI) was the ranking minority member. He was pretty slick, I must say, and ran circles around Warner and the other members. He introduced a new fact to the equation, revealing that the FBI had actually briefed Congress nineteen times since 1996 on Kindred Spirit. These were briefings for the intelligence committees and most likely represented updates, brief and terse, on the state of the case. Given how little the FBI had done, it would be interesting to know what these briefings actually contained.

After these pleasantries, Ed Curran led off. He too had constantly bitched about Moler and the Office of the Secretary stalling and delaying implementation of CI reform, but there was no mention of this in Ed's statement. Only praise for Richardson.

Then it was my turn. In my opening statement, I discussed the implications of the department's failure to act in response to Freeh's recommendation that Lee be taken out of access to classified information: "Mr. Chairman, I am not sure that we will ever know how much damage has been done to U.S. national security as a result of this inaction." I was right, of course, because Lee had made at least one additional tape of classified nuclear weapons information in 1997 that was never recovered.

I described the Energy Department's efforts to bury the Kindred Spirit case and how Moler and Pena had effectively done so for about two years—especially after the 1997 FBI study found that the labs were not up to even minimal standards of security and counterintelligence. I described the department's efforts to suppress other intelligence information and Moler's denial to Congress of information on this case.

I concluded with three main points: First, I said that I did not believe that the conduct of effective, nonpoliticized intelligence was any longer possible at DOE, that there was just too much interference from the administration's political appointees. Second, that I believed the entire episode raised serious questions about the credibility of the national labs, their ability to protect our nuclear secrets, and the tendency of so many lab managers to "prevaricate," "respond with vague and evasive answers" and even "lie" in response to legitimate inquiries. DOE officials were as bad, if not worse. The whole premise of the administration's policy on maintaining our nuclear arsenal without testing hinged on the "credibility" of the labs. Lab managers and their political bosses in Washington had to tell the truth about the integrity of the nuclear stockpile. Could these managers be trusted to tell President Clinton the truth if they believed that one of our nuclear warheads wouldn't work—and that the only way to fix it would be to return to live nuclear testing in Nevada? The labs' handling of security and counterintelligence—a real "stewardship" issue—should have raised questions about their overall credibility. Finally, while I supported Richardson and his efforts at reform, I questioned the long-term effectiveness of these reforms, given that many of the people actually implementing them were the same people who had been blocking such reforms for the past two years.

The question period focused mostly on the memo I had written Moler and how it had been handled. Warner seemed totally uninterested in the larger issues I had raised and preferred to focus on minor details about my interactions with Moler. Levin walked me through the sequence of events and made clear that neither Berger nor anyone else in the White House had stopped DOE from going to the Hill. Which was true—in 1996, but not in 1997 or 1998. A former senior DOE official later told me that he was certain that

Moler was under instructions from the White House to keep Kindred Spirit away from Congress from 1997 on.

To Senator Inhofe's credit, his questioning sought to show that this was not just about the W88, but that PRC acquisitions extended to other areas of the U.S. nuclear program. He didn't get far with that because of security restrictions on this information. Berger had been claiming that the 1996 briefing was general and nonspecific, and Inhofe asked me to refute that, which I did. (Later, Charlie Curtis gave a background interview to the *New York Times* confirming that the 1996 briefing had been anything but "nonspecific.") Then Inhofe asked:

"Would you submit to a polygraph test concerning your allegations and statements about Moler?"

"Absolutely," I replied.

During his question time, Senator Jeff Sessions (R-AL) focused on Moler's denial of information to the Hill, but also brought up her failure to act on Freeh's 1997 recommendations about Lee.

When Moler's turn to testify came, she denied everything or blamed it on me. She was more prepared than she had been in some of the closed sessions. For example, at one closed hearing she claimed that Louis Freeh had been urging her to fire Wen Ho Lee but she didn't have the authority to do that. Now her story was that she expected me to take care of Lee, although she didn't explain how I was supposed to have done that. She also had brought a lawyer along with her, which didn't appear to inspire confidence on the part of many committee members. Inhofe repeated his request that she take a polygraph, but she refused to give him a straight answer and danced around the question. Inhofe told me later that he never intended to give either one of us a polygraph, but he anticipated that I would say yes and Moler would refuse or evade the question altogether.

Paul Richenbach, her staff guy, came next. It had been Richenbach who was the action officer fielding congressional requests for Moler in 1998. He had witnessed Moler telling me that Congress only wanted to harm President Clinton on his China policy. In her testimony, Moler had vehemently denied making that statement and Richenbach backed her up: he claimed to have had no knowledge of any requests from Congress for briefings in 1998 and said that Moler certainly had not denied any such request. My executive assistant had personally handed Richenbach my memo detailing these requests. Richenbach had stood right next to Moler when she denied these, saying that Congress only wanted to hurt the President on his China policy.* Now he was claiming that neither one of these events ever happened. Not that he couldn't remember, which was the usual response, but that these didn't happen—period. One congressional aide later told me that a number of senators on the Republican side discussed perjury proceedings against Richenbach, but knowing they would have to rely on Clinton's Justice Department to carry out the investigation, they decided it wasn't worth it.

But I was truly unprepared for what came next. Ric Bloodsworth, my former counterintelligence deputy, began his testimony by sidestepping all the key issues and essentially giving Moler a free pass on all of her stalling and obstruction of CI reform. He hadn't seen this, he hadn't heard that, he had no firsthand knowledge of her efforts to block or delay counterintelligence reform, in fact she seemed very committed to such reforms and had worked hard on them. I couldn't believe my ears, but Moler and her allies, both among the DOE staff sitting behind her and over on the Democrat side of the senators' platform, were grinning ear to ear. My main eyewitness had just cut my legs right out from under me. What could he possibly have been thinking? For months he had suffered right along with the rest of us in meaningless paper exercises, drawing up more options and more options while days and then weeks slipped away and still no CI reform. Bloodsworth had firsthand experience with Moler's efforts to block the Presidential Decision Directive and he knew that she had ignored Freeh's recommendation to remove Wen Ho Lee's access to nuclear weapons secrets. For months he had regaled my office staff with stories of Moler's incompetence and ineptitude and her efforts to block CI reform. Now he was saying the exact opposite—and not for the last time.

I am not sure I have ever experienced a more stunning and unexpected betrayal, after all we had been through: the pushing

---

*See page 205 above.

and pulling of the labs on counterintelligence, the battle to bring a recalcitrant Energy Department around to accepting the President's mandate to reform CI, and so forth. I had gotten Bloodsworth promoted and made sure he received the Intelligence Community's highest medal for all his work at DOE. It wasn't as though I were asking him to lie for me, just tell the truth about what had happened. After the hearing, Warner's chief aide, Les Brownlee, came over to me and said, "Bloodsworth sold you right down the river, didn't he? Who do you think got to him?"

Things basically petered out at that point. Warner concluded the hearing by saying that further closed sessions would be held. But if they were, I wasn't invited. I don't really know if Warner did anything else on this. The audience must have been left wondering what they had just heard. Serious, damning charges from one side and complete denials, "it never happened," from the other. One thing should have been very clear to me then: Everyone else who had helped fight these battles to plug the gaps in lab security was now abandoning ship. I was in this alone.

The media coverage the next morning was mostly straightforward. The *New York Times* article focused on the White House's efforts to downplay or minimize the PRC's nuclear thefts.[3] The *Times* characterized Moler's responses skeptically, saying she couldn't recall discussions about briefing requests or explain how the 1998 briefing memo was found in her safe. It repeated my statements about NSC official Gary Samore's comments on using the labs as a tool of engagement and quoted Samore's claim that he was joking when he made that statement. The reporting was balanced, capturing the "on the one hand, on the other" nature of the testimony.

The *Washington Post* also covered the hearing, and even reprinted my oral presentation on the editorial page on April 13. To its credit, the *Post* said: "In many papers and newscasts, Trulock's extraordinary testimony was lost amid coverage of the war in Kosovo, the Paula Jones contempt decision, and the Susan McDougal verdict. So here, in his own words before the Senate, is Notra Trulock's story."[4] But in its reportage of the hearing, the *Post* took a different spin. Essentially, the *Post* highlighted DOE's role in screwing up this case and cited my references to Moler and other

DOE officials as causing the delay in improving security.[5] In contrast to the *Times,* the *Post* made no mention of Samore or of White House efforts to play down PRC spying. Instead, the *Post* interpreted what I had said as giving credit to President Clinton and the White House for making necessary reforms.

Three days later, I was back on the Hill in open testimony again. This time, the venue was on the House side, before the Armed Services Committee. The purpose of this hearing was to look into Moler's gag order on me during the closed hearing of the same committee back in October 1998. Congressman Duncan Hunter (R-CA) blistered Moler throughout the hearing. He told Moler that they didn't want her at that hearing in the first place, but that she had called three times insisting that she be present and give testimony. He recounted the difficulty he'd had in getting my testimony up to his staff, his questioning of Moler regarding what she had removed, and how upset he was that Richardson had yet to provide the original draft of the 1998 testimony. Of course, I had already given it to our Congressional Affairs Office, but they were sitting on it in hopes that Hunter would give up.

I opened the testimony by admitting that I had not been forthcoming with information about Kindred Spirit at last fall's hearing. I related my understanding of what the committee was interested in, how that contrasted with the directions I had received from Moler, and how relieved Richenbach had been after that hearing when we hadn't spilled the beans on Kindred Spirit. I also apologized to the committee, Rep. Hunter and Rep. Floyd Spence, the committee chairman, for not being able to tell the whole truth in my testimony.

Moler's performance was even lamer this time. Hunter just kept after her on the same question: Why didn't you tell us about Kindred Spirit? You sat right next to Trulock in the hearing, you told us that you were there to tell us the truth, and when we asked you, you didn't tell us. Her response was classic:

MR. HUNTER: Why didn't you tell us?
MS. MOLER: You asked Mr. Trulock to review the losses that had occurred. You did not ask me, sir, to review the losses that had occurred.

MR. HUNTER: Didn't you feel you had a duty to us to tell us the whole truth as you had been sworn to do? You had your subordinate sitting side by side with you.
MS. MOLER: Yes, I did.

Moler then tried to read her opening statement rather than respond. But Hunter wasn't about to let up. All she could offer was that Hunter had asked me the questions and not her. She denied editing my testimony. She also stated that she had never withheld testimony from Congress out of concern about the President's China policy: "Those accusations are false."

Hunter was all over her on that one:

MR. HUNTER: But you did sit in a hearing under oath when I asked the question, have any losses occurred at our national nuclear laboratories, and you said nothing about the loss that we are talking about.
MS. MOLER: Neither Mr. Trulock nor I said anything about that. With the benefit of hindsight, that was a mistake, sir, and I apologize for that.

Further along there was a discussion of her gag rule:

MR. HUNTER: Did you ever instruct Mr. Trulock not to tell Congress about the loss of the nuclear weapons secrets at Los Alamos?
MS. MOLER: Mr. Trulock was under the direct instructions that information about this program should be handled through the appropriate channels. I was never aware of a request from a committee of Congress for Mr. Trulock to discuss this information with the Congress.
MR. HUNTER: So you never gave him a general admonishment, "Don't tell anybody about this loss?"
MS. MOLER: He was under very specific instructions to limit dissemination about this program; that is correct. But he never received a request to my knowledge that he shared with me.
MR. HUNTER: Who gave the instructions?
MS. MOLER: Secretary Pena and I both did.

. . . .

MR. HUNTER: Do you recall yourself giving him any instructions to not tell us about this in any way?

MS. MOLER: I do not recall giving him any specific instructions, but it is entirely possible I did. I well understood this was restricted data.

As I recall, there was one more public hearing that spring. In May, the Senate Energy and Natural Resource Committee held a public hearing. This committee authorizes all the non-defense DOE budget and it also holds confirmation hearings on the secretary and the other appointed officials. Its chairman, Senator Frank Murkowski (R-AK) was notorious for his temper and was taking that temper out on officials testifying before him. But I didn't see any of that, at least directed at me.

The hearing was held on Thursday, May 20. Murkowski stated in his opening that the purpose of this hearing was to look at the damage to national security from Chinese espionage at DOE's nuclear weapons labs.[6] At least he didn't mince words or beat around the bush like Senator Warner. Further, he noted the dismal state of security:

> We seem to get new revelations from time to time, particularly in the newspapers every week. It's pretty hard to believe that any of our secrets are safe, not even our warheads legacy code for submarines, or for that matter, our reentry vehicles.
>
> In open session, I cannot go into detail about what has been lost, but suffice to say that our national security has been compromised because of the rather cavalier attitude that officials had about lab security. And I'm convinced from the exposure I've had so far that this is going to be the greatest breach of our national security in the history of our country.
>
> What we're doing today is to demand answers to why this loss occurred and who bears the responsibility. What we heard from the lab directors two weeks ago is that you can still walk out of the most secret rooms in the lab, having downloaded a disk similar to this [at this point he held up a 3.5-inch floppy disk—I had an answer for this in my prepared remarks], a disk that could contain nuclear legacy codes and basically nobody knows it. You can simply walk out.

Murkowski also quoted a statement from a DOE security whistle-blower: "If there is a problem, classify it, hide it and get rid of the people who brought it up." There is no more apt description of DOE's modus operandi than that.

Not to be deterred, Murkowski also got after the FBI for refusing to show up at his hearings. The FBI had repeatedly refused to participate in any of the open congressional sessions. Murkowski's explanation for this:

> Quite frankly, I question whether they're hiding behind a smoke-screen of national security to cover up their blunders in the case. Clearly they're pointing the finger at one another. We've heard and we will probably hear more from today's DOE witnesses that the FBI and the Department of Justice handling of this case was highly unusual, to coin a phrase, and apparently unlike any other case.

In my remarks, I emphasized how often the warnings we had given over the years had been disregarded. I was still incensed about the discovery of Lee's massive transfer of nuclear secrets to an unclassified network, which had gone undetected for years, and about the failure of the labs, the Energy Department and the FBI ever to take warnings about the vulnerability of these networks seriously. I had repeatedly warned the labs and Vic Reis and Ken Baker and everyone else about the PRC's interest in our nuclear simulation codes and even was able to specify Los Alamos as a target.

> By early 1996, we at the Department had become sufficiently concerned about reports that we were getting on Chinese efforts to acquire nuclear weapons simulation codes—that is, the legacy codes—that we began briefing this widely. By 1997, we had centered on Los Alamos as the most likely target of these Chinese activities. We warned DOE, laboratory officials, and senior officials throughout the U.S. national security community on this issue many times.
>
> What was done to follow up with our warnings? In short, as we now know, nothing was done. Since few took the threat seriously, why bother taking any extreme measures, such as searching computer files of individuals?

... But I think the record shows that no one in a responsible position at the Department of Energy in the office of the secretary, security affairs, or in defense programs, nor at the laboratories in a security or a weapons management position took our warnings seriously enough to check the prime suspect's computer.

At one point I held up a plastic computer disk that could be inserted into any computer's floppy drive and then locked with a key. I told the committee that this disk, which cost about $15, had been installed on all the computer workstations in the Intelligence Office and that it was an obvious solution to the problem Murkowski had raised in his opening remarks. That was my last appearance in public on the Hill, at least until later that fall.

Most of the real action was taking place behind closed doors anyway. On the Senate side, the Governmental Affairs Committee and Murkowski's Energy and Natural Resources Committee held closed sessions. Surprisingly, the Intelligence Committee in the Senate didn't do much more; on the House side, there was one closed Intelligence Committee meeting, but it was fairly lackluster. Between Murkowski and the GAC, though, I learned a lot more about what had been going on the past four years. For example:

- I learned that Charlie Curtis, as he was departing DOE in 1996, had instructed Ken Baker to brief the incoming secretary on Kindred Spirit at the earliest possible moment. He didn't do it himself because Pena didn't have the appropriate clearances yet.
- I learned that FBI had tried to look at Lee's computer in 1996. I had no idea that there had ever been such an exchange between the FBI and Los Alamos. Of course, the Los Alamos contract counterintelligence officer, Terry Craig, had made a serious mistake. He didn't know Lee had signed a security waiver, and believing he hadn't, Craig thought that Lee had a reasonable expectation of privacy. *On his workstation, inside the vault in X Division!* This still strikes me as the single biggest blunder in the whole case.
- I learned, for the first time, about the FBI's relationship with the Lees during the 1980s. I didn't know until that hearing

that the FBI had employed the Lees as information assets right up to 1991. Had I known it when we were doing the Administrative Inquiry, I would have halted the inquiry and gone to the FBI to ask what was going on. Maybe FBI Headquarters didn't know about this relationship, but now I could begin to understand why FBI Albuquerque did so little on this case.

- Much of the GAC hearing was taken up with the Justice Department's refusal to grant a Foreign Intelligence Surveillance Act (FISA) application to the FBI for technical coverage of Wen Ho Lee. I didn't know that the FBI hadn't even attempted to obtain a warrant until July 1997, more than a year after they opened the case. (Recall that the FBI had told us that they would have such a warrant in thirty to sixty days.) This was to become the subject of great controversy. Justice established a much higher threshold for "probable cause" for the Lee warrant than it had ever set for any other case. FBI Albuquerque's neglect of the case—failing to look at the other leads, for example—gave Justice the ammunition it needed to turn down the FISA request.

As this round of closed hearings finished, it was clear to me that there was a whole lot more to this case than had seemed in the beginning. In particular, now it appeared that the FBI had a long relationship with the Lees, stretching back to 1982 or earlier. I'd known nothing about this at DOE. Moreover, one of the Hill staffers had uncovered Lee's security file. The file Dan Bruno had seen in 1995 had been "reconstructed" after DOE Headquarters had "lost" Lee's original security file. The file Dan saw mentioned the FBI's polygraph of Lee in the early 1980s, but the file this congressional aide had obtained was apparently the original file and contained considerably more derogatory information about Wen Ho Lee. Neither the congressional aide nor his boss, Senator Pete Domenici, shared the file with me. The only hint the aide would give me was that the story of Lee's involvement with the Livermore scientist in 1982, the polygraph the FBI gave him in 1984, and some other information were very damning to his case. Given this, no wonder that Domenici questioned how Wen Ho Lee had ever managed to keep his security clearance. Once, Domenici said, "If only DOE and the FBI had done their job right in the first place, Lee would never have had a clearance after the mid-1980s." But he would never repeat those remarks in public.

DURING THIS SAME period, I was getting a lot of requests to appear on the television political talk shows. Many of these came into DOE's Public Affairs Office and I didn't learn about them until much later. This office would tell media people that I didn't want to talk about any of this, on or off the record. A few enterprising types got through to the secretary at the Office of Intelligence or even to my voice mail, among them Larry King. Most of these were turned down on my behalf by DOE Public Affairs. The department's public affairs officer told me that Secretary Richardson would allow no one but himself to appear on the *Larry King Show*.

One request, however, I would not turn down and that was from *Meet the Press*. Like many, I had been watching this program since I was quite young, and Tim Russert, the current host, always seemed fair in his questioning. He had been all over this story and talked about it the day after the *New York Times* report appeared on March 6. So I agreed to do the interview, although I had never done this kind of television before. Richardson approved this request because he thought I would set the record straight on the case and clear up some of the confusion, according to a later statement by a department spokesperson.

I was scheduled to appear on Sunday, May 23, 1999, along with Rep. Chris Cox. Russert was very kind to me; I don't know if he could tell I was nervous, but we chatted several minutes in the "green room" before the taping began. William Safire, the *New York Times* columnist, and Rep. Bob Barr (R-GA) were also on the program. The show is taped about an hour before it appears, at least here in Washington, D.C. Russert plows straight through. There are breaks for commercials, when you can catch your breath a bit, but there is no rehearsal and he just fires away at you.

I stuck to my "script": yes, there had been Chinese espionage at the nuclear labs (at least two cases confirmed, one likely, and possibly more).[7] Cox verified this and claimed that about 70 percent of his "classified" report would actually see the light of day. Russert walked me through the Sandy Berger briefings at the White House. (He had really been working Berger over on who knew what, when, and Berger had changed his story at least once already.) We then went over the department's efforts to bury the story. With the exception of DOE officials, my responses to Russert basically gave the Clinton administration good marks for their actions after Richardson had taken over. Of course, we had to rake Moler over the coals, but I went out of my way to praise Richardson and his efforts to fix this problem.

Russert also pointed up the President's tap-dancing on this topic. Clinton had been Clinton, of course, when he was first asked, "Can you assure the American people that under your watch, no valuable nuclear secrets were lost?" Clinton replied: "Can I tell you there has been no espionage at the labs since I've been president? I can tell you that no one has reported to me that they suspect such a thing has occurred. To the best of my knowledge, no one has said anything to me about any espionage which occurred by the Chinese against the labs during my presidency." Russert drew the correct conclusion: Berger never told the President about any of this. Cox claimed to have met with Clinton in April, but Clinton's press statement had been given in March, so who knows? I dodged, not too artfully, Russert's question as to whether it was conceivable to me that nobody would have told the President. I wasn't about to answer that while I was still working in the Clinton administration. And it is perfectly conceivable that Berger never told him; Berger probably had a whole list of things that Clinton didn't want to know.

Russert asked me how serious I thought the damage would turn out to be. I said: "I think the potential is on a magnitude equal to the Rosenberg-Fuchs compromise of the Manhattan Project information. So, I concluded in my personal view that the potential damage is very significant." I was referring not just to suspicions about Wen Ho Lee and the mid-1980s compromise of the W88 information, but to everything we had learned about PRC acquisitions over the past four years plus our new knowledge about Lee's compromise of every nuclear warhead designed by Los Alamos. I still consider the probability that the PRC will develop and field mobile long-range missiles capable of striking not only our homeland but also U.S. military forces throughout the Pacific to represent very significant potential damage.

A week later, Russert was back on this theme, hammering away at Richardson this time. Richardson, along with the rest of the administration, was doing a lot of spinning and damage control. When the Cox Report had been released earlier that week, he had proclaimed, "There is no evidence of a wholesale loss of information."[8] And he had picked up the theme that no Chinese warhead modernization had yet taken place from Walpole's Intelligence Community Damage Assessment. When asked about the Cox Report's conclusion about PRC acquisition of classified information on seven warheads, Richardson responded that there were "three confirmed cases of espionage." He listed the 1970s neutron bomb, the 1980s W88 and the 1990s. "There is no question that the Chinese got some of our nuclear secrets."

Then Russert closed the trap.

MR. RUSSERT: Then here's my problem. If Mr. Cox sent a report to the White House in January of '99 saying there were suspicions of ongoing Chinese espionage, and you just said in September of '98 you suspected ongoing Chinese espionage at the labs, why did the President in March 1999 say that "no one has reported to me they suspect such a thing has occurred?"
SEC'Y RICHARDSON: Tim, again, we got into this at the last show. What is very clear is that what the president meant was that there was no espionage loss. There is no evidence of espionage loss at the labs during this period.

Pretty lame, huh? Richardson in the previous breath had just referred to "confirmed" espionage in the 1990s. But he wasn't done yet. He promised "firings and demotions at the Department of Energy" and stressed that his department would run on "accountability."

The biggest whopper was in response to a question from Russert about me.

MR. RUSSERT: Mr. Secretary, let me show you and our viewers a photograph. This was taken Friday. It's you and our guest from

last week, Notra Trulock, who works for the Department of Energy. You gave him a bonus and an award commending his service, and, yet, one year ago this very month, he was demoted—demoted in the Department of Energy. Why the turnaround within a year?
SEC'Y RICHARDSON: Well, I wasn't there a year ago, but I can tell you that this man did exceptional service. He can stay at the Department of Energy. He's a key member of my team. He is acting deputy director, and his service to this country is very important. That's why I rewarded him. He can stay.
MR. RUSSERT: Will he be given a permanent job, no longer acting?
SEC'Y RICHARDSON: If he wants to, he can stay. I want him to be part of my team. He's done some very, very valuable service to the country. He was persistent. He raised this issue. He's the one that discovered it first, that it's not the walk-in. He's the one in the Department of Energy officials that brought this to the attention of the U.S. government.

It is true that after my appearance on *Meet the Press,* Secretary Richardson had presented me with a Monetary Award for Special Act or Service. I had kept my end of the bargain by praising Richardson and his efforts to reform DOE counterintelligence. On May 27, 1999, Richardson held a ceremony in the Intelligence Office and presented me with a check for $10,000 ($7,500 after taxes) and a certificate reading:

> Over a four-year period of 1995–1999, you have performed a series of exceptional acts which benefited the national security of the United States. Moreover you have displayed extraordinary analytic skills, persistence, and have been undeterred in revealing the scope of the intelligence collection program of the Peoples Republic of China. In doing these things, you have performed an important service for your country.

I thought it was a nice gesture, but Richardson also played it for his own political purposes. Going into the conference room, I was told that CNN would be there with a reporter. I am willing to bet that this was the first such award in the history of the Energy Department to be televised and it was certainly the first time a TV camera crew had ever been inside the intelligence vault at the Energy Department. Pierre Thomas was the reporter and I tried to answer his questions in a straightforward manner. Richardson told me later that he had encountered fierce resistance from his staff of political appointees, who had tried to talk him out of the award and then urged him to cut it to $5,000 or less.

On the brighter side, I also received some very nice correspondence from across the country thanking me for my service. One lady wrote telling me that she was nominating me for *Time* magazine's Man of the Year. Others wrote praising my "integrity," "courage" and so forth. I even got a letter from a former colleague at Los Alamos thanking me for finally exposing the lab, but also telling me that nothing had really changed down there. These were truly appreciated, if a little embarrassing. After all, I still thought I was just doing my job. Another theme that came through: Don't let the bastards get you down. But I was fast losing that fight.

EIGHT

Backlash

... and Trulock, a persistent, irritating man who resembles Star Trek's
Captain Kirk ... "Because of his personality," said an administration
official who deals with nuclear security, "it doesn't take long before
you just blow off what he has to say."
—*Philadelphia Inquirer*
June 2, 1999

I don't know about the Captain Kirk part, but I certainly was
persistent, if not irritating, about security vulnerabilities at the
labs and the threat of Chinese nuclear espionage. And so it
was inevitable that sooner or later the backlash initiated by the
Clinton administration would reach the media and Capitol Hill.
Too much was at stake: careers and reputations, billions of dollars
in program budgets, jobs and, oh yes, China. China was the topic
of a raging, if not great, debate and the administration was still
under fire for accepting campaign contributions from the People's
Liberation Army. Had the topic been Russian espionage or espionage by just about any other country, I'm not sure that there would
have been so much controversy. But China was and is different.
Because of Clinton's complex interactions with the PRC—personal,
political and electoral—the message about Chinese nuclear espionage was bound to come under attack.

The irony, of course, is that when the scandal first broke,
administration officials quickly conceded that espionage did indeed
occur. Both Sandy Berger and Bill Richardson admitted this and
that the administration had been slow to respond.[1] Berger had
declared on national television, "There's no question that they [the
PRC] benefited from this." Richardson made numerous television
appearances in which he acknowledged Chinese espionage against
his labs, but assured the American public that "their nuclear secrets

are now safe at the labs."[2] White House officials were probably surprised by the easy success of their damage control. By the end of that summer, the White House was celebrating the disappearance of the issue from the nation's news media. Gary Samore, the NSC nonproliferation director, was telling reporters, "Isn't it incredible how a story like this can get started and then it turns out to be totally false. The Cox report has been totally invalidated. Not a single one of its conclusions stands up to close scrutiny."[3] But it wasn't as effortless as it seemed. The White House had established a warroom operation to "manage" the Chinese nuclear espionage story.[4] James Kennedy, who handled the Clintons' impeachment counteroffensive and later became Senator Hillary Clinton's press agent, ran the operation.[5] The main objective of this campaign was to shift blame away from the White House and, if possible, make the whole thing just go away.

The White House got some help from unexpected quarters. The FBI launched its own major damage-control operation, doing everything it could to avoid the harm to its public image and reputation that its own performance in this case merited. The FBI's investigation had been "a paradigm of how not to manage and work an important espionage case," and its mistakes and failures in an investigation that "involved allegations of espionage as significant as any the United States Government is likely to face" were inexplicable and in some instances staggering.[6] Put simply, the FBI never devoted the resources or the management attention to this case that such allegations would normally warrant.

The FBI's John Lewis, who ran the National Security Division until 1998, had retired into a plush job with Goldman-Sachs, and after an interim period, a new assistant director, Neil Gallagher, took over the Wen Ho Lee case in late November 1998. The following February, Louis Freeh appointed him to represent the FBI in the upcoming congressional hearings. I first met Gallagher that spring and was immediately struck by two things. First, he didn't know a thing about the cooperation and interaction between the FBI and DOE that now stretched back to 1995. On every question, he had to consult his briefing books or his notes. Second, he seemed more concerned about protecting the Bureau's image than anything else. For example, in one hearing I characterized the outcome of

the April 1997 meeting in Los Alamos between the FBI, Energy and
the lab as a "quid pro quo"—we would leave Wen Ho Lee in place
and the FBI would press to wrap the case up. Gallagher immediately denied the existence of any such deal, claiming that Energy
had decided on its own to leave Lee in place. "Uh-oh," I remember thinking.

Gallagher's tack in congressional testimony and probably with
the media was to overstate the role and importance of the Energy
Department's 1996 Administrative Inquiry. He told the Senate Governmental Affairs Committee in mid-1999 that "he had full credibility in the [AI] report," that he could find no errors in it, and that
it made a compelling case for focusing on Los Alamos.[7] Gallagher
would repeatedly depict the Administrative Inquiry as if it were
the last word in the FBI's investigation and not what it should have
been—the prologue to a full FBI field investigation.

Of course, that ignored the recommendations of Special Agent
"F. Jeff Maines" for the investigation that he believed the FBI should
conduct *after* the Bureau received the AI report in May 1996, but
never did. There was also the problem of the other investigative
leads contained in the original AI report that the FBI had ignored,
including those from Livermore Lab. Gallagher's expressions of
high confidence in the AI finally got him in hot water on Capitol
Hill as more people learned of the actual contents of the report.

The Bureau was coming under increasing criticism for its
many mistakes in the case. The Thompson-Lieberman Senate Statement referred to "investigatory missteps, institutional and personal
miscommunications, and—we believe—legal and policy misun-
derstandings and mistakes at all levels of government."[8] The statement went on to lump the FBI in with Energy and Justice and
declared that "all must share the blame for our government's poor
performance in handling this matter." As has become clear in the
aftermath of the September 11, 2002, terrorist attacks, the Bureau
is notoriously thin-skinned and devotes much of its time and effort
to protecting its public image—often at the expense of the truth.

So the FBI switched tactics. No longer was the AI portrayed
as complete and thorough. Now it was "complete junk" and a "piece
of crap." This assessment came from the FBI's Albuquerque field
office, which had been responsible for running—and botching—

the case for over three years. The field office was subsequently charged in a Justice Department report with "neglect, faulty judgment, bad personnel choices, inept investigation, and inadequate supervision of that inept investigation."[9] The same office that was led by managers who had consistently failed "to recognize or appreciate the gravity of the case."[10]

FBI officials, both at Albuquerque and in the Washington Headquarters, began promoting the idea that the DOE Administrative Inquiry was to blame for all the FBI mistakes of the past four years, just as it would blame Ed Curran for withholding the transcripts of Lee's December polygraph from them. Albuquerque's new assistant SAC, Will Lueckenhoff, led the charge, suddenly discovering all kinds of "problems" with the 1996 AI report: selection criteria that were too "narrow," conclusions that were not "supportable," a time frame for the potential compromise that was "questionable," and a focus "unduly" on persons with comprehensive access to the W88 classified information.[11] To make this case, though, the bureau had to conceal the role played by FBI Headquarters officials in the 1995 approval of the AI's methodology and then their uncritical acceptance of the 1996 report. And how to explain the role of Special Agent "Maines" in the conduct of the AI? Despite the fact that "Maines" had made some of the key decisions regarding Wen Ho Lee, Gallagher would now describe his part merely as one of "assistance," with full responsibility for the AI belonging solely to the Energy Department.[12]

FBI officials blamed DOE for "misleading" them and causing them to focus on the wrong crime and the wrong suspect. In particular, they would claim that DOE misled the FBI regarding the nature of the "predicate" of the investigation and, consequently, the FBI spent four years investigating the wrong crime, or perhaps there never had been a crime after all.[13] I thought the FBI understood full well the predicate: that the PRC had acquired classified data on the W88 warhead and that this compromise had materially assisted the Chinese nuclear weapons program. What could be clearer than that? The FBI has hidden behind classification so as to conceal their interpretation of what was actually communicated to the Bureau in the AI report.

In a number of publicly available documents, the Bureau asserts that it was told that the W88 classified information could only have come from within the weapons division (X Division) at

Los Alamos and that Wen Ho Lee was our only suspect. But our list of potential investigative leads included scientists from both Los Alamos and Livermore, and I had heard Energy investigators repeatedly tell the FBI that the Bureau should also be looking at Defense Department facilities and Navy contractors. Former attorney general Janet Reno specifically criticized the Bureau in congressional testimony in 1999 for failing to investigate leads from Livermore provided by DOE in 1996. She told the Senate Judiciary Committee that the FBI had focused on Los Alamos, but "the DOE inquiry focused both on Los Alamos and the Lawrence Livermore Laboratory."[14] Bureau spokesmen and some lab scientists would also claim that there had been widespread dissent to the Kindred Spirit Analysis Group's 1995 findings, dissent that had been suppressed in the transmission of these findings to the FBI. But the only dissenter was Bobby Henson, and his dissent took the form of criticizing the KSAG findings for being too weak. He pushed the KSAG to declare that a spy at Los Alamos had assisted the Chinese and he even had some candidates, including his former supervisors Danny Stillman and Terry Hawkins. I thought Henson was way over the top and I was satisfied with the KSAG conclusions, while taking note of Henson's dissent.

The assault had begun in early 1999, but was publicly acknowledged in a letter from Janet Reno and Louis Freeh to Congress the following October, announcing that the FBI had decided to "reopen" the W88 investigation:

> Our decision to take this action in regard to the investigation into the compromise of U.S. nuclear technology is the result of two separate inquiries. First, there were investigative concerns raised by the FBI Albuquerque field office that began to develop in November 1998, regarding deficiencies in the DOE Administrative Inquiry. Second, after Senate Governmental Affairs Committee staff raised questions, we started to reexamine flawed analysis in the conclusions drawn in the DOE Administrative Inquiry.[15]

This was pure FBI spin, and at the highest level. In November 1998, the Albuquerque field office had been trying to convince Washington to grant an application to begin technical surveillance on Wen Ho Lee, an application that had stressed Lee's propensity to commit espionage. There is the "not guilty" memo sent to Washington by Albuquerque SAC Dave Kitchen in late January 1999. Relying on DOE's word that Lee had passed his polygraph, Lee's own statement that he hadn't done anything wrong, and his personal endorsement of Lee as being "cooperative," Kitchen concluded that Lee hadn't done it and proposed to shut down the investigation. The Senate Judiciary Committee would later observe, "Any comments from Mr. Kitchen regarding flaws in the Administrative Inquiry must be viewed in the context of the Albuquerque division's bungling of the Kindred Spirit investigation."[16] It would label Kitchen's recommendation to shut down the investigation "nothing short of outrageous." But Louis Freeh, his boss, would echo all Kitchen's criticisms in later congressional testimony.

Ironically, the FBI had also brought back Steve Dillard to head up a task force to reexamine the case. "Ironically" because Dillard had been the FBI's section chief during a crucial phase of the Kindred Spirit investigation, from late 1996 to 1998. Dillard had failed to inform his supervisors about his section's growing concerns about Albuquerque's handling of the Lee investigation or its mismanagement and diversion of agents dispatched by Washington to help with the case. He had also misled Congress about the investigation and Lee's status at the lab. Now he was back—supposedly to look at what had gone wrong the first time around.

By late October 1999, Secretary Bill Richardson had had enough of FBI carping about the Administrative Inquiry. He wrote to Freeh complaining:

> ... I think there has been a tendency to overstate the adverse influence that DOE's technical analysis and preliminary investigative support had on the conduct of the Kindred Spirit investigation. There also has been, in my opinion, an over-emphasis on the degree to which DOE input served to limit the FBI's investigative work.... [T]he fact is that all of the decisions to limit the scope of the investigation were clearly, mutually agreed-upon by DOE and the FBI, based on security and other concerns.[17]

Richardson was right and deserves credit for defending his agency's work. Of course, Freeh ignored Richardson's letter, and the FBI's campaign to discredit the Administrative Inquiry continued unabated. In particular, the FBI sought at every turn to downplay the role Special Agent "F. Jeff Maines" played in the Administrative Inquiry and especially any reference to his part in focusing on Wen Ho Lee.

Senator Charles Grassley of Iowa would later confirm in a public hearing that the FBI had been trying to distance itself from its role in the Administrative Inquiry:

> Mr. Trulock, the documents that we reviewed as part of this investigation confirm what you say about the FBI giving its blessing to the Administrative Inquiry. So I want to state for the record that that is the case, because the FBI has tried to absolve itself of that concurrence.[18]

A former Grassley aide also told me that the FBI had conducted a "whispering campaign" on Capitol Hill intended to destroy my credibility with the congressmen and senators. When I heard this, I recalled one FBI agent telling me that Gallagher was furious when he saw these same senators accepting testimony from me about what had happened as "gospel."

Los Alamos National Laboratory would soon join in the offensive against the AI. There had been some personnel changes down at Los Alamos, too. Sig Hecker had stepped down as director and was replaced by John Browne, whom I had worked for at the lab in the early 1990s. Browne became the new director after a struggle between Senator Pete Domenici and University of California selection officials. Domenici regarded the university's candidates as insufficiently experienced in national security, whereas Browne had worked these issues at both Livermore and Los Alamos and he seemed the best candidate, although some of Domenici's aides considered him too weak for the job. Mostly, congressional aides and Energy Department officials were glad to see Hecker go. Many thought he was a terrible manager, and under his command Los Alamos had repeatedly missed deadlines on construction projects and was far behind in its Stockpile Stewardship obligations. The change of management, however, did nothing to take the heat off Los Alamos, which was taking a beating on Capitol Hill and in the national media.

On March 8, 1999, at Secretary Richardson's direction, Browne had fired Wen Ho Lee. The same day, Richardson named Lee in an on-the-record interview with the *New York Times* and other Washington reporters, citing Lee's failure to report his contacts with PRC nuclear scientists, his failure to make full disclosure to security officials on these and other matters, and his mishandling of classified information as reasons for his dismissal. Richardson did not yet know about Lee's computer tapes. But the harsh criticisms of the lab only increased. Los Alamos seemed to represent all that was wrong with the Energy Department and its national labs: arrogant, profligate and scornful of even the most fundamental requirements of security and counterintelligence.

About a week after Lee was fired, Los Alamos' senior managers met to plot their own damage control strategy. Not long after the lab fired Lee, Karl Braithwaite, a former aide to Senator Edmund Muskie who ran Los Alamos' congressional lobbying office, held a brainstorming session on how to cope with all the "bad publicity" the lab was getting. Present at the meeting were Terry Hawkins, the lab's resident China expert, and Bob Vrooman, its former counterintelligence chief, who had retired a year earlier from Los Alamos but was now back as a consultant. Their objective was to develop a campaign to deflect attention away from the lab by demonstrating that the W88 compromise couldn't possibly have come from Los Alamos, if indeed it had happened at all. Hawkins would begin spreading the word to anyone who would listen that the Chinese couldn't have replicated the W88 and he knew that the PRC's new nuclear warhead was actually "longer" than the W88. (Just how he "knew" this is unclear.) Besides, the Chinese certainly didn't have the technical expertise to deploy such a weapon on long-range ballistic missiles anyway. He had been to China, after all, had met the Chinese nuclear scientists and toured their facilities.

In truth, Hawkins had been meeting with Chinese nuclear scientists for several years and they had convinced him that their warhead developments represented no threat to the United States. He, in turn, communicated a very benign picture of the PRC nuclear program to intelligence, defense and congressional officials in Washington. According to Hawkins, the Chinese were only concerned for the safety of their nuclear warheads, and he believed we should be helping them—a view that any acknowledgement of Chinese nuclear espionage would seriously discredit. It would also diminish the influence of Hawkins and of Los Alamos in U.S. decision-making on future lab-to-lab interactions with the PRC. Hawkins found a very receptive audience at DOE Headquarters and among both Democrats and Republicans on Capitol Hill, especially on the Senate Select Committee on Intelligence. He also began giving background briefings to the media on his critique of the Chinese nuclear espionage case.

Vrooman, on the other hand, would attack the Energy Department's Administrative Inquiry for its "premature" focus on Wen Ho Lee and other so-called flaws. Vrooman's motives were far more prosaic than those of Hawkins: he told reporters that he was "going public" to save his professional reputation.[19] For good reason, as it turns out, since all of the alleged events of this case, including Wen Ho Lee's illegal computer transfers, had happened on his watch as lab CI officer. After the FBI had recommended against further interactions between the Lees and PRC scientists, he approved continued contacts between Sylvia (and presumably Wen Ho) Lee and the Chinese in 1989, even though he suspected that the PRC was eliciting classified information from them. He had stood by when the FBI made a feeble effort to access Lee's computer in 1996, and he had made no effort to link the FBI's interest in Lee's computer activity to Los Alamos computer security monitoring capabilities.

Had Vrooman put the FBI in touch with lab computer security experts in 1996, Lee's illicit transfers might have been detected before he could make his 1997 tape containing the very latest Los Alamos computer codes and the most sensitive information on the W88 warhead. On his own initiative, Vrooman rejected Louis Freeh's recommendation to remove Wen Ho Lee from access to nuclear secrets in 1997 and left him in place for another fifteen months.

Albuquerque FBI chief Dave Kitchen's "not guilty" memo on Wen Ho Lee came in handy for Vrooman, who could now claim that the Bureau never thought there was much to this case in the first place; and so did Wackenhut's botched polygraph.[20] Vrooman would also be the first to play the race card as part of the Los Alamos damage control strategy. Hawkins would operate on the inside, lobbying the administration and Capitol Hill, and Vrooman would take his criticisms public. Los Alamos would find very sympathetic ears for their lob-bying efforts in three key reporters—Walter Pincus and Vernon Loeb of the *Washington Post* and Bill Broad of the *New York Times.*

Loeb would later admit that he was under intense pressure from his editor, Jackson Diehl, after the March 6 *New York Times* article had scooped the *Post.* He said that he was caught "flat-footed" even though his partner, Walter Pincus, had already covered most of the details of the case in a February article.[21] Thanks to Vrooman, he would get a sensational new angle on the story.

Bill Broad was the *New York Times'* science reporter and was well known within the Energy Department labs. Hawkins, Vrooman and Bobby Henson, among others, worked with Broad over the sum-mer to reshape the *Times'* coverage of the story. By September, Broad was writing that the Chinese had achieved the breakthroughs on their own, citing Terry Hawkins as saying that all nations' nuclear weapons "look alike" and that China's advances had "more to do with physics than espionage."[22] Despite the existence of the walk-in document, which even Vrooman had referred to as a "smoking gun" in 1995, Broad now quoted a top administration official as saying, "we don't have a smoking gun." He repeated Hawkins' claim that China's new warhead was longer than the W88.

In his book *My Country versus Me,* Wen Ho Lee makes an inter-esting assertion regarding the *New York Times'* coverage of his story. He says that in midsummer 1999, his lawyer threatened to cut off the *Times* if the newspaper didn't change its coverage of the Lees' story. Lee says the threat worked: "Later, when other *New York Times* reporters began to write about my case and the stories became more balanced, my lawyers resumed answering their questions."[23] Broad certainly helped by airing Los Alamos' "doubts" about the original espionage allegations.

The Clinton administration got a lot of help from Capitol Hill, and not just from Democrats. Reports from committees chaired by Republicans, issued in the aftermath of the hearings, provided accounts of the Kindred Spirit investigations, especially the Admin-istrative Inquiry, that were shaded, distorted and just plain wrong. And the labs' supporters on Capitol Hill, Democrats and especially Republicans, pulled out all the stops to protect the labs from any further "embarrassment" over their dereliction in the protection of our nuclear secrets.

The President's Foreign Intelligence Advisory Board had also been tasked to look into this mess and issued its report in June 1999. That report went a long way toward shifting blame away from the administration onto DOE and the labs. And given that the espionage involved the Chinese and that the FBI's main suspect was Asian-American, it was probably inevitable that race and ethnicity would become issues sooner or later.

Taken together, this combination enabled the administration to evade any responsibility whatsoever for its handling of the Chinese nuclear spying scandal. Administration officials, speaking anonymously of course, claimed that there had been no Chinese nuclear espionage after all, whatever its own representatives may have admitted publicly. And none of this would have been possible without congressional Republicans leaving the field at precisely the key moment. The Cox Report was quietly shelved and Congress spent most of its time in devising schemes to protect the labs — mostly from more stringent security regulations.

To cinch the deal, the White House campaign began to turn personal, employing the same scorched-earth tactics that had worked so well against all other Clinton opponents. How I fell into that category when I continued to hold my end of a bargain with Secretary Richardson still mystifies me. Early on, after the *New York Times* article, an emissary from Richardson approached me with a "deal": If I wouldn't criticize him in public, Richardson would "stand by me." Now, "stand by" means different things to different people, but Richardson's emissary guaranteed that the secretary would have nothing but "nice" things to say about me in public. I didn't have much to lose at that point. And Richardson did seem to be trying to make some changes and implement counterintelligence and security reform. So I consistently gave him credit in public for what he was trying to do. But I didn't pull any punches on the old regime when this catastrophe had unfolded, and I think Richardson finally had to choose between me or Pena and Moler. Of course, he opted to defend *their* record and leave me twisting slowly in the wind, a time-honored Washington tradition.

The first shots were fired as the unclassified version of the Cox Report was about to be published. Just before its release, White House officials had warned the media that it would produce classified information to discredit any report that went too hard on the Clinton administration. The White House would claim that the published version did not square with the classified version and that it could prove that Cox and company had relied on "worst-case scenarios."[24] Most reporters ignored Chris Cox's claim that the unclassified version of the report contained nearly 70 percent of the material published in the classified version.

In response to questions about Chinese nuclear espionage, administration spokesmen would continually refer to the conclusions of the Intelligence Community's Damage Assessment: no Chinese strategic force modernization and no new nuclear warhead deployments had yet taken place. No harm, no foul. There was a classified version of the Damage Assessment, which differed little in content from the Cox Report, but it was hidden away from the public by classification rules. The administration took pains to carefully limit its distribution, even inside the government.

Second, the *Washington Post* began to question the credibility of some of the intelligence information used by the Cox Committee to make its judgments. In particular, the *Post* raised questions about the "walk-in document."[25] The *Post* reported that CIA had been "deliberately fed" this document by Chinese intelligence sources. "Why would the Chinese do this?" was a question that had been under debate since at least 1996 and now was out in the open. Chris Cox mostly bungled his attempts to explain this, saying that maybe they had been trying to intimidate the U.S. or maybe they made a "mistake." Not surprisingly, the *Post* found a number of experts willing to dismiss the walk-in document and its evidence of Chinese nuclear espionage out of hand. Terry Hawkins, Los Alamos' China expert, quoted Sun Tzu, the ancient Chinese military philosopher, in speculating that the Chinese sought to stir up such turmoil to dissuade "top Chinese nuclear physicists" from joining the nuclear labs. Cox and the committee were made to look rather ridiculous by supposedly relying so heavily on one "tainted" source. DOE officials like Under Secretary Ernie Moniz kept pushing this red herring by spreading distorted versions of how the walk-in document was acquired and what was really in it around Capitol Hill. Moniz got so far out with his "perception management campaign" that the CIA actually protested to Richardson about his deputy's distortions of CIA activities. Energy Department officials and lab scientists also began to "leak" to the media that perhaps the information in the walk-in document wasn't accurate, after all.

Supposedly, Los Alamos scientists had reviewed the document in mid-1999 and this time uncovered some "inaccuracies," which they now used to raise even more questions about the investigation with the local FBI, on Capitol Hill and in the media. Los Alamos scientists shared their findings with the Albuquerque FBI agents, who latched onto this to further their own crusade to blame all of Albuquerque's failures on the original Administrative Inquiry. That Los Alamos would find "inaccuracies" is ironic since its own scientists—Carl Henry, John Richter, Alan Riley and Larry Booth— had repeatedly checked the W88 information in the document in 1995 and 1996. Tom Cook had repeatedly pronounced the data in the walk-in document accurate to "three significant figures." But now other scientists would claim that the data were more likely taken from "interface control documents."

A Los Alamos scientist named John Kammerdiener led the charge on this allegation. He told reporters that the W88 data in the walk-in document had come from documents that describe which parts of the bomb would be built by Energy and which by the Defense Department and its contractors.[26] According to Kammerdiener, Wen Ho Lee would not have had access to the data in the walk-in document, but rather blueprints and internal dimensions. Kammerdiener would also claim that he had told me all this in 1995. The FBI gobbled up his story, since it would "prove" that we had misled them all along. Kammerdiener's account found its way into a later Justice Department review that echoed the Bureau's criticisms of DOE.

There are some problems with Kammerdiener's story. First, I do not recall him among Mike Henderson's selections to be on the KSAG back in 1995. I can recall clearly the faces of many of the scientists arguing and debating in my conference room over that summer, 1995, but I have no recollection of Kammerdiener being among them. Second, at least a dozen highly experienced nuclear weapons designers examined the data in the walk-in document. These scientists had nearly a hundred live nuclear tests to their credit and had designed much of the U.S. "enduring nuclear stockpile," but somehow they couldn't tell the difference between interface documents and warhead blueprints? I think arguing that they were unable to distinguish the source of the data in the walk-in document strains credulity. How was Kammerdiener so smart and all the rest of these highly respected nuclear warhead designers so dumb?

Last, of course, is Kammerdiener's claim to have told me all this in 1995 while he was on a three-month stint in my office. My first recollection of meeting Kammerdiener is in 1998. I had seen him around Los Alamos, but I didn't know, for example, that he was married to one of the Los Alamos program managers whom we funded. My recollection is that he came to Washington in 1998 for a short tour. He and I worked on a project together in this period, and I do recall having some conversations with him, Richter and Cook about the W88 data during this time, but nothing before that. Kammerdiener should get a medal from the FBI and Vrooman, however, because he gave them the out they were desperately seeking.

Vrooman began spreading the claim that the W88 information that the Chinese had acquired was held at many locations throughout the nuclear weapons complex and not just at the Energy Department labs. According to him, this proved that Wen Ho Lee could not have provided such information to the Chinese and that the Administrative Inquiry was deeply flawed. Of course, Dan Bruno had repeatedly told the FBI that very thing, and at least once in Vrooman's presence. But Vrooman ignored this and claimed that more that five hundred people, mostly in the Defense Department, had received documents with "Restricted Data" information on the W88. In his August 1999 press release, he declared that

> a rather detailed description of the W88 had a distribution of 548 copies, of which only 180 copies are within the DOE complex. The rest of the addresses are in the Defense Department, military services (including the National Guard), and other government agencies and contractors such as Lockheed Missile and Space Corporation.[27]

Vrooman led reporters to believe he was referring to documents available during the period of our investigative focus—1984 to 1988. But he was later forced to admit that the document he referred to had been produced in 1996—eight years after our 1988 cutoff.

And Moniz knew better. Not long after the scandal broke, I was summoned to his office and told to bring the walk-in document with me. Robin Staffins, the Livermore scientist now working in Moniz's office, and Joan Rohfling were there with him, demanding to review the information in the document. Staffins read it over carefully, especially the descriptions of the W88, and gulped. "Yeah," he said, "it's all in there." I was dismissed and left Moniz, Rohfling and Staffins all staring at each other, wondering what to do next.

But Moniz didn't stop with the walk-in document. After news broke of Wen Ho Lee's illegal computer activities in late April, Moniz repeatedly told senators and congressmen that Lee had placed only unclassified information on the unprotected computer network at Los Alamos. Once, I accompanied him to a meeting with Congressman Fred Upton (R-MI) to discuss Kindred Spirit. When Moniz told Upton that Lee had downloaded only some unclassified hydrodynamic codes, I couldn't help but contradict him in front of the congressman. Not a career-enhancing move. I was called on the carpet when I got back to the department and was never invited to accompany Moniz again on his trips to Capitol Hill.

Next, the President's Foreign Intelligence Advisory Board jumped into the act. The origins of the PFIAB stretch back to the Eisenhower administration. Its mission is to "assess the quality, quantity, and adequacy of intelligence collection, of analysis and estimates, of counterintelligence, and other intelligence activities."[28] That's a pretty broad mandate, and the board has had a roller-coaster ride over the years. Jimmy Carter abolished it altogether and tried to destroy the history in its files. These treasures were saved only through the efforts of a secretary who understood their significance. During the Reagan years, the board was fairly influential, but less so during the first Bush administration. Its composition, leadership and access to the President have always determined the value of the board.

Warren Rudman, a former U.S. senator, was Clinton's appointee as chairman of the PFIAB. Rudman was known around town as a thoroughly nasty guy, always quick to spring to the defense of the status quo. He had played a memorable role during the confirmation hearings for Bob Gates as director of Central Intelligence in the Bush administration. His cross-examination of intelligence officers who had alleged that Gates had participated in the politicization of intelligence on the former Soviet Union was intemperate and demeaning. In conservative political circles, he was commonly known as a RINO, "Republican in name only." He left the Senate years earlier, but continued to hang around Washington serving on prestigious boards and blue-ribbon panels. He was the perfect selection to head Clinton's PFIAB. As a nominal Republican he gave Clinton top cover, but was certain to defend the White House at the end of the day.

When the scandal broke, Clinton had tasked the PFIAB to examine structural and managerial problems in the Energy Department's security and counterintelligence operations. I met with the PFIAB investigators several times, but only once with Rudman, who treated me like a criminal. During my session with him, he badgered me about the Administrative Inquiry. And that was it. No questions about the PRC nuclear espionage, the walk-in document, the four years' worth of intelligence analysis the labs had done on the threat to DOE, all the roadblocks we had encountered trying to reform counterintelligence—nothing. All he wanted to know was why we focused on Wen Ho Lee. "We didn't," I replied. I told him repeatedly that we had identified other investigative leads for the FBI, but the Bureau didn't follow up on them. Of course, he had Dan Bruno's "investigator's note" that talked of Lee's access, opportunity and motive; but no matter how I tried to place that in context or refer to the other "investigative leads" or remind him that Dan was expressing his "opinion," Rudman was interested only in Lee and Los Alamos. "What focus on Los Alamos?" I asked again. "What about the Livermore leads?" But he simply didn't want to hear about that, nor did he ask whether the FBI had ever come back for more information on any aspects of the AI.

Not surprisingly, the PFIAB did indeed produce a scathing report on the "adequacy" of measures taken by DOE to meet the security threat. The report confirmed what many others and I had been saying about DOE's approach to security and CI for years:

1. The labs were and continue to be a major target of foreign intelligence services.
2. Security and CI problems had been documented and were well understood for more than twenty-five years.
3. Security and CI had been relegated to a low-priority status for decades.
4. Organizational disarray, managerial neglect and a culture of arrogance—both at DOE Headquarters and at the labs themselves—conspired to create an espionage scandal waiting to happen.
5. The nature of the intelligence-gathering methods used by the People's Republic of China poses a special challenge to the U.S. in general and the weapons labs in particular.

The PFIAB's conclusion on the labs' attitude toward security was scathing:

> When it comes to a genuine understanding of and appreciation for the value of security and counterintelligence programs, especially in the context of America's nuclear arsenal and secrets, the DOE and its weapons labs have been Pollyannaish. The predominant attitude toward security and counterintelligence among many DOE and lab managers has ranged from half-hearted, grudging accommodation to smug disregard. Thus the panel is convinced that the potential for major leaks and thefts of sensitive information and material has been substantial. Moreover, such security lapses would have occurred in bureaucratic environments that would have allowed them to go undetected with relative ease.[29]

Moreover, the report affirmed my public testimony that Moler and her allies in the DOE bureaucracy had blocked, resisted and delayed reform and had even fought the implementation of the Presidential Decision Directive:

> Never before has the panel found an agency with the bureaucratic insolence to dispute, delay and resist implementation of a Presidential directive on security, as DOE's bureaucracy tried to do to the Presidential Decision Directive No. 61 in February 1998.[30]

While chiding officials for initially moving too slowly, the PFIAB report congratulated the Clinton administration for its forceful action, the speed and scope of its response to the crisis, and the PDD and some of Richardson's initiatives. Finally, the report recommended abolishing the Office of Intelligence, replacing it with a small staff mainly to exercise liaison with the Intelligence Community, and turning all of the labs' analytic assets over to the CIA. At the encouragement of Richardson and Sanchez, I sent a letter to Rudman noting the irony of recommending the abolishment of the office whose efforts had led to a Presidential Decision Directive and forced the administration finally to confront the threat of nuclear espionage. I faxed my letter over to Rudman directly, and then promptly forgot about it. I was surprised to hear from *Washington Post* reporter Walter Pincus that the PFIAB had provided a copy of my letter to him. Rudman replied in an open letter containing some vile allegations about my "wildly inaccurate assertions and reckless accusations" and my "misread[ing of] professional disagreements as personal affronts." As if that weren't enough, he then wrote, "[Y]our comments approach a fevered pitch of hysteria and confusion," and "intentionally or unintentionally, you have repeatedly marketed fiction as fact."[31]

The *New York Times* covered the PFIAB report in a fairly straightforward manner. It cited Rudman's findings that the bureaucracy was dragging its feet and that Richardson had overstated his claim that the nuclear secrets were now safe, and noted the long string of CI failures within DOE.[32] At the *Washington Post,* reporters were still looking for an angle or an approach different from the *Times.* The first story published in the *Post* on the PFIAB report, July 7, 1999, emphasized the PFIAB criticisms of the conduct of the Kindred Spirit investigation. In particular, the *Post* cited the PFIAB report as cutting

> to the quick of the spy case at Los Alamos, asking why the FBI and the DOE's chief spy hunter, Notra Trulock, focused virtually all their energy on one nuclear physicist at the lab, Wen Ho Lee, without hard evidence that classified warhead data obtained by the Chinese came from Lee or anyone else at the fabled home of the atomic bomb.[33]

"Chief spy hunter"? That was a new one. I guess this is the *Post's* interpretation of the PFIAB's question regarding the possibility that W88 information was also located in places other than Los Alamos and that only one inquiry was opened. That is a stretch, to say the least. Suffice to say, there is not a word in the entire PFIAB report about Wen Ho Lee or the conduct of the DOE Administrative Inquiry.

I can't say that I hadn't been warned about the *Washington Post,* ironically, by a senior official of the Washington Post Company itself. Earlier that spring, this official warned me to "watch out for Walter Pincus." I was surprised and asked what he meant. He said that Pincus's wife was close friends with Mrs. Clinton and had received a high appointment to the intelligence section of the State Department—the Bureau of Intelligence and Research. Further, Pincus and his wife had been frequent guests of the Clintons at Camp David. His warning was clear: I should expect the worst from the *Washington Post.* But up to this point, I thought Pincus's coverage had been fair enough, if somewhat forgiving of the White House.

Now, however, the tone of the *Washington Post's* coverage shifted dramatically. Over the summer, Pincus and his co-reporter, Vernon Loeb, hammered away at me personally. They accused me of all sorts of wrongful and even illegal actions in the conduct of the 1995–1996 Administrative Inquiry. For example, they said the PFIAB report criticized "Trulock and other investigators for focusing almost exclusively on Lee when there was not solid evidence that he, or anyone else at Los Alamos, was the source of classified information that China had somehow obtained about the W88."[34] The two reporters claimed that "Trulock has come under mounting pressure in recent weeks as two government reports and a growing number of intelligence and security officials sharply criticize him for singling out Wen Ho Lee, a Chinese-American physicist at Los Alamos, as the government's prime espionage suspect."[35]

So now, in addition to being the DOE's "chief spy hunter," I had also "singled out Wen Ho Lee." Where was this stuff coming from? I wondered. Obviously, from Bob Vrooman and the FBI, but the key to the reporters' objectives was clear:

But most of the experts who have looked into the suspected Chinese espionage have concluded that it is not clear exactly how much classified data China has obtained or where the information came from. There is also a continuing debate about the value of the information and whether China has used it to update its nuclear arsenal.

The other government report mentioned in the *Washington Post* is the "Statement" issued by Senator Fred Thompson (R-TN) and Senator Joe Lieberman (D-CT), the chairman and the ranking minority member of the Senate Governmental Affairs Committee, that I referred to earlier. They had held closed hearings in June totaling nearly thirteen hours, with twenty witnesses.[36] I had participated in at least one such session and learned several new and surprising things. There were no CIA officials, mostly Justice and the FBI. The Bureau and Justice spent most of their testimony explaining what had happened to the FBI's Foreign Intelligence Surveillance Application for technical coverage of Wen Ho Lee. Vrooman revealed the former relationship between the FBI and the Lees, but the FBI had never once breathed a word to us of their previous association with the Lees. The FBI's prime, and only, suspect once worked for the FBI as an informational asset? This was a stunning development. But the Thompson-Lieberman Committee failed to address it either in the hearings or in its report.

When the testimony was finally over, the committee staff went off to write up Thompson and Lieberman's statement. When the report was finally issued on August 5, 1999, I couldn't believe what I was reading. First, the statement falsely claimed that the DOE inquiry had focused specifically on Los Alamos and that we had constructed a "matrix" to identify possible suspects there. Second, it made no mention of Livermore or the fact that there were ten other investigative leads besides the Lees on the list we sent over to the FBI in May 1996. The statement noted that the Lees stood out "in the minds of the DOE investigators" because of Mrs. Lee's aggressive efforts to interact with PRC visitors and Dr. Lee's previous brush with the FBI in 1982, but failed to mention that the FBI had an ongoing preliminary investigation of Lee under way in 1994 and 1995.[37]

Pincus and Loeb of the *Washington Post* continued to pile on. Their August 6 article on the Thompson/Lieberman Statement falsely reported two of its key conclusions.[38] First, the *Post* claimed the report "notes that it is still unclear whether any secrets were really stolen," a continuation of the *Post's* campaign to minimize any damage from Chinese espionage. In fact, the Governmental Affairs Committee report had taken no position on whether W88 or other nuclear weapons information had been compromised. This was not within the scope of the GAC inquiry and, unlike the PFIAB, they had stuck to their charter. In fact, I can recall no instance in any hearing in which the finding that China had acquired W88 warhead information was ever challenged. More ominously, the *Post* raised the specter of Wen Ho and Sylvia Lees' ethnicity as a factor in their selection as suspects.

Their factual "errors" were bad enough to elicit a letter to the editor of the *Post,* signed by both Senator Thompson and Senator Lieberman, which was published on August 26, 1999. Besides stating that the committee took no position on espionage and was satisfied with the Intelligence Community Damage Assessment, Thompson and Lieberman wrote:

> The article accurately recounts these three factors considered in the analysis [of Lee] but then *invents* a fourth: that the Lees "were Chinese American." Let the record be clear:
>
> The evidence we have seen and heard provides no basis for the claim that the initial DOE-FBI inquiry focused upon the Lees because of their race. Only much later in the process, did the investigation consider the Lees' ethnicity—and then only because, according to FBI counterintelligence experts, Beijing's intelligence actively tries to recruit Chinese American scientists working in sensitive U.S. facilities. [Emphasis added.][39]

Thompson and Lieberman were referring to the FBI's application for a warrant to establish technical coverage of Lee in 1997. This application had included the FBI's assessment that "It was standard PRC intelligence tradecraft to focus particularly upon targeting and recruitment of ethnic Chinese living in foreign countries (i.e., Chinese-Americans)."[40] This was not a theory that we had subscribed to at DOE during the conduct of the Administrative Inquiry.

I SUPPOSE IT was inevitable, given the Clinton administration's obsession with "diversity," that at some point race and ethnicity would become the central issue in this case. Certainly in 1995 we had heard a lot from the FBI and the CIA about the PRC's practice of targeting Asian-Americans in its espionage efforts. But our experience was that the PRC would try to elicit information from anyone foolish enough to engage in dialogues or discussions that could end up in classified matters. Our list of twelve leads had some Asian-Americans on it in addition to Caucasians. Race or ethnicity was not a criterion used to put people on or take people off the list of potential investigative leads. I can recall no indication on the lists that we sent to the FBI of race or ethnicity, only place and date of birth.[41] I never saw or heard any racial remarks or references to ethnicity from Dan Bruno, Chuck Washington or any other of our DOE counterintelligence investigators. Washington's Kindred Spirit cover memo of May 16, 1996, certainly made no mention of ethnicity or race.

The Clinton administration had already played the race card to deflect criticism in the campaign finance scandals, many of whose principal players were either Asian-Americans or Asian nationals. But I was still rocked when the race card was hauled out against me. At the time it still seemed to come out of nowhere, and it was (and still is) deeply offensive. Not surprisingly, the *Washington Post* was the first to hurl these charges. Chagrined at having been scooped by the *New York Times* on the espionage story from the outset, the *Post* reporters latched onto a different but equally sensational angle.

Throughout the congressional hearings, both open and closed, the issue of race or ethnic profiling was never once raised. Bob Vrooman, the Los Alamos counterintelligence chief, sat through the congressional hearings and, while he had many criticisms of the Administrative Inquiry, he never once mentioned race or ethnic profiling. Sometime around August 17, 1999, Vrooman issued a press release to the *Post* and the *New York Times* after the DOE inspector general had recommended him for a reprimand for his rejection of Freeh's recommendation on Wen Ho Lee. In his press release he dropped the race bomb: "It can be said at this time that Mr. Lee's ethnicity was a major factor" in his selection as the "prime suspect" in the W88 compromise.

This time, the *Post* would not be scooped by the *New York Times*. *Post* reporter Vernon Loeb published Vrooman's allegations virtually verbatim on August 17. Identifying Vrooman as a "high-ranking participant" in the investigation who was "breaking a long public silence," Loeb hit hard on the racism theme. He mentioned in passing that Vrooman had been singled out for disciplinary action, but this was subsidiary to the allegations about race and ethnicity. He cited Vrooman as claiming that thirteen Caucasians were left out of the investigation, but failed to note that Vrooman made no effort to bring this to the attention of the FBI or DOE.

The *New York Times* ran with the Vrooman story the next day. Instead of Gerth and Risen, who had done the initial investigative reporting on this story, Bill Broad wrote this article.[42] He repeated Vrooman's allegations verbatim, except that Vrooman's claim was now up to "83 people" who had not been investigated.[43]

Why had Vrooman waited nearly three years to raise these issues if he truly believed them? Not once over the course of Kindred Spirit had any such objection or concern been raised by any of the participants. I was unaware of any such communication between Vrooman and our own CI shop or between Vrooman and the FBI—because there was none. Now here he was making these allegations in print. And the media was just jumping all over them. The *Post*'s August 17 story was rerun on the wire services and soon I was having to deny that I was a racist.

Two more Energy Department employees came forward to "substantiate" Vrooman's allegations to Loeb. One was Chuck Washington, whom Loeb cited as providing the *Post* with a copy of a memorandum in which he had recommended the case be closed for lack of evidence. I scratched my head trying to imagine, what memorandum? I could recall no such memo from Washington or anyone else. It turned out to be the classified memo that Washington had included on the AI on May 16, 1996, recommending stylistic fixes to the report.[44] In it, Washington had recommended that the "report [not the "case" as Loeb had written] should be CLOSED, rather than PENDING." Washington then went on to recommend that DOE CI open a "Monitor Investigation to Monitor the FBI investigation," or "open a Joint Investigation." If Loeb had the memorandum, as he claimed in the article, did he understand the difference between closing a report and closing a case? Or did he deliberately change the wording to support his ongoing campaign against the Wen Ho Lee investigation?*

In addition to publicizing Washington's patently false claim, Loeb then cited Washington as claiming that:

> he told Trulock that he was unfairly singling out Lee and another Chinese American scientist at Los Alamos when numerous others had similar access to secrets. And Washington alleged that Trulock was motivated at least in part by a desire to win a larger budget for Energy's relatively small intelligence office, which he headed.
>
> "Trulock used to say, 'We need one good espionage case to make this program grow,' " Washington said last week in an interview. "He said, 'There's one spy out there, and we're going to find him.' "

That allegation was patently false, but Loeb never contacted me for a comment. Washington had his own axe to grind: I had declined to make him the director of CI in 1996, after Ken Baker, my boss, had promised him the job before I came on the scene. He was the classic disgruntled, vengeful ex-employee who filed discrimination complaints against nearly all of his supervisors, including Ed Curran in 1998. Unhappy because Curran would not give him a senior management job in the new CI shop, Washington refused to come to work for ten months. He was not on suspension or anything like that; he simply didn't show up for work each day. At any other intelligence agency in the government or in the private sector, he would have been suspended, had his clearance revoked and probably been fired. But not at DOE. Richardson permitted him to continue drawing his $90,000-plus salary throughout this period and took no action against him.[45]

FBI agents supporting a Justice Department review of the case considered Washington so unreliable that they didn't interview him, even though they interviewed dozens of others. But Loeb was only interested in the sensational allegations made by Washington and didn't bother to check his track record.

---

*See page 116 above.

The *Post* kept pummeling me. On August 26, there was another front-page headline: "Allegations of Bias Hurt Case against Spy Suspect; Inquiries Find Flaws in Targeting of Lee." I was truly amazed to read the list of things I had supposedly done over the previous few years. For example, Loeb claimed that I had drawn up the "first list of suspects" and "drafted an investigative road map for FBI investigators that clearly identified Lee and his wife as prime suspects," and that I laid out a "trail of evidence" for the FBI, and that I "developed" the initial list of twelve suspects, and that I "lacked any hard evidence against Lee and singled him out as a suspect because of his ethnicity." In addition to his DOE sources, Loeb was clearly picking up the FBI's efforts to shift blame back onto DOE for screwing up the Lee investigation. I was anointed as the "guiding force behind the probe."

But the *Post* still wasn't done. It published yet another article on August 29, in which I was branded not only a racist, but also a "dangerous demagogue," in the words of one of my detractors. An unnamed "senior Energy Department official" called me a "great impostor" and went on to say, "He got what he wanted—his moment on stage. He was the star of the show. That's what he lived for." My favorite line was this: "Trulock the inside intelligence analyst and reformer had become Trulock the whistleblower." References were made to my "ego and slashing style."

Secretary Bill Richardson, who had reason to know all of this was bunk, just stood by. But most disappointing was the response of the Republicans on the Hill. Recall that Senator Warner's staff had told me, don't worry, we'll protect you. Where were Warner and all of my alleged Republican friends now? Nowhere to be seen or heard. They had vanished.

THE LAST STRAW for me was the release of the Energy Department's inspector general report. Practically every agency in Washington, with the exception of the FBI, has an inspector general. This post is supposed to be the "junkyard dog" of any department, ever on the lookout for waste, fraud and abuse. The inspector general looks into allegations of potential lawbreaking by federal employees, conducts audits and inspections, and generally is supposed to ensure that departmental and, in DOE's case, lab contractors comply with orders, policies, health and safety requirements, and use sound management and fiscal procedures. All members of the Intelligence Community have inspectors general. At CIA and other big intelligence agencies, the IGs focus solely on intelligence matters. At DOE and other cabinet departments, like State, the IG is spread thinner. In short, the IGs are the last line of defense, especially in such gray areas as the politicization of intelligence. But specific breaches of conduct, such as withholding information from Congress, are clearly within the purview of the IG. Above all, the inspector general is supposed to protect employees from retaliation by management for reporting wrongdoing or mismanagement.

Secretary Richardson had promised the American public a full investigation of what had gone wrong in the Kindred Spirit case. On *Meet the Press* and elsewhere, he talked of firings and reprimands for all those responsible for blocking efforts at reform and for stalling Wen Ho Lee's removal from access to nuclear secrets. He promised the American public that the department would be run on accountability. Now it was time to keep his promise. The IG inspectors put on a good show of taking statements and conducting interviews of all the participants. They later claimed to have conducted ninety-seven interviews with DOE, lab and even FBI officials. I learned that they were also up on the Hill interviewing congressional aides. The IG investigation kicked off in late March or April, but delivery of a final report was delayed several times. In May, during the congressional hearings, constant reference was made to the investigation. Jeff Bingaman and other Democratic senators pleaded with colleagues to await the outcome of that report before holding any more hearings. At one such hearing on May 20, 1999, Bingaman said that Richardson had told him the IG report was finished.[46] About ten days later, Richardson confirmed this in an appearance on *Meet the Press*. Curiously, the report was not finally released until August 12, 1999, and it has never been made public.

According to Energy Department insiders, the inspector general presented a draft of its report to Richardson sometime in May or early June 1999. It was pretty hardhitting, and the language was straightforward and sharp. Those who have seen this draft say that it recommended reprimands for Moler and others. But that is not the report that would finally be released by Richardson.

In the final report, all this was removed and the department's mishandling of the case was whitewashed. The recommendations for reprimands, at least for the political appointees, were removed. The IG report treated Moler's denial of congressional oversight as a "he said, she said" issue.

> The Inspector General's two month investigation examined allegations that Department officials blocked or prevented briefings to former Secretary Pena or the Congress about potential espionage at the labs. In the course of its investigation, the Inspector General's office conducted 82 interviews. They found that witnesses possessed varying degrees of recollection and there were conflicting versions about the reporting of LANL espionage allegations to the Secretary and the Congress. Despite a number of primary and follow-up interviews designed to clarify key matters, they were not able to reconcile the conflicting information. As a consequence, the Inspector General could not establish with any certainty that any Departmental official, knowingly or intentionally, improperly delayed, prohibited, or interfered with briefings to Mr. Pena or to the congressional intelligence committees.[47]

What about Charlie Curtis's testimony that he had directed Ken Baker in 1996 to make sure that Pena knew about Kindred Spirit as early as possible? What about Betsy Moler's refusal to allow the House Intelligence Committee to receive the Kindred Spirit briefing in mid-1998? What about all the congressional testimony or even the PFIAB report that had confirmed my allegations about the stalling and delays that blocked implementation of counterintelligence reforms? But there was no reference to any of these issues.

Richardson issued a press release that essentially glossed over the key issues and recommended three lab employees at Los Alamos for reprimands. The three were Sig Hecker, the former director, and Bob Vrooman and Terry Craig, the lab's counterintelligence officers. While Vrooman and Craig had clearly been derelict in their duties, Hecker was mostly the victim of incompetence on the part of his subordinates. If he was worthy of a reprimand, what about Moler and the others? But no further action was to be taken.

To add insult to injury, I heard about the press release from a friend outside the department. I didn't know that the report had been issued or that DOE was putting out a press release. I called the DOE press officer, who said, "Gee, I guess we should have told you."

On August 23, 1999, I sent an e-mail to Gregory Friedman, the DOE inspector general. I wanted him to know that I considered his report to be "nothing more than a whitewash and a perpetuation of the Department's efforts to cover up the malfeasance of a number of both political appointees and federal employees as well." I added:

> The Inspector General is the last line of defense for the Department's intelligence organization against the violations of the rules and policies that govern intelligence throughout the Federal branch. Three times the Office of Intelligence has looked to the Inspector General for support and protection in the Office's efforts to manage intelligence within the rules of EO 12333 and the Attorney General's Guidelines for Intelligence Activities at the Department. Three times you looked the other way and, in so doing, furthered the efforts of those seeking to discredit and diminish the role of intelligence management in the Department.

I wrapped up my e-mail to Friedman by saying, "In sum, your report is unworthy of the efforts and hard work of the members of the Office of Intelligence."

In retrospect, I believe that Senator Pete Domenici, the labs' patron saint, intervened in the preparation of the IG report. When I read it, I recalled a strange incident with him that had happened during one of the closed hearings back in the spring. Domenici called me to follow him outside the hearing room.[48] We went into one of the side rooms. He closed the door and then turned to me and said, "Haven't I protected you over at DOE?" "Yes," was my reply, for I knew that either he or his staff had called Moniz and told them to leave me alone. "Well, you are going to see some things that you won't understand," he said, "but just keep your mouth shut and everything will turn out fine." I was puzzled at the time, but he turned and walked out of the room before I could ask what he meant.

Now I knew. He had put the fix in on the IG report. Domenici had saved Baker, a particular favorite of his, and Moler from being reprimanded and had his congressional aide deny any conversation with Moler about a Kindred Spirit briefing for him. I had heard this exchange with my own ears; I will never forget Moler putting down the phone and saying, "I can't believe I just said no to Pete Domenici." I can't imagine what the senator's motives were; maybe he thought that too much damage was being inflicted on Los Alamos and the other labs.

"Keep your mouth shut and keep your job." This was what the last four years had been about? I couldn't agree that the "future of the national labs," as Domenici and others put it, was worth more than protecting our nuclear secrets. Some day a future adversary might use the information gained from penetration of the labs to kill American troops, sink our aircraft carriers, or even destroy our cities.

NINE

Aftermath

The FBI's failures in the Wen Ho Lee investigation should not be
blamed on the AI. . . . This perception has also unfairly undermined
the government's credibility on the ethnic/racial profiling question
and seriously damaged Notra Trulock's reputation and career.
—Senate Judiciary Committee
    December 2001

When I walked out of DOE for the last time on August 23, 1999, I thought that I could go back to working quietly—in the shadows, so to speak—in the intelligence field that had absorbed my adult life. I had done my job and achieved some of what I had set out to do. DOE and the labs had finally been forced to confront the reality of the foreign intelligence threat. My successors, Ed Curran and his staff, had the manpower and the budgets to do the counterintelligence job right. More importantly, they had the attention of the American public, which I thought would translate into authority, since no lawmaker wanted to look "weak" in dealing with espionage threats. DOE Intelligence had survived and would now be able to resume its important contributions to national security. Even security at the Energy Department seemed to have benefited—it too was now an independent office reporting directly to the secretary. No more political interference in security, intelligence or counterintelligence. Personally, things had been rough, but I had survived and thought that now I could get on with my professional life outside of government.

I joined TRW, a large defense/aerospace contractor, the day after I left the Energy Department. TRW offered me a nice salary and a signing bonus, so I was confident that my future would be bright there. I was promptly assigned to a project management role in a very large modernization program in support of the National

Security Agency. It involved a long commute to the job site, but it was a relief to be out of the DOE cauldron.

As I began my next job, I was disappointed to learn that the National Security Agency was not immune from the general decline of intelligence during the Clinton administration. The agency, which had been so capable and confident up to the early 1990s, was now floundering. Study after study had uncovered serious deficiencies in leadership and direction. Recommendations were ignored and the NSA continued to operate as if nothing were wrong. Sounded a lot like the Department of Energy.

Two such studies commissioned in 1999, one by an outside team and a more important one by a group of NSA employees, came out at the same place. NSA had been experiencing a "leadership crisis" for the better part of the 1990s. The result: NSA's capabilities, so critical to our nation's security, were declining rapidly. The NSA study group warned, "Absent profound change at NSA, the nation will lose a powerful weapon in its arsenal."[1] NSA had changed a lot since my time there in the late 1970s, and not for the better. I hoped to help fix the problem in some small way.

But I didn't count on being summoned to testify on Capitol Hill once more. Congressman Duncan Hunter wanted to rehash Betsy Moler's role in blocking congressional notification of Kindred Spirit and in failing to follow FBI director Louis Freeh's recommendation to remove Wen Ho Lee from his X Division office yet again. I was to be his prime witness. I told him this was really unfair; I had done my part and now just wanted to get on with my life. But Hunter wouldn't take no for an answer and finally threatened me with a subpoena.

Secretary Richardson was reported to be very unhappy when he learned of Hunter's plans. The congressman intended to go over the inspector general's assessment and Richardson probably didn't want too much congressional scrutiny of the doctored report. He called TRW and pressured them to prevent my appearance, but my bosses just threw up their hands—what could they do if Hunter subpoenaed me? I knew nothing good would come of this.

The hearing was held November 10, 1999, and was just a dreary repetition of all that had gone before. Federico Pena, the former secretary of DOE, was also present. I would say one thing and Betsy or Pena would deny it. Then they would make some outrageous claim and I would deny that. Richardson need not have worried about the inspector general's report; it was all hidden behind classification restrictions and couldn't be discussed.

What a waste of time and trouble this all was, contributing nothing to the public record of the Kindred Spirit case. But it did ruin my future at TRW. Few defense contractors, dependent on the federal government for business, can withstand the ill will of a major customer like the Energy Department that my appearance at the hearing generated, particularly on top of the racism allegations launched by Bob Vrooman, Chuck Washington, and Wen Ho Lee's lawyers. I suddenly found myself without any responsibilities. TRW officials told me that Richardson and others from within the Energy Department were urging them to get rid of me. TRW professed to be unable to find any work for me. I sought out program managers at TRW to offer my experience and services. Every time I interviewed with one of these managers for a position, there was initial enthusiasm, replaced after a few days by vague, evasive promises to "get back to me." Of course, I never heard from them again. Although I was still technically on the payroll, I couldn't find any real work to do. My supervisors regularly held staff meetings that excluded me. I submitted proposals for projects at various Intelligence Community agencies, but invariably these were torpedoed by "senior" managers in the Intelligence Community or sometimes even by TRW. I was finally terminated on June 30, 2000. The day I left, one of the senior officers of the company told me that TRW had caved in to "pressure from the Office of the Secretary" at the Energy Department. Efforts by Congressman Hunter and even a prestigious TRW consultant failed to sway TRW officials under the gun from DOE to get rid of me. TRW had a huge contract with the Energy Department and wilted under the threat of losing it.

I desperately sought employment with other defense contractors around Washington, but even old friends at companies like Lockheed-Martin wouldn't return my phone calls or letters. They told me that I was just too "radioactive" as long as Bill Clinton was President.

MEANWHILE, THE U.S. government was deciding what to do about Wen Ho Lee. In December 1999, the Justice Department filed a 59-count indictment accusing him of mishandling classified information. Months had passed since Lee's transfer of classified nuclear warhead data onto the Los Alamos unclassified computer system and computer tapes had been uncovered. The FBI had opened a criminal case code-named "Sea Change" to find out what Lee had done with the missing computer tapes. As surely as night follows day, Sea Change owed its existence and success to Kindred Spirit. Had it not been for the efforts of Dan Bruno and others, the FBI would never have stumbled onto Lee's illegal computer activity.

If the FBI had moved with any dispatch in 1996 or 1997, they could have uncovered the massive nuclear weapons data files that Lee had placed on the Los Alamos network, but their dithering cost the U.S. dearly. Besides the tape he made in 1997, there were reports that hackers suspected of an affiliation with a PRC government institute attacked the Los Alamos network and removed a large number of files in late 1998 or early 1999, just about the time when Lee began to realize he was under suspicion.[2] The government knew how vulnerable that network was and had recorded hundreds of attacks on it during that period. The government also knew that Lee had accessed these files during one of his trips to Taiwan in 1998; before his trip, he had called the computer help desk and gotten instructions on how to access the files from outside the lab.[3] By early 2000, the government still didn't know if someone else had acquired the files from outside the lab. The lab had kept records of outsiders logging onto the system, but these records didn't include which files had been accessed.

Once the FBI began to understand the gravity of Lee's computer activity, it focused a massive amount of resources on the case and searched the entire Los Alamos computer network for traces of Lee's activity. What it uncovered was stunning.

Beginning in 1988, Lee had transferred onto the unclassified Los Alamos computer network and later onto computer tapes about 1,600 files totaling more than 800 megabytes of classified information. That is the equivalent of about one and a half compact discs. Lee painstakingly removed all classified markings from this material before making these transfers. He placed copies of classified

briefings on Los Alamos nuclear warheads, as well as other classified materials, on the unclassified computer system. At least twice,
and perhaps three times, a system developed at Los Alamos titled
the Network Anomaly Detection and Intrusion Recording System
(NADIR) flagged Lee's massive file transfers: once in 1993, probably again in 1994, and in 1997. Not once did the Los Alamos office
responsible for running this system inform Los Alamos security or
counterintelligence. The technology did its job, but there was human
failure of astounding proportions. A Los Alamos official would later
claim that she didn't know Wen Ho Lee was a suspect and therefore took no notice of his activity. But of course from 1994 on, he
was an FBI espionage suspect. And FBI sources had reported that
Lee had helped the Chinese with computer codes and software, so
it would have been logical to monitor his computer activity. But
neither Bob Vrooman nor the FBI alerted Los Alamos computer
security officials to Wen Ho Lee's status. Nor did Vrooman or his
deputy, Terry Craig, tell the FBI about NADIR, which could have
been searched for Lee's "anomalous" computer activity.

At the time of Lee's indictment, the government thought he
had made ten tapes. They recovered three in his office. So now the
government believed there were seven missing tapes containing
source codes, input decks and data files, including the W88 tape.
Source codes include data used for determining by simulation the
validity of nuclear weapons designs and for comparing bomb test
results with predicted results. Input decks or input files contain
electronic blueprints of the exact dimensions and geometry of this
nation's nuclear weapons, including our most sophisticated modern warheads. Data files contain protocol libraries for nuclear bomb
testing, reflecting the data from actual tests of nuclear weapons;
data concerning nuclear weapons bomb test problems, yield calculations, and other nuclear weapons design and detonation information; and information relating to the physical and radioactive
properties of materials used to construct nuclear weapons. The
tapes contained information for both the primary and secondary
devices in as many as twenty thermonuclear warheads in our current arsenal.[4]

As was his practice throughout, Lee—through his counsel—
denied that he had downloaded any classified information onto

unprotected systems and claimed that he had only put unclassified data on those systems. Some of his supporters tried to argue
that even if the information was classified, this was a common practice at Los Alamos. But the FBI did a thorough forensics scrub of
the Los Alamos computer network in April 1999 and could find no
trace of such activity by other Los Alamos scientists. Moreover, lab
management and the FBI let it be known that they would like to
talk to any other lab scientist claiming to have moved classified
information to the unprotected Los Alamos system. Not surprisingly, no one came forward. When confronted with evidence that
he had moved classified data, Lee, true to form, changed his story
and now claimed that he had destroyed the missing tapes. The government refused to accept his word—at least at this point in the
case.

If the Justice Department thought Wen Ho Lee would agree to
a plea bargain in return for telling them the location of the tapes,
trading information for modified sentences in the manner of most
other U.S. spies, it was dead wrong. Lee obtained talented legal
counsel and fought the government every step of the way. When
the presiding judge returned the indictment in December 1999, he
also denied bail to Lee. The government had argued that Lee's refusal
to give up the seven missing computer tapes constituted a serious
danger to U.S. national security. Lee stuck to his claim that he had
destroyed them. So he was held in solitary confinement in a federal facility outside Santa Fe to prevent him from passing information about the tapes to anyone else. That decision to keep him
locked up was made at the White House in early December 1999
with Janet Reno, Louis Freeh, Bill Richardson, George Tenet and
Sandy Berger present.

For John Kelly, the U.S. attorney from the New Mexico district prosecuting the case, in order to implement the "special administrative measures" that would hold Lee in solitary confinement,
Secretary Richardson would have to certify that "unauthorized disclosure of classified information would pose a threat to the national
security and that there is a danger that the inmate will disclose
such information." Air Force General Eugene Habiger, now retired
and the director of security at Energy, urged Richardson to make
the required certification:

In my judgment such a certification is warranted to enable the Department of Justice to take whatever steps are reasonably available to it to preclude Mr. Lee, during the period of his pretrial confinement, any opportunity to communicate, directly or through other means, the extremely sensitive nuclear weapons data that the indictment alleges Mr. Lee surreptitiously diverted to his own possession from Los Alamos National Laboratory.

Shortly thereafter, Richardson wrote to Attorney General Janet Reno that "the unauthorized disclosure of classified information described in the above indictment would pose a threat to the national security and there is a danger that Mr. Lee will disclose such information." So if Kelly and the Justice Department put Lee in solitary, Bill Richardson turned the key on his cell door.

At a bail hearing in late December, lab scientists offered vivid testimony about the potential value of the tapes that Lee had created. Los Alamos' associate director for nuclear weapons programs, Dr. Stephen Younger, labeled these tapes "priceless" and said, "The codes and databases that were downloaded represent a complete nuclear weapons design capability, everything you would need to install that capability in another location, everything." He went on to argue that:

These codes and their associated databases, and the input files combined with someone that knew how to use them could, in my opinion, in the wrong hands, change the global strategic balance. They enable the possessor to design the only objects that could result in military defeat of America's conventional forces. The only threat, for example, to our carrier battle groups. They represent the gravest possible security risk to the United States, what the president and most other presidents have described as the supreme national interest of the United States, the supreme national interest.

He concluded that the seven missing tapes represented "a complete portable nuclear design capability which could be installed on a super computer center or even lesser computer capabilities."[5]

Younger took a lot of heat from some in DOE and elsewhere for this assessment, especially his reference to "chang[ing] the global strategic balance." The United States deploys an extremely robust and sophisticated nuclear arsenal matched only by the former Soviet Union. It would take decades for other countries to catch up to these two powers. But that really wasn't the point. The information on the tapes could help a country with an existing nuclear weapons program, like China, to modernize its arsenal, or Taiwan, with a sophisticated science and technology base, to create one. By making its weapons less vulnerable and more effective, this would immeasurably enhance the deterrent value of the Chinese force— possibly enough to deter the United States from intervening in a regional conflict involving China.

Still looking to limit the political damage to Los Alamos, Energy officials tried to play down the potential consequences of Lee's actions and alleged that Younger had overstated the importance of the missing data. Some senior Energy officials even labeled him "wacky" for his assessment of the potential damage. Not surprisingly, Younger is no longer at Los Alamos.*

Another Los Alamos scientist, Richard Krajcik, who as deputy director of X Division at Los Alamos was one of Lee's immediate supervisors, labeled the tapes the "crown jewels of the United States' nuclear weapons program." Krajcik said that Lee's tapes represented a chilling collection of codes and files.

> Chilling in the sense that it contained the codes important to doing design or design assessment files important to determine geometries, important successfully tested nuclear weapons. It contained important output setups, nuclear output setups. It contained devices across a range of weapons, from weapons that were relatively easy to manufacture, let's say, to weapons that were very sophisticated and would be very difficult to manufacture. It contained the databases that those codes would require to run. And for someone who used those codes to incorporate them into any kind of calculations that were made in terms of designing something new or checking something old, it was all there.[6]

---

*He now runs the Defense Department's Threat Reduction Agency, located outside of Washington, D.C.

Later testimony elaborated on Lee's care in assembling the tapes. The president of Sandia National Lab testified that the tapes

> were very carefully designed to be loaded with the subroutines that would be needed for each design code to be placed right behind the design code. And so I believe they should not require a lot of additional instruction. In other words, the collection of files was more than just a collection of files—it had been assembled so as to ensure that data files called for in the codes were available at the right place, making it possible for the codes to actually run when executed.[7]

Lee's defense claimed that the operating manuals had not been included with the codes and therefore the codes themselves would be impossible to use. But this testimony indicated that was not the case. It also raises the question of just whom Wen Ho Lee had made these tapes for—obviously someone who might not have access to a full set of operating manuals.

Given such testimony, the presiding judge had little choice but to continue to hold Wen Ho Lee without bail—for the next nine months. Setting aside for a moment the government's assertions about the dangers of Lee compromising the tapes if allowed bail, I am fairly certain that a key part of the prosecution's strategy was to coerce a confession from Lee. This was a variation on the FBI's approach to the Peter Lee case in 1997. In that case, the FBI wanted a sentence that would put Peter Lee into detention with hardened criminals, in hopes that he would sing like a bird. I don't think this was a kinder, gentler FBI. The Bureau and John Kelly must have thought that solitary confinement was the way to extract a confession from Wen Ho Lee.

At the bail hearings and in General Habiger's solitary confinement recommendation, much was made of the threat that Lee might surreptitiously communicate the whereabouts of the tapes to a foreign intelligence officer. The FBI had searched his house, car and office, and had maintained physical surveillance on him since earlier that summer—but still hadn't obtained a warrant to monitor his telephone conversations. Why did they wait nearly eight months after the discovery that there were missing tapes to suddenly become worried about the risks of Lee's unfettered communications?

But Wen Ho Lee's legal team executed a brilliant defense strategy composed of three distinct elements. First, they attacked the government's contention that the tapes were as precious as depicted in the testimony given at the December bail hearing. Second, they portrayed Lee as a target of "selective prosecution" based on his ethnicity and race. And finally, they painted Lee as the innocent victim of a vengeful government intent on indicting someone, anyone, to justify its four-year espionage investigation. They benefited greatly from an inexplicably inept prosecution and from a very sympathetic media that was extremely sensitive to issues of "diversity." A media strategy was a key part of the overall approach to freeing Wen Ho Lee. His lawyers issued press releases and made sure that court documents supporting their three basic themes got to friendly journalists.

Lee's first get-out-of-jail card came from the scientists his lawyers produced to challenge the prosecution's expert witnesses on the importance of the missing tapes. A surprising cast of prestigious former Los Alamos scientists, including Dr. Harold Agnew, a former Los Alamos National Laboratory director, assisted Lee. Agnew was joined by Dr. Walter Goad, an "emeritus" at LANL. The bona fides of these two scientists should have been tarnished a bit by the fact that neither had been in the bomb-building business for at least two decades and neither had actually reviewed the data contained in Lee's tapes. (Agnew had stepped down as director in 1979. Goad had worked on "computational biology" since 1970.)[8] Agnew and Goad both claimed that the codes would be of little value to any country with a nuclear arsenal—in marked contrast to the prosecution's expert witness testimony.

But the defense was able to produce one witness who did know the importance of the information on the missing tapes. Dr. John Richter came to Lee's assistance when he testified that prosecution's allegation that possession of the codes could alter the global balance of power was vastly overstated. Moreover, Richter claimed that 99 percent of the information Lee had downloaded was unclassified and widely available in the public domain. This testimony was surprising to many; after all, Richter was the author of the memo that started this whole saga in 1995. Yet it was Richter's testimony that turned the judge around on the question of the value of the information on the tapes. Richter believed the government was wrong to incarcerate Lee and was happy that his testimony was decisive in undermining the government's case. He told a reporter, "If I had any influence in getting him out, I figured that's a payback."[9] Payback for exactly what was not clear. Richter's testimony stunned many of his Los Alamos colleagues, who began calling him "Wen Ho Richter."

Lee's defense attacked the importance of the tapes from a different angle as well. They employed a tactic known as "graymail," which involved the threat to expose classified information in an open courtroom in the defense of their client. One of Lee's lawyers, John Cline, had employed the technique successfully to defend a CIA client during the Oliver North prosecution in the late 1980s. The defense team claimed that the tapes were not nearly as valuable as the prosecution had argued, because the codes were full of bugs and errors. Instead of the "crown jewels," Lee and his lawyers claimed, the codes were "crown junk." They argued that they would need to introduce actual nuclear warhead blueprints into a trial to refute the prosecution's claim that the tapes contained electronic warhead blueprints. Back in December 1999, Janet Reno had promised to drop the case if it appeared that classified information would be revealed in the course of a trial.[10] Graymail is not an automatic winner for defendants, because the prosecution may substitute unclassified descriptions of the information in question. Rather than fight through this process, however, the government folded at the first whiff of graymail—long before the case even got to trial.

Beyond graymail and the war of the experts, the defense was able to use the prosecution's own words against it. The information Lee had placed on the tapes was classified Secret/Restricted Data. The defense raised doubts in the court's mind by questioning why the information was only classified Secret, by definition the loss of which "could be expected to cause serious damage to national security." Given the prosecution's characterization of the potential consequences of this information, the defense wondered why the tapes weren't classified Top Secret. The loss of Top Secret information "could be expected to cause exceptionally grave damage to the national security." Changing the global strategic balance or destroying U.S. aircraft carriers sounded like a lot more than "serious" damage to national security.

The prosecution was caught flat-footed on this one. The prosecutors hadn't bothered to check basic classification manuals to make sure their expert witness testimony would track with the government's classification guidelines. Had they done so, they also would have learned that very little atomic energy information (Restricted Data) within the Energy Department or at the National Labs is marked Top Secret, and that the classification of even the details of a nuclear warhead design had been no higher than Secret/Restricted Data stretching back decades.[11] It was a specious argument, but it helped the defense when the prosecution failed to rebut it effectively.

Inevitably, the prosecution's lack of an effective response to these challenges supported the defense's strategy to sow confusion and uncertainty in the mind of the presiding judge, by now Judge James A. Parker, a Reagan appointee. It worked, too. Judge Parker bought the defense's assertions that much of the material was available in open literature and that the nuclear weapons data on the tapes weren't really all that significant. His order releasing Wen Ho Lee from pretrial detention was based in part on the defense's arguments that the missing tapes would be of "very limited use to the PRC or any other foreign country with a nuclear arsenal."[12]

And yet, less than six weeks later, Richter recanted his claim that 99 percent of the information Lee downloaded was unclassified. The following exchange between Richter and Senator Arlen Specter took place during a Senate Judiciary Committee hearing on October 3, 2000, in the Dirksen Senate Office Building. Richter was under oath at the time.

> SEN. SPECTER: Well, when you testified, Dr. Richter, that 99 percent of it was unclassified, you were talking about the source codes and not about the data files and the input decks, right?
> MR. RICHTER: Exactly. That's exactly right.
> SEN. SPECTER: Well, focusing for just a moment on the input decks, what was there about that classification which was restricted or very serious data?
> MR. RICHTER: This is some of the details of how we build our front-line nuclear weapons. Now I've spent a good deal of my career, latter—in the latter days, trying to figure out what other nations' nuclear weapons are.

SEN. SPECTER: Well, are you saying, as to the material in the input decks, that although classified, it was available to other nations?

MR. RICHTER: It shouldn't be. It should not be.

SEN. SPECTER: Well, a few moments ago, you said that everybody—so many nations know how to build nuclear weapons that it doesn't change the global strategic balance. Now, as to the input decks, would that be something known to other nations?

MR. RICHTER: No, it shouldn't be. This is the way the United States chooses to build its nuclear weapons.

SEN. SPECTER: Well, as to the input decks, to what extent did Dr. Lee make disclosures on input decks which were not available— disclosures not available to other nations?

MR. RICHTER: He shouldn't have done it.

SEN. SPECTER: Well, was that among the materials that Dr. Lee did in fact disclose?

MR. RICHTER: I'm afraid yes. Yes, indeed. I saw one of the input files myself.

SEN. SPECTER: And what was that input file which you saw?

MR. RICHTER: It was the—shows the primary of the W88.[13]

Richter stuck to his assertion that the missing tapes could not alter the global strategic balance, but he did admit that his statements to the judge were incorrect. I was present at this hearing and it was painful to watch a scientist whom I had respected and admired humble himself like this.

SEN. SPECTER: Dr. Richter, you have been quoted as testifying before Judge Parker that at least 99 percent of the nuclear secrets that Dr. Lee downloaded to tapes were unclassified. Is that an accurate statement?

MR. RICHTER: It's an accurate statement regarding the codes. I still maintain that. The material properties—I don't think I was referring to that at the time. If I did say it—mean—say it that way, then I didn't mean it, and I was—I erred.[14]

Specter, a former prosecutor, knew the right questions to ask Richter. Why didn't the government's prosecutors? But it was too late; Wen Ho Lee was already free.

Steve Younger was also at that hearing. He reiterated his judgment that "the information contained on the tapes made by Dr. Lee could, in the wrong hands, pose a grave danger to the national security of the United States."[15] Younger was asked if he still believed that the secrets assembled by Lee on the tapes represented the crown jewels of nuclear security. His response: "If the design of the most sophisticated nuclear weapons on the planet are not the crown jewels of nuclear security, I don't know what is."

The prosecution didn't have to rely just on the testimony of lab scientists like Younger, although this should have been enough. In February 2000, the U.S. Intelligence Community had also produced an unclassified damage assessment of the potential value of the missing tapes, just as it had produced an assessment of the implications of PRC acquisition of U.S. nuclear weapons information in April 1999. This assessment was more "balanced" than the testimony offered by Steve Younger and other lab scientists, but still concluded that "the information contained on the tapes would be useful to anyone who already has some nuclear weapons background. It also could be useful in blackmail scenarios or published on the Internet by domestic anti-government organizations." With regard to contributions to specific foreign nuclear programs, the assessment made the following observations:

> China would likely continue pursuing its existing designs, which have been enhanced by information already obtained from the United States, although the information on these tapes would provide China more detailed design information and more robust tools for designing weapons, which could help with a future, smaller advanced weapon.
>
> Countries with nuclear weapons programs but little or no testing—such as India, Pakistan, North Korea, Iran—would find the information very useful, helping with design efforts and probably accelerating the development of boosted fission weapons and thermonuclear designs, increasing yields from a few to up to hundreds of kilotons or more.
>
> Countries with limited or no programs—Taiwan, Japan, South Korea, Germany—but with high technological capabilities would be able to use the information to accelerate any efforts to pursue

a nuclear weapons program, and allow them to start at a much higher technical level.

The assessment carried the usual caveats found in products of the U.S. Intelligence Community, but underscored the importance of getting the tapes back under U.S. custody. There is no indication that the prosecution ever introduced this assessment into the detention hearings.

WITH REGARD TO the second part of their strategy—playing the race card—Lee's legal team conducted a vigorous public relations campaign on the theme of selective prosecution. They made sure that reporters and the major media outlets got copies of all their court documents. Bob Vrooman and Chuck Washington provided affidavits to the defense team alleging that Lee had been the victim of ethnic profiling and racism; they faxed copies of these directly to Vernon Loeb of the *Washington Post*. Their message was very straightforward: that Lee had been "singled out" for prosecution because he was Chinese-American, and that somehow I was the culprit and mastermind of the campaign to get him. The fact that I had been out of government for months by the time the government got around to indicting Lee didn't seem to carry much weight with his defense team, his supporters, or much of the national media. Lee's legal team and his community of supporters needed a "Mark Fuhrman," the infamous Los Angeles detective in the O. J. Simpson case. They managed to make the racism label stick to me long enough to help get Lee out of jail. This campaign helped them to mobilize public opinion and raise money for the Wen Ho Lee defense fund, particularly in the Asian-American community, and gave them a readymade "villain" on which to focus their public relations efforts. They established and controlled a website to ensure broad distribution of their defamatory accusations against me and to support their fundraising activities.

The Lee defense was handed this "get-out-of-jail" card by Bob Vrooman, the former Los Alamos counterintelligence officer, and others who had first raised the spurious issues of racism and ethnic profiling. Lee's lawyers contacted Vrooman in December 1999 after Lee's indictment. After Vrooman agreed to help them, the lawyers ensured that he would become a media star so as to gain wide exposure for his allegations. He appeared on *CBS News* and ABC's *Nightline,* and became a regular speaker at college campuses across the country. He gave speeches with such grandiose titles as "Ethics, Integrity and National Security: The Other Side of the Story"; "Professionalism, Security and Civil Rights"; and (my favorite) "The Courage to Be: A Case Study." The *Washington Post* alone quoted or cited him in twenty articles beginning in August 1999. Copies of his speeches and interviews were posted at various sites on the Internet, including Wen Ho Lee's website.

All of Vrooman's allegations were directed at me personally and my supervision of the 1995–1996 Administrative Inquiry. Each time he spoke publicly he upped the ante—each allegation becoming more expansive and more damaging to me than the last. Like Senator Joe McCarthy and his list of "Reds" in the State Department during the 1950s, every time Vrooman cited the number of lab employees who should have been on the initial list of "investigative leads" sent to the FBI in 1996, that number grew. He claimed that 30, then 70, then 83, and finally just "lots" of others should have been on the list, but weren't because they weren't Asian-Americans. He claimed that individuals on the list of investigative leads didn't have security clearances or access to the W88 information. Vrooman claimed that I was prejudiced against Asian-Americans and alleged that I made statements that Asian-Americans shouldn't be allowed to work on classified U.S. nuclear weapons programs.

He cited Attorney General Janet Reno's 1999 testimony to show that DOE had ignored other potential leads with "a motivation, perhaps greater than Wen Ho Lee." According to Vrooman, all these "other logical suspects, at least at Los Alamos, were not ethnic Chinese."[16] But Vrooman had twisted the attorney general's testimony to make his point. In truth, Reno was criticizing the FBI for not investigating the other potential leads during the 1997 dispute between the Justice Department and the FBI over the warrant for technical surveillance of Lee: "if you look at the original DOE report, there were perhaps other leads that could have been followed."[17] She was clearly referring to the FBI's failure to pursue these other leads in the context of her testimony about Justice's failure to approve a warrant for technical coverage of Wen Ho Lee.

And what about the individuals who didn't have clearances? It turns out that these people were included among the files of travelers to China in the 1980s provided by Vrooman to Dan Bruno. Dan had eliminated them when he winnowed the list down and they never got close to his final list of twelve, despite Vrooman's allegations—they didn't have security clearances, after all. Finally, it seemed that it was only Vrooman who could recall my alleged statements about Asian-Americans; he could not produce any other eyewitnesses to back up his claims.

When Vrooman finally had to testify about these matters under oath, he was unable to come up with a single instance of racism or racial profiling by DOE or me against Lee. In the same Senate Judiciary Committee hearing in which Richter had recanted his statements about the classification of Lee's tapes, Vrooman was asked to provide examples of the role that racism had played in the Wen Ho Lee investigation. Save for one 1999 discussion between the FBI and the Justice Department, he couldn't come up with any.

> SEN. GRASSLEY: Mr. Vrooman, would you—I'd like to have you elaborate on your comment that whenever Dr. Lee's motive was discussed, it come down to ethnicity. Could you be more specific about what was said, and by whom?
>
> MR. VROOMAN: The first example that comes to mind is during the Thompson-Lieberman hearings [held in 1999]. They were in closed session. Can I do that here? Would you prefer I—
>
> SEN. GRASSLEY: I'll let the chairman make a ruling of whether or not he could say something here that was said in the closed Lieberman hearing.
>
> SEN. SPECTER: Well, I think that depends upon whether—depends really on Mr. Vrooman's assessment as to the proprietary for a statement in an open hearing. That is really best judged by the witness.
>
> SEN. GRASSLEY: Okay. I would ask you to tell us if you feel like you can, because I'd like to get as much of this out in the open as we can.
>
> MR. VROOMAN: Well, the Department of Justice representative asked the FBI what Lee's motive was, because it was not clear to him, and the response was an elaboration on how the Chinese focus their efforts on ethnic Chinese.

SEN. GRASSLEY: Okay.

MR. VROOMAN: That's one example, and there are others of conversations over the years as this investigation proceeded that that was the only motive.

SEN. GRASSLEY: Okay. Could you point to any documentation that would back up the point that you've just made, or the points that you've—

MR. VROOMAN: No, sir, I cannot.

SEN. GRASSLEY: Or the points that you've made about ethnicity being a prime concern.

MR. VROOMAN: I don't believe there are any documents.[18]

Another obvious question had to do with why Vrooman had failed to come forward with his allegations in 1996, 1997 or 1998. Besides Chuck Washington, Vrooman was unable to produce any other "witnesses" to support his charges of "ethnic profiling." The question was put to him in the Senate hearing in October 2000 by Senator Specter. Vrooman responded, "My supervisor, who is the Lab's director, told me that he wanted to improve my relationship with Mr. Trulock, and what I was about to say would not have done that. So we decided, as a matter of course, to let the FBI have the case."[19] During his sworn deposition, taken by my lawyers in November and December 2001, he denied that his "supervisor" had ordered him not to tell me of his concerns back in 1996, and his "supervisor," Sig Hecker, could not recall any such discussion with Vrooman.

Lee's lawyers scored a coup when their public relations expert got Wen Ho Lee a very sympathetic interview on *60 Minutes*. During that interview, he stayed on the same theme that the lawyers were pounding me with: that he had been selected for prosecution because he was Chinese. Lee had also stretched the truth in his interview with Mike Wallace by claiming that he was the "one Oriental or Chinese people working on the top secret for last eighteen years," and that this was the reason he had become the scapegoat for all the lab's security problems. In fact, Wen Ho Lee was not the only Chinese-American working in the Los Alamos nuclear weapons program; two Chinese-Americans outranked him, and he had two other Chinese-American colleagues in X Division.[20] Lee's lawyer had repeatedly objected to questions posed by Wallace, but *60 Minutes* agreed to edit out all the objections and interruptions when it finally aired the show.

Besides the *60 Minutes* interview, *CBS News* ran stories stating outright that Wen Ho Lee was a "scapegoat—someone to blame for the alleged theft of masses of American top secret nuclear weapons information by China." It had obtained copies of the December 23, 1998, Energy Department polygraph of Wen Ho Lee. This file, which contained the scores given Lee's responses to the examiner's questions, was classified at the time and was leaked from within DOE to Lee's lawyers or *CBS News.* The network's reporter, Sheryl Attkisson, and her editors slanted the news report, which ran on February 4, 2000, to make it appear that Lee had passed the December 23, 1998, polygraph with flying colors and that the FBI had arbitrarily "reversed" the results of that exam. She cited former FBI agent Richard Keifer, then the chairman of the American Polygraph Association, as saying that "he had never been able to score anyone so high on the non-deceptive scale" and that "somebody is making an error" to explain the discrepancies between the Energy Department's and the FBI's subsequent reading of the polygraph results.[21] After *CBS News* ran the piece, Keifer claimed that he had been quoted out of context and that Attkisson's piece "was manipulated to suggest wrongdoing by the government."[22] Once he had the opportunity to review Lee's polygraph charts, Keifer agreed with other polygraph experts and the FBI's polygraph quality control team that the Energy Department's exam questions were structured in such a way as to ensure that Lee scored highly non-deceptive on the test. It was Energy that had made the "errors," but neither Attkisson nor *CBS News* ever reported as much.

CBS and Attkisson struck again a couple of months later. This time she ran a piece based on Vrooman's allegations that Lee had been singled out before the Administrative Inquiry had even begun, continuing the theme of Lee as scapegoat.[23] She gave Vrooman a forum to make possibly the most outrageous allegation in the whole case. Speaking of the list of twelve potential investigative leads we had provided to the FBI in May 1996, she quoted Vrooman saying:

"It appeared to me like it was a bogus list, to give the appearance of doing a legitimate investigation," Vrooman says. "There's one person on there who doesn't have a clearance. There are other people on there who don't have access to nuclear weapons information. The investigators just told me, Well, look, I know it's Lee and, ah, we just need some other names to make this thing look good."

Attkisson interviewed me, but most of that tape never made it into her piece. She introduced me as "the man credited with pushing the theory of Lee as the prime suspect from the very beginning."

These allegations became an important component of Lee's defense strategy as well as the heart of his public relations campaign. The defense filed motions asserting that the government had engaged in "unconstitutional selective prosecution."[24] One such motion specifically cited Vrooman's allegation that "Trulock held the belief these [Asian] American citizens could not be trusted like other Americans." According to Vrooman, Trulock made such statements "when he was personally assisting the criminal investigation of Dr. Lee."* Lee's lawyers claimed that "Trulock's statements that American citizens who are 'ethnic Chinese' should be barred from sensitive jobs at LANL are a violation of federal civil rights statutes that prohibit racial discrimination for employment." The motion also quoted Chuck Washington regarding my alleged "singling out of Lee."

The government's feeble response to these allegations left many believing that there might be some merit to them. The prosecution argued that the issue of my alleged racism or ethnic bias was irrelevant since I had played no role in the decision to prosecute Wen Ho Lee for downloading classified information on his tapes. It made no effort to refute these allegations, despite the fact that the prosecution had available numerous declarations and even a multivolume Justice Department report documenting that the allegations were completely false. The government's inept response

---

*Sea Change was the criminal investigation of Lee's computer activity. I played no role in that. My involvement with the FBI was limited to the counterintelligence investigation Kindred Spirit.

only fueled speculation that Lee's defense team was on the right track. Judge Parker, in his ruling announcing Lee's plea bargain in September 2000, implied that the government had accepted Lee's plea in order "to avoid its discovery obligations on the selective prosecution issue."[25]

IN RESPONDING TO the defense's "selective prosecution" strategy, the government stumbled badly, perhaps most egregiously in ignoring the report of the attorney general's review team on the FBI, DOE and Justice's handling of this case. Sometime in mid-1999, Janet Reno had commissioned a review of the Wen Ho Lee case.[26] The review was conducted by Justice Department prosecutors, headed by a senior prosecutor named Randy I. Bellows, and an FBI supervisory special agent and two other special agents. (Ironically, one of those agents had been detailed to the Energy Department's counterintelligence office in the early 1990s.) The team collected and reviewed over 42,000 documents from the FBI, CIA, Justice and the Energy Department. They also conducted nearly 170 interviews of all the participants (and some scientists who were not) in the Lee case. They started with Lee's initial encounter with the FBI in 1982 and carried the investigation up to early 1999, right to the point at which the FBI opened its Sea Change criminal phase of the case.

This report, known as the Bellows Report, had been completed by May 2000 and was available to the prosecution during the Wen Ho Lee proceedings. At any point, the prosecution could have produced this report to refute the defense's allegations of selective prosecution and ethnic profiling. But it didn't. The report was classified, but volumes of classified material were introduced into the trial and the judge could have reviewed the report *in camera.*

What did the Justice Department report conclude? The investigators could find no evidence of racial bias against Lee or any other Asian-American in the conduct of the Energy Department Administrative Inquiry. The report claimed that the Administrative Inquiry had many serious problems, but racism was not among them. Lee's name was on the list of investigative leads provided to the FBI in 1996 not because he was Chinese-American, but because of his previous contacts with PRC nuclear scientists and the existence of two counterintelligence investigations into Lee, one of which was ongoing in 1995. The Justice Department report shows that the AI did not focus exclusively on Asian-Americans, that no group of files was ever assembled of only Asian-Americans, and that no filters were ever applied to sort out only Asian-Americans. The "protocol" approved by me directed Dan Bruno and the team to review each and every file.[27]

The Justice Department report reveals that it was Bob Vrooman who had singled out Wen Ho and Sylvia Lee to the Bruno-"Maines" team during their 1996 visit at Los Alamos; that these were the only names he provided to the team; and that he didn't provide information on any of the "others" he would later claim should have been on the list. Nor did the Justice Department turn up any records or information that Vrooman ever expressed his "concerns" to anyone in the FBI prior to 1999.

I don't know why the prosecution didn't use these materials, so readily available to them, to refute the allegations of racism, ethnic profiling and selective prosecution. The Bellows Report is harshly critical of the FBI and the Justice Department, along with Energy, for the overall handling of the case. It appeared that the government would rather be painted as racially motivated in its prosecution of Lee than expose the FBI's disastrous management of the case. After all, the only person who would suffer from this was me.

The prosecution failed to refute the testimony of Lee's expert witnesses and failed to rebut Lee's allegations of selective prosecution and ethnic profiling. It couldn't come up with a reasonable theory of why Lee made the tapes or what he intended to do with them. The government was extremely reluctant to argue that he had made them to assist the People's Republic of China, even though Lee had admitted helping the Chinese with computer codes and software. For some reason, the government dated Lee's first illegal computer activity to 1994, though in fact he had started moving classified information onto the unclassified Los Alamos computer network in 1988—around the time of his second trip to Beijing. By highlighting 1994, the prosecution avoided the inference to a link to the Chinese, but opened the door to a theory that Lee feared he would be fired from Los Alamos and made the tapes to help his employment prospects—the prosecution's theory, which the defense never subscribed to. But the prosecution could never decide just where it was that Lee would seek employment with these tapes containing America's nuclear weapons secrets in hand. When pressed to cite the foreign countries where Lee might be seeking employment with the tapes, the prosecution cited Singapore, Great Britain, Hong Kong and Australia, among others. There must have been some snickering in the courtroom as the prosecution read out this list.

And then, suddenly, it was over. The government's arguments for holding Lee in solitary confinement were undermined by its own mistakes at least as much as by Lee's defense strategy. For example, a key FBI agent testifying back in December 1999 in the detention hearing had misled the presiding magistrate judge about Wen Ho Lee's statements to a colleague concerning Lee's use of the colleague's password and access control. The agent had testified that Lee told the colleague that he wanted to download a resumé, while the colleague said that Lee told him he wanted to download some files. In his book, Lee said that he didn't tell his colleague about the classified files because the colleague didn't have the appropriate security clearances. (Never mind that the computer was outside the security perimeter, in an unclassified area.) When I read about the FBI's misleading testimony, I thought the key point was that Lee hadn't told the colleague that he was downloading classified files onto computer tapes. But Judge Parker seemed more offended by the FBI agent's misleading testimony than by Lee's actions.

Second, the defense discovered that the materials Lee had downloaded were designated PARD files. PARD stands for Protect As Restricted Data, a security designation intended to govern the handling of computer printouts of these files. PARD didn't mean that the files were unclassified, just that the computer printouts would eventually be subject to a classification review. When that review was finished on Lee's materials, the files were deemed to contain information classified both Secret/Restricted Data and Confidential/Restricted Data. Then much was made of the fact that such data may be transmitted via registered mail. On that one, the government shot itself in the foot. I had never been comfortable with sending such information through the U.S. mail system, but security officials had approved this long ago. These decisions were made to facilitate handling of this material and in no way diminished the sensitivity of the tapes. But the prosecution should have anticipated that Lee's defense would raise these issues.

Faced with the prospect of losing its motion to retain Lee in solitary confinement and the failure of its strategy to coerce a confession from him, the government cut a deal with Lee's lawyers: time served—227 days in solitary confinement—and a small fine in return for Lee revealing what he had done with the tapes. The government would drop 58 of the 59 counts in the original indictment if Lee would just tell the prosecutors what he did with the tapes. The deal was held up a few days after Lee admitted that there weren't 7 missing tapes, but more like 17 or maybe 20. He had made additional copies of the tapes, but didn't even tell his lawyers about these until the last minute. Yet the government still accepted the plea bargain and on September 13, 2000, Wen Ho Lee walked out a free man. A convicted felon, but a free man with his lab pension intact and a lucrative book and movie deal, said to be worth $650,000. Lee claimed that he had never voted, never owned a gun, and had no desire to be a politician, so the felony conviction didn't seem to bother him much.[28] The government also granted him immunity from further prosecution in return for the tapes.

FBI director Louis Freeh justified the plea bargain by claiming that this was the government's "best opportunity to protect the national security by finding out what happened to the seven missing tapes, as well as the additional copies of the tapes that Dr. Lee has now admitted to having made."[29] Freeh promised further interrogations and polygraphs to ensure that Lee carried out his end of the plea bargain.

And what did the government get? Nothing. Lee stuck to his story that he had erased the information on the tapes and thrown them in a Dumpster, and he refused to disclose why he had made them in the first place. In his book, he claims that he moved the classified information onto the unprotected system and then made the tapes to back up his work in the event that the Los Alamos computer system crashed. But any scientist, indeed anyone who uses a computer, worries about that. Los Alamos had one of the most powerful computing centers in the world and had made provisions for exactly this contingency. It had well-established procedures for the creation and secure handling of backup computer tapes. All the codes and information that Lee downloaded onto tapes had been stored on backup tapes held in a secure location for years. Wen Ho Lee knew that Los Alamos computer experts could help him protect his work and still safeguard the lab's nuclear secrets. But Lee chose not to go to these experts; he chose to ignore his security obligations and make his own tapes surreptitiously. His claim that he was simply making backup tapes—tapes that the government has never found—remains unconvincing to many.

Later that fall, FBI agents were seen digging in the huge trash dump outside of Los Alamos, but the tapes they found were not from Lee's collection. Government debriefings of Lee were unproductive, and after months of searching, the government offered limited immunity to Mrs. Lee in return for any information she could provide them on the missing tapes. She said that she may have seen some tapes, but didn't know if these were classified or not. The government was left only with Wen Ho Lee's word and, as the FBI knew from its two decades of experience with Lee, unless he was confronted with irrefutable evidence or a polygraph, that word wasn't worth much at all.

PREDICTABLY, A FIRESTORM of criticism broke out in the national media in the aftermath of the plea bargain, fueled in part by President Clinton's criticism of his own Justice Department's incarceration of Lee. Clinton pronounced himself "troubled" by the department's behavior and its potential abuse of executive authority.[30] Never mind that the decision to hold Lee in solitary confinement prior to his trial was made by Clinton's national security advisor, Sandy Berger, and other administration officials meeting in the White House in December 1999.

The *Wall Street Journal* pronounced the whole thing a "diversion."[31] Wen Ho Lee took the fall for all of the Energy Department's security flaws and loss of secrets exposed by the Cox Report, the PFIAB and others over the summer of 1999. And Bill Richardson's advisors had urged him to fire Lee to show how tough he was and that he was cleaning people like Lee out of the department.

I think the FBI and Justice also went after Lee so hard to cover up for their mistakes in the Kindred Spirit investigation. Despite the mountain of circumstantial evidence against Lee warranting a full counterintelligence investigation of him, the FBI did next to nothing for three years and then pronounced him not guilty in January 1999—only to have him fail one of their own polygraphs, reveal still more details about his contacts with PRC nuclear scientists that fueled further suspicions about him, and then to learn by accident that he had been building a personal library of nuclear warhead design for more than a decade.

But the focus of most of the press accounts was on racial profiling and racism—and my alleged role in "singling out Wen Ho Lee." Former Berkeley radical and Kim Il Sung admirer Robert Scheer, writing in the *Los Angeles Times,* claimed, "Trulock Is Source of Botched Lee Case."[32] Relying exclusively on the Vrooman and Chuck Washington statements, he wrote, "Trulock, a former Energy Department intelligence officer, has relentlessly and almost single-handedly pursued Los Alamos scientist Wen Ho Lee for years." Scheer cited Washington's claims that I had assaulted him, that I held racist views against minority groups and had victimized other minorities.[33]

Not to be outdone, another *Los Angeles Times* reporter, Bob Drogin, wrote that I had insisted that Lee was the only suspect and that I was a "self-described knuckle-dragger" and a "hard-charging ideologue with little patience for those who did not agree" with me.[34] I wondered about the "self-described knuckle-dragger" reference and I finally got the chance to ask Drogin where he got it. He said that I had described myself in that manner during my congressional testimony. When I checked, I found that what I had really said was that "those people advocating those measures were *repeatedly labeled* 'Cold Warriors,' 'knuckle draggers,' and even 'McCarthyites' " by DOE managers (emphasis added).[35]

But the prize for the most distorted "reporting" goes to Edward Klein, who authored "The Hunting of Wen Ho Lee," published in *Vanity Fair* in December 2000.[36] Klein introduced all sorts of new "facts" into this story, such as his assertion that I wrote the original Administrative Inquiry that was transmitted to the FBI. That I identified Wen Ho Lee as the only suspect with access, opportunity and motivation. That I was a careerist intent on using the Lee case to further my own prospects. He repeated Vrooman and

Washington's allegation that I had selected Lee because he was Chinese-American. And then finally, when it appeared that the case had come to a dead end, "in his Javert-like zeal, Trulock urged F.B.I. director Louis Freeh to launch a vigorous investigation." When I began to refute these charges in a telephone conversation with Klein before publication, he cut me off, saying that his wife was yelling at him that it was time to go. He never called me back.

NO ONE CAME FORWARD to dispute these charges—none of my former employees at Energy and certainly none of my "protectors" on Capitol Hill. Senator Warner and Congressman Cox refused to return my phone calls. The chairmen of the Intelligence Committees, Senator Shelby and Representative Goss, ignored my requests for assistance. From time to time, reporters would call seeking a comment on Lee's allegations, but for the most part the media simply took these charges as gospel. One night I was watching a program on Fox News hosted by Paula Zahn, a TV personality I had always liked. "What about this guy Notra Trulock?" she asked one of her guests in a tone suggesting that maybe I was a notch above Charlie Manson or some other criminal, but not by much.

I had simply been trying to do my job throughout the Kindred Spirit case, so why was I now being depicted as the villain? I spent hours poring over the few documents and reports that had been released by the government or Congress about the case. I badgered former colleagues and associates: What did we do wrong? How did this thing go so badly off track? The more I read and thought about this case, the more puzzled I became about how the various 1999 inquiries, both on Capitol Hill and by the administration, could have been so slanted. According to these, the Energy Department Administrative Inquiry was the main source of the FBI's mistakes in the case. We at Energy had focused too early on Los Alamos and Wen Ho Lee to the exclusion of other possible sources of the W88 compromise.

But that didn't track with what we had actually done in the Administrative Inquiry. The list of potential investigative leads that we had provided to the FBI in 1996 contained twelve names, each and every one worthy of at least a preliminary FBI investigation. Focus on Los Alamos? The list included scientists from Livermore; but we had also repeatedly told the FBI to look at the Defense

Department, the Navy and Navy contractors, hadn't we? Was the methodology and approach Dan Bruno had employed flawed or wrong in some fashion? But hadn't the FBI, in the persons of the two section chiefs from FBI Headquarters, Jerry Doyle and then Steve Dillard, approved Bruno's approach? Hadn't a seasoned FBI counterintelligence expert, Special Agent "F. Jeff Maines," teamed with Dan to conduct the Administrative Inquiry? The FBI had pulled "Maines" off after the Los Alamos leg of the inquiry, but he had contributed to the final report and even congratulated Dan for his efforts.[37]

The more I thought about this and the more I read, the more convinced I became that the FBI had set out to make Energy and me personally the scapegoat for its mistakes and failures. I was especially convinced after I read the Thompson-Lieberman Senate report and the President's Foreign Intelligence Report over and over again. Nobody reads footnotes, but my background and years of experience as a military Sovietologist had trained me to pay careful attention to them. And finally I found at least the beginning of an explanation.

In a footnote to the Thompson-Lieberman statement, I read the following:

> When the FBI had learned on or shortly after October 31, 1995 that DOE was looking into Lee in connection with the W88 matter, however, it had suspended its inquiry into the separate FBI lead pending the outcome of the DOE inquiry. This suspension— which occurred on November 2, 1995—was undertaken in order to avoid interfering with the Wen Ho Lee inquiry. Gallagher, GAC II transcript, at 7-12.

Neil Gallagher, the FBI's associate director, told the Thompson-Lieberman committee that DOE had already identified Lee before it began the AI, and the FBI called off the inquiry into Lee's 1993 meeting with Hu Side because of Energy's decision to pursue Lee.

Put simply, this testimony was false. The report cites Gallagher telling Thompson and Lieberman that DOE was "looking into Lee" by October 1995, but Bruno didn't turn up Lee's name until their visit to Los Alamos in February 1996. It was during this visit that Vrooman had singled out Lee for his suspicious contacts with the Chinese.[38] I first learned of Lee in a memo Bruno sent me in April 1996 tagging Lee as a possible suspect. So how could DOE warn the FBI off of Wen Ho Lee in early November 1995?

Obviously, DOE didn't warn the FBI off its preliminary investigation of Lee in 1995, but Special Agent "Maines," preparing to accompany Bruno on the lab visits, could and did. In fact, that is precisely what Neil Gallagher told the committee behind closed doors: that "Maines" had told the Santa Fe resident FBI agent, "Dick Lowenthal," to back off the Wen Ho Lee preliminary investigation in November 1995. This was later confirmed by a Justice Department report that cited the conclusion of "Maines" that "it was decided Lee could be the subject at some point of the Albuquerque Case Kindred Spirit" and that during a meeting at FBI Headquarters on November 2, 1995, "Maines" requested that "Lowenthal" undertake no interview of Lee at that time.[39] Decided by whom? "Maines," "Lowenthal" and "Greg Smith" of the FBI. So who had focused on Wen Ho Lee and Los Alamos "too early" in the case? Not Energy, but the FBI. This was due in large part to the FBI's "long history with Wen Ho Lee."[40] A history that the Energy Department knew very little about, as it turns out.

Convinced that FBI officials had misled the various investigative committees, deliberately or otherwise, and that the Energy Department Administrative Inquiry was getting a bum rap as a result, I tried to set the record straight. I wrote letters to Louis Freeh and to Senators Thompson and Lieberman refuting Gallagher's false and misleading statements before the Senate committee. In my letter to Freeh, I underscored the consequences of Gallagher's misleading testimony:

> Whatever his purpose, however, one result has been to discredit the good work done by DOE in support of the FBI in 1995–1996. Intentionally or otherwise, Gallagher's testimony has had the effect of damaging my professional integrity and personal reputation. His portrayal of DOE actions has left me open to allegations of racism and harsh criticism for my role in this affair.
>
> Frankly, I expected better of the FBI.[41]

Neither Thompson nor Lieberman ever replied. Eventually I got a reply from the FBI, but not the one I expected.

A congressional aide to Senator Trent Lott, still the majority leader at the time, had urged me to write a history of Kindred Spirit, at least from my perspective—what I had seen and experienced and how the administration, including the FBI, had responded to my warnings about Chinese nuclear espionage. Over the course of a few months in early 2000, I put together a paper that ran about sixty pages or so, detailing my experiences. I was careful to keep classified material out of the paper; all the classified files were still at DOE and I tried to carefully document and source any fact or number that I included. In keeping with the obligations that went along with my security clearances, I sent the paper down to the special security officer at the Energy Department for a classification review. This officer, who had been promoted into that job by me, declined to review the paper. "Not my job," she claimed. Since I was no longer working for the Energy Department, she said that my paper would have to be reviewed by the government agency that held my security clearances now that I was with TRW. But when I talked to TRW's security officers, they said that agency had no obligation to review my paper and it was up to the Energy Department. A real Catch-22 situation.

So I sent the paper to a few former intelligence officials and congressional staffers around town, in hopes that at least these people would get my side of the story. The paper was very critical of the Clinton administration, the Energy Department and the FBI. I had no intention of publishing it, but when I was forced out of TRW, Rich Lowry, the editor of *National Review,* accepted a shorter version, which was published under the title "Energy Loss." I chose *National Review* because I thought it was widely read on Capitol Hill and I still had some hope that some senators or congressmen might recognize the gravity of the situation.

But the only response I got was from the FBI. Although I had submitted the paper, the Energy Department had refused to conduct the necessary review. The FBI used this as a pretext to come after me.

On July 14, two agents from the FBI Washington field office entered the townhouse I was renting and seized the computer on which I had prepared the paper. They coerced "consent" from my roommate, who owned the townhouse, but they took the computer without a search warrant. When I asked the agents why they were taking the computer, they responded, "Someone thinks there is classified information in the paper."

"Who?" I asked.

"We don't know, we are just following orders," they responded.

Their excuse for seizing the computer was the "threat" of a hacker breaking into my computer and stealing classified information. I couldn't help but think that Wen Ho Lee got a better deal than I did when it came to his "expectation of privacy" and Fourth Amendment rights. After all, the FBI hadn't touched his computer for years because of their sensitivities about these issues. During their interrogation of me that Friday night, the two FBI agents asked repeatedly whether I had any classified documents in the house or had placed classified documents on my computer. Despite their efforts to elicit incriminating information, neither agent Mirandized me before the interrogation. Earlier that day they had questioned my roommate about my friends, my acquaintances, anyone else who might have a copy of the manuscript, whom I called on my cell phone.

A few days later someone broke into our townhouse, searched through my files and papers, and wounded my dog. I called the police, and an officer came to the townhouse, looked around and wrote it up as a "suspicious incident." When the news media asked them for a copy of the report, a police spokesperson told the reporter that my dog had done it. That did generate a funny headline: "Pooch Main Suspect in Trulock Burglary."

I fully expected an indictment or some form of a target letter from the FBI telling me I was under investigation. To try to stave this off, I contacted Fox News, which sent a camera crew out to the townhouse. The images of dangling wires where a computer hard drive used to be were pretty effective. John McLaughlin asked me to come on his Sunday talk program, *One on One,* and was very helpful in publicizing the case. McLaughlin said that he had been told, "There is a body of opinion that says those who are 'out to get you' are going to try to morph you into John Deutch and Wen Ho Lee on the basis of this raid on your computer."[42]

The *Washington Times* published a blistering editorial entitled "Target Trulock":

After all these many Clinton years of Chinese espionage during which, coincidence or not, nuclear codes have been downloaded, satellite technology has gone missing, top-secret hard drives have been "lost," supercomputer technology has been sold and nuclear facilities have all but gone up in smoke, Americans may now finally rejoice that the nation's security is assured: the FBI has seized Notra Trulock's desktop computer.

The editorial went on to call for a "thorough investigation into whether Mr. Trulock has indeed been subjected to the forces of intimidation and retaliation that this administration has become so accustomed to wielding."[43]

The FBI made sure there would be no such investigation, at least on Capitol Hill. The Bureau took the unprecedented step of targeting Senate committee staffs for e-mails I had sent to them. Staff members of the Senate Armed Services and Senate Judiciary Committees received an e-mail from the Office of Senate Security after FBI agents visited that office trying to "find out whose ears Trulock has on the Hill."[44] The FBI wanted copies of any e-mail message to senators or their staffs that I had sent anytime over the previous five months. Not surprisingly, with few exceptions, notably Arlen Specter and Bob Smith (R-VT), most senators and their staffs ran for cover. Senator Smith tried to elicit help from John Warner, the chairman of the Senate Armed Services Committee and my home state senator. Warner ignored Smith's and my own appeals for help. In retrospect, I wish I had sent some e-mails to Democrats.

I had heard that the FBI was desperate to find some classified material in the manuscript and was pushing the CIA hard to make a criminal referral on me to the Justice Department immediately. A public interest law firm in Washington, Judicial Watch, took up my case and I credit them for keeping me out of jail. Weeks turned into months and there was still no word from the FBI. The bureau seemed content to keep me in limbo. I suppose FBI officials thought this would be the best way to silence me—just keep the threat of prosecution hanging over my head.

Sometime in late summer, a producer from *60 Minutes* expressed an interest in hearing my "story." I had been approached by *60 Minutes* when the *New York Times* article first appeared, but I declined to talk to them. I had also met with representatives of NBC's *Dateline* who were interested in the story. But I was still in the government and figured that Bill Richardson and the Energy Department would forbid me to appear on these programs. But now I was out of government and out of work, and had nothing to lose.

The producer, Richard Bonin, worked for Leslie Stahl. I didn't see Stahl until the day of the taping, but spent a lot of time with Bonin and his assistants. "We want your side of the story," they repeatedly emphasized. So I told them the story over and over again. I told them everything—the bogus allegations of racism, the FBI's retaliation against me for criticizing their handling of the Wen Ho Lee case, the obstacles to counterintelligence reform at DOE, the whole thing. I gave them documents, pictures of me receiving an Intelligence Community award, everything I could think of to help them with the story. Although initially Bonin seemed eager to get the story on the air, things began to drag out. The *New York Post* ran a small item alleging that Mike Wallace, who had done the Wen Ho Lee *60 Minutes* piece the summer before, was blocking Stahl's story. True or not, the pace of Bonin's efforts did seem to pick up after that.

Bonin and his crew interviewed a lot of people, including Ed Curran and Dan Bruno, the DOE investigator who had run the Administrative Inquiry. Bruno told them—on camera—that I had played no role in putting Wen Ho Lee or anyone else's name on the list that went to the FBI. He emphasized that he and Special Agent "Maines" had made the list, based on their review of records at the labs. I thought that was rather compelling and would go a long way to clearing my name.

Bonin had tons of B-roll shot of me walking around Washington. (B-roll is the filler that shows like *60 Minutes* use to get some video into their show segments. Generally, it depicts people sitting at their desks or wandering around looking at trees.) In my case, they mostly used shots of me walking alongside the Energy Department or framed against the Capitol Dome. But they also depicted the missing computer by filming the cabinet where it had been stored and the dangling wires. They had a camera crew follow me around at a Judicial Watch dinner. Judicial Watch is politically very conservative and has some fairly notorious clients—like Gennifer Flowers, one of Bill Clinton's women. I suspected that the *60 Minutes* crew wanted to film me embracing Flowers or something like that, so I kept my distance.

Finally I was invited to travel to New York for the on-camera interview with Stahl. She was very gracious and I felt comfortable going through the interview. Bonin had insisted that I "reveal" that I had been one of the *New York Times'* sources for its March 1999 article. My lawyers didn't seem to think any harm could come from it, so I described for Bonin exactly what I had told Jim Risen the year before. No classified information; I didn't reveal Wen Ho Lee's name or anything like that. The interview itself was fairly straightforward.

I was pretty nervous when the segment finally aired in December 2001. It wasn't a bad piece, although Stahl vastly overstated my role in the Administrative Inquiry. But that's what she was hearing from the FBI, I'm sure. Ed Curran was used as the counterpoint to many of the things I said on camera. Obviously, Ed had changed his tune since I had last seen him and now he seemed more of a spokesman for Richardson and the FBI. Stahl made a huge deal out of my being the "deep throat" for the *New York Times* article. Curran then blamed me for damaging the investigation and harming Wen Ho Lee and his family. There hadn't been much of an investigation in the first place and it was Bill Richardson who had leaked Lee's name to the media, but Curran followed the administration's line that it was all my fault. Stahl implied that I had gone off the deep end and Ed confirmed that he had seen me "go off" on people who disagreed with me.

What *60 Minutes* left out, of course, was the Dan Bruno interview. Bruno essentially refuted—on camera—all the disinformation the FBI had been spreading around about my role in the Administrative Inquiry. I guess that would not have made for good TV, but why not have on the guy who had actually done the inquiry? It was disappointing that he got left on the cutting room floor, but I had come to expect that sort of thing by now.

Judicial Watch filed lawsuits against FBI officials Louis Freeh and Neil Gallagher for violating my First and Fourth Amendment rights in their invasion of my home. Initially thrown out by a local federal court, the First Amendment claim at least was upheld on appeal. The court's written opinion noted correctly that the FBI had not received a criminal referral from the Energy Department (nor the CIA, for that matter). According to the appeals court, the timing of the seizure, about two weeks after *National Review* published "Energy Loss," raise[s] a reasonable inference that the interrogation and search were retaliatory. Thus, we hold that it was clearly established at the time of the search that the First Amendment prohibits an officer from retaliating against an individual for speaking critically of the government.[45]

The appeals court decision was unanimous on my First Amendment claim, but upheld the local court's rejection of my Fourth Amendment claim on a split decision. As I read the opinion, it appears that the majority acknowledged my claim, but granted the FBI limited immunity "because a reasonable officer in their position would not have known that the search would violate clearly established law."[46] "Why not?" I wondered. And one judge writing the dissenting opinion made the same point:

> The owner of password protected computer files has a clear expectation of privacy in those files that is protected by the Fourth Amendment. . . . This should have been abundantly clear to any reasonable law enforcement officer operating in the year 2000.[47]

I sued Wen Ho Lee, Bob Vrooman and Charles Washington for defamation when they claimed that I was a racist and had singled out Lee because he was ethnic Chinese. It was this effort at litigation that finally compelled the Justice Department to publish a heavily redacted version of the Bellows Report, which demonstrated that there had been no racial profiling in this case. During the discovery portion of this case, Wen Ho Lee said under oath that he doesn't think he was indicted because he is Chinese, that he had never told his lawyers to allege that he was investigated because he is Chinese-American, that he didn't agree with Robert Vrooman's allegations that he was singled out due to his ethnicity, that he had never experienced racism, and that he doesn't understand the term "racial profiling."[48] He was forced to admit that the government had valid reasons for investigating him, as did Vrooman when he finally had to testify under oath. After months of discovery and legal maneuvering, just days before the trial was to commence, the Justice Department intervened to have the case dismissed on national security grounds. Justice submitted a secret affidavit by

CIA director George Tenet in support of its claim that state secrets might be imperiled if the trial was allowed to continue.

And how did the counterintelligence reforms fare within the Energy Department and at the labs after all the dust had settled? In mid-2000, the House Intelligence Committee commissioned Paul Redmond, a retired CIA counterintelligence expert, to undertake an evaluation of CI reforms within DOE. The Redmond Report, issued in July 2000, gave Ed Curran high marks for effort and good intentions, but noted some enduring shortfalls in the CI program.[49] It applauded Ed's programs to identify and cope with insider threats and it noted that he still had the attention and support of the energy secretary, Bill Richardson. Both the Headquarters and the lab CI offices had finally hired a solid cadre of trained investigators and Curran had established a team of inspectors to conduct annual checks on the state of DOE's CI program. The report identified some of the lingering problems confronting Curran, including training and awareness, cyber CI and polygraph testing. The latter area, in particular, encountered a hard push back from the labs; Sandia had even commissioned a study to refute the polygraph's effectiveness as an investigative tool and there was outright hostility at the other labs. Bill Richardson's exempting of his political appointees from the polygraph, even though many were handling the same information as lab scientists, did nothing to build trust between scientists and CI officers on that issue.

Beyond these findings, the Redmond Report made two very significant predictions about the future of CI in the Energy complex. First, Redmond dismissed the assurances that "all is well" coming from Richardson and elsewhere within DOE Headquarters as "nonsense":

> Problems and deficiencies caused by decades of nonfeasance and neglect cannot be fixed overnight. Such statements serve only to strengthen the position of those at the laboratories who would wait out the effort to improve CI and thus make the job all that much harder.

More ominously, Redmond issued a caution about the dilution of Curran's authority over counterintelligence inherent in the creation of the National Nuclear Security Administration by Congress. Curran was already fighting a rearguard action against the plan, which had the effect of eliminating Ed's authority over CI programs at the nuclear weapons labs, the source of all the trouble in the first place. Richardson proposed keeping Ed "dual-hatted" in charge of CI for both the new organization and the Energy Department, but that arrangement would not withstand congressional demands that the new law be implemented as written.

In fact, when it established the National Nuclear Security Administration, the U.S. Congress snatched defeat from the jaws of victory—at least in the area of counterintelligence and security reform. Since early in the Clinton administration, departmental managers like Vic Reis, the assistant secretary in charge of the weapons labs, as well as their congressional supporters had been frustrated by the declining share of the DOE budgets going to the weapons labs and a supposed lack of attention by Secretary O'Leary and her successors. Seizing on the espionage scandal and the PFIAB's findings of decades of management neglect and organizational disorder, Congress mandated a reorganization of the Energy Department in mid-1999. Led by Pete Domenici, the Senate came up with a scheme to create a semi-autonomous agency within the Energy Department to oversee the nuclear weapons labs, complete with separate and parallel management organizations for counterintelligence and security. Vic Reis probably saw an opportunity to create a completely indepedent agency—along the lines of the National Aeronautics and Space Administration (NASA) or the old Atomic Energy Commission, with himself as the director—while Domenici wanted to free the weapons labs from the burdens of Washington oversight.

The new organization, created by the National Defense Authorization Act for FY 2000, was signed into law in October 1999 for implementation by March 1, 2000. Boiled down to their essentials, the express objectives of the National Nuclear Security Administration were to ensure that the Science Based Stockpile Stewardship program, the substitute for live nuclear testing, worked, and to enhance safeguards against future espionage at the labs. But in Senate hearings, Democrats expressed particular reservations about the division of authority over counterintelligence. They correctly noted the risks of diffusing responsibility for CI: "If we care about preventing espionage at these laboratories, then we need the simplest and clearest lines of authority and responsibility here—lines that go directly to the top of the department." Recall that the key FBI findings about DOE counterintelligence in 1997 had singled out the lack of centralized authority and clear lines of accountability as critical deficiencies. The whole point of Presidential Decision Directive 61 had been to fix exactly those deficiencies.

But Senator Domenici and his colleagues waved off these reservations and established the position of "administrator" to run the weapons labs, created separate offices of "Defense Nuclear Counterintelligence" and "Defense Nuclear Security," and then simply transferred other Energy Department organizations, like the Office of Nonproliferation and National Security, into the administration. In most cases, this meant that many of the same people who had fiercely resisted CI and security reform got to carry on their resistance from within the new structure.

Richardson had bitterly opposed congressional efforts to divide his department and, after losing by overwhelming margins in both the Senate and the House, tried to circumvent the new law by dual-hatting his hand-picked management team to run both the new administration and what was left of the Energy Department. By so doing, he faced allegations of "unconstitutional" violations of the principle of separation of powers, and threats from Domenici and others to pull the weapons labs out of DOE altogether. In defense of his actions, he argued that the new structure, if implemented as envisioned by Congress, would simply enhance the "institutional isolation and arrogance" cited in the PFIAB report. But of course, that was the underlying objective of the whole legislative initiative: to protect the labs from too much oversight and interference from Washington, regardless of how poorly lab managers had performed over the years on security and counterintelligence.

Initially Ed Curran served as both the Energy and the Defense nuclear CI chief, but in 2001 his authority over the weapons labs was delegated to a new "chief for defensive counterintelligence," Kathy Eberwein, the former congressional aide from the House Intelligence Committee. Eberwein had no prior CI experience and certainly no operational experience running CI cases, contrary to the PFIAB's recommendation that this position be filled by an experienced FBI counterintelligence expert. The Congress made sure she had plenty of funding to spend at the labs, but practically no staff of her own.

Security fared no better under the National Nuclear Security Administration. Former DOE security officials reported that the same old faces were showing up in the new administration's security positions and it was back to business as usual. A government watchdog group reported that the nuclear labs had yet to close vulnerabilities in cybersecurity, noting that nothing had been done to prevent a repeat of Wen Ho Lee's illegal computer transfers.[50] Under the new organization, the labs continued to fail security exercises even when the tests were "dumbed down"; labs fudged the results of self-assessments; and the lab protective forces continued to deteriorate. And as before, the new administration squashed anyone who dared to voice publicly any concerns about security failures.

And there the matter stands. I spent my entire career working for the federal government, either directly or as a contractor. I had held the highest security clearances the government grants. I had tried to protect my country against a security breach that could come back to haunt it some day in a catastrophe that would make the events of September 11 look like a warmup pitch.

I did my best to protect America against Chinese nuclear espionage. I love this country, but sometimes I can't help but feel that my country has abandoned me; I know that my government has. Would I do it all again? Frankly, I just don't know.

Appendix A

MEMORANDUM

May 16, 1996

TO: NOTRA TRULOCK

FROM: CHUCK WASHINGTON

SUBJECT: KINDRED SPIRIT

I received the report about an hour and a half ago. I read the first 7 pages and the Internal Data Pages (IDP - yellow pages). The rest of the report consists of lists of names. I did not dwell on the lists, because I wanted to get the report to you ASAP, since the FBI said they would open after they received our report.

My thoughts on the report:

-The Summary should provide an overview of the pertinent discoveries; it does not.

-The body of the report really doesn't tell us much. If you do not receive the IDP (yellow pages - which only go to OEI and FBI), the report doesn't shed much light on the situation.

-Much of the information in the IDP duplicates information identified in the body of the report.

-The report should be CLOSED, rather than PENDING, because no leads are set forth, and in the IDP it is stated that there is really nothing left to be done. We should consider publishing a CLOSED report and opening a Monitor investigation to Monitor the FBI investigation, or open a Joint Investigation, based upon a request for assistance from the FBI. Based on what we know now, I think we should not expend anymore OEI efforts on this without a tasking (verbal is okay; written is better) from the FBI, because we are mighty close to becoming involved in an espionage investigation, which we do not have the authority to do.

-Several typing errors, that I marked in pencil. In most cases these errors do not negatively impact the understandability of the report.

-On future reports we must fix the report writing format.

I have not discussed this with Dan. Your call on how you wish to proceed.

Appendix B

Los Alamos
Los Alamos National Laboratory
Los Alamos, New Mexico 87545

memorandum

TO: Distribution   DATE: December 13, 1989

FROM: Robert S. Vrooman   MAIL STOP/TELEPHONE: G733/5-2448

SYMBOL: ADO/ISEC:89(C)

SUBJECT: MEETING ON PEOPLE'S REPUBLIC OF CHINA (PRC) CONTACTS

On December 11, 1989, Bob Vrooman, ADO/ISEC; Harold Sullivan, N-6; and Sylvia Lee, N-6, met to discuss Sylvia's role in arranging official contacts between Laboratory Staff and the PRC. Vrooman explained the purpose of the meeting was to clarify responsibilities and protect Sylvia from unauthorized infringement on her time. Vrooman was also concerned about the motives of the PRC in cultivating her as their point-of-contact. Sylvia understood and agreed with this concern.

Sylvia explained how she came to be involved in this and agreed to the following:

- Sylvia will forward all incoming requests for assistance from the PRC to George Kwei.

- Her personal relationship and correspondence with the PRC are her own business. By her own choice she will keep Dave Bibb, FBI, apprised of these.

- Vrooman will advise the Los Alamos Staff to either deal directly with the PRC or with George Kwei if assistance is needed.

I concur with the above: _____
                                                    Sylvia Lee

Date: _____12/15/89_____

RSV:jb

Cy: Sylvia Lee
    ISEC File

Distribution:
    John T. Whetten, ADET, MS A107
    Allen J. Tiedman, ADO, MS A120
    L. Harold Sullivan, N-6, MS K557
    Dave T. Bibb, FBI, Santa Fe (Handcarried)
    George H. Kwei, CLS-2, MS D437
    Horace H. Sprouse, OS-12, MS G727
    CRM-4 (2), MS A150

EXHIBIT
5
Vrooman

WHL 001329

Attachment 2   "IN CONFIDENCE"

Appendix C

```
Filename:       ciCC Response.doc
Directory:      A:\Counterintel
Template:       C:\Program Files\Microsoft
  Office\Office\Normal.dot
Title:          COX COMMISSION RESPONSE
Subject:
Author:         R.P. Eddy
Keywords:
Comments:
Creation Date: 01/06/99 1:49 PM
Change Number: 1
Last Saved On: 01/06/99 2:07 PM
Last Saved By: R.P. Eddy
Total Editing Time: 19 Minutes
Last Printed On:   06/13/00 3:42 PM
As of Last Complete Printing
  Number of Pages: 1
  Number of Words: 193 (approx.)
  Number of Characters:  795 (approx.)
```

COX COMMISSION RESPONSE

WHAT IS IN THE REPORT?

1) Findings:
   a) Summary of the Trulok findings (i.e.
   b)

2) Recommendations:
   a) Mostly innocuous reporting requirements except:
      i) DOE and other agencies must do a damage assessment
         to submit to the Hill.

WHAT IS LEAKED?

- Detailed specifics of Trulok briefing.
- Details on the _kindred spirit_ disclosures.
- Depth and benefits of _____ per Trulok's
  point of view.

WHAT ARE WE DOING?

1) Curran on-the-record explaining:

   - CI penetrations are from the 80's
   - We are well underway to strengthening the program
   - Fixes already in place, more robust steps underway,
     why these fixes are important
   - PDD and new steps to strengthen the program because:
     A. Program was poor until 90's,
     B. new post-cold war threat environment,
     C. disclosure in 90's of poor program in 80's and PDD
        and program strengthening due to and

2) Using lab experts to make a new DOE review of the
   _ks_ Trulok used to create his assessments.
   Create a new more measured "DOE position" on _____
   _ks_ .

DOE00083

Appendix D

Intelligence Community Damage Assessment of China's Acquisition of U.S. Nuclear Weapons Information

Chinese strategic nuclear efforts have focused on developing and deploying a survivable long-range missile force that can hold a significant portion of the U.S. and Russian populations at risk in a retaliatory strike. By at least the late 1970s the Chinese launched an ambitious collection program focused on the U.S., including its national laboratories, to acquire nuclear weapons technologies. By the 1980s China recognized that its second strike capability might be in jeopardy unless its force became more survivable. This probably prompted the Chinese to heighten their interest in smaller and lighter nuclear weapon systems to permit a mobile force.

China obtained by espionage classified U.S. nuclear weapons information that probably accelerated its program to develop future nuclear weapons. This collection program allowed China to focus successfully down critical paths and avoid less promising approaches to nuclear weapons designs.

- China obtained at least basic design information on several modern U.S. nuclear reentry vehicles, including the Trident II (W-88).
- China also obtained information on a variety of U.S. weapon design concepts and weaponization features, including those of a neutron bomb.
- We cannot determine the full extent of weapon information obtained. For example, we do not know whether any weapon design documentation or blueprints were acquired.
- We believe it is more likely that the Chinese used U.S. design information to inform their own program than to replicate U.S. weapon designs.

China's technical advances have been made on the basis of classified and unclassified information derived from espionage, contact with U.S. and other countries' scientists, conferences and publications, unauthorized media enclosures, declassified U.S.

weapons information, and Chinese indigenous development. The relative contribution of each cannot be determined.

Regardless of the source of the weapons information, it has made an important contribution to the Chinese objective to maintain a second strike capability and provided useful information for future design.

Significant deficiencies remain in the Chinese weapons program. The Chinese almost certainly are using aggressive collection efforts to address deficiencies as well as to obtain manufacturing and production capabilities from both nuclear and nonnuclear sources.

To date, the aggressive Chinese collection effort has not resulted in any apparent modernization of their deployed strategic force or any new nuclear weapons deployment.

China has had the technical capability to develop a multiple independently targetable reentry vehicle (MIRV) system for its large, currently deployed ICBM for many years, but has not done so. U.S. information acquired by the Chinese could help them develop a MIRV for a future mobile missile.

We do not know if U.S. classified nuclear information acquired by the Chinese has been passed to other countries. Having obtained more modern U.S. nuclear technology, the Chinese might be less concerned about having their older technology.

Notes

ABBREVIATIONS

NYT   *New York Times*
WP   *Washington Post*
WSJ   *Wall Street Journal*
WT   *Washington Times*

PROLOGUE

1. Bellows Report, p. 184.
2. Specter Report, p. 22.
3. PFIAB Report, p. ii.
4. PFIAB Report, p. 38.
5. Bellows Report. p. 41.
6. Bellows Report, p. 183.

TWO: SETTING THE STAGE

1. Bill Richardson served on the House Intelligence Committee, but a former staff director of that committee told me that he used the committee to pay for his globe trotting and made no substantive contribution to the deliberations of the committee. Senate Republicans pointed to the lack of security credentials as a symptom of the Clinton administration's disregard for national security and vowed to appoint a national security expert if given the opportunity. Ironically, they confirmed President Bush's appointee, a one-term U.S. senator with even less national security experience than Clinton's appointees.
2. Paul Redmond, "America Pays the Price of Openness," WSJ, June 2000.

3. The name of the office has been changed back to "Classification."
4. Congressman Curt Weldon (R.-PA), Press Release, "Newsstand Nukes: It Was O'Leary," 23 August 1999.
5. Hamza, *Saddam's Bombmaker.*
6. Gertz, *The China Threat,* p. 209.
7. Sworn Deposition of Robert Vrooman, 17 November 2001.
8. Stober and Hoffman, *A Convenient Spy,* pp. 71, 77.
9. See, for example, Robert Vrooman, "Professionalism, Security, and Civil Rights," IEEE Public Forum, Los Alamos National Laboratory, 14 December 1999.
10. Stober and Hoffman, *A Convenient Spy,* p. 77.
11. Stober and Hoffman, *A Convenient Spy,* p. 77.
12. PFIAB Report, p. 2.

THREE: TO BUILD A BETTER BOMB

1. Special Report of the Senate Select Committee on Intelligence, United States Senate, 6 January 1999 to 15 December 2000, Report 107-51, August 2001, p. 16.
2. Bill Gertz of the *Washington Times* has reported that a blue-ribbon panel review of CIA's China reporting found that reporting to be "biased and slanted toward a benign view of the emerging communist power." If true, this bias would account for some of the reports generated by CIA in the Kindred Spirit matter. See Bill Gertz, "Panel Finds CIA Soft on China," WT, 6 July 2001.
3. Cox Report, vol. 1, p. 72.
4. The Bellows Report has redacted all references to the memo other than the date of its submission to me. Bellows Report, ch. 6, p. 238.
5. Cox Report, vol. 1, p. 72.
6. Cox Report, vol. 1, p. 72.
7. This refers to what is known as a "source code" or the set of instructions that can be given to a computer to perform a calculation simulating a physical event. Source codes for thermonuclear weapons designs model and simulate events that closely resemble test data from past nuclear weapons tests. They address such matters as detonation, high-explosive burn, hydrodynamics, radiation transport, neutron transport, thermonuclear burn, and weapons aging and degradation. This is taken from a subsection entitled "Nuclear Weapons Terminology" in the Wen Ho Lee indictment, December 1999.
8. The Bellows Report notes, "Trulock respected Richter's judgment in the area of nuclear weapons design." True, but I was hardly the only person who held Richter in high esteem. Bellows Report, p. 240.
9. Bellows Report, p. 240.
10. Notra Trulock III, Acting Deputy, Office of Intelligence, DOE, "Damage to National Security from Chinese Espionage at DOE Nuclear Weapons Laboratories," Statement for the Record to the Committee on Energy and National Resources, U.S. Senate, 20 May 1999, p. 2.

11. Cox Report, vol. 1, p. 60.
12. William J. Broad, "Spies vs. Sweat: The Debate over China's Nuclear Advance," NYT, 7 September 1999.
13. See especially Matthew Purdy, "The Making of a Suspect: The Case of Wen Ho Lee," NYT, 4 February 2001. This "retrospective" omits any reference to the role played by Booth, probably to his immense relief.
14. Bellows Report, p. 249.
15. For some reason, Henson felt that he never got the credit he deserved for his role in uncovering the espionage. Nevertheless, it was Richter's assessment that triggered the whole case.
16. Bellows Report, p. 255.
17. Schlesinger is a Washington "big foot" who has served various Presidents as secretary of defense, director of the Office of Management and Budget, and director of CIA. He was the first secretary of the Energy Department, which was formed in the Carter years. He serves on numerous boards and panels and he remained influential throughout the Clinton administration, despite some obvious differences with Clinton policies. He is especially protective of the Energy Department and maintains very reliable sources within the department to make sure he keeps in touch with developments there. One of those very reliable sources was Baker.
18. Bellows Report, p. 349.
19. The Bellows Report claims, "Trulock initially contemplated forming only a LANL team, with CIA [redacted] participation, to validate the initial assessment." Regrettably, the source of this claim is redacted. In truth, I had no such intention; I always intended that the peer review would include scientists from both labs. I have wondered how Bellows was able to divine my "intentions."
20. The Bellows Report says the group first met on July 10, 1995.
21. Cox Report, vol. 1, p. 87. In fact, there are multiple variants of the W70, which was designed to be the nuclear warhead for the U.S. LANCE tactical missile. One of the variants was the enhanced radiation or neutron bomb. Readers may recall the furor over U.S. plans to deploy this weapon in Europe in the late 1970s. The warhead was commonly characterized as useful for killing people but not destroying buildings, etc. Then President Carter gave in to the European anti-nuclear movement and canceled the planned deployment.
22. Bill Cleveland told me that he got the shock of his life when he ran into the former Livermore scientist in the Beijing airport sometime in the mid-1980s. Cleveland was escorting some Livermore officials, but never expected to see an FBI espionage suspect free to travel to China.
23. U.S. nuclear warhead development takes place along a well-defined timeline and is divided into phases. Prior to phase three, Livermore and Los Alamos develop competing designs to meet the military customer's stated requirements. Once a design is selected, the

warhead is said to enter the third phase of its development. Later phases deal with manufacturing and production, deployment with military units, and retirement and dismantlement. Bellows Report, p. 305.

24. PFIAB Report, Appendix, p. A-3.
25. Defense Estimative Brief, Nuclear Weapons Systems in China, DEB-49-84, 24 April 1984, pp. 3–4.
26. Defense Estimative Brief, p. 3.
27. As of this writing, this document is still posted online at http://www.gwu.edu/~nsarchiv/news/19990521/01-01.htm.
28. Cox Report, vol. 1, p. 76. Of course, the Cox Report was prepared in late 1999. At the time the KSAG was meeting in midsummer 1995, the PRC had conducted fewer than forty such tests.
29. I am aware that a former lab director, Harold Agnew, made some assertions at variance with this assessment during his defense of Wen Ho Lee. I can only say that I don't know when Agnew made his visits to the PRC, but a careful review of trip reports turned up no such information. The only data that was available to the KSAG on PRC diagnostic capabilities were contained in the unclassified trip report discussed here.
30. Specter Report, p. 18.
31. PFIAB Report, pp. 30–31.
32. Cox Report, vol. 1, p. 83.
33. Reno Testimony, p. 27.
34. Declaration of Robert A. Messemer, 21 July 2000. Messemer was an FBI supervisory special agent in charge of all national security investigations in New Mexico at that time.
35. David Wise, "Inside the Chinese Spy Mystery," *GQ*, November 1999, pp. 288–89.
36. Nearly all of the paragraphs of the Bellows Report referring to the walk-in document have been redacted. But in a congressional hearing conducted on October 3, 2000, the following exchange was entered into the record:

> SEN. SPECTER: ... Mr. Vrooman, the documents were provided to this subcommittee just last night, that I want to start with, which is a memorandum from ["Greg Smith"], which says—["Greg Smith"] of the FBI, Albuquerque office—"on August 25, 1995, Bob Vrooman, who oversees counterintelligence(s), advised Los Alamos National Laboratory's report regarding Kindred Spirit will be provided to Notra Trulock of the DOE headquarters in approximately two weeks. Further a 'quote' 'smoking gun has been found' close quote. Vrooman learned of the information from Diane (Soran)."

Vrooman claimed to have no recollection of this; then, in closed testimony just after this public hearing, he admitted that he did recall this and acknowledged that the term "smoking gun" referred to the walk-in document. I don't know why he could not acknowledge this in public.

37. Author's interview with confidential sources, 2000.
38. Bellows Report, p. 309.
39. Cox Report, vol. 1, p. 73.
40. Huan, "China's Strategic Nuclear Weapons," p. 134.
41. Bellows Report, p. 309.
42. When the FBI interviewed one of the Kindred Spirit participants in fall 1996, he said that the only debate was over the importance of the information. Specter Report, p. 17. Henson would later claim that I discarded the group's conclusions and adopted his harder line. Not true. I also thought Henson was pursuing a personal vendetta against some of his lab supervisors.
43. Specter Report, p. 17.
44. Bellows Report, pp. 235–36.
45. I distinctly recall a KSAG briefing to Curtis sometime in the fall of 1995, perhaps November. No one else seems to recall this meeting and the Bellows Report claims there is no reference to such a meeting in the Kindred Spirit chronology. No member of the KSAG recalls such a meeting. When I interviewed Curtis, however, he did recall such a meeting as part of his preparation for a meeting with DCI Deutch.

FOUR: WHO DONE IT?

1. Bellows Report, p. 153, n. 219.
2. Bellows Report, p. 276.
3. Bellows Report, p. 266.
4. Reno Testimony, p. 5.
5. Reno Testimony, p. 18. On p. 27 of her declassified testimony, Attorney General Janet Reno said, "The espionage at issue that created the whole problem, occurred sometime between 1984 and 1988. It was done, the W88 was gone."
6. Zhongwen and Zongxiao, *Sources and Techniques of Obtaining National Defense Science and Technology Intelligence.*
7. See the Cox Report, vol. 1, pp. 80–83. For a specific example of this technique, see Cox Report, vol. 1, pp. 88–90.
8. PFIAB Report, p. 3.
9. Most notably, John C. Browne, later to become Los Alamos director, returned from a trip to China in 1985, recommending no further visits by Los Alamos scientists. His advice was ignored.
10. See James Risen, "In China, Physicist Learns, He Tripped between Useful Exchange and Security Breach," NYT, 1 August 1999. It was certainly the FBI that told the Cox Committee about the Keyworth case. One account claims Keyworth was actually spying on the Chinese for the CIA and Bob Vrooman was his case officer. Stober and Hoffman, *A Convenient Spy,* pp. 49–57.
11. Messemer declaration, 21 July 2000.
12. Bellows Report, p. 385.
13. Anderson would claim in 1999 that he told Bruno and Special Agent "Maines" that the W88 information was widely distributed

throughout the U.S. nuclear weapons complex. But "Maines'" 1996 written record of the Anderson interview contradicts Anderson's later claim. Bellows Report, p. 360, n. 527. Interviews with a former Los Alamos counterintelligence official confirmed "Maines'" record that Anderson only told the visitors about W88 nuclear tests.

14. During his defense, Vrooman asserted that Wen Ho Lee seldom visited the room where warhead models were kept. Big deal; the only time most of the labs scientists visited the Blue Room was when they had VIP visitors and wanted to impress them with models of the warheads designed at Los Alamos. The Blue Room was kept locked, and when I finally got the tour, we had to wait for a secretary to come down to unlock the room.

15. Bellows Report, p. 384.

16. Bruno to "Maines" correspondence, 14 March 1996.

17. Bellows Report, pp. 370, 371.

18. Personal Communication with the author, 19 March 2000.

19. Bruno deposition. Controversy re: editing, p. 26.

20. Final version of FBI electronic communication provided to U.S. Senate by FBI Assistant Director Neil J. Gallagher, published in U.S. General Accounting Office letter to Senators Specter, Grassley and Torricelli, 28 June 2001, from Robert H. Hast, Managing Director, Office of Special Investigations.

    "In 1996, Energy completed an Administrative Inquiry, which (1) concluded that classified information concerning the W-88 warhead was most likely compromised at the Los Alamos National Laboratory and (2) identified Wen Ho Lee and 11 other suspects in espionage."

    Published on Federation of American Scientists website.

21. Specter Report, p. 16.

22. Reno Testimony, p. 34.

23. Reno Testimony, pp. 7, 15.

24. Memorandum from Chuck Washington to Notra Trulock, Subject: Kindred Spirit, 16 May 1996.

25. Specter Report, p. 16.

26. Specter Report, p. 17. The report cites an FBI interview with "Maines" conducted in 1999.

27. Specter Report, p. 16.

28. Sworn Deposition of Terry L. Craig, Los Alamos, New Mexico, 17 November 2001.

29. See Statement for the Record of Attorney General Janet Reno and FBI Director Louis Freeh on "Investigation and Prosecution of Dr. Wen Ho Lee," before the Senate Select Committee on Intelligence and the Senate Judiciary Committee, Washington, D.C., 26 September 2000, p. 8.

30. Cox Report, 87.

31. Dan Bruno memo, 29 April 1996.

32. Bellows Report, p. 156.

33. Bellows Report, p. 657.

NOTES **359**

34. Bellows Report, p. 657.
35. In 2000 we learned that they had never installed the device. Everyone in Washington and even poor Sig Hecker operated under the assumption that X Division had such a device for four years, when the X Division types had taken the money allocated for the device and spent it on something else.
36. Bellows Report, p. 401.
37. There are several official sources to verify the number of leads included in the report we sent to the FBI. For example, Robert H. Hast, Managing Director, Office of Special Investigations, United States General Accounting Office, lists 12 "suspects in espionage" in Energy's Administrative Inquiry. See Robert Hast, "FBI Official's Congressional Testimony Was Inaccurate Because He Failed to Present Certain Information That Had Been Made Available to Him about the Wen Ho Lee Investigation," United States General Accounting Office, 28 June 2001.
38. Bellows Report, ch. 4, p. 81.
39. Personal communication with the author, 6 September 2000.
40. Specter Report, pp. 11–12.
41. Reno Testimony, p. 8.
42. This account is based on multiple sources, including a declassified court affidavit by Special Agent "Marvin Long," 13 April 1999; O'Melveny and Myers press release, "A Reply to Misleading Press Reports Concerning Dr. Wen Ho Lee," 6 May 1999; Bellows Report, pp. 26–46.
43. This account is based on the Specter Report, pp. 8–11.
44. In his book, Lee claimed that once Taiwan had asked him for a copy of an unclassified research paper. He gave it to them, but was "less than candid" about his other dealings with the Taiwanese. Wen Ho Lee, *My Country versus Me.* See also Reno Testimony, p. 8; Specter Report, pp. 8–11.
45. Specter Report, p. 10.
46. Lee, *My Country versus Me,* p. 270.
47. Bellows Report, p. 26.
48. Bellows Report, p. 41; Specter Report, pp. 8–11.
49. Bellows Report, p. 531.
50. This account is bsed on multiple sources including the O'Melveney and Myers press release, 6 May 1999; the Thompson-Lieberman Statement, 5 August 1999, pp. 14–15; and the Bellows Report, p. 47.
51. Bellows Report, p. 534.
52. Vrooman memo.
53. O'Melveney and Myers press release.
54. Quoted in Stober and Hoffman, *A Convenient Spy,* p. 75.
55. "Marvin Long" Affidavit, 13 April 1999.
56. Lee, *My Country versus Me,* pp. 112–13.
57. Stober and Hoffman, *A Convenient Spy,* p. 101.
58. *USA v. WHL,* Notice of Intention to Offer Evidence Pursuant to Rule 404(b) of the Federal Rules of Evidence, Criminal No. 99-1416 (JP), p. 4.

59. O'Melveney and Myers press release.
60. Specter Report, p. 21.
61. Vrooman memo.
62. Specter Report, p. 76. The quote is from an FBI "source" cited in a 1998 FBI request for electronic surveillance of Lee.
63. Bill Gertz, "Experts Still Suspect Lee of Spying for China," WT, 18 August 2001.
64. Deposition of Wen Ho Lee, 10 October 2001, p. 71. When he was fired from the lab, he was making $82,000.
65. Cited in Edward Klein, "The Hunting of Wen Ho Lee," *Vanity Fair,* December 2000, p. 146.
66. Specter Report, pp. 75–76.
67 "Marvin Long" Affidavit, p. 4.
68 Stober and Hoffman, *A Convenient Spy,* p. 143.
69. Specter Report, p. 76.
70. Wise, *The Spy That Got Away.*
71. The reference is from the Bellows Report, p. 399.
72. Bellows Report, p. 131.
73. Bellows Report, p. 617.
74. Reno Testimony, pp. 20, 15.
75. Specter Report, p. 18.
76. Specter Report, p. 18.
77. Bellows Report, p. 63.
78. Bellows Report, p. 610.
79. The Specter Report contains the best account of this confusing episode.
80. Bellows Report, p. 474.
81. Bellows Report, p. 661.
82. Bellows Report, p. 672.
83. Bellows Report, p. 672.
84. Reno testimony, p. 33.
85. Bellows Report, p. 476.
86. This stunning revelation came from Senator Patrick Leahy's September 2001 speech. Bill Gertz also uncovered indications that Beijing also "issued a blunt warning that the outcome of the Peter Lee case could upset China-US relations." Gertz, *The China Threat,* p. 152. See also, Bellows Report, p. 183.
87. Bellows Report, p. 183.
88. Bellows Report, p. 197.
89. At Headquarters we did pick up Ray Wickman, who had "retired" rather than comply with the Justice Department's handling of the Chinese campaign finance scandal.
90. GAO, 26 September 1996, p. 1.
91. GAO, 26 September 1996, p. 2.
92. Quoted in Stober and Hoffman, *A Convenient Spy,* p. 166.

FIVE: THE HORSE HAS LEFT THE BARN

1. My deputy director later told a DOE inspector general investigator about these discussions, but the IG apparently ignored her testimony.
2. DOE press release, "Secretary Pena Terminates Brookhaven Contract: Pena Says This Step Necessary to Build Public Trust," 1 May 1997.
3. Cox Report, vol. 1, p. 87.
4. Cox Report, vol. 1, p. 68.
5. Cox Report, vol. 1, p. 61.
6. Cox Report, vol. 1, p. 100.
7. Dr. Thomas L. Cook, "HPC Acquisition and China: Impact of the Acquisition of High Performance Computers on the Chinese Nuclear Weapons Program," LANL NIS-p(U)-98-254.
8. Cox Report, vol. 1, p. 111.
9. PFIAB Report, p. 19.
10. The FBI had assigned two new agents fresh out of training to Albuquerque to work the Kindred Spirit case. These two agents were immediately "diverted" to other cases by the Albuquerque SAC.
11. Bellows Report, p. 88.
12. Bellows Report, p. 97.
13. Bellows Report, p. 95.
14. See Alison Mitchell, "Warning on China Never Got to Him, Clinton Contends," NYT, 11 March 1997. I was starting to wonder if anybody ever told this President anything. Jerry Doyle is also mentioned in this article. He left the case in November 1996 and Steve Dillard took over. The FBI told us Doyle was going to the field, New Jersey I think, but here he was turning up in Washington working on the Chinese campaign finance case.
15. Author's interview with Elgie Holstein, January 2002.
16. Testimony before the Military Procurement Subcommittee, House Armed Services Committee, 10 November 1999, p. 32.
17. FBI records indicate that Freeh would not learn about this case until two days later, on 31 July 1997. Bellows Report, pp. 202, 206–9.
18. Cohen was the token Republican in Clinton's cabinet. He had a reputation as a "smart" senator and I had encountered him several times during testimony before the Senate Intelligence Committee. Cohen had come in for much criticism for presiding over the rundown of the U.S. military during his tenure as secretary of defense.
19. One Senate report characterized it this way: "Director Freeh met with Deputy Energy Secretary Elizabeth Moler to tell her that there was no longer any investigatory reason to keep Lee in place at LANL, that DOE should feel free to remove him in order to protect against further disclosures of classified information." Another Senate report says, "FBI Director Freeh advised DOE Deputy Secretary Moler and Intelligence Chief Trulock that there was no

longer any investigative need to keep Lee in place and that he could be moved to a less sensitive post."

20. Bellows Report, p. 664.
21. This account is taken from the Bellows Report, pp. 664–65.
22. As the Bellows Report would later note, "When the Director of the FBI speaks, that is, by definition, the FBI's official position."
23. Bellows Report, p. 664, n. 891.
24. Bellows Report, p. 668.
25. Bellows Report, p. 494.
26. Reno Testimony, p. 13.
27. Thompson-Lieberman Statement, pp. 7–9.
28. Quoted in Specter Report, p. 22.
29. U.S.-China Security Review Commission Report, chapter 7, "Proliferation and Chinese Relations with Terrorist-Sponsoring States," July 2002.
30. Quoted in Kenneth R. Timmerman, " 'Shoot the Messengers': Criticize U.S. China Policy and Kiss Your Career Goodbye," *American Spectator,* December 1999/January 2000.
31. Timmerman, "Shoot the Messengers."
32. James Risen, "White House Is Said to Ignore Evidence of China's Spying," NYT, 13 April 1999.
33. Bellows Report, p. 333.
34. Bellows covers up for the CIA as well, saying that "brevity" led the CIA to modify its paper. It's much more likely that people like Jack Downing, a member of our DOE SAG but by now the new chief of the CIA's Directorate of Operations, wouldn't be party to such blatant politicization.
35. See the discussion in the Bellows Report, p. 668.
36. General Accounting Office, "DOE Needs to Improve Controls over Foreign Visitors," GAO/RCED-97-229, 25 September 1997.
37. PFIAB, Appendix, p. A-11.
38. This was confirmed to me by a senior NSC official, who saw the letter from the labs stating their "non-concurrence" and strongly recommending that DOE do likewise.
39. See PDD/NSC 61 Energy Department Counterintelligence, February 1998, online at http://www.fas.org/irp/offdocs/pdd-tscm.htm.
40. Bellows Report, p. 670.
41. Bellows Report, p. 667.
42. Bellows Report, p. 668.
43. Bellows Report, p. 670.
44. Department of Energy press release, "Pena Appoints Director for Nonproliferation and National Security," 14 November 1997.
45. "Report on the Investigation of Peter Lee," p. 1.
46. J. Michael Waller, "DOE 'Green Book' Secrets Exposed," *Insight Magazine,* 16 July 2001, online edition.

SIX: THE TRUTH COMES OUT

1. PDD 61; PFIAB Report chronology.
2. PFIAB Report, p. 37.
3. Garwin, speaking later to the NYT, claims that "he dismissed the notion as whimsical." To whom, one wonders. Other members of the commission state categorically that he said no such thing and made no objection on this point. So much for scientific integrity. Matthew Purdy, "The Making of a Suspect: The Case of Wen Ho Lee," NYT, 4 February 2001.
4. Cox Report, p. 221. The committee has been criticized in some quarters for not fulfilling this part of its mandate.
5. Cox Report, vol. 1, p. 69.
6. *Sales or Security? Supercomputers and Export Controls.*
7. Department of Energy, Office of Intelligence, Technical Intelligence Note on Computers, Nuclear Weapons, and U.S. Security, 6 May 1998, as quoted in Cox Report, vol. 1, p. 107.
8. Cox Report, vol. 1, p. 101.
9. Cox Report, vol. 1, p. 61.
10. Cox Report, vol. 1, p. 73.
11. Cox Report, vol. 1, p. 85.
12. Bellows Report, p. 673.
13. Specter Report, p. 33.
14. Walter Pincus, "Interrogation of Lee Raises New Questions, Sources Say," WP, 4 February 2001, p. A2.
15. FBIS, "Celebrating Thirty Years of Chung-Shan Science Research Institute."
16. A sting operation involves the use of an agent portraying himself as working for another foreign government and attempting to elicit information from a suspect on that basis. Specter Report, p. 28.
17. Specter Report, p. 36.
18. Laurie P. Cohen and David S. Cloud, "How Federal Agents Bungled the Spy Case against Lee," WSJ, 8 December 2000. The single best media account of the FBI's handling of this case to date.
19. Specter Report, p. 575.
20. This account is based on the Specter Report, pp. 28–30. Other details are from the Bellows Report, pp. 602–4, 615, 573.
21. Specter Report, p. 29.
22. Bellows Report, p. 578.
23. Stober and Hoffman, *A Convenient Spy,* pp. 159–60.
24. Bellows Report, p. 600.
25. Bellows Report, p. 575, 581.
26. Timperlake and Triplett, *Year of the Rat.*
27. I did have the chance to talk about this with Ray Wickman, who had retired from the FBI and was now working for us. Wickman had been deeply involved and told me that Chinese efforts had started out against the Congress—trying to buy influence and so forth. Gradually, however, the White House became the focus of their campaign.

28. Bellows Report, p. 622.
29. Cox Report, vol. 1, p. 63.
30. Cox Report. vol. 1, p. 93.
31. Cox Report, vol. 1, p. 93.
32. Hearing of the Administrative Oversight and the Courts Subcommittee of the Senate Judiciary Committee, 3 October 2000.
33. Bellows Report, p. 675.
34. Bellows Report, p. 634.
35. T Division stands for Theoretical Division, a component of Los Alamos that focuses heavily on applied mathematics, modeling and simulation, equations of state. Much of its work is unclassified and performed outside the security perimeter.
36. David Kitchen memo, FBI, 22 January 1999.
37. Bellows Report, p. 639.
38. Bellows Report, p. 642.
39. Kitchen's other criticisms have been redacted from the Bellows Report.
40. Bellows Report, pp. 643–44.
41. Specter Report, p. 76.
42. Specter Report, p. 48.
43. Bellows Report, pp. 120–22.
44. Bellows Report, p. 646–47.
45. Bellows Report, p. 646.
46. Specter Report, p. 45.
47. Affidavit, "Marvin Long," Special Agent, Federal Bureau of Investigation, 13 April 1999 (declassified).
48. Freeh testimony, p. 9.
49. Bellows Report, p. 213.
50. Bellows Report, p. 2.
51. Thompson-Lieberman Statement, pp. 14, 16.
52. "Marvin Long" Affidavit.
53. I couldn't help but be struck by the irony of this. Early in O'Leary's days, DOE changed the name of the Office of Classification to the Office of Declassification. The new office was shoving declassified DOE material out the front door as fast as it could. All of this was rationalized by mantra-like references to the "public's right to know." Now the very same people were prepared to make sure that the public would never see this information. Another pattern established under Pena and Moler and continued under Richardson: declassification is fine, as long as it doesn't embarrass the department. In that case, bury everything under a blanket of classification.
54. Carla Ann Robbins, "China Received Secret Data on Advanced U.S. Warhead," WSJ, 7 January 1999.
55. Walter Pincus, "U.S. Cracking Down on Chinese Designs on Nuclear Data," WP, 17 February 1999, p. A7.
56. James Risen and Jeff Gerth, "China Stole Nuclear Secrets from Los Alamos, U.S. Officials Say," NYT, 6 March 1999, p. 1.

57. Messemer declaration, p. 2.
58. I have never understood why the government argued in its indictment that Lee's activity began in 1993. That is when he started making tapes, but he actually began moving files in 1988. Late in the pre-trial detention arguments, the government finally introduced additional evidence of Lee's activities going back to 1988. It was too late then.
59. Bellows Report, pp. 446–47.
60. Bellows Report, p. 402.
61. Bellows Report, p. 400.
62. Jeff Gerth and Jim Risen, "1998 Report Told of Lab Breaches and China Threat," NYT, 2 May 1999.
63. Stober and Hoffman, *A Convenient Spy,* p. 99.
64. Stober and Hoffman, *A Convenient Spy,* p. 99.
65. Key Findings: The Intelligence Community Damage Assessment on the Implications of China's Acquisition of US Nuclear Weapons Information on the Development of Future Chinese Weapons (U).
66. "Declassify the Cox Report," WT, 1 April 1999.
67. The White House, "Response to the Report of the Select Committee on U.S. National Security and Military/Commercial Concerns with the People's Republic of China," 25 May 1999.

SEVEN: TESTIMONY

1. Shippers, *Sell Out: The Inside Story of President Clinton's Impeachment.*
2. Senate Armed Services Committee hearing, transcript, 12 April 1999, p. 1.
3. James Risen, "White House Said to Ignore Evidence of China's Spying," NYT, 13 April 1999.
4. "Inside the Chinese Espionage Coverup," WP, 13 April 1999. I wonder years from now who will remember or even think about Paula Jones or Susan McDougal?
5. Walter Pincus, "DOE Officials Faulted in Probe, Efforts to Tighten Security at Nuclear Labs Allegedly Blocked," WP, 13 April 1999.
6. Senate Energy and Natural Resources Committee hearing, 20 May 1999.
7. The following account is drawn from National Broadcasting Co. Inc., NBC News Transcripts, *Meet the Press* (10:00 AM EDT), 23 May 1999.
8. NBC News Transcripts, *Meet the Press,* 30 May 1999.

EIGHT: BACKLASH

1. David Sanger, "Clinton Aides Admit Lapses on Espionage by Chinese," NYT, 7 March 1999.
2. NBC News Transcripts, *Meet the Press,* 30 May 1999.
3. Kenneth R. Timmerman, " 'Shoot the Messengers': Criticize U.S. China Policy and Kiss Your Career Goodbye," *American Spectator,* December 1999/January 2000.

4. Gertz, *The China Threat,* p. 128.

5. Kennedy is cited as a White House spokesman who handled responses to criticisms of the administration by the Congress in a number of press articles of that time.

6. Bellows Report, p. 56.

7. Cited in the Specter Report, p. 49.

8. Thompson-Lieberman Statement, p. 2.

9. Bellows Report, p. 68.

10. Bellows Report, p. 68.

11. Bellows Report, p. 127.

12. U.S. General Accounting Office, Robert H. Hast letter to Senators Specter, Grassley and Torricelli, 28 June 2001, p. 2.

13. Bellows Report, p. 236.

14. Reno Testimony.

15. Specter Report, p. 47.

16. Specter Report, p. 48.

17. Specter Report, p. 14.

18. October 2000 testimony.

19. Dan Stober, "Ex-Official at Lab Raised Concerns of Racial Bias," *San Jose Mercury-News,* 17 December 2000.

20. Stober and Hoffman, *A Convenient Spy,* pp. 231–32.

21. Lucinda Fleeson, "Rush to Judgment," *American Journalism Review,* November 2000, pp. 1–2.

22. William J. Broad, "Spies vs. Sweat: The Debate over China's Nuclear Advance," NYT, 7 September 1999.

23. Wen Ho Lee, *My Country versus Me,* p. 132.

24. Gertz, *The China Threat,* p. 128.

25. Vernon Loeb, Walter Pincus, "Planted Document Sows Seeds of Doubt; Spy Experts Wonder What China Hoped to Reap," WP, 28 May 1999, p. A3.

26. This account is taken from Stober and Hoffman, *A Convenient Spy,* pp. 207–8.

27. RobertVrooman statement, 17 August 1999.

28. Executive Order 12537, President's Foreign Intelligence Advisory Board, 28 October 1995.

29. PFIAB Report, pp 2–3.

30. PFIAB Report, p. 6.

31. Al Kamen, WP, 25 June 1999.

32. James Risen, "Report Scolds Bureaucracy for U.S. Nuclear Lab Lapses," NYT, 15 June 1999.

33. Vernon Loeb, Back Channels The Intelligence Community A Key Panel Asks: Why Only One Spy Probe," WP, 7 July 1999, p. 17.

34. Vernon Loeb and Walter Pincus, "Espionage Whistleblower Resigns," WP, 24 August 1999. p. 1.

35. Loeb and Pincus, "Espionage Whistleblower Resigns."

36. Thompson/Lieberman Statement, 5 August 1999.

37. Thompson/Lieberman Statement, p. 3.

38. Walter Pincus, "China Spy Probe Bungled, Panel Finds; Senators Say U.S. May Never Know if Atomic Secrets Were Lost," WP, 16 August 1999, p. A1.
39. On the Chinese Espionage Investigations, 26 August 1999, p. A24.
40. Thompson/Lieberman Statement, p. 7.
41. Chapter 7 of the Bellows Report confirms this, p. 386.
42. Broad clearly sees himself as a "science guy," and colleagues told me that he even wears a white lab coat when he is working. He made some snide remarks about my "lack of formal training" in nuclear physics.
43. William J. Broad, "Official Asserts Spy Case Suspect Was a Bias Victim," NYT, 18 August 1999.
44. To my knowledge, DOE never "investigated" Washington's breach of security. His offense was far more serious than the trumped-up charges Bill Richardson used to run Ed McCallum out of the department that same summer.
45. Chuck Washington sworn deposition, 27 November 2001, pp. 63–64.
46. Senate Energy and Natural Resources Committee hearing, p. 3.
47. Department of Energy press release, p. 3.
48. The hearing was before the Thompson-Lieberman Governmental Affairs Committee on 9 June 1999.

NINE: AFTERMATH

1. See "New Enterprise Team Recommendations, The Director's Work Plan for Change," 1 October 1999, p. 1, and External Team Report, "A Management Review for the Director," NSA, 22 October 1999.
2. Bill Gertz, "Hackers Linked to China Stole Documents from Los Alamos," WT, 3 August 2000, p. A1.
3. Bellows Report, p. 401.
4. "Nuclear Weapons Restricted Data Downloaded by Dr. Lee on Portable Tapes," Statement for the Record of Attorney General Janet Reno and FBI Director Louis J. Freeh on "Investigation and Prosecution of Dr. Wen Ho Lee" before the Senate Select Committee on Intelligence and the Senate Judiciary Committee, Washington, D.C., 26 September 2000.
5. Bellows Report, pp. 403–4.
6. Bellows Report, pp. 402–3.
7. Quoted in Specter Report, p. 69.
8. Specter Report, p. 6.
9. Specter Report, p. 70.
10. Specter Report, p. 57.
11. Arvin S. Quist, "Security Classification of Information," Oak Ridge National Laboratory, April 1993.
12. USA v. Lee, Memorandum of Opinion, No. CR 00-1417 JP, 31 August 2000.

13. Hearing of the Administrative Oversight and the Courts Subcommittee of the Senate Judiciary Committee, 3 October 2000.
14. Senate Judiciary Subcommittee hearing, 3 October 2000.
15. Senate Judiciary Subcommittee hearing, 3 October 2000.
16. Robert Vrooman, "What Went Wrong?" New Mexico Chapter of the Association of Chinese-American Engineers and Scientists, Albuquerque, New Mexico, 19 February 2000.
17. Reno Testimony.
18. Senate Judiciary Subcommittee hearing, 3 October 2000.
19. Senate Judiciary Subcommittee hearing, 3 October 2000, p. 31.
20. Stober and Hoffman, *A Convenient Spy*, p. 243.
21. Specter Report, p. 41. See CBS.com, "Wen Ho Lee's Problematic Polygraph," 4 February 2000.
22. Specter Report, p. 43.
23. CBSnews.com, "Wen Ho Lee: Scapegoat or Spy," 19 May 2000.
24. *United States of America v. Wen Ho Lee,* Criminal Case 99-1417, "Motion for Discovery of Materials Related to Selective Prosecution," 23 June 2000.
25. Specter Report, p. 73.
26. Bellows Report, p. 19.
27. Bellows Report, pp. 381–88.
28. Lee, *My Country versus Me,* p. 312.
29. Statement for the Record of Attorney General Janet Reno and FBI Director Louis J. Freeh on "Investigation and Prosecution of Dr. Wen Ho Lee" before the Senate Select Committee on Intelligence and the Senate Judiciary Committee, Washington, D.C., 26 September 2000.
30. Marc Larey, "Clinton Doubts Scientist's Race Influenced Case," NYT, 16 September 2000.
31. "The Wen Ho Lee Diversion," WSJ, 19 September 1999.
32. Robert Scheer, "Trulock Is Source of Botched Lee Case," *Los Angeles Times,* 5 September 2000.
33. To bolster his credibility, Scheer identified Washington as a "decorated Vietnam veteran." Not quite, since Washington didn't join the Air Force until 1973; the closest he ever got to Vietnam was a tour in Udorn, Thailand, after the war was long over; and even Washington didn't claim to be an actual Vietnam veteran—only a "Vietnam era veteran." It was interesting that Scheer would use Washington's supposed Vietnam experience to promote his claims, given Scheer's own antiwar record.
34. Bob Drogin, "Column One: How FBI's Flawed Case against Lee Unraveled," *Los Angeles Times,* 13 September 2000.
35. Hearing, Damage to National Security from Chinese Espionage at National Labs.
36. Edward Klein, "The Hunting of Wen Ho Lee," *Vanity Fair,* December 2000.
37. Bill Cleveland, the Livermore counterintelligence officer, considered the final report of the AI to be a good, professional job. Cleveland had 22 years of experience and headed the China Squad

out of the San Francisco/Oakland FBI field office. FBI officials regularly consulted him about Chinese intelligence operations and methodologies, especially as the Chinese go after the Energy Department National Labs.

38. The Bellows Report indicates that Lee was certainly known to the FBI; Vrooman had met with "Maines" and "Smith" back in 1988 to discuss Wen Ho Lee. Bill Cleveland and his staff knew about Lee from the 1982 investigation and at least one of Bill's staff had mentioned Lee to the FBI in December 1995. Then there is the case of the mysterious "notes" supposedly written sometime in June or July 1995. No one recognizes the handwriting, but the notes make reference to Lee and a number of other potential "suspects." I never saw these notes, nor was I aware of the various discussions between the FBI and individuals at Energy or in the labs. It is certainly incorrect to say that Energy was looking into Lee in 1995, when the director of intelligence (me) had never heard of him at that point.
39. Bellows Report, p. 232.
40. Freeh testimony.
41. Letter to Louis J. Freeh, Director, Federal Bureau of Investigations, 3 March 2000.
42. PR newswire, 21 July 2000.
43. WT, 28 July 2000.
44. Paul Sperry, "FBI Fishes Senate E-mail for Trulock: Agents Demand Staffers Search In-boxes for Any Messages from Whistleblower," *World Net Daily*, 6 July 2000.
45. *Notra Trulock, III v. Louis J. Freeh, et al.*
46. *Notra Trulock III v. Louis J. Freeh, et al.*, p. 8.
47. *Notra Trulock III v. Louis J. Freeh, et al.*, p. 11.
48. Deposition of Wen Ho Lee, 10 October 2001, pp. 71, 74, 235, 243.
49. *Report of the Redmond Panel.*
50. Project on Government Oversight, *U.S. Nuclear Weapons Complex: Security at Risk*, October 2001.

Bibliography

Appeal from the United States District Court for the Eastern District of Virginia, *Notra Trulock III v. Louis J. Freeh, et al.,* No. 00-2260, 28 December 2001.

Department of Energy, Office of Intelligence, *Technical Intelligence Note on Computers, Nuclear Weapons, and U.S. Security,* 6 May 1998.

Department of Justice, *Attorney General's Review Team on the Handling of the Los Alamos National Laboratory Investigation,* May 2000, p. 41. (Bellows Report)

FBIS document, *Celebrating Thirty Years of Chung-Shan Science Research Institute,* CPP200000711000135, 1 August 1999.

Gertz, William. *The China Threat: How the People's Republic Targets America.* Washington: Regnery Publishing, 2000.

Hamza, Khidir, with Jeff Stein. *Saddam's Bombmaker: The Terrifying Inside Story of the Iraqi Nuclear and Biological Weapons Agenda.* New York: Scribner, 2000.

Huan, Major General Yang. "China's Strategic Nuclear Weapons." In *Chinese Views of Future Warfare,* edited by Michael Pillsbury. Washington: National Defense University, 1997.

Lee, Wen Ho, with Helen Zia. *My Country versus Me.* New York: Hyperion, 2001.

President's Foreign Intelligence Advisory Board. *Science at Its Best,*

Security at Its Worst: A Report on Security Problems at the U.S. Department of Energy. June 1999. (PFIAB Report)

Project on Government Oversight. *U.S. Nuclear Weapons Complex: Security at Risk.* October 2001.

Shippers, David. *Sell Out: The Inside Story of President Clinton's Impeachment.* Washington: Regnery Publishing, 2000.

Statement of Senator Fred Thompson and Senator Joseph Lieberman, Governmental Affairs Committee. *Department of Energy, FBI and Department of Justice Handling of the Espionage Investigation on the W88 Warhead.* 5 August 1999. (Thompson/Lieberman Statement)

Stober, Dan, and Ian Hoffman. *A Convenient Spy: Wen Ho Lee and the Politics of Nuclear Espionage.* New York: Simon and Schuster, 2001.

Timperlake, Edward, and William C. Triplett II. *Year of the Rat: How Bill Clinton Compromised U.S. Security for Chinese Cash.* Washington: Regnery Publishing, 1998.

U.S. Congress, U.S.-China Commission. *The National Security Implications of the Economic Relationship between the United States and China.* Report to the Congress of the U.S.-China Security Review Commission. July 2002.

U.S. House of Representatives. *Report of the Redmond Panel: Improving Counterintelligence Capabilities at the Department of Energy and the Los Alamos, Sandia and Lawrence Livermore National Laboratories.* The House Permanent Select Committee on Intelligence, 106–687. 21 June 2000. (Redmond Report)

U.S. House of Representatives. *Report of the Select Committee on U.S. National Security and Military/Commercial Concerns with the People's Republic of China.* Declassified. 25 May 1999. (Cox Report)

U.S. House of Representatives. *Sales or Security? Supercomputers and Export Controls.* National Security Report, National Security Committee, vol. 2, no. 2, April 1998.

U.S. Intelligence Community. *Key Findings: The Intelligence Community Damage Assessment on the Implications of China's Acquisition of US Nuclear Weapons. Information on the Development of Future Chinese Weapons.* May 1999. (U)

U.S. Senate. *Damage to National Security from Chinese Espionage at National Labs.* Energy and Natural Resources Committee. 20 May 1999.

U.S. Senate. *Hearing of the Administrative Oversight and the Courts Subcommittee of the Judiciary Committee.* 3 October 2000.

U.S. Senate. *Report on the Government's Handling of the Investigation and Prosecution of Dr. Wen Ho Lee.* Subcommittee on Department of Justice Oversight, Committee on the Judiciary. 20 December 2001. (Specter Report)

U.S. Senate. *Report on the Investigation of Peter Lee.* Subcommittee on Department of Justice Oversight, Committee on the Judiciary. 20 December 2001.

U.S. Senate. *Special Report of the Senate Select Committee on Intelligence.* 6 January 1999 to 15 December 2000. Report 107–51. August 2001.

U.S. Senate. TOP SECRET HEARING (Declassified Version), online version. Committee on the Judiciary. 8 June 1999. (Reno Testimony)

Wise, David. *The Spy That Got Away: The Inside Story of Edward Lee Howard.* New York: Random House, 1988.

Zhongwen, Huo, and Wang Zongxiao. *Sources and Techniques of Obtaining National Defense Science and Technology Intelligence.* Beijing, 1991.

Index